GERMAN
WORKERS'
CULTURE

GERMAN

WORKERS'

CULTURE

❧❦❧

IN THE UNITED STATES
1850 to 1920

EDITED BY HARTMUT KEIL

Smithsonian Institution Press

Washington and London

Editor: Joanne Reams
Designer: Linda McKnight

Library of Congress Cataloging-in-Publication Data

German workers' culture in the United States, 1850 to 1920.

   Bibliography: p.
   Includes index.
   1. German Americans—Employment—History.   2. German
Americans—Social life and customs.   3. German Americans
—History.   4. Labor and laboring classes—United States
—History.   I. Keil, Hartmut, 1942-
HD8081.G4G45   1988   331.6'2'43073   87-600478
ISBN 0-87474-558-6

British Library Cataloging-in-Publication Data available

10   9   8   7   6   5   4   3   2   1

Manufactured in the United States of America

♾ The paper used in this publication
meets the minimum requirements of the
American National Standard for
Permanence of Paper for Printed Library
Materials Z39.48-1984.

Contents

List of Illustrations

Introduction

HARTMUT KEIL

This collection of essays intends to explore the culture of German immigrant workers in America's industrial cities from the mid-nineteenth century through World War I. It focuses on a major aspect of the social history of German workers that the Chicago Project has been studying in the midwestern metropolis for the same time period. In addition, however, this book's scope of inquiry is extended to include cities like New York and Milwaukee with strong German working-class representations. Since German urban immigrant communities were similar with regard to population, work, living conditions, institutional and organizational networks, and leisure and cultural activities, we hope that this collection will contribute to a general understanding of the basic patterns of German working-class culture in the United States during the period under investigation.

Until recently, German immigration into the United States was not readily associated with the history of America's working class. Social and cultural prejudices against immigrants from eastern and southeastern Europe, nourished by key spokespersons of Anglo-American society and resulting in increasingly restrictionist policies in the early decades of the twentieth century, worked to the advantage of older immigrant groups, among them the Germans, many of whom had already become accepted members of American society after a process of group integration sometimes extending over two or three generations. As a consequence, the majority culture was ill prepared to appreciate internal group differences; from its vantage point, it perceived the German-American community as a homogeneous ethnic group united by an alien culture and a foreign language. More importantly, however, Germans were regarded as a typical immigrant population of socially mobile achievers, quickly disburdening themselves of ethnic traditions and loyalties to become part of mainstream American society. This perspective coincided with the traditional melting-pot concept of unhindered, desirable, and swift assimilation.

In this frame of reference, the facts that the majority of German immigrants were lower class and that most immigrants to urban areas added to America's industrial working population were passed over by immigration, ethnic, and even labor historians. The latter concentrated on organizational activities of German workers in the emerging American labor movement, showing practically no interest in cultural issues, except for a limited focus on political ideology. On the one hand, German-American working-class radicalism was given sole, and often disproportionate, attention; on the other, it was described as an isolated phenomenon, seemingly without a viable social base among German immigrant workers and detached from their everyday lives and concerns. Thus working-class radicals came to be seen as a marginal group in terms of ethnicity, class, and ideology. This view was shared by German-American filiopietistic historians who emphasized the contributions of German immigrants to American society and culture. They suppressed such alternative, "un-American" currents as running counter to the image they wanted to create.

By contrast, ours is a social historical approach that wants to analyze the interrelation between social processes, economic developments, political decisions, and cultural phenomena. In line with that perspective, this book's purpose is fourfold: First, it will place the culture of German immigrant workers in its social, economic, and political contexts. We must understand this culture as arising from the mass immigration of workers, as connected with ethnic settlement as well as artisan and skilled work patterns, and as grounded in labor and ethnic institutions partly transferred from the German labor movement. This means that it was firmly anchored in the German immigrant community at a time when the character of this community was largely working-class.

Second, the book wants to recover a sense of the forms and contents of this culture as well as of its networks. What were its distinct media of expression? To what extent and in what way was it original, or did it adopt available forms and themes? Are we justified in describing it as a genuinely radical subculture, or did it share some of the values of German high culture? We must also understand that this working-class culture was not strictly confined to specific radical organizations but provided workers with a common cultural ground, even extending beyond them to overlap with—sometimes even to include—groups that, like the Turners and freethinkers, were indebted to the European radical republican tradition.

Third, it is important to analyze the uses to which this culture was put. If it was a culture of performance and agitation, intimately tied into the everyday activities of the working-class community, then the perspective of the participants is the adequate yardstick to be applied when evaluating its impact. Apparently working-class culture was not an outworn and ossified relic but fulfilled essential practical and conceptual needs for the community.

Finally, we must ask how relevant the culture of German immigrant workers was for an emerging multiethnic American working-class culture and for American society at large. Although it is necessary to look into the group mechanisms and internal functions of this subculture, we must not forget the larger social and political context by which its options were defined and delimited. In what ways did it compete for recognition in the marketplace of "public culture" (a term recently coined by Thomas Bender)? To what degree was it recognized or submerged in that process?

The concept of culture as applied in this collection is therefore not uniform. It reflects the insights of the ongoing debate that culture is a complex system operating on different levels of the social structure. Thus the transfer, application, and changes of cultural traditions are analyzed in order to identify their function in a new social context and to describe the system of meaning and values that defined the everyday life of German immigrant workers. Relational and communicative aspects—the occasions and performative contexts when cultural forms and symbols were used, the networks of identification and solidarity within the community —are especially accentuated. When discussing German working-class culture as an alternative (sub)cultural system set against other competing subsystems as well as against the majority culture, the focus is widened to include at least implicitly issues of power and subordination. Although pursuing quite different topics from their own distinctive perspectives, Ruth Seifert in her essay and Heinz Ickstadt in the concluding essay explicitly view culture as a system to which the political categories of interest and dominance are central.

The collection attempts to include essential areas and developments of German working-class culture without claiming comprehensive coverage. In the opening essay, Hartmut Keil describes the institutional and individual transfer of German cultural traditions and the resultant patterns of communication and interchange between the German Social Democracy and the German-American working-class movement. He argues that the transmission of ideology was intimately tied into the process of mass immigration, that it depended heavily on the participation of intellectuals with prior experience in German working-class organizations and went hand in hand with the creation of a substantial institutional network. His second essay, on a German immigrant neighborhood in Chicago, shows, however, that it is not enough to characterize German-American working-class culture and institutions merely as expressions of an imported and therefore alien tradition. Firmly grounded in an immigrant community sharing common class and ethnic experiences on the basis of work, home, and leisure, working-class culture interpreted immigrant workers' shared experiences in, and confrontations with, an unfamiliar and often hostile society and offered them help and guidance in their everyday needs. In this effort, more often than not, it was fiercely opposed by middle-class and religious institutions and values.

Artisan traditions also contributed substantially to the emerging working-class culture, both in Germany and the United States. Not only did they precede the Civil War in urban centers like Chicago, when a dense network of artisan institutions was established that readily integrated newcomers into the life of the community, but they continued to serve as the institutional and intellectual foundation for the working-class movement. Using three examples of artisan institutions in his essay "Artisan Culture and the Organization of Chicago's German Workers in the Gilded Age," John Jentz illustrates particular resources that artisan culture provided to German craftsmen, whether it be fellowship, intellectual stimulation, organizational strength, or a sense of personal independence. Although becoming increasingly anachronistic amidst the rapidly expanding industries of Chicago, artisan traditions often provided elements of organizational continuity when workers' efforts at founding modern labor institutions made but slow progress or were threatened by economic crisis and political pressure.

In their essay "Elements of German Working-Class Culture in Chicago, 1880 to 1890," Hartmut Keil and Heinz Ickstadt locate the roots of German workers' radicalism as much in the depressing social and economic conditions they encountered in the city as in German radical traditions. Substantially involved in Chicago's labor movement in a decade of industrial and labor unrest, they tried to transcend ethnic barriers within the working class by employing familiar cultural forms for this purpose. Although European Jacobinism shared some common ground with American republicanism, German Socialist and anarchist cultural values and life-styles, as documented in their festivities, leisure activities, and literary expressions, differed significantly from those of American labor traditions as advocated by the Knights of Labor. However, German workers made use of their reservoir of organizational forms and interpretative models by redefining them within the new context of work and everyday life.

The German Social Democracy claimed to have solved the question of woman's social position through its class analysis of capitalist society. German-American Socialists who had avidly absorbed August Bebel's treatise of this subject also believed that they stood on safe theoretical ground. As Ruth Seifert demonstrates in her essay, "The Portrayal of Women in the German-American Labor Movement," by analyzing both the theory as repeatedly expounded in the Socialist press and the praxis of male behavior as related through women's letters, also in the press, the definition of woman's proper role in the Socialist movement was more a reflection of male needs in a working-class context than of female emancipation. The letter writers' theoretical frame of reference was not only one of class, but also one of gender. They grappled with ascriptions of femininity that were both part of their identity and cultural coercion.

The following three essays deal with important institutions of German workers' culture in Chicago. Renate Kiesewetter analyzes the German-language labor press, which was indispensable as the mouthpiece of the organized German workers in the city. It also served as a communicative center for the German-American labor movement at large and as a vital link to the international labor network. Kiesewetter demonstrates that the founders of the two Chicago papers *Vorbote* and *Chicagoer Arbeiter-Zeitung* were well acquainted with institutional precedents established by the German Social Democracy. They copied organizational structures, like that of the cooperative publishing company, adapting them to specific needs arising form the American context. Although the papers carried news especially relevant to the city's German workers and their organizations, they also tried to serve a wider audience. In addition, the papers took on the function of cultural media, reporting on festivities, theater performances, and concerts, and disseminating essays, poems, short stories, novels, and even plays in their pages.

Among the papers' subscribers could be found saloon keepers. Klaus Ensslen's essay characterizes German-American working-class saloons as semipublic social centers for specific neighborhoods that provided recreational facilities (often for the whole family), exchange of communication, and other indispensable services like meeting halls, for trade unions and parties, and job agencies. Complementing the brewing industry's interest in expanding the beer market, German immigrants insisted on their cultural tradition of public drinking in saloons, halls, and beer gardens, and this against the dominant society's efforts at imposing the temperance norms buttressed by a puritanical work ethic. However, they could not prevent the eventual interpenetration of older ethnic and the new leisure habits of the emerging American mass culture, as documented in the substantial changes that beer gardens underwent.

In her essay "Popular and Working-Class German Theater in Chicago, 1870 to 1910," Christine Heiβ describes the German theater as an ethnic minority institution that had to adjust to the rules of a profit-oriented cultural industry. Alongside the regular German theater catering to the upper and middle classes, there were numerous neighborhood-based popular theaters performing in Turner and public halls and attracting the lower middle and the working class, as well as the openly propagandistic theater of the labor movement, enacted at summer picnics and political or popular festivals. The working-class theater sometimes joined forces with the commercial popular theater to attract larger audiences, and in the late 1880s comedies and farces imported from Bismarck's Germany formed the stock of popular repertoire even for Socialist amateur theaters. However, the labor press also encouraged workers to attend regular theater productions touching on working-class interests, proclaiming professional performances as a presentation of art suitable for the education of the masses.

That the culture of the labor movement saw itself as the virtual guardian of German classical culture, is emphasized by Heinz Ickstadt in the essay "Workers' Literature in Chicago—Old Forms in New Contexts." Providing biographical information on several important German-American writers, he points out their traditional classical education and analyzes formal and stylistic continuities in their literary production as well as new elements with respect to subject matter. There was a scarcity of talent in the German-American labor movement, however, and high cultural standards were maintained only so long as authors were drawn to the United States from Germany. When the ranks of the German immigrant working class were thinning out around the turn of the century, editors and writers increasingly and nostalgically lamented the loss of support for, and vitality of, the movement and its culture.

This decline can be observed within other institutions of the German immigrant community as well. Two essays by Ralf Wagner and Bettina Goldberg bring into view two German immigrant organizations stemming from a radical tradition that preceded the rise of the labor movement. Originating from the Vormärz period, both the Turner and the freethinker movements worked for an enlightened, liberal democratic society free from autocratic rule. Substantial numbers of both groups' members immigrated to the United States after the Revolution of 1848–49, where they established national organizations. However, Wagner and Goldberg analyze the local level—primarily Milwaukee, but also Chicago in the case of the Turners—in order to demonstrate the communal context in which the activities of these associations were especially important. They quickly adjusted their radicalism to the pressures of the new society, first by turning attention to American themes like slavery, then by reluctantly giving in to the increasingly conservative mood of the membership (the Turners) or accepting a marginal place within the German-American community (the freethinkers). The Haymarket tragedy of 1886 forced radicals of all persuasions to take a clear stand; as a consequence of that event, German-American radicals had to form coalitions in order to survive the conservative onslaught. Thus Socialists, Turners, and freethinkers became the supporters of a particular brand of reform radicalism as represented for example in the Social Democratic party of Milwaukee.

The last two essays try to locate the transitions between German working-class culture and American popular mass culture and entertainment. Berndt Ostendorf traces the contributions of several well-known German-American musicians to a diverse American musical tradition drawing upon various ethnic sources, and especially upon the second generation of immigrants. Giants like Theodore Thomas and the Damrosch family were profusely idolized and recognized, since they helped transfer the European (and specifically German) classical music to the United States and founded and gave repute to major symphony orchestras and choirs. By contrast, the significant additions by the Dressers and Witmarks to a commercialized popular music became submerged. The composers and publishers themselves kept a low ethnic profile in a market defined as genuinely American. Moreover, believing high culture to be the major German contribution to America's musical heritage, representatives of the German-American community disassociated themselves from popular music, which they considered trivial and shallow and a debasement of German high cultural traditions.

The concluding essay by Heinz Ickstadt introduces the majority culture's perspective on the immigrant lower class and discusses their concern with social control as a means of maintaining Anglo-American cultural values against the onslaught of competing cultural traditions.

Thus upper-class and progressive reformers tried to transform the "Black City" of urban chaos into the "White City" of genteel cultural idealism. Leaders of the German working class attempted in turn to preserve an autonomous ethnic working-class culture against the pressures of environment and social degradation. At the same time, a new urban or mass culture emerged, which slowly eroded ethnic as well as genteel cultural ideals. Even though these various attempts to create a new society or a culturally coherent "Civic Order" eventually failed, they gave rise to a great variety of social and cultural institutions, opened up new possibilities for cultural participation and integration, and led to a less hierarchical and more differentiated vision of Chicago as multiethnic metropolis.

Like all similar collections, this volume is marked by certain omissions in the spectrum of relevant topics. Among the more obvious gaps is the absence of separate essays on the issues of religion and education. In a limited way, these questions are touched upon in some essays, for example when describing the role of the Catholic church in Chicago's Northwest Side German neighborhood, the freethinkers' position toward the established churches, their attitude, as well as the Socialists' views, on education and the practical steps taken to offer alternative instruction. A thorough discussion of working-class family life is another topic one might wish to find more extensively treated, although some light is thrown on this issue in the neighborhood essay and the essay "The Portrayal of Women in the German-American Labor Movement."

Topical omissions can be partly explained by the fact that these essays reflect various stages of the Chicago Project's work on a "Social History of German Workers in Chicago, 1850–1910." Several individuals and institutions contributed to this interdisciplinary and international project according to their research interests and resources. Thus, the project, which was conducted at the America Institute of the University of Munich and funded by the Volkswagen Foundation from 1979 to 1983, cooperated with the John F. Kennedy-Institute for North American Studies at the Free University of Berlin, as well as with the Newberry Library in Chicago. Student and research assistants shared time on the project with faculty members and fulltime project staff. Other students joined in with our work when they decided to write their theses about related thematical aspects. All of these groups are represented in this collection. Although the majority of essays have been written for this volume, not all of them are new. Six essays previously published in German journals are here included in translated and revised versions.

The numerous persons who contributed to the Chicago Project cannot all be mentioned here. However, I would like to specifically thank those directly involved in this collection: Burt Weinshanker, who translated the essays "Immigrant Neighborhoods," "Elements of German Working-Class Culture," "The Portrayal of Women," "German-American Labor Press," "German-American Working-Class Saloons," "Popular and German Working-Class Theater," "Turner Societies," and "Radical German-American Freethinkers" (including quoted materials; in other cases, translations were by the authors); Richard Hellinger, who helped provide several illustrations; my colleague Klaus Ensslen, who generously gave his time critically revising the manuscript; Ruth Seifert, who relieved me of some editorial chores in the final editing stage; Cornelia Fellhauer, who helped prepare the index; and the staff of the Smithsonian Institution Press—Daniel Goodwin and Ruth Spiegel, who safely steered the manuscript through the publishing process, and Joanne Reams, who performed a magnificent copyediting job.

CHAPTER 1

German Working-Class Immigration and the Social Democratic Tradition of Germany

HARTMUT KEIL

High hopes for a victory of the United Labor party in the New York City mayoralty election in the fall of 1886 were nourished by the encouraging facts that, for the first time, different factions in the city's working class, including the Socialist Labor party dominated by German Socialist immigrants, had been able to lay aside their political antagonisms for a pragmatic coalition, and that in Henry George they had found a creditable candidate for the city's highest office. But it was George himself who—after failing to gain the necessary plurality despite an impressive voter turnout—disavowed this coalition only some months later by repudiating the Socialists as political allies. Their philosophy, George maintained, was irreconcilable with American political culture and traditions. Individualism was so "strongly rooted in all the habits of thought of the peoples of English language" that "socialism of the German school can never make the headway here that it has on the continent of Europe."[1] He elaborated in the *Standard*: "German socialism is so confused and confusing in its terminology, so illogical in its methods; it contains such a mixture of important truths with superficial generalizations and unwarranted assumptions, that it is difficult—at least for people of English speech—to readily understand its real meaning and purpose."[2] For him, "state socialism" was "an exotic born of European conditions that cannot take root and flourish in American soil."[3]

George was only one in a long line of politicians and scholars who have consistently described the Socialist movement in the United States as being sectarian, foreign, and imported. They have tended to see the German radical tradition brought over by immigrant workers and intellectuals as a unified ideological system, overlooking important differences and variations. Yet the German radical culture trying to gain a foothold in America had many faces, and it was reflected in diverse traditions and groups, such as freethinkers and radical Republicans, communitarians and land reformers, Lassallean and Marxist Socialists, Social Democrats and anarchists. Extended German working-class immigration and ideological transfer resulted in a multiplicity of class and cultural experiences that defy easy categorization.[4]

This essay will explore the ideological roots of the radical German-American working-class tradition, their transfer from Germany to the United States, the continuing close relationship between German Social Democrats and German-American Socialists, as well as the transformation of these radical traditions in the new social context.

THE GERMAN SOCIAL DEMOCRATIC PERCEPTION OF AMERICAN SOCIETY

In their views of the United States, German Socialists partook in a long liberal-democratic tradition that emphasized the revolutionary and liberalizing impact of the republican experiment.[5] American independence was a tremendous boost for suppressed longings in Germany to be freed from the despotism and tyranny of feudal domination and absolutist monarchism. Such aspirations were projected on the new republic by the literary tradition of the Sturm und Drang period as well as by the Enlightenment, which hailed the American Revolution as a new stage in the progress of humanity.[6] The historical event of American independence was rationalized into an ideological symbol of the universal aspirations of humanity, and its practical result, as codified in the American Constitution, was soon accorded the rank of an inviolable political canon.[7] Such a view of America did not mirror the reality of American institutions and life, but, rather, universal ideals to be aspired to in the European context of the Napoleonic era and the Wars of Liberation.

The emerging political liberalism in the repressive restoration period continued to center its attention on the American Constitution. In the opinion of liberals, it had transformed their own as yet unattained ideals of personal and political rights and freedoms into a practical reality. The United States, therefore, became the symbol of political freedom; thus, during the Hambach Festival in 1832, which united diverse radical groups in a common demonstration for national unity and political rights, cheers were voiced on "the united free states of Germany" in obvious reference to the United States of America.[8] The radical democrats of the Young Germany movement, sometimes living in exile in France and Switzerland, helped popularize republican ideals in rousing poems and songs that often were but thinly veiled calls for action. Poems of the Vormärz period were later incorporated by the Social Democrats as an integral part of their revolutionary tradition and aspirations. Thus a general and basically uncritical enthusiasm for America's "great democracy"[9] prevailed among radical democrats as well as liberals during the Revolution of 1848–49. At democrats' and workers' mass meetings, the Stars and Stripes was always displayed alongside the Tricolor and the revolutionary red flag.[10] It was especially the democratic Left that pointed to the American federal system as an example to be followed, asking for a new German federal state with a "constitution along the lines of North America with accompanying republican institutions."[11] Although the Revolution of 1848–49 miserably failed to accomplish this goal, the liberal-democratic ideal of America, which had guided its leaders and followers significantly, persisted into the 1870s.[12]

Parallel to this liberal-republican debate ran a current of popular enthusiasm for the American Republic, grounded less in constitutional and political ideals than in hopes of material rewards. Surpassing idealistic motives in importance in its long-term consequences, material ambition led to mass emigration from Germany in the middle of the century at the very moment when liberal aspirations had been shattered. Contemporary fiction popularized the expectation that in America everything would turn out well; one only needed to live there for a while in order to return as a well-to-do, respected person. Novels and short stories, as well as popular plays written and widely performed in the latter half of the nineteenth century, presented the stereotypical "rich uncle from America" admired by relatives and friends upon his visit in the Old Country.[13] Emigrants' guides often were no less biased, raising false hopes of easy settlement and quick material success in the New World.[14] But it was above all the "reports of republican happiness spread by emigrated Germans in hundreds of thousands of letters among their fellow countrymen back home"[15] that decisively shaped the masses' perceptions and expectations.

The German Social Democracy incorporated certain elements of the liberal-republican tradition while trying to come to terms with the strong undercurrent of mass opinion in favor of the United States and the resulting mass emigration. It was the refusal of the German states and, later, the German Reich to grant fundamental civil rights that helps explain, at least in part, the unprecedented success of the Socialist party in Germany. The Marxist Erfurt program of 1891, which replaced the party's program passed at the Gotha Unity Congress in 1875, still contained in its second part those typically democratic demands that had been partially realized in the United States.[16] When evaluating the relative accomplishments of different nations with respect to civil and democratic liberties, German Socialists continued to look favorably upon the American Republic.[17]

The Socialists took an ambivalent position toward mass emigration from Germany to the United States, however. They blamed domestic economic, social, and political conditions for the exodus. Although they were resolutely opposed to any legal restriction of emigration, they did not encourage the move abroad.[18] On the other hand, the American Republic continued to attract persons who were politically persecuted in Germany. Since the 1820s, revolutionaries of various persuasions had chosen America for their temporary or permanent home. Socialists made no exception; in the late 1870s and early 1880s, when the Social Democrats were harassed increasingly by state authorities until their party was outlawed by Bismarck's Anti-Socialist Law of 1878, many exiled and persecuted Socialists chose to emigrate to the United States.[19] The party, however, reaffirmed its position that "social grievances cannot be eliminated by mass emigration."[20] The resolution by the International Workingmen's Association on emigration, passed in 1873 by the General Council and stating that "emigration of workers does not contribute to the emancipation of the working class, but only transfers the battleground," was quoted with obvious approval by the party's paper, Volksstaat.[21] The New Yorker Volks-Zeitung also opposed mass emigration, since it served as a "safety valve against the revolution" in Germany.[22] The Sozialdemokrat, published in Zurich, joined in this evaluation of the "emigration fever," which "we must deplore and fight."[23] When some party leaders emigrated despite such warnings, these moves were openly branded as "desertion" and "cowardly acts."[24] Instead, the "soldiers of the revolution" were admonished to "stay home"; it was their "duty to hold out on the battleground."[25] Paraphrasing a sentence written by Johann Wolfgang von Goethe, Wilhelm Liebknecht coined the famous rallying slogan: "Our America is in Germany!"[26]

Figure 1.1. Wilhelm Liebknecht, photographed in Chicago during his visit in 1886 in the studio of Julius Vahlteich's wife. Vahlteich, former secretary to Ferdinand Lassalle (founder of the General German Workingmen's Association) and Social Democratic member of the German Diet, made his home in Chicago in 1883 after emigrating to the United States two years earlier.

THE SCOPE OF SOCIALIST IMMIGRATION

Because of its very nature as ideological transfer, Socialist immigration cannot be quantified with any degree of accuracy. Professed Socialists known to have been active in the German labor movement before coming to the United States certainly numbered in the hundreds or even thousands. But the mass of immigrants, of course, were not asked to register their political beliefs upon entering the country. In the absence of reliable statistics, wild guesses have been offered on various occasions. After passage of the Anti-Socialist Law of 1878 in the German Reich, the American press carried the news that a mass exodus of Socialists was imminent; there were even rumors that Bismarck's administration encouraged such emigration from the Reich in order to rid itself of malcontents, revolutionaries, and incendiaries.[27] American authorities and politicians were sufficiently worried to seek new legislation keeping such persons off its shores, and they tried to get expert opinion to substantiate their suspicions of high immigration figures for this group of political immigrants.[28]

In the absence of reliable statistics, an informed guess as to the numbers of Socialist immigrants must be based on knowledge of the origins and the social makeup of mass emigration, the composition of the German-American labor force, fragmentary indicators of actual Socialist immigration, and the character of German-American labor organizations.

German mass emigration in the nineteenth century was triggered by the social upheavals resulting from agrarian reforms and industrialization.[29] Their uneven and regionally deferred impact established the pattern of gradual change of origin of the areas of emigration. Until the middle of the century, southwestern and western German states (Württemberg, Baden, and the Bavarian Palatinate) predominated, whereas afterward northeastern and eastern Prussia took the lead. This development has been interpreted as evidence of the predominantly agrarian composition of the German emigration. An article in the *Neue Zeit*, the intellectual mouthpiece of the German Socialists, maintained that mass emigration originated in regions that, because of their economic structure, were largely unaffected by the emerging German Social Democracy.[30]

However, one must not overlook the fact that substantial numbers of artisans and skilled workers emigrated in the earlier as well as the later period. Regions with mixed economies, including trades, handicrafts, and industries, such as western and central Germany, supplied a "relatively high number of emigrants,"[31] and their occupations reflected the economic structure. Emigrants from Saxony, one of the early industrial regions in Germany and a stronghold of the Socialist party, tended to come from declining trades and handicrafts. The desolate state of the home and textile industries caused thousands of weavers to emigrate from there.[32] American consuls in other areas of Germany also noted the relationship between depressed industrial conditions and the emigration of workers.[33] It is also significant that emigration from agrarian regions tended to decline compared to that from urban-industrial areas during the second half of the nineteenth century. Since more than 70 percent (about 3.5 million) of the German immigrants came after the American Civil War, a continuously high and rising absolute number of artisans and skilled and industrial workers contributed to this enormous population movement.

The urban concentration and the occupational distribution of the German-American work force corroborate this conclusion. Even at midcentury the proportion of Germans settling in large cities was way above that of the U.S. urban population,[34] and it continued to rise steadily along with continued mass immigration from Germany; by the turn of the century, more than half of all German-Americans lived in cities with a population of more than twenty-five thousand.[35] The importance of industrial employment among German immigrants is confirmed by occupational patterns. Of the two most important sectors of the economy, industry (where some 35 percent were employed) clearly came before agriculture. Artisans and skilled workers, in this connection, were the most important groups in the industrial work force, since they formed the backbone of trade unions as well as of the emerging Socialist party in Germany. These two groups also contributed large numbers of immigrants to the United States, as can readily be seen from a profile of the thirteen numerically most important occupations of German immigrant workers other than laborers for the years 1870 to 1890. In each of the three census years, these trades constituted about 60 percent of the German American industrial work force.[36] Traditional crafts in building, food processing, and the furniture and metal industries predominated. Although threatened by industrialization, these crafts apparently survived because of the constant replenishment of their ranks by new immigrants who tried to escape from the pressure of social dislocation and occupational degradation in the Reich.

The immigration of substantial numbers of German skilled workers supplied an enormous potential of persons inclined to holding socialist convictions and remaining Socialist supporters or at least sympathizers after settling in the United States. Evidence of such continuities is most conclusive on the organizational level. The membership of the International Workingmen's Association, the Socialist Labor party, the International Working People's Association, and local party organizations was made up overwhelmingly of German immigrants, as the often-voiced complaints about the foreign stamp of these labor organizations made abundantly clear. More than 80 percent of the Socialist Labor party members in New York City between 1878 and 1881 had German names.[37] Not only were labor unions often founded by Socialists, but there were also heavy concentrations of Socialists in those very unions whose trades were dominated by, or had a large share of, German workers.[38]

A look at the local level confirms the impact that German Socialist immigrants had on trade-union organization. Unionism in Chicago, for example, dated from the 1850s, when the carpenters, carriage and wagon makers, tailors, typographers, and other workers organized, and when a central body was formed toward the end of the decade, even taking over nationwide functions for all German workers' associations in the United States. Chicago's labor organizations, like the national union movement, did not survive the Civil War, so that new beginnings had to be made, starting in the mid-1860s. It was during the depression years from 1873 to 1878, however, that the trade-union principle of organization was securely established among German workers, when the tailors', cigarmakers', furniture workers', typographers', and the building trades' unions, most of them led by Socialists, were able to hold out. Radical leaders managed to put their unions on a solid financial basis, working out a system of benefits and insurance that would tie new members more permanently into the organization. The trade unions set up unemployment, sickness, and life insurance and strike funds. It was this institutional solidification under an experienced radical leadership in times of severe crisis that accounted for their important role. The *New Yorker Volks-Zeitung* was therefore justified in writing in 1880 that Socialists themselves had founded "many and numerous unions."[39] The National Executive Committee of the Socialist Labor party, in its report for the year 1880, also stated proudly that "in almost all towns unions are headed by socialists."[40]

The ideological conflicts that arose in several unions as well as in the Socialist parties since the late 1870s were often caused by recently immigrated German Socialists who tried to uphold rigorous socialist principles, usually according to the precedents set by their respective organizations in Germany. As a rule, these Socialists emigrated as individuals; petty harassment by police and legal authorities, discrimination in the work place, and bleak prospects of economic betterment were the breeding grounds for such a decision. Even in cases of forced political exile, a combination of motives contributed to the decision to emigrate. Although the practice of discriminating against labor organizations and Socialist workers predated the time when the Anti-Socialist Law was in effect (1878–90), this period witnessed the clearest instances of politically motivated emigration of Socialists that can be documented. On several occasions, the government used a clause in the infamous law authorizing the eviction of party and union members when a state of emergency had been declared over a large urban area. Of the hundreds of Socialists from Berlin, Hamburg, and Leipzig who were thereby forced to leave their homes and work, at least one-fourth emigrated to the United States in groups or individually.[41]

By exiling these Socialists, the government intended to destroy the labor movement's infrastructure, at least on the local level. Therefore it banned persons who had carried out more or less important party functions. Although information about them is fragmentary, it shows that more than two-thirds actively served the party, in local elections and support committees, in official party and union functions, as organizers, and as press agents. Others had been delegates to regional or national labor conventions and candidates or deputies for regional or national parliaments.[42] The loss of these experienced Socialists was keenly felt.

Was this resource of experience actually introduced into the German-American labor movement? On one hand, it seems that many Socialists, who had been active in Germany and who upon their arrival were taken care of by the Socialist Labor party (SLP) and other labor organizations, soon became alienated from the SLP. They joined the large group of "drop-outs," those "many thousands of the oldest, most experienced, and theoretically clear-headed comrades holding themselves aloof" whose inactivity was deplored again and again in the German-American labor press.[43] On the other hand, almost half of the exiled Socialists became active in the labor movement, although their functions took on a different importance. Few were delegates to party and union conventions, perhaps because of the language barrier. The local level became more important than in Germany. These Socialists now had to prove themselves in routine duties, in heading party sections, and in educational and agitational work, whereas press and publishing were of smaller dimensions and confined to fewer persons.

Although mass immigration from Germany provided an important supply of skilled industrial workers sympathizing with the German Social Democracy and forming a sizable group of potential supporters for the emergent labor movements in American industrial cities, it was the experienced leadership also immigrating from Germany in substantial numbers that was indispensable in founding a variety of labor organizations, thereby supplying the necessary institutional base for a German-American labor movement.

THE TRANSFER OF INSTITUTIONS
AND CULTURE

The transfer of German working-class institutions and culture was intimately connected with mass immigration. This cannot be taken simply as a matter of course; other ways, totally unrelated to population movements, are conceivable of how ideas can be transferred. The factual coincidence in this case, however, had important repercussions on the mechanisms of transfer—on its direction and reception, on its duration, and even on its content.

First, an intricate communications network developed between the Socialist movements in Germany and the United States.[44] This was not evenly balanced, because the German Social Democracy, as the progenitor of the German-American Socialist movement and as the theoretically most advanced and electorally most successful Socialist party, assumed from the beginning the role of shining example to be emulated. It was therefore essential to remain informed of the development of theory, tactics, and organization in the parent party, and to receive guidelines for action. But the network served other more practical and individual needs as well.

Basically, there were three channels of communication: private correspondence between leading Socialists, in which official matters and background developments were discussed; personal exchanges through visits of Socialist leaders and other individuals; and the labor press (party, trade union, and local daily and weekly papers). The latter was the most important of the three, since it was widely circulated and covered a broad spectrum of needs, serving both the rank and file and the leadership as well as outsiders who wished to be informed of events in the labor movement. The extent to which labor papers were read and information between them exchanged on both sides of the Atlantic is remarkable; as early as 1874, seventeen German-language labor papers published in Germany and other European countries were advertised for sale in the Chicago *Vorbote*.[45] The German-American labor press quoted the German *Demokratisches Wochenblatt* and its successors *Volksstaat* and *Vorwärts* as well as local Socialist papers as the main sources for European labor events. Several papers, like the *Arbeiter-Union* and the *New Yorker Volks-Zeitung*, also hired prominent Socialist leaders such as Wilhelm Liebknecht or Julius Vahlteich as regular correspondents for Germany.[46] Official announcements, proceedings of party and union conventions, and important new theoretical and political publications were often reported verbatim or serialized. After 1878, when the publication of Socialist papers was forbidden under the Anti-Socialist Law, the flow was reversed in favor of the more numerous German-American labor publications. The editors of the *Sozialdemokrat* in Zurich, the major center of Socialist communication in the 1880s, received all German-language labor papers from the United States and exploited them thoroughly for pertinent information.

The German-language labor press, in both Europe and America, also served individuals who had more practical concerns, as is documented by

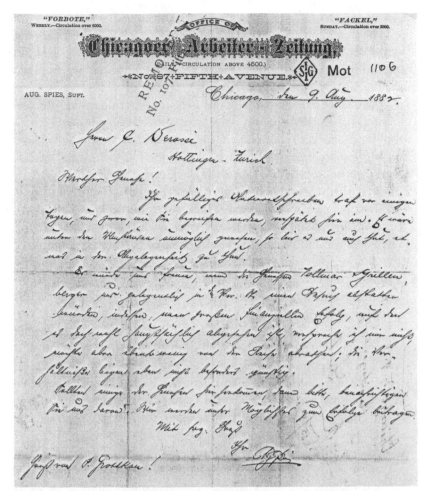

Figure 1.2. *Letter by August Spies to Carl Derossi of the* Sozialdemokrat *in Zurich, Switzerland, the German labor paper published in exile while Bismarck's Anti-Socialist Law was in effect. Spies expresses some doubt as to the advisability of another agitation tour through the United States planned for two prominent German Social Democrats.*

short notices, appeals, and advertisements in the *Sozialdemokrat* specifically addressed to, or inserted by, persons wanting to emigrate. Here comrades publicly announced their intention, and were in turn bid farewell by those staying behind and recommended to Socialists in the New World.[47]

Countless receipts for money sent by individuals and organizations from prominent and obscure places in the United States and information on work conditions in specific trades and cities are testimony to the extent and internationality of this network of communication, practical help, and solidarity.[48]

The practice of exchanging and using information from all available sources was founded not only upon an ideological agreement among the publishers, but also on common experiences, personal contacts, and friendships in Germany. With few exceptions, German-American labor papers were edited by journalists who had learned their job in Germany. Some of them were hired while still there because of a shortage of qualified people in the United States. After the late 1870s, however, there was an oversupply, when many arrived who had lost their means of livelihood because labor papers were banned.[49] Voluntary and forced transatlantic job mobility in this profession thus tended to reinforce the continuity of perspective of the German-American labor papers and the flow of information between them and the corresponding publications in Europe.

In its formative stages, the German-American labor movement leaned heavily on the German example, imitating its organizational structures and functions. In order to become established and accepted, however, new associations could not operate in a vacuum of pure socialist theory, but had to observe the needs of immigrant workers. Ideological transfer was therefore closely tied into the actual practice of establishing and maintaining working-class institutions in immigrant neighborhoods. In addition to the usual lower-class social setting the immigrants had known in Germany, they were now part of a marginal ethnic culture. Ethnic and cultural overtones tended to have considerably more weight within the German-American working class than within the German, especially when it came to conflicts with other immigrant groups and with the dominant culture. When Socialist institutions had to contend with class and cultural issues at the same time, socialist principles sometimes were neglected for concerns immediately touching upon everyday life. Thus the associational life flourishing in these immigrant working-class neighborhoods cannot be approached simply from an ideological perspective, but must also be understood for its social functions.

This associational network of German immigrant neighborhoods cannot be analyzed thoroughly in this context.[50] Instead, to take but one example of an institution that reached beyond individual neighborhoods, the Socialist party will be discussed in order to demonstrate how organizational structures were transferred from Germany. Immigrant Socialists admired the German Social Democracy above all for its quick electoral growth since the mid-1870s, which was taken as outward proof that its theoretical position was also most advanced. They were proud that it was in Germany, "the center of Europe," the "recognized cradle of modern science," that the "communistic science was put to the severe test of proving its inner validity" and that it had "obviously passed it." The Socialist movement had thereby "found an intellectual center."[51]

The unification of Lassalleans and Marxists at the Gotha Unity Congress in 1875 was also seen as a model to be followed quickly. The different German Socialist groups had taken a foothold in the United States before. Now the attempts at unification were closely watched by German-American Socialists, who welcomed them as an incentive to similar efforts of their own. In April 1875, the Chicago *Vorbote* published an article demanding the unification of the three existing factions—the International Workingmen's Association, the Labor party of Illinois, and the Social Democratic Workingmen's party of North America—by pointing to the expected unification of the two German wings of the labor movement and by explicitly suggesting that the example be copied.[52] When unity was accomplished in Germany seven weeks later at the Gotha Unity Congress, the *Vorbote's* editor, Conrad Conzett, pleaded for a similar move. He sought to underscore the necessity for such a step by quoting from a private letter that Wilhelm Liebknecht had written to him, in which he had declared: "Now it is to be hoped that in America, too, unification will be accomplished, putting an end to the itching for special alliances. You only need the goodwill of those who are sincere in their convictions. In Germany the obstacles were certainly larger than over there. And yet we succeeded. Where there is a will there is a way."[53] In an appeal issued by a "Unification Committee of the Two Socialist Factions in Chicago," the German example was cited again.[54] The Workingmen's party of the United States emerged one year later at Philadelphia as a result of these and similar efforts.

The party's organizational structure, as well as its goals and tactics, reflected its orientation toward the German party. For several years, political actionists gained the upper hand, seeing participation in elections as the right path to recognition and growth. They tried to emulate the German strategy, ignoring warnings by experienced internationalists against premature political action and instead insisting that institutions, liberties, and rights granted in the American political system had to be used. The party also adopted the principle of centralization, placing ultimate power into the national convention and creating a strong national executive controlled by a board of appeals. Its goals consisted of principles and demands almost identical with those of the German party.[55]

There were many such instances of institutional transfer. Other secondary associations, as well as specific forms, contents, and enactments of German working-class culture, were also initially brought over from Germany. These included insurance and benefit societies, educational clubs and schools, singing and theater societies, typical forms of celebration and leisure, and a radical literary tradition used to cultivate common ideological identification and class solidarity.[56] However, even after the initial transfer, the continued vitality of working-class institutions and culture depended on uninterrupted immigration of skilled workers and Socialists from Germany and on the intimate interrelationship with the German Social Democracy. Organizational, ideological, and cultural traditions were thus maintained by an intricate network of immigration, personal communication, and institutional imitation.

THE AMERICANIZATION OF GERMAN
WORKING-CLASS RADICALISM

Henry George's repudiation of socialism in 1887, following his defeat in the 1886 New York mayoralty election, confronted German-American Socialists once more with the indisputable fact that years of ceaseless agitation and efforts at organization all too often had failed to translate into lasting results. Frustrated Socialists tried to find explanations for this disappointing lack of organizational progress. The several answers they offered revealed both the sincerity of their concern and their feeling of helplessness in the face of social and economic circumstances that, according to their understanding, should have made for a powerful working-class movement but instead had eroded it time and again. They held themselves responsible for this outcome, but they also blamed the specific conditions of American society.

In his article "Nationality and Socialism" in the *New Yorker Volks-Zeitung* Sergej Schewitsch explained that socialism stood above any nationality.[57] However, "national character" could influence the form of organization and the plan of agitation, and socialism had to adapt to such national peculiarities. In a follow-up article, "Theory and Life," Schewitsch stated that the mentality of the Anglo-Saxon people was averse to any abstract theory.[58] Others shared his observations; in a letter to the same paper, the opinion was voiced that "it was much easier to agitate among the immigrant element of the population than among those born in this country," because French and German immigrants seemed to be "intellectually more enlightened"[59] than the "practical-minded" American workers who had inherited this characteristic from England.[60] John (Johann) Most's *Freiheit*, still published in London at that time, agreed that Americans devoted all their energy to physical work and were therefore behind "in intellectual matters"; their "fundamental trait" was "a most blatant instinct of acquisition."[61]

On the other hand, Henry George's harsh comments implied a failure on the part of German Socialists to adapt to American conditions. Many German radicals tended to agree partly with his indictment. All too often, Socialist immigrants haughtily conceived of America as an industrializing country waiting to be made over in the German image by their missionary zeal. Despairing soon of such an ineffective approach, many Socialists then confined themselves to supporting the Social Democratic party in Germany and identifying with its obvious advances rather than with the Socialist Labor party, which suffered repeated setbacks. They thereby reinforced their self-imposed isolation.[62] German-American labor papers, however, kept reminding their readers that actual developments were distinct from "notions conceived in the heads of German Socialists in the United States who apply German standards to the completely different conditions here."[63] It was wrong to keep principles untainted by staying away from unfamiliar social movements; instead, the motto should be: "Go ye into all the world and preach the Gospel among the Gentiles."[64]

One indispensable element was knowledge of the English language. Workers could not content themselves with the claim of middle-class papers that it was "the mission of German-Americans" to preserve German traditions and the German language, wrote the *New Yorker Volks-Zeitung*. Learning English thoroughly was not to be taken as a betrayal of one's native tongue, but as a means to more effective agitation. There was no sharper weapon than colloquial English. The paper admonished its readers to attend a language course offered in the numerous evening schools.[65] During his American journey, Wilhelm Liebknecht also addressed this burning issue. In a speech in Brooklyn, he exhorted his listeners to learn the language of their adopted country: "I tell you, study, and learn English above all else. It's a mistake that my fellow countrymen learn so little English. They must know the ways of Americans and therefore I tell you learn."[66]

English-language Socialist papers were also sadly lacking, and German Socialists made repeated efforts to supply them. The Chicago *Socialist* was financed by the overwhelmingly German membership of the Socialist Labor party, as were the *Leader*, the *Workmen's Advocate*, and the *People* in later years. Likewise, Albert Parsons published the *Alarm* in the offices of the *Chicagoer Arbeiter-Zeitung*. From early on, German Socialists also tried to reach workers through leaflets and pamphlets written in English, an undertaking impeded by the lack of native speakers. German-Americans who were relatively fluent in English, like F. A. Sorge, A. Jonas, A. Douai, A. Hepner, and later G. Hoehn, filled the gap.[67] Since these pamphlets explicitly referred to American conditions, they were preferred for agitational purposes over translations of German tracts reflecting German conditions.

Such activities could not hide the fact, however, that German radicals could score their most important organizational victories among the ethnic group of German immigrants. Given the large concentrations of German skilled workers in specific branches of industry and in certain regions and cities, this comes as no surprise. Here were the natural starting points of a common national and cultural heritage, from which radicals could draw for more than three decades. The labor movement used such ethnic traditions, which proved to be powerful cement when joining workers on the basis of a common craft and common skills. Reaching out from here, the English language was an important medium not only for communicating with American workers, but also for finding common ground with immigrant workers of other nationalities who, like the Germans, used their own cultural and work traditions for establishing effective organization. The eventual acceptance of the English language may have had more to do with demographic changes, especially the replacement of the immigrant generation by their American-born children, than with conscious efforts of the kind described above.

Generational changes among German workers and shifts in the composition of the American working class had mellowed the pure and uncompromising German-American radicalism of the 1870s and 1880s as the century came to a close. The increasing tempo of industrial reorganization since the 1880s and the restructuring of work toward homogenization had displaced German skilled workers, and especially traditional crafts, from the center of the production process. Second-generation sons and daughters also left aside outworn occupational prospects, looking instead for jobs in new-growth industries. Thus, at the very time that strong union organization had been established, after years of struggle on the craft basis as propagated by the American Federation of Labor, industrial development toward mass production and the reception of the new immigrants into the working class had already outmoded such forms of organization. German radicals who had matured in the 1870s and 1880s had grown old, and the membership for whom they could speak was decreasing. Labor radicalism after 1900, as expressed in new forms of organization like the Industrial Workers of the World, was carried by other population groups. German radicals tended instead to identify themselves with the Socialist party, in which they saw the culmination of their search for close cooperation between the party and the trade unions.[68] Ironically, the radical tradition scored its most visible organizational advances in places like Milwaukee, where it discarded revolutionary goals for a complacent reform radicalism along the lines of German reform socialism, thus becoming almost indistinguishable from progressive local reform groups. It was only able to do so, however, because it had finally brought together the trade unions and the party in a common municipal program.[69] In this context, Americanization was almost equivalent to giving up the radical goals of the 1880s. Thus German-American socialism was curbed even before the restrictive internal measures accompanying the entry of the United States into World War I were put into effect by the government.[70] Whatever heritage and traditions it had contributed to an American radicalism either had been absorbed by multiethnic organizations before the war years or became lost as German working-class organizations gradually thinned out.

NOTES

1. "The New Party," *Standard*, 30 July 1887.

2. "Socialism and the New Party," *Standard*, 6 August 1887.

3. The United Labor Party and Socialism," *Standard*, 13 August 1887.

4. Cf. Hermann Schlüter, *Die Anfänge der deutschen Arbeiterbewegung in Amerika* (Stuttgart, 1907; Philip S. Foner and Brewster Chamberlin, eds., *Friedrich A. Sorge's Labor Movement in the United States: A History of the American Working Class from Colonial Times to 1890* (Westport, CT, 1977). The standard books on the liberals escaping to the United States after the failure of the Revolution in 1848 are Carl Wittke, *Refugees of the Revolution: The German Forty-Eighters in America* (Philadelphia, 1952) and A. E. Zucker, ed., *The Forty-Eighters: Political Refugees of the German Revolution of 1848* (New York, 1950).

5. For a general introduction to the literature, cf. Hildegard Meyer, *Nord-Amerika im Urteil des deutschen Schrifttums bis zur Mitte des 19. Jahrhunderts. Eine Untersuchung über Kürnbergers "Amerika-Müden". Mit einer Bibliographie* (Hamburg, 1929); and Paul C. Weber, *America in Imaginative German Literature in the First Half of the Nineteenth Century* (New York, 1926). Also Rolf Engelsing, "Deutschland und die Vereinigten Staaten im 19. Jahrhundert. Eine Periodisierung," *Die Welt als Geschichte* 18 (Stuttgart, 1958): 139; and Günter Moltmann, *Atlantische Blockpolitik im 19. Jahrhundert. Die Vereinigten Staaten und der deutsche Liberalismus während der Revolution von 1848–49* (Düsseldorf, 1973), 39. Meyer and Weber also point out a highly critical perspective on America originating with the romantic period; it emphasized the ahistorical and therefore artificial nature and the uncivilized character of American public and social life. This kind of cultural criticism, which continued unabated throughout the nineteenth century, was often expressed in the German-language labor press in the United States as well.

6. Ernst Fraenkel, ed., *Amerika im Spiegel des deutschen politischen Denkens. Äußerungen deutscher Staatsmänner und Staatsdenker über Staat und Gesellschaft in den Vereinigten Staaten von Amerika* (Köln/Opladen, 1959), 20. Meyer, *Nord-Amerika*, 10; Rolf Engelsing, "Deutschland und die Vereinigten Staaten," 141.

7. Engelsing, "Deutschland und die Vereinigten Staaten," 141f.

8. Meyer, *Nord-Amerika*, 33f.; cf. also Engelsing, "Deutschland und die Vereinigten Staaten," 146.

9. The term was used by the historian Friedrich von Raumer; it is quoted by Meyer, *Nord-Amerika*, 44.

10. Cf. Eckhart G. Franz, *Das Amerikabild der deutschen Revolution von 1848/49. Zum Problem der Übertragung gewachsener Verfassungsformen* (Heidelberg, 1958), 105.

11. "Erster Bericht der demokratischen Partei der deutschen constituirenden National-Versammlung vom 1. August 1848," quoted in Franz, *Amerikabild*, 106.

12. Engelsing, "Deutschland und die Vereinigten Staaten," 146.

13. Meyer, *Nord-Amerika*, 10.

14. Thus, according to Rudolph Cronau, Gottfried Duden's *Bericht über eine Reise nach den westlichen Staaten Nordamerikas und einen mehrjährigen Aufenthalt am Missouri (1824–1827)*, published in 1829, triggered an emigration fever; and Gustav Koerner, in his refutation *Beleuchtung des Dudenschen Berichtes über die westlichen Staaten*, published five years later, observed: "In many families it was read day by day on the eve embarking for the New World, and became an authoritative source for their information"; cf. Weber, *America*, 115–19; the quotation is from Weber, 117; cf. also Meyer, *Nord-Amerika*, 23f.

15. *Allgemeine Zeitung*, 16 April 1848, quoted in Franz, *Amerikabild*, 108. Cf. Fraenkel, *Amerika im Spiegel*, 35, who emphasizes the "Utopian expectations that wide masses of the German people had of America as a land of unlimited opportunities. In more than one sense for the lower classes of Continental Europe the USA was the myth of the 19th century"; the poet Johann Wolfgang von Goethe wrote that "America was then (1775), perhaps still more

than now (1818), the Eldorado of all who found themselves restricted in their present circumstances," *Dichtung und Wahrheit,* quoted in Weber, *America,* 87.

16. Cf. "Programm der Sozialdemokratischen Partei Deutschlands," reprinted in *Dokumente und Materialien zur Geschichte der deutschen Arbeiterbewegung,* vol. III: March 1871–April 1898, Institut für Marxismus-Leninismus beim Zentralkomitee der SED, ed. (Berlin, 1974), 383f.; cf. also Alfred Vagts, *Deutschland und die Vereinigten Staaten in der Weltpolitik,* vol. I (New York, 1935), 612.

17. Vagts, *Deutschland,* 612f. concludes:

> For parliamentary-practical socialism . . . friendship with America would mean the approximation to more freedom, but also the realization of certain socialist Utopias, like originally the preservation of America's colonial policy, and later . . . the American militia system. . . . Out of friendliness to America the German Social Democracy came to historically wrong conclusions about some developments in the United States.

Fraenkel, *Amerika im Spiegel,* 35f. also emphasizes the pro-American attitude of *Vorwärts,* the party paper, in the 1890s.

18. E.g., *Volksstaat,* No. 65, 14 Aug. 1872; No. 17, 26 Feb. 1873.

19. Hartmut Keil, "German Socialists Exiled under the Anti-Socialist Law, 1878–1890," chapter 3 of "Deutsche sozialistische Einwanderer in den USA im letzten Drittel des 19. Jahrhunderts. Lebensweise und Organisation im Spannungsfeld von Tradition und Integration," (Habilitation thesis, Munich, 1985); and Dirk Hoerder and Hartmut Keil, "The American Case and German Social Democracy at the Turn of the Twentieth Century, 1878–1907" in *Why Is There No Socialism in the United States. Pourquoi n'y a-t-il pas de socialisme aux États-Unis?* Jean Heffer and Jeanine Rovet, eds. (Paris, 1988), 141–65.

20. *Volksstaat,* 4 Jan. 1873.

21. *Volksstaat,* 17 May 1873; cf. also 22 Aug. 1873.

22. *New Yorker Volks-Zeitung (NYVZ),* 1 July 1881; cf. also 10 Aug. 1880; 25 Apr. 1881, 10 July 1881.

23. *Sozialdemokrat,* 13 Feb. 1881.

24. *Volksstaat,* 17 May 1873; cf. the comments on the occasion of the emigration of Julius Vahlteich and F. W. Fritzsche, two prominent socialists and former members of the German Parliament, in *Sozialdemokrat,* 19 and 26 June 1881; 21 July 1881; *NYVZ,* 27 June, 4 and 6 July 1881; also Keil, "Deutsche sozialistische Einwanderer," 137; Sozialistische Arbeiterpartei Deutschlands, *Verhandlungen des Parteitags der deutschen Sozialdemokratie in St. Gallen. Abgehalten vom 2. bis 6. Oktober 1887* (Hottingen–Zürich, 1888), 9; and "Gegen die Ausreißerei," *Sozialdemokrat,* 13 Oct. 1888.

25. *Volksstaat,* No. 17, 26 Feb. 1873.

26. *NYVZ*, 3 Nov. 1878 and 13 Nov. 1880; *Sozialdemokrat*, 16 Jan. 1880 and 20 Feb. 1881. The slogan appears in the *Volksstaat* as early as 1873, cf. 4 Dec. 1873. The *NYVZ* remarked that "a more opportune saying has not often been sent out into the world," 3 Nov. 1878. The slogan derives from a remark by Lothario, one of the characters in Goethe's *Wilhelm Meisters Wanderjahre*. Having served in the American War of Independence, Lothario returns home to his old estate and exclaims: "Here or nowhere is America!" Cf. Weber, *America*, 89.

27. "German Socialism in America," *North American Review* 128 (April and May 1879): 372–67, 481–92; cf. also the reaction to that article in the *NYVZ*, 20 and 23 March 1879.

28. U.S. Congress, House of Representatives, "Testimony of Johann Most," *Testimony Taken by the Select Committee of the House of Representatives to Inquire into the Alleged Violation of the Laws Prohibiting the Importation of Contract Laborers, Paupers, Convicts, and other Classes*, 50th Cong., 1st Sess., Washington, DC, 1888, Misc. Doc. 572, 246–53.

29. For overviews see Wolfgang Köllmann and Peter Marschalck, "German Emigration to the United States," *Perspectives in American History* 7 (1973): 449–554; Mack Walker, *Germany and the Emigration 1816–1885* (Cambridge, MA, 1964); Peter Marschalck, *Deutsche Überseewanderung im 19. Jahrhundert. Ein Beitrag zur soziologischen Theorie der Bevölkerung* (Stuttgart, 1973); Klaus J.Bade, "Die deutsche überseeische Massenauswanderung im 19. und 20. Jahrhundert: Bestimmungsfaktoren und Entwicklungsbedingungen," in *Auswanderer-Wanderarbeiter–Gastarbeiter: Bevölkerung, Arbeitsmarkt und Wanderung in Deutschland seit der Mitte des 19. Jahrhunderts*, Klaus J. Bade, ed., vol. 1 (Ostfildern, 1984), 259–99; Bade, ed., *Population, Labour and Migration in 19th- and 20th-Century Germany*, German Historical Perspectives, vol. 1 (Leamington Spa, 1987); and Wilhelm Mönckmeier, *Die deutsche überseeische Auswanderung. Ein Beitrag zur deutschen Wanderungsgeschichte* (Jena, 1912).

30. "Die deutsche Auswanderung," *Neue Zeit* 3 (1885): 253–57; cf. also the commentary to this article in *NYVZ*, 20 June 1885.

31. Köllmann and Marschalck, "German Emigration," 535.

32. *NYVZ*, 4 Dec. 1881; for emigration from Saxony see Hildegard Rosenthal, *Die Auswanderung aus Sachsen im 19. Jahrhundert (1815–1871)* (Stuttgart, 1931).

33. See, e.g., U.S. Congress, House, *Consular Reports on the State of Labor in Europe*, 46th Cong., 1st Sess., Washington, DC, 1878, H. Doc. 5; and U.S. Congress, House, *Reports of Diplomatic and Consular Officers Concerning Emigration from Europe to the United States. . .* , 50th Cong., 1st Sess., Washington, DC, 1889, Misc. Doc. 572, pt. 2.

34. The definition of "large cities" is not consistent here, since the census, which provided the only figures available for the purpose, changed the base number for the population.

35. U.S. Bureau of the Census, *Twelfth Census, 1900: Population*, pt. 1 (Washington, DC, 1901), clxxvi.

36. Bureau of the Census, *Compendium of the Ninth Census, 1870* (Washington, DC, 1872); *U.S. Tenth Census, 1880: Population*, pt. 1 (Washington, DC, 1883), 753ff.; *U.S. Eleventh Census, 1890: Populatiion*, pt. 2 (Washington, DC, 1897), 486–89.

37. Analysis of membership lists of the Socialist Labor party, New York; nationality

was not given, but it can be assumed that most persons with German names had immigrated; Socialist Party Collection, Tamiment Institut, Bobst Library, New York University. This finding is consistent with the general observation on the predominance of Germans in the Socialist Labor party in the secondary literature.

38. For overviews of the organizational activities of German Socialists, see *Friedrich A. Sorge's Labor Movement*, Foner and Chamberlin, eds.; Schlüter, *Anfänge der deutschen Arbeiterbewegung;* and Hermann Schlüter, *Die Internationale in Amerika: Ein Beitrag zur Geschichte der Arbeiterbewegung in den Vereinigten Staaten* (Chicago, 1918).

39. *NYVZ*, 21 June 1880.

40. *NYVZ*, 22 May 1881.

41. Cf. Heinzpeter Thümmler, *Sozialistengesetz §28. Ausweisungen und Ausgewiesene 1878–1890* (Berlin, 1979); Ignaz Auer, *Nach zehn Jahren. Material and Glossen zur Geschichte des Sozialistengesetzes* (London, 1889); Helga Berndt, "Die auf Grund des Sozialistengesetzes zwischen 1881 und 1890 Ausgewiesenen aus Leipzig und Umgegend. Eine Studie zur sozialen Struktur der deutschen Arbeiterklasse und Arbeiterbewegung" (Dr. phil. diss., Humboldt University, Berlin/East, 1972).

42. For the functions of exiled Socialists in the labor movement before and after emigrating, see Keil, "Deutsche sozialistische Einwanderer," 173–182.

43. E.g., in *NYVZ*, 12 Oct. 1889; *Sozialist*, 15 Jan., 30 April, 6 Aug., 3 Sept. 1887; 7 Jan., 21 and 28 July, 4 Aug. 1888; 8 March 1890; cf. also Gretch, letter to Eichle, Evansville, 19 Nov. 1889, Box 3; Brown in Boston, letter to Emil Kreis, 26 July 1883, Box 6, Socialist Labor party papers, State Historical Society of Wisconsin, Madison.

44. See Hoerder and Keil, "The American Case."

45. *Vorbote*, 30 May 1874; such advertisements often appeared in the German-language labor press.

46. Wilhelm Liebknecht wrote regularly for the *Arbeiter-Union* from April 1869 to September 1870, and Julius Vahlteich for the *NYVZ* before his emigration to the United States in 1881.

47. See Hoerder and Keil, "The American Case."

48. See, e.g., *Sozialdemokrat*, 10 Nov. 1881; 23 Jan., 13 Feb., 2 March 1882; 23 March, 5 April, 10 and 17 May 1883; 14 Aug., 27 Nov. 1884; 27 Aug. 1885; 5 March, 17 June 1886; 27 April 1889; cf. also Hoerder and Keil, "The American Case."

49. In an interview in mid-October 1878, two journalists who had just arrived in New York from Germany voiced their opinion that if the Anti-Socialist Law were paassed, "of course many of our editors and journalists will lose their means of existence. A goodly number of them will probably emigrate to America," *NYVZ*, 16 Oct. 1878.

50. For other examples, see Dorothee Schneider-Liebersohn, "Gewerkschaft und Gemeinschaft. Drei deutsche Gewerkschaften in New York 1875–1900" (Dr. phil. diss., University of Munich, 1983); Kathleen Neils Conzen, *Immigrant Milwaukee, 1836–1860: Accommodation and Continuity in a Frontier City* (Cambridge, MA, 1976); Agnes Bretting,

Soziale Probleme deutscher Einwanderer in New York City 1800–1860 (Wiesbaden, 1981; Christiane Harzig, "Chicago's German North Side, 1880–1900: The Structure of a Gilded Age Ethnic Neighborhood," in *German Workers in Industrial Chicago, 1850–1910: A Comparative Perspective*, Hartmut Keil and John B. Jentz, eds. (DeKalb, 1983), 127–144; and Hartmut Keil, "Immigrant Neighborhoods and American Society: German Immigrants on Chicago's Northwest Side in the Late Nineteenth Century," in this volume.

51. Adolf Douai in *Vorbote*, 15 June 1878; such praise was reiterated in countless variations; see, e.g., *NYVZ*, 16 Nov. 1881 and 7 June 1885, when the German Social Democracy was named the "guiding star of the European and American working classes" and the "trailblazer for all other movements in other countries."

52. Jakob Winnen, "Die Aufgabe der verschiedenen Arbeiter-Organisationen in der Jetztzeit," *Vorbote*, 3 April 1875.

53. Quoted by Conrad Conzett in *Vorbote*, 10 July 1875.

54. "Aufruf an alle Mitglieder der IAA, sozial-demokratischen Arbeiter-Partei von Nord-Amerika und der Arbeiterpartei von Illinois zur Gründung einer neuen, einheitlichen sozialistischen Arbeiterorganisation von Amerika," dated Chicago, 13 July 1875; in *Vorbote*, 17 July 1875.

55. Keil, "Deutsche sozialistische Einwanderer," 324–41.

56. For analyses, see Hartmut Keil and Heinz Ickstadt, "Elements of German Working-Class Culture in Chicago, 1880 to 1890," in this volume; Heinz Ickstadt and Klaus Ensslen, "German Working-Class Culture in Chicago. Continuity and Change in the Decade from 1900 to 1910," in *German Workers*, Keil and Jentz, eds., 236–52; for an example of the communal context in which German-American working-class culture flourished, see the collection of documents, Hartmut Keil, ed., *Deutsche Arbeiterkultur in Chicago von 1850 bis zum Ersten Weltkrieg. Eine Anthologie* (Ostfildern, 1984); the (translated) American edition is *German Workers in Chicago: A Documentary History of Working-Class Culture from 1850 to World War I*, Hartmut Keil and John B. Jentz, eds. (Urbana, 1988); for a recent analysis of German working-class culture see Vernon L. Lidtke, *The Alternative Culture: Socialist Labor in Imperial Germany* (New York, 1985).

57. *NYVZ*, 4 Aug. 1878.

58. *NYVZ*, 11 Aug. 1878. The same arguments were taken up once more in a series of articles by the same author, "Socialism on Anglo-Saxon Ground," *NYVZ*, 8, 15, 22, and 29 Aug. 1880.

59. *NYVZ*, 15 Oct. 1879.

60. *NYVZ*, 15 Aug. 1880.

61. *Freiheit*, 4 Sept. 1880.

62. Cf. Hoerder and Keil, "The American Case."

63. Conrad Conzett, "Der Weg zum Ziele," *Vorbote*, 12 Aug. 1876.

64. Alexander Jonas, "Die Socialdemokratie und die neue Arbeiterpartei," *NYVZ*, 5 Dec. 1886.

65. Edward Thimme, "Die deutschen Arbeiter und die englische Sprache," tenth anniversary issue of *NYVZ*, 28 Jan. 1888.

66. "Wilhelm Liebknecht in Brooklyn," *NYVZ*, 24 Sept. 1886.

67. E.g., Friedrich Adolph Sorge, *Socialism and the Worker* (New York, 1876); Alexander Jonas, *Reporter and Socialist: An Interview Explaining the Aims and Objects of Socialism* (New York, 1885); Adolf Douai, *Better Times!* (Chicago, 1877); Adolf Hepner, *Immoral and Unconstitutional: Our Accessorship Laws. . .* (New York, 1890); Gustav A. Hoehn, *Labor and Capital and the Object of the Labor Movement* (St. Louis, 1893).

68. Cf. Charles Leinenweber, "The Class and Ethnic Bases of New York City Socialism, 1904–1915," *Labor History* 22 (Winter 1981): 31–56, for evidence of the composition of the Socialist party in New York.

69. Cf. Robert Mikkelsen, "The Social Democratic Party of Milwaukee, Wisconsin: A Study of Ethnic Composition and Political Development," (Diss., Oslo, 1976); Elmer A. Beck, *The Sewer Socialists: A History of the Socialist Party of Wisconsin 1897–1940*, 2 vols. (Fennimore, WI, 1982); Joseph Anthony Kunkel, III, "The Ideological Party in American Politics: The Case of the Milwaukee Social Democrats" (Ph.D. diss., University of Minnesota, 1980). For the close cooperation between party and trade unions that made electoral success possible, see the completely different situation in Reading, PA, as analyzed by Henry G. Stetler, *The Socialist Movement in Reading, Pennsylvania 1896–1936: A Study in Social Change* (Philadelphia, repr., 1974).

70. Cf. Howard Quint, *The Forging of American Socialism: Origins of the Movement* (Indianapolis, 1964); Morris Hillquit, *History of Socialism in the United States* (New York, 1971); Ira Kipnis, *The American Socialist Movement: 1897–1912* (New York, 1952); James Weinstein, *The Decline of Socialism in America 1912–1925* (New York, 1969).

CHAPTER 2

Immigrant Neighborhoods and American Society
German Immigrants on Chicago's Northwest Side in the Late Nineteenth Century

HARTMUT KEIL

I n the latter half of the nineteenth century, Chicago witnessed unparalleled growth, making it the second-largest commercial, industrial, and population center in the United States.[1] German immigrants played a decisive role in this expansion: From the 1850s until World War I, they and their American-born children made up between 25 and 35 percent of the total population. Whereas 5,000 Germans lived in Chicago in 1850, there were more than 200,000 a generation later in 1884, prompting the *Chicagoer Arbeiter-Zeitung* to write of a "German city in America."[2] By the turn of the century, the census registered more than 440,000 residents in Chicago of German descent. They remained the city's largest ethnic group until after World War I.[3]

As a result of this high proportion of Germans in the city, several German neighborhoods emerged in various sections of Chicago (see Fig. 2.1). This essay will focus on one of these German neighborhoods—an area on Chicago's Northwest Side, bordering the industrial belt on the North Branch of the Chicago River.

POPULATION AND RESIDENTIAL STRUCTURE

Milwaukee Avenue, running northwest to southeast, linked the Northwest Side to both the city center and the large industrial zone on the nearby West Side, thus offering Northwest Side residents a variety of job

Figure 2.1. Map of Chicago including mid-1880s city limits and the German neighborhoods.

opportunities. These, in turn, had a marked effect on the population structure. The section of the city to the northwest, however, was topographically open; rapid development by construction and real estate companies, along with continued population growth, resulted in an extensive incorporation in 1889, which pushed the municipal borders farther outward. At the same time, there was increasing westward expansion—sometimes into residential areas—of companies that had originally been located along the industrial belt. Coupled with the flow of new immigrants and immigrant groups into the old residential areas close to the city, this industrial expansion led to a geographic and ethnic redistribution of the population.[4]

In 1870, when Chicago's population was approximately 300,000, there were already more than 25,000 people living in the Fourteenth Ward on the Northwest Side; but it was not until later that the Northwest Side witnessed rapid expansion. One important impulse was provided by the Great Fire of 1871, which destroyed one-third of the houses on the West and North Sides, as well as in the downtown districts of the city, but left the Northwest Side unscathed. Many people from other parts of the city who had lost their homes settled there permanently. Population growth in the Fourteenth Ward continued to be disproportionately high during the last decades of the nineteenth century, so that in 1900 more than 290,000 inhabitants—almost one-sixth of Chicago's total population—lived on the Northwest Side.[5]

Even though more than twenty ethnic groups contributed to this development, Scandinavians, Poles, and Germans were the most important, and the Germans represented by far the largest.[6] However, these groups did not intermingle randomly; instead, they tended to form regional centers according to ethnic and class-specific criteria (though there was considerable overlapping on the peripheries; see Fig. 2.2). Business streets, and especially Milwaukee Avenue, provided services for all groups and functioned not only as borders between ethnic neighborhoods, but also as public areas where the different groups met and interacted.

Economic and social status were decisive factors in territorial allocation. The Irish lived in the unhealthy quarters close to the Chicago River, where they initially found unskilled factory work. In the 1880s, they were to a large extent supplanted by the Poles, who also sought work as unskilled labor. By contrast, from the 1870s onward, the Scandinavian colony near the furniture companies south of Chicago Avenue grew into

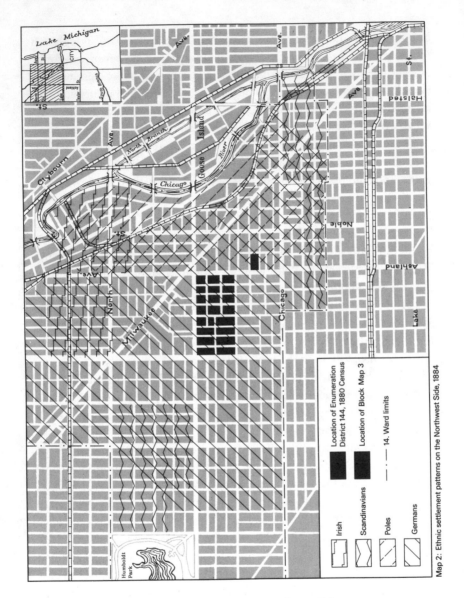

Figure 2.2. Ethnic settlement patterns on the Northwest Side, 1884.

an important neighborhood, since most Scandinavian workers found employment in the woodworking and metal industries on the nearby West Side. Beginning in the 1860s, the Germans formed a neighborhood along the western side of Milwaukee Avenue. Although it remained intact until after the turn of the century, it kept expanding west and northwest, so that the center of the German population continually gravitated to the outer city sections. The quality of life in this extensive area varied considerably, but on the whole, the western sections of the district were healthier and less populated.[7]

Beginning around the middle of the century and corresponding to the relatively late formation of the German neighborhood on the Northwest Side, there was also a clear shift in the regions of emigration, from southwestern to northeastern Germany. In 1880, a census inspector painstakingly registered the regional origins of immigrants in an enumeration district of the German neighborhood. His findings confirm the predominance of Germans from northern and northeastern regions, and they also provide insight into how the neighborhood was spatially differentiated by origin and occupation (see geographical location in Fig 2.2).[8] Most of the inhabitants of this district, which comprised some twenty blocks, were German immigrants and their families. Not even 2 percent of the household heads, however, belonged to the American-born second generation. Three-fifths came from northeastern Germany—four-fifths from northern Germany all told, if one also includes the general designation "Prussian" (which cannot, however, be divided into more specific regions). By contrast, not even one-fifth came from the older regions of emigration in southwestern, western, and central Germany. This relative homogeneity of the population can also be seen in other characteristics, such as a high percentage of family immigration, direct immigration to Chicago, and a low proportion of skilled workers. Only 15 percent of the immigrants from the northeastern provinces of Germany, as against almost two-thirds of the immigrants from industrial areas like Silesia and Saxony, were employed in Chicago as skilled workers. Unskilled immigrants from the same province preferred to live with each other in one street, whereas skilled German workers and artisans lived next door to skilled immigrants of other nationalities. Thus eleven of thirteen families on Samuel Street came from Pomerania, and, with one exception, all household heads were unskilled workers. Only one family from Mecklenburg had strayed into the street (the thirteenth family indicated "Prussia" as their region of origin); most people from Mecklenburg lived together on Dudley and Thomas Streets, five blocks farther west. By contrast, of the thirty families living together in a block of houses in Paulina Street, almost half were skilled workers, and they came from Scotland, England, Denmark, France, Maine, and New York, as well as from western Prussia and Hesse. Thus ethnic and regional ties were stronger for German immigrants from rural areas than for skilled workers, whose occupational status overshadowed ethnic differences.[9]

As was the case throughout Chicago, the typical German household on the Northwest Side was working-class, with the nuclear family as the basic unit.[10] In 1880, the average German household in Chicago comprised five people. Relatives seldom lived in the family; if they did, it was mostly younger people who, though old though to work, were still single and had possibly immigrated at a later date than the others. To take in strangers, however, was rare and as a rule limited to categories of people like master artisans, who rented rooms to journeymen working for them, or widows for whom taking in boarders was often the only source of income. For most single men and women seeking lodging, there were numerous boarding houses near the downtown districts, varying in quality and cost. By contrast, the German section on the Northwest Side was a family neighborhood. Its population was also correspondingly young, though not because of recent immigration. In 1884, the number of children aged sixteen or younger (i.e., as a rule dependent children living in the family) made up more than two-fifths of the population in the Fourteenth Ward—well above the city average. This high proportion of young people was typical of immigrant neighborhoods, whereas in boardinghouse districts and those wards where a large proportion of the population was American, it was considerably lower.[11]

What were the living conditions like in this neighborhood? One block of houses, still occupied primarily by Germans in 1900, was the object of a contemporary study. It pointed out typical characteristics that—with certain qualifications for the new residential areas farther west near Humboldt Park—held true for the neighborhood as a whole.[12] This block was built according to the grid-square layout of Chicago, which, in contrast to the irregular patterns of European cities, was planned arbitrarily on the drawing board (see Figs. 2.1 and 2.2).[13] Real estate tax, calculated according to street frontage, also played a decisive role in partitioning property. Lots in Chicago were generally 25 feet wide and 125 feet deep, as was also the case in the block of houses in question (see Fig. 2.3).[14] To take full advantage of this restricted width, the houses were often built adjacent to each other, leaving only a narrow passageway on one side to the backyard.

Construction was much influenced by the available material. Wood, transported by boat from northern Michigan and Wisconsin, was the cheapest building material. Until well into the twentieth century, the character of immigrant and working-class neighborhoods was marked by the invention (in 1833) of the so-called balloon, or frame, house. Making the traditional beam structure superfluous, these houses could be built within a week and were thus able to satisfy the immense need for accommodation. At best, these light structures could only support two stories over the basement. Immigrant neighborhoods in Chicago were consequently structured in a completely different way than, for instance, those in New York, or the tenement sections in Berlin. In time, older frame houses made way for multistory brick buildings; but instead of being torn down, they were moved into the backyard, where—provided with a set of steps to the second floor—they then housed two families instead of the original one.[15] In addition, more and more houses were built along the narrow alleys that separated the backs of the lots. These houses were put up close to the sheds and wooden shacks where garbage was kept and where primitive toilets had been constructed.

Increasingly dense construction led to a lack of natural light and ventilation in the house. George T. Nesmith, investigating the living conditions in a typical block on the Northwest Side for Northwestern University Settlement, confirmed: "I have seen more than one double bed-room which received its only air and sunshine filtered through an unventilated odorous living-room."[16] In addition, he found but one bathroom in all of the houses he inspected. Water closets, when present, had to be shared by three families; as a rule, there was one water tap in the house, but sometimes there was only one water tap for two families or a mere hydrant in the backyard.[17] As for washing clothes, the women had even greater problems; since there was no other place to dry the wet clothes, the living room had to suffice:

A living room surfeited with the heated odor of dirty soapsuds is not an ideal place to stay in, and a family, obliged to eat their noon-day meal with clammy clothes hanging about their heads are not apt to prolong the dinner unduly. Nevertheless only three tenements were found that had laundries in the basement, and not many more which provided a place for the drying of clothes on rainy days.[18]

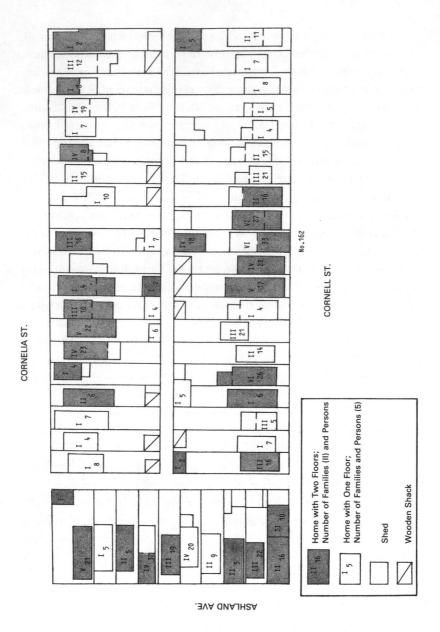

Figure 2.3. The block of houses in the German Northwest Side neighborhood bordered by Cornell Street, Ashland Avenue, Cornelia Street, and an alley.

Some of the streets, used by children as playgrounds, were in pitiful condition. If they were paved at all, it was with blocks of hardwood. When there was no storage room for coal, or when, because of a lack of funds, only small quantities could be bought at a time—often from deceitful dealers demanding inflated prices—residents were sorely tempted to use these hardwood blocks for fuel. Inadequate garbage collection, puddles of stagnant water, foul-smelling trash thrown onto the streets, a lack of toilets and sewerage made for filthy conditions that contributed to one of the highest child mortality rates in Chicago.[19]

Such conditions held true for the block formed by Cornelia and Cornell Streets, Ashland Avenue, and an alley (see Fig. 2.3). In 1886, only six of the fifty-eight houses were made of stone; the others, of the usual wood. Along the back alleys one can see sheds and wooden shacks, but also a few houses, the number of which would more than double by the turn of the century so that construction became increasingly dense. Even in the mid-1880s, the buildings on about half the lots took up 50 percent or more of the space. The houses were one- or two-story structures, and, except for two food stores, one butcher shop, and one tailor shop, they served exclusively as living quarters.[20] Between one and ten families lived on each lot; those ten families were found at 162 Cornell Street, where three houses had been built on more than 80 percent of the lot. Of the 135 families living in the block, only 5 rented out rooms to people other than relatives. On the average, each household comprised five people, but there were also one-person households and those with ten members. Only two household heads were single; the overwhelming majority were married (90.4 percent); and most of the rest, widows (8.1 percent). This is also reflected in the age structures: While three-fifths of the men were between thirty and fifty years old, a slightly higher proportion of the female household heads were over fifty.

German families were in a clear majority in that block (83.7 percent). Some three-fourths of them came from northern sections of Germany; only one household head was born to German parents in Chicago. With the exception of a few businesspeople and white-collar workers, as well as a few in private service, the household heads were almost exclusively workers, and some 40 percent of them were skilled (mainly carpenters, joiners, tailors, and painters). Jobs in the woodworking, metal, and construction industries were dominant. Among the unskilled (38.5 percent), about one-third worked in larger firms—steel, picture-framing, furniture, and shoe factories. Typically, over 90 percent of the unskilled workers, but barely 60 percent of the skilled, came from northern sections of Germany.

In more than one-third of the families, children—sometimes several—also worked. This was apparently necessary to supplement the family income, especially in larger families with seven or more members and in families where the household head was a common worker. Still more typical were working children in families where the father had died. In all such cases—regardless of whether the widow worked as a cleaning woman, a nurse, or a midwife—at least one child was employed. Moreover, almost all the women with paying jobs were single; among the housewives, only four indicated that they had an additional job.

Given the confined and unhealthy living conditions in this and the neighboring blocks, it is not surprising that there was a desire to move to areas where new houses had been built. Although the lots were not larger, additional development (of, for instance, the rear sections of the lots) was rare. But who could afford a simply furnished house, some 6 by 9.5 yards, for which the realtor S. E. Gross was asking fifteen dollars a month (see Fig. 2.4)?[21] Only the "working aristocracy" or families with several working members were in a position to do so.

INDUSTRIAL, COMMERCIAL, AND OCCUPATIONAL STRUCTURES

Job opportunities for the Northwest Side's population were limited to industries within easy reach, and they were determined essentially by four factors. One employment sector was represented by the small commercial and trade businesses within the neighborhood, those which directly addressed the needs of the local residents and expanded in proportion to the enormous increase in population. At first, businesses were located primarily along Milwaukee Avenue and in the surrounding streets, but in time crafts and stores also gained a foothold in the new residential areas. Then there was the industrial belt stretching along the North Branch of the Chicago River, which attracted thousands of unskilled and semiskilled workers. They worked in the numerous lumber, coal, and brick yards, in sawmills, construction yards, and various utility companies, but also in the North Chicago Rolling Mills and in more than a dozen tanneries. Skilled and semiskilled workers, especially metal and furniture workers, found

Figure 2.4. This broadside from 1883 advertises solid brick cottages on Chicago's Northwest Side in both English and German.

jobs in the factories on the nearby West Side (the center of these industries). And one must not underestimate the significance of the downtown districts, where, in the mid-1880s, over 40 percent of all the jobs in Chicago were located.[22] From an early date, Milwaukee Avenue connected the Northwest Side to the downtown area (first by horsecar, then in the 1880s by cablecar), facilitating access to these centrally located jobs. But the Northwest Side was still close enough that workers who could not afford the daily ride could walk to work. For the overwhelming majority of workers, closeness to the work place was the decisive factor when it came to choosing accommodations. Every weekday morning, Milwaukee Avenue was thronged with people rushing to work:

> The workday began in the dark hours of the early morning, as early as 4 A.M. for those with over two or three miles to walk (since they could not afford . . . streetcars that cost 10¢ which was two hours wages for the

women and children). By six o'clock thousands of men, women, and
children were trudging down streets like Milwaukee Avenue . . . dinner
buckets in hand, not to return until early evening.[23]

These job opportunities were reflected in the occupational structure
among heads of German families on the Northwest Side. In 1880, two-
thirds of all the households were working-class households, and this figure remained more or less constant until 1900. In this sense, the
Northwest Side was typical for German families throughout all of Chicago. But a comparison with the city's German North Side shows that
there were also significant differences between the neighborhoods. On
the North Side, the lower middle class was more highly represented. In
1880, moreover, with relatively fewer working-class residents, there was a
much greater proportion of skilled workers and artisans, and a correspondingly smaller proportion of unskilled workers.

By 1900, the composition of the working-class population on the
Northwest Side had also shifted in this direction. Unskilled laborers de-
creased by 13 percent, whereas skilled workers increased by 11.6 percent,
pushing their proportion above the city's average. The expansion of the
industrial belt offered them additional job opportunities (for instance, in
large bakeries, in the garment and construction industries, and in the
breweries). As was the case of the city at large, the lower middle class registered the largest increase. Various factors coincided here. For one, the
younger generation, having gone to school in Chicago and become familiar with the English language, had access to positions that were closed to
the older immigrant generation (like white-collar jobs in offices and department stores), particularly since at this time the tertiary sector expanded, absorbing a disproportionately large number of workers in the
downtown districts. In other parts of the city, too, commercial and service
institutions in the city had increased, in part because the enormous
growth in the population led to the emergence of additional shopping
streets and centers. In this context, it should be noted that the Northwest
Side had become the largest German section in the city.

By 1880, the neighborhood had sufficient businesses from the building and food trades; there were also commercial services and home industries like tailoring, shoemaking, and cigarmaking. A wide occupational
range was thus offered to the Germans of this neighborhood, in their immediate vicinity and for their immediate needs. In small- and medium-
sized workshops, one generally found that master, journeymen, and
apprentices all shared the same national origin. People working in such an

environment had no immediate need to learn English as an interethnic medium. Thousands of other workers, however, had to leave their neighborhoods to work in the nearby industrial zone.[24] They were employed in the large factories on the nearby West Side and on the North Branch of the Chicago River. Three-fourths of the tanners lived on the Northwest Side, where all Chicago's tanneries were located along the river (the rest of the tanners lived on the other side of the Chicago River). None of them had to travel more than 1.3 miles to work—a distance easily covered by foot.[25]

The widespread consequences of industrialization affected not only skilled labor. An analysis of the furniture workers living in the German neighborhood north of Chicago Avenue showed that highly qualified German cabinetmakers depended on the nearby furniture factories for employment, and that when wages began to stagnate, they faced the devaluation of their craft. At the same time, with increasing frequency, the furniture industry began hiring German immigrants' sons, many of whom had been born in the United States. Although semiskilled and therefore paid less, they apparently preferred to work in these companies, where, in contrast to some other branches and smaller shops, there was steady work throughout the year.[26] Equally desirable were jobs in the metal industry, where wage rates were relatively high for qualified workers.

The situation was completely different for cigarmakers. In 1880, this was still a traditionally German trade, strongly represented on the Northwest Side.[27] Three-quarters of the 236 cigarmakers in this section of the city were German immigrants, and one-third of them were American-born children of German immigrants. More sons and daughters than fathers worked as cigarmakers, so that the trade had a young work force: One-third were under twenty-one years of age and two-fifths between twenty-one and thirty. In each case the fathers had a different occupation from their children's; these were neither small family businesses, where the boys and girls had to help out, nor occupations handed down to the next generation. Among workers in this trade one can distinguish three groups, each with a different background. First, there were the skilled cigarmakers who worked in small shops and rolled quality cigars. Most had learned their trade in Germany, and many had come from southwestern and northern Germany, regions with an important cigar industry. They found work on the Northwest Side, where the number of shops had jumped to some forty between 1870 and 1880; by the turn of the century, that number had doubled.[28] On Milwaukee Avenue, the center of the industry, were sweatshops like Hanson's shop, where thirty-five men, young women, and children were employed. Although the unreasonable work conditions in Hanson's shop were the object of repeated vehement protests by the Socialist Labor party's alderman in the Fourteenth Ward, the municipal factory inspectors found no fault with them.[29] With no prior experience, it was possible to develop skills demanded by shops like Hanson's within a few weeks. Thus the trade offered employment for the second group seeking work—the newly arrived immigrants. In contrast, for instance, to fathers among furniture workers, three-fifths of whom had been living in the city for at least five years, the same proportion of fathers in the cigar trade had been there for less than five.

The third group consisted of children in unskilled jobs. Because heavy immigration assured entrepreneurs of a virtually inexhaustible reservoir of young, cheap labor, the circumstances under which children in the industry had to work remained unchanged, though repeatedly denounced by the union.[30] Similar to the textile industry, which absorbed mainly young girls and women, the cigar industry declined without significant mechanization; it was weakened primarily by the depression of wages and the displacement of production from artisans' workshops and medium-sized businesses to the sweatshops.

Retail trade was especially important for the neighborhood. The burgeoning German lower middle class was composed of white-collar workers on one hand and small-businesspeople and retailers on the other. Among household heads of the immigrant generation, there were almost three times as many retailers (13.6 percent in 1880, 13.8 percent in 1900) as white-collar workers (4.9 percent in 1880, 5.3 percent in 1900), whereas the figures for second-generation household heads were just about even, for 1880 as well as 1900. If second-generation sons and daughters are included, white-collar employees outnumbered retailers and businesspeople by a factor of three.[31] However, it was these establishments that played a decisive role in shaping the ethnic character of a neighborhood. They offered a complete supply of ethnic commodities—above all food and other specialties—and emphasized their ethnic character by usually advertising them in German. There were sections of Milwaukee Avenue were one could buy clothes, watches, jewelry, hardware, furniture, cigars, piece goods and notions, sewing machines, baking products, meat and other foods, and natural beverages and spirits—all in adjacent German stores. The shopping street, with its clusters of ethnic institutions, thus represented the most visible expression of the German neighborhood. One must therefore ask how, and to what extent, institutions generally influenced the communications network and identity of this neighborhood.

INSTITUTIONS, ASSOCIATIONS, AND EVERYDAY CULTURE

Cities in late nineteenth-century America witnessed enormous population changes.[32] The rapid increase brought about by immigration was supplemented by other forms of geographic mobility, such as intracity migration of blue- and white-collar workers looking for jobs, and the migration of seasonal agricultural workers drifting back into the city. Within the city, too, established classes moved to the city's periphery and to suburban residential areas, and members of the poorer classes frequently changed living quarters, often within the same neighborhood.[33] What consequences did this mobility have for immigrant neighborhoods, and what were the elements of their continuity? An investigation of bakeries and saloons on the German North Side showed that the establishments survived longer than their original ownership or lease.[34] Continuity is even more evident in institutions like churches or assembly halls, which represented large investments and served a broader population. That is why institutional changes lagged behind demographic changes in the German neighborhood on the Northwest Side. The Aurora Turner Society, for instance, gave up its old hall, close to the city, more than a decade after the center of the German population had moved outward; the Catholic St. Boniface Church held out several years longer, even though the ethnic composition of the parish kept shifting. Not until 1916 was the church finally relinquished to the Polish population.[35] These brief illustrations indicate that an analysis of local institutions can shed light on continuity and change within immigrant neighborhoods.

There was hardly a German association or club in Chicago that was not firmly anchored in a neighborhood. The most important exception was the German Society, which was founded in 1854 to help needy immigrants and thus lent assistance primarily to Germans newly arrived in Chicago or passing through the city en route to other destinations. It was not until later that the German Society also began helping needy German families living in Chicago.[36] Membership in all other associations, regardless of whether they were mainly ethnic, union, social, church, or charitable, was limited to the neighborhoods. Even organizations for fellow expatriates like the *Plattdeutsche Verein* (Low German Society) were subdivided into sections based on geographical location within the city. As the Northwest Side expanded, it was not so much the membership of existing sections that multiplied; rather, new sections were rapidly

Figure 2.5 Membership certificate, Order of the Sons of Herman, depicting scenes from the Battle of the Teutoburg Forest in A.D. 9, won by the Cheruscan duke Hermann (really Arminius) after whom the order was named, and, at the bottom, illustrations of the order's services, along with its motto, "Friendship, Charity, and Loyalty."

established. In 1883, for instance, there was only one section of the *Plattdeutsche Verein* on all of Chicago's West Side, but by 1896—on the Northwest Side alone—there were fifteen "guilds" with some sixteen hundred members.[37]

Benevolent Societies and Neighborhood Welfare

This multifaceted, neighborhood associational network served the vital function of providing for social welfare needs. Based on a sample of seven lodges, this function will be looked at in more detail.[38] Originally transferred from England, the lodge system preserved many ritual elements from Free Masonry. Lodges in the United States intensified assistance and support for members, beginning in the 1830s. A national insurance system, initiated by the private sector, did not begin to emerge until the end of the century. This and, more importantly, the fact that there were practically no legally anchored social welfare provisions, led to the enormous growth of the lodge system.[39] German immigrants participated to a considerable extent. They founded their own orders, such as the *Harugari* (Order of Harugari) and the *Hermannssöhne* (Sons of Herman), and formed subgroups of existing organizations, such as the *Druiden* (Druids) and the *Sonderbare Brüder* (Odd Fellows).[40] In 1883, there were at least twenty-six sections of such German and American orders; twenty-two of these were composed primarily of Germans, a fact often reflected in the names (*Humboldt, Körner, Hoffnung, Teutonia, Germania, Goethe,* and *Wallenstein*).[41] The German lodges explicitly referred to the preservation of German culture and language as one of their essential tasks (as, for instance, the Order of Harugari).[42] The statutes of the Robert Blum Lodge No. 58 of the Odd Fellows, founded in Chicago in 1849, also prescribed that "all business and transactions of this lodge shall be conducted in the German language."[43]

The lodges more closely analyzed here belonged to the Order of *Harugari* (two sections), the *Hermannssöhne*, the *Druiden*, the Ancient Order of United Workmen, the Independent Order of Mutual Aid, and the Jewish Order Kesher Shel Barzel.[44] The number of members in each ranged from 25 to 174. Almost three-fourths of the members lived on the Northwest Side; the rest, who lived in other sections of the city or outside Chicago, had probably also once lived in the northwestern part of the city.

Figure 2.6. Membership certificate, Independent Order of Redmen, with imaginary scenes from American Indian life and the order's motto, "Liberty, Beneficence & Brotherly Love."

Within the neighborhood itself, there were also geographical concentrations for members of individual lodges. While members of the *Körner* Lodge, for instance, were concentrated on Milwaukee Avenue and adjacent streets between Erie and Augusta Streets, members of the Chicago Lodge No. 91 lived farther north; those of the Chicago Lodge No. 88 of the Jewish Order were concentrated in the quadrant formed by Division, Noble, and Augusta Streets and Ashland Avenue around the center of Milwaukee Avenue. As far as national origins—above all German— were concerned, the lodges also differed considerably. In the *Körner* Lodge, only one member was not of German descent, and he came from Austria. In the Fort Dearborn Lodge, the non-German members—more than 40 percent—came primarily from Scandinavia, Great Britain, Ireland, and the United States. By contrast, few second-generation German-Americans were members. This meager representation concurs with findings that, with the exception of the *Hoffnung* Lodge, almost all members were household heads. Their ages were correspondingly high; in our sample, the extremes were the *Hoffnung* Lodge on the one hand, where 70 percent of the members were thirty years old or younger and half the members were household heads, and on the other hand the Jewish Order, which did not have even one member that young and all of the members were household heads. In the latter case, the high proportion of Jewish immigrants born in Germany, compared with the origins of Jewish immigrants overall, is also worth noting. The membership was composed of old German-Jewish immigrants from southern and southwestern regions of Germany who did not mix with east European Jews; not one member, for instance, was Polish or Russian. Nor is it surprising that the members of the Jewish Order had lived in Chicago for some time. More than 80 percent had been in Chicago for at least six years (in contrast to an average 72.5 percent for all seven lodges—an above-average figure in itself).[45] Nearly half of its members belonged to the middle class and were employed mainly in retail trades, especially the garment trade. Most of the skilled workers were employed as tailors.

In almost all seven lodges, there was a relatively high ratio of businesspeople to workers, in comparison to the occupational structure of the neighborhood. (Exceptions were the *Hoffnung* Lodge, with more than three-fourths workers, and the West Chicago Grove, whose proportion more or less reflected the neighborhood's occupational structure.) Unskilled workers made up a conspicuously small fraction of the members. The most highly represented occupations among skilled workers were the woodworking industry (16.1 percent), the building and construction industry (15.3 percent), and the metalworking industry (10.4 percent), though the proportions varied from lodge to lodge. The high number of tanners in the Fort Dearborn Lodge (21.5 percent of the skilled workers) and in the West Chicago Grove (12.5 percent) is also surprising, since it is way above their actual representation among German skilled workers on the Northwest Side (0.2 percent).

This membership analysis conveys the picture of a socially and economically established class that could afford to insure itself against illness and unexpected misfortune, in some cases several times over. Even within these seven arbitrarily selected German lodges, there were some dozen cases of dual membership.[46] Other associations—church, for instance, or trade—presumably contributed to multiple membership as well.

But there were, of course, numerous families who could not afford membership in mutual benefit associations. How did they protect themselves? It is difficult to ascertain exact details about the undocumented, informal assistance that took place between individuals and families. In certain exceptional situations, there was a willingness to sacrifice and a desire to help those in need—when, for instance, flood catastrophes in the United States and in Germany resulted in organization representatives setting out on fund-raising campaigns,[47] or when individuals from the neighborhood were assisted directly by means of "benefit events." In the latter case, for instance, public entertainment evenings were held in the Aurora Turner Hall and in Nutzhorn's Hall on behalf of two orphans or a "sick comrade."[48] But these actions were also initiated in associations. It is revealing that the deceased father of the two orphans was a member of two lodges, and the sick person belonged to the *Lehr- und Wehr-Verein* (Education and Defense Society). For nonmembers in need, there were citywide institutions like the German Society, other private relief organizations like the Chicago Relief and Aid Society, settlements, or the county's public assistance funds. Members of neighborhood associations or churches often mediated so that aid was more easily accorded; but the overwhelming majority of the people from the Northwest Side seeking aid from the German Society were affiliated neither with an association nor with a church.[49] In these cases, even slight disturbances in the everyday routine could have disastrous repercussions; when, for instance—due to unemployment, sickness, an accident at work, or the disappearance or death of a husband—the rent could not be paid and the family was literally put out on the street; or when there was no money for food, clothing, medicine, and heating materials. Here one sees how necessary it was to be tied into some institutional network, and, at the same time, how impossible it was to take part in associational life for those who lacked the necessary means.

Social Functions and Entertainment

One German visitor, who wanted to familiarize himself personally with conditions among the German-American working class before the turn of the century, found that the importance of the associations lay not so much in their charitable functions, but rather in their attempt to satisfy a need for sociability. He correctly perceived the lack of accessible public entertainment in Chicago, though he did not try to explain the reason for the need.[50] The most important factor was the cramped living quarters, which, inhibiting any sort of social life in one's own home, increased the desire to escape and relax, if only for a little while. In this sense, associations represented an extension of the domestic sphere for the lower classes as well as a semipublic communicative framework.[51] These institutionalized encounters took place in neighborhood saloons; their back rooms or, in larger establishments, "halls" served as meeting places for most organizations, most of which did not have their own buildings. In addition, many informal contacts were made in the saloons (mainly for men; for housewives, the shops had a similar function); but German neighborhood saloons differed from those of other ethnic groups in that they were more family oriented.[52]

The location of saloons on the Northwest Side illustrates the priority given to them in the poorer residential areas between the river and Milwaukee Avenue and around the shopping streets like Milwaukee, Chicago, and North Avenues as well as Division Street, all of which could be easily reached by those living west of Milwaukee Avenue (see Fig. 2.7). The multifunctional character of the saloon becomes especially apparent in the larger establishments. A varied clientele frequented the bars; near the companies along the river, for instance, workers regularly dropped in after their shift.[53] On weekends, the saloons were geared more toward the family; there were advertisements promoting the food and special Sunday afternoon musical programs. The back rooms and halls—rented by associations, trade unions, and political parties—were used not only for regular weekly business meetings,[54] but frequently also for social gatherings (sometimes determined by specific annual events), which explicitly included family and friends.[55] To step up business, saloon keepers sometimes took the initiative and offered variety shows, light farces, or other forms of entertainment on their premises.[56] Differences in entertainment between the small saloons and large halls were minimal. Associations usually sponsoring this light entertainment were—regardless of any ideological differences—basically agreed on its content and style. Conspicuous,

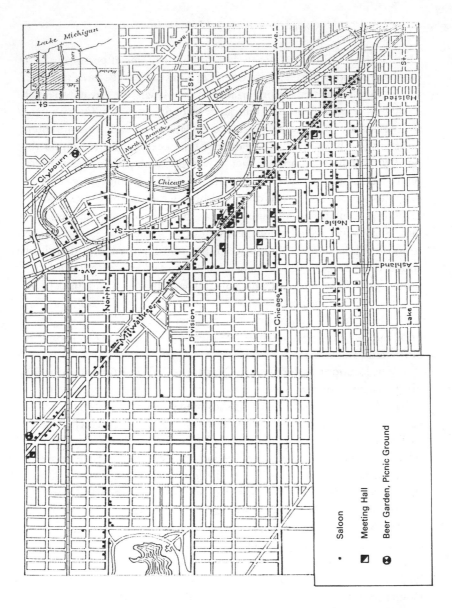

Figure 2.7. Location of saloons, public halls, and beer gardens on Chicago's North-west Side, 1885.

however, was a constant pattern of festivities that conformed to the available space and the importance of the event.

The Aurora Turner Hall was the largest assembly hall in the German section on the Northwest Side. The events held there over the course of one year, from the fall of 1883 to the summer of 1884, offer an impressive example not only of the wide range of activities and sponsors, but also of the way various needs were often met by a single event.[57] (The regular business meetings, evening debates, and informative gatherings held by the hall's landlord, the Aurora Turner Association, are not included.) The hall was used for residents' meetings concerning matters of immediate neighborhood concern, like the improvement of the streets and sewer systems or the neglect of the schools. The hall was also used for evening entertainments, concerts, balls, Turner and theater performances sponsored by trade unions, and by Turner, singing, and regional societies, by lodges, and Socialists. When the editors of the *New Yorker Volks-Zeitung* and of the *Freiheit*, Alexander Jonas and John Most, appeared in May 1884, the Socialist Labor party and Chicago's International Working People's Association used the hall for agitational meetings centering around the topics "What the Socialists Want and How They Want It" and "Who We Are and What We Want." Influential local politicians, in turn, used the hall as a political podium when they took part in a benefit event.

Every lodge and union section on the Northwest Side went to great pains when planning its anniversary celebration and, if possible, an annual ball; the more important events were held in the Aurora Turner Hall, since their sponsors wanted to reach a broad audience. On such occasions, an association's activities went beyond its specific membership and became general neighborhood events. During the carnival season especially, there was one ball after another. As a rule, the regularly scheduled evening entertainment—orchestral, vocal, and instrumental music, as well as recitals, one-act plays, and even complete comedies—was followed by a dance, advertised in large print in the preliminary announcements. Events were held almost exclusively on weekends (Saturday evening and Sunday afternoon and evening), on holidays, and on nights preceding holidays; the time and energy demanded by work left no other choice. At these events, of course, as in the saloons, substantial quantities of beer and wine were consumed. It is perhaps not so important to ask which of these diverse elements were most appreciated by the audience, but rather to note that these regular programs were accepted as adequate entertainment by a wide range of spectators over the years.

In warmer weather—by the end of May at the latest—institution-alized recreation took place outside. Saloons opened their gardens, and picnics were held in the big beer gardens and parks (notably Ogden's Grove on Clybourn Avenue). Hardly a weekend in June and July passed without a handful of picnics, organized by associations, political parties, and trade unions. Not oriented toward any single neighborhood, several sections of a lodge—like the Order of Harugari—might get together and organize a picnic for all Germans in Chicago. Some of these were espe-cially ambitious, preceded by a parade through the streets to Ogden's Grove, where the actual picnic was to take place. There were attractions for young and old: concerts, song and dance, and, at night, Bengal lights or even fireworks. One generally found family-oriented elements of popular ethnic entertainment and sociability that were a seasonal continuation of the events offered in the halls.

Alternative Cultural Subsystems

To this point, emphasis has been placed on the ethnic and cultural similar-ities among Germans living in this neighborhood. It was natural that these social and festive traditions were seen by German immigrants as the only right form of spending leisure time; but viewed from outside, especially from the perspective of the American middle class, these traditions seemed highly questionable. German gemütlichkeit was quite alien to puritanical values, especially when immigrants presumed to drink wine and beer in public places, much less to sing and go to the theater on Sun-days and holidays. The American middle class perceived the German eth-nic group as homogeneous in its cultural tradition or, conversely, perceived ethnic solidarity as an attempt to assert a sense of identity vis-à-vis social and cultural pressures from the dominant culture.

But this outside view must not blur the fact that there were also con-siderable social, regional, religious, and political differences within the German population of this neighborhood, differences reflected institu-tionally on many levels. The religious diversity is itself remarkable: In 1880, along with German Roman Catholic parishes, there were Lutherans (split into three subdivisions), Baptists, Adventists, Methodists (two de-nominations), a Jewish congregation, and freethinkers.[58] The political spectrum ranged from the two established parties, the Democrats and Re-publicans, to the Social Democrats, Socialists, and anarchists. Accord-ingly, diverse cultural manifestations were available, but they were not used arbitrarily. It seems more justifiable to speak in terms of alternatives, even of cultural subsystems, which were strictly separated from each other and which—though existing side by side in the same ethnic neighborhood—competed or even feuded with each other.[59]

This can be illustrated by looking at two antagonistic groups—the Roman Catholic St. Boniface parish and its offshoot, St. Aloysius, on the one hand, and the labor movement in its varying organizational forms on the other. St. Boniface Church was founded in the 1860s; in the 1870s, it expanded so rapidly that additions and new buildings (including a new church in the 1880s) were necessary to keep pace. By the early 1890s, the parish had grown to more than six hundred families. In addition, the influx to the new residential areas along Humboldt Park necessitated the foundation of a further parish, St. Aloysius Church, which already numbered four hundred families by the end of the 1880s.[60] Parish life went beyond the religious sphere and was organized into various associations meant to include all members so that institutions outside the church would become superfluous. Thus there were mutual benefit associations similar to those of the lodges (because the lodges were secret organizations, they were rejected by the Catholic church), and sections of the Foresters of Illinois and the Knights of America. Women were organized in charity groups (such as the Christian Mothers' Society and the Rosary Society), while the girls belonged to the Young Ladies' Sodality, where they organized picnics, dances, theater performances, and other events. For the boys there was the St. Raphael Young Men's Sodality, which provided for sport meetings, bowling, camping, and theater performances. Although bazaars or picnics were sometimes held in the neighborhood's large halls or beer gardens rented for the occasion, most parish events were conducted in the church's own rooms. But the most important expression of this attempt to attain institutional independence was represented by the parish school as an alternative to the public school. Founded in 1868, St. Boniface School reached its peak in 1902–03 with almost one thousand pupils.[61] One offshoot from its activities was the strong attention paid to the preservation of the German language. The parish was also involved in charitable establishments like St. Aloysius Church's St. Elisabeth Hospital, the St. Vincent de Paul Society, and charitable nuns' orders. The hospital was open to all faiths.

The labor movement also represented an alternative value system that frequently assumed an oppositional character. But the labor movement resorted to the wide range of already existing institutions, which, in part, it ultimately sought to reform and use for its own purposes (like the public school system).[62] In various associations the overwhelming majority of members belonged to the working class, so that—with the exception of trade unions, party sections, and political clubs—the focus was on developing political objectives within the already existing organizations. The lodge system, for instance, was a controversial associational form within the labor movement, particularly since it represented serious competition to the trades' mutual benefit societies and later to union health and accident insurance. While attacking the lodges' rituals and hierarchical structure, the labor movement nevertheless tried to secure the cooperation of neighborhood lodges when it came to celebrations and other events. Such cooperation was also achieved with various other associations from 1879 to 1886; the result was a political coalition between the working class and the lower middle class in the Fourteenth Ward, which was even able to elect a Socialist alderman for four years. Following the Haymarket bombing, the Aurora Turner Society—the most important link between the radical wing of the labor movement and the liberal middle class—gave its unconditional support to the arrested and sentenced anarchists (among them one of its members, August Spies); it also initiated mass meetings where residents of the Northwest Side protested the death sentence.[63] When the sentence was carried out in November 1887, an enormous number of residents accompanied the funeral procession down Milwaukee Avenue; most of the executed had lived on the Northwest Side.[64]

Even though the labor movement was firmly anchored in institutional relations, and its success in the early organizational phase was directly dependent on this neighborhood basis, its objectives went beyond these narrow confines, encompassing local and national forms of organization. The German-language *Chicagoer Arbeiter-Zeitung* required the support of all of Chicago's working class, just as class solidarity had to address repeated questions transcending local and ethnic boundaries, if the labor movement wanted to be taken seriously as a political force.

CHANGE AND DISSOLUTION

In the preceding pages, reference has been made to demographic and institutional developments that led to constant changes in the physical appearance and the population structure of the Northwest Side. What long-term effects did these developments have on the neighborhood's social structure?

At the turn of the century, the German population had grown sub-

stantially and was spread over a much larger area than twenty years earlier. Only one-third still lived in the original Fourteenth Ward; the remaining two-thirds, in the outer districts that had been incorporated in
1889.[65] This redistribution was not due to the depopulation of the old
German neighborhood; in absolute figures, the number of German residents living there had increased. But rather, the center of the German
population had shifted, and—even if it did not occur immediately—this
inevitably heralded the dissolution of the old neighborhood. Especially
among workers, there was a disproportionately high push toward the
city's periphery; in 1900, more than 70 percent of Chicago's working
class lived outside of the 1889 city limits (and comparatively speaking,
more unskilled than skilled workers), as against not quite 60 percent of
the middle class. But a rise in social status explains only part of this geographic mobility. House prices and rent were cheapest on the outskirts
of the city, and when unskilled workers understandably sought to escape
the overfilled and unhealthy slums, they were forced to move farthest
away.

Beyond noting general tendencies, it is difficult to ascertain just how
this shift in population affected specific groups of the German population. But another look at the residents in the block of houses formed by
Cornelia and Cornell Streets and Ashland Avenue, this time in 1900, offers some insight into what kinds of changes had taken place in the old
German neighborhood.[66] Since 1880, there had been great fluctuation
among the population—only 12 percent of the families were still living
there in 1900. Nevertheless, the number of residents had remained remarkably stable, while the number of families had increased by 17 percent;
the average family size had dropped to 4.3 members (from 5.0 in 1880). To
a considerable degree, this was a function of the altered age structure;
among male heads of household, for instance, more than 25 percent (as opposed to 16.1 percent in 1880) were over fifty years old. (The proportion
of women over fifty was much higher than in 1880.) The advanced life
cycle of the Germans becomes especially clear when compared to the
Poles, who now made up more than one-tenth of the population: More
than two-thirds of the Polish , but not even half of the German heads of
household, were under forty years old. The second generation, constituting 8.2 percent, was much more pronounced than in 1880 (0.7 percent).
All told, the proportion of Germans in this block had dropped to some 75
percent, while the proportion of other ethnic groups had risen to more
than 20 percent.

These older people belonged to the group that remained in the neighborhood, but they remained only under certain circumstances. This group comprised primarily thirty house owners, most of whom had succeeded, after years, in paying off the mortgages on their property; grown older, they could rent out apartments and be assured of a more or less steady income. More than 80 percent of them had immigrated to the United States prior to 1880,[67] the rest between 1880 and 1885, though the latter still had more to pay off on their houses then the former. Only half of the owners still worked at jobs; the others had already retired. A high percentage (30 percent) was composed of widows whose husbands had died during the twenty years since 1880. The advanced ages of neighborhood residents in general is reflected in the fact that 20 percent of all household heads (5.1 percent in 1880) were no longer working. While middle-class and skilled trades had remained relatively constant, unskilled and service jobs—which made up more than half of the total in 1880—had dropped dramatically by 15 percent. Thus this group of people, who were more or less economically secure, and who had settled in the block when the residential section was still being built, contributed to the neighborhood's continuity. At the same time, however, the group's advanced age points to a break in generational succession, a break anticipated by the marked changes in the demographic structure of the block.

Similar developments took place on the institutional level. The pattern has already been seen in the cases of St. Boniface Church and the Aurora Turner Hall. They were originally established in the center of the German neighborhood or in a residential area in anticipation of its rapid population, which then actually ensued, so that the institutions assumed a central geographical and social location. Subsequent continued geographical and demographical expansion of the neighborhood led to the founding of branch institutions farther away from the core of the city. The original buildings were then taken over by other advancing ethnic groups (on the Northwest Side, the Poles and later the Italians) or by businesspeople, who used them for new commercial purposes (the Aurora Turner Hall was made into a movie theater after 1900).

The displacement of the neighborhood also brought about considerable changes in the relationship between workplace and home, and hence in the local communications network. A more pronounced separation between place of employment, local institutions, and residential areas led to the increasing importance of the private sphere. In this sense, the altered neighborhood structure helped solidify middle-class life styles, which were geared primarily toward the private and individual as opposed to the local and communal. If, from the 1890s onward, industrialization led to the increasing segmentation of work,[68] the process of urbanization brought on a corresponding segmentation of the domestic and the familial spheres.

NOTES

1. Chicago's population development from 1850 to 1900 was as follows: 1850, ca. 30,000; 1860, 110,000; 1870, 300,000; 1880, 500,000; 1890, 1,100,000; 1900, 1,700,000. The figures are taken from the U.S. censuses on population published for the years in question.

2. *Chicagoer Arbeiter-Zeitung (ChAZ)*, 30 Aug. 1884. The figures are taken from that year's *School Census of the City of Chicago, Taken May 1884*. The German population is defined as immigrants and their children who were born in the United States; i.e., the criterion for the immigrant generation is the country of birth—the Prussian provinces and the kingdoms and principalities within the borders of the German Reich of 1871—and for the second generation the father's country of birth.

3. Bureau of the Census, *U.S. Twelfth Census, 1900: Population*, pt. 1 (Washington, DC, 1901), 796–99. Cf. also Hartmut Keil, "Chicago's German Working Class in 1900," in *German Workers in Industrial Chicago, 1850–1910: A Comparative Perspective*, Hartmut Keil and John B. Jentz, eds. (DeKalb, IL, 1983), 19–38.

4. For the development of the Northwest Side, see Barbara Mercedes Posadas, "Community Structures of Chicago's Northwest Side: The Transition from Rural to Urban, 1830–1889" (Ph.D. diss., Northwestern University, 1976).

5. Calculated on the basis of the *School Census*, taken every two years, 1880–98.

6. The figures were taken from the *School Census* of 1884 and 1898. These were the only years when questions were posed pertaining to national origin.

7. Cf. the detailed precinct analysis in Hartmut Keil, "Einwandererviertel und amerikanische Gesellschaft. Zur Integration deutscher Einwanderer in die amerikanische städtisch-industrielle Umwelt des ausgehenden 19. Jahrhunderts am Beispiel Chicagos," *Archiv für Sozialgeschichte* XXIV (1984): 54–61.

8. Chicago Project, America Institute, University of Munich, Analysis of Households in Enumeration District No. 144, *U.S. Census on Population 1880*, manuscript schedules; and *Robinson's Atlas of the City of Chicago, Illinois*, vol. IV (New York, 1886), plate 23. For figures on distribution according to regions in all of Chicago, see Bessie L. Pierce, *A History of Chicago*, vol. 2: *The Rise of a Modern City, 1871–1893* (New York, 1957), 516. For the national distribution of German immigrants from the various regions of the German Reich, cf. Walter D. Kamphoefner, *Westfalen in der Neuen Welt* (Münster, 1982), 86–122.

9. The tradition of traveling artisans also brought those in Europe into closer contact with other groups and nationalities.

10. In 1880, almost three-fourths of all households were working-class households; in 1900, the proportion was still more than two-thirds. Three-fourths of all German families were nuclear families; in addition, relatives lived in 9.7 percent of the families, 6.9 percent of the families let out rooms, and 8 percent had household help. But this picture shifted considerably as one moved from one class to another. In the upper middle class only one-fourth of the families were nuclear families, and more than one-half had maids; by contrast, more than four-fifths of the working-class households consisted of nuclear families; Chicago Project, Analysis of 2,222 German Households in 1880, *U.S. Census on Population,* manuscript schedules.

11. In Precincts 3, 4, 9, 11, 12, and 18, where the proportion of American inhabitants was more than 40 percent, the proportion of children up to sixteen years old was between 16.8 and 28.7 percent; *School Census,* 1884.

12. George T. Nesmith, "The Housing of the Wage-earners of the Sixteenth Ward of the City of Chicago" (M.A. thesis, Northwestern University, 1900).

13. For city planning and development see John W. Reps, *The Making of Urban America: A History of City Planning in the United States* (Princeton, 1965); Allan R. Pred, *The Spatial Dynamics of U.S. Urban-Industrial Growth, 1880–1914* (Cambridge, MA, 1966; Richard C. Wade, *The Urban Frontier: The Rise of Western Cities 1790–1830* (Cambridge, 1959); Sam Bass Warner, Jr., *The Urban Wilderness: A History of the American City* (New York, 1972); Homer Hoyt, *One Hundred Years of Land Values in Chicago* (New York, 1970).

14. Hoyt, *One Hundred Years,* 429.

15. Nesmith, "Housing," 12; Robert Hunter, *Tenement Conditions in Chicago* (New York, repr. 1970); Thomas Lee Philpott, *The Slum and the Ghetto: Neighborhood Deterioration and Middle-Class Reform, Chicago 1880–1930* (New York, 1978), 6–41; Agnes Sinclair Holbrook, "Map Notes and Comments," *Hull-House Maps and Papers* (New York, repr. 1970), 3–26.

16. Nesmith, "Housing," 52.

17. Nesmith, "Housing," 52ff.

18. Nesmith, "Housing," 53.

19. Nesmith, "Housing," 50, 74–79.

20. Information on the structure of the houses from *Robinson's Atlas,* IV, plate 21; on the population from the manuscript schedules, "Enumeration District No. 142," *U.S. Census on Population 1880.*

21. For a discussion of living conditions of German working-class families in Chicago in the early 1880s, see "Earnings, Expenses, and Condition of Workingmen and Their Families," in Illinois Bureau of Labor Statistics, *Third Biennial Report* (Springfield, IL, 1884), 135–414. Cf. also Hartmut Keil and Heinz Ickstadt, "Elements of German Working-Class Culture in Chicago, 1880 to 1890," in this volume.

22. *Report of Department of Health of the City of Chicago for the Year 1886: Report of the Tenement and Factory Inspectors 1886* (Chicago, 1887), 68.

23. Unknown author, quoted in William J. Adelman, *Haymarket Revisited* (Chicago, 1976), 80.

24. By itself, the available data do not indicate the location of place of employment. For instance, one cannot unequivocally ascertain whether a cabinetmaker worked in a small workshop or in a furniture company. Nevertheless, for some branches other circumstantial data indicate a close interrelationship between place of employment and place of residence. There was, for instance, an above-average representation of furniture and metal workers in this neighborhood, as was also the case with those unskilled and semiskilled workers who, instead of giving an exact occupation, listed only the branch in which they worked ("works in furniture factory"). The 1880 census tried to convey as exact information as possible; "works in" was supposed to define a different occupational category than that of a skilled worker ("cabinetmaker"). Nevertheless, we do not know how consistent the individual census takers were.

25. Chicago Project, Sample of 2,222 German Households: Geographic Distribution in 1880, *U.S. Census on Population 1880.*

26. Cf. John B. Jentz, "Chicago's Furniture Industry and Its Work Force from 1850 to 1910: A Social and Economic Framework for Interpreting the German-American Furniture Workers and Their Unions," in *Impressions of a Gilded Age: The American Fin de Siècle,* Marc Chénetier and Rob Kroes, eds., (Amsterdam, 1983), 287–300; John B. Jentz, "Skilled Workers and Industrialization: Chicago's German Cabinetmakers and Machinists," in *German Workers,* Keil and Jentz, eds., 73–85.

27. Chicago Project, Analysis of the Cigarmakers on the Northwest Side on the Basis of the U.S. Census on Population 1880. Cf. also Hartmut Keil and John B. Jentz, "German Workers in Industrial Chicago: The Transformation of Industries and Neighborhoods in the Late 19th Century" (Paper given at the Annual Convention of the Organization of American Historians, Detroit, April 1981).

28. Chicago Project, Analysis of the Chicago Business Directories for 1870, 1880, 1890, and 1900.

29. *ChAZ,* 10 and 13 March, 4 April 1880.

30. During a strike in 1883, the Cigarmakers' Union protested that a company employing girls from ten to thirteen years old payed them only one dollar per one thousand cigars, whereby wages were often deducted for alleged substandard quality. The girls complained that they were not allowed to talk while they worked, that monetary penalties were imposed, and even that the clock was turned back in order to extend work hours; *ChAZ,* 16 and 17 May 1883.

31. Chicago Project, Analysis of the Lower Middle Class According to Occupation and Generation for Chicago's German Population in 1900, Sample of 1,532 German Households, *U.S. Census on Population 1900.*

32. Cf. Stephan Thernstrom, "Urbanization, Migration, and Social Mobility in Late Nineteenth-Century America," in *Towards a New Past: Dissenting Essays in American History,* Barton J. Bernstein, ed. (New York, 1969), 158–75; Stephan Thernstrom and Peter R.

Knights, "Men in Motion: Some Data and Speculations about Urban Population Mobility in Nineteenth-Century America," *Journal of Interdisciplinary History* 1 (1970): 7–35.

33. Stephan Thernstrom, "Working Class Social Mobility in Industrial America," in *Essays in Theory and History: An Approach to the Social Sciences*, M. Richter, ed. (Cambridge, MA, 1970), 221–38; Thernstrom and Knights, "Men in Motion;" Paul F. Cressey, "Population Succession in Chicago: 1898–1930;" *American Journal of Sociology* 44 (1938–39): 59–69; Kenneth Kann, "Working Class Culture and the Labor Movement in Nineteenth Century Chicago" (Ph.D. diss., Berkeley, 1977) 29f.; Hartmut Keil, "Die deutsche Amerikaeinwanderung im städtisch-industriellen Kontext: das Beispiel Chicago 1880–1900," in *Auswanderer–Wanderarbeiter–Gastarbeiter: Bevölkerung, Arbeitsmarkt und Wanderung in Deutschland seit der Mitte des 19. Jahrhunderts*, Klaus J. Bade, ed. (Ostfildern, 1984), 378–405.

34. Christiane Harzig, "Chicago's German North Side, 1880–1900: The Structure of a Gilded Age Ethnic Neighborhood," in *German Workers*, Keil and Jentz, eds., 127–44.

35. For the history of the Aurora Turner Society, see "Der Aurora Turnverein," *Westen*, 15 and 22 Nov. 1896; *ChAZ*, 11 May 1896. For the history of St. Boniface Church, see Rev. F. L. Kalvelage, *The Annals of St. Boniface Parish 1862–1926* (Chicago, n.d.) and J. C. Bürgler, *Geschichte der Kathol. Kirche Chicago's. Mit besonderer Berücksichtigung des katholischen Deutschthums* (Chicago, 1889).

36. Cf. John B. Jentz and Hartmut Keil, "From Immigrants to Urban Workers: Chicago's German Poor in the Gilded Age and Progressive Era," *Vierteljahrschrift für Sozial– und Wirtschaftsgeschichte* 68 (1981): 52–97.

37. *ChAZ*, 24 June 1883, 20 Jan. 1896.

38. Based on the membership lists in the *Chicago Directory of Lodges and Benevolent Societies for the Year 1883* (Chicago, 1882).

39. The *Chicago Directory* of 1900 lists more than two thousand lodges.

40. Alexander J. Schem, *Deutsch-amerikanisches Conversations-Lexicon. Mit specieller Rücksicht auf das Bedürfnis der in Amerika lebenden Deutschen*, 11 vols. (New York, 1869–74). Cf. the respective entries on the "Druidenorden" (vol. 2, 765f.), "Harugari" (vol. 5, 191ff.), "Hermann's Söhne" (vol. 5, 281), "Rothmänner" (vol. 9, 459f.) and "Sonderbare Brüder" (vol. 10, 309ff.).

41. The figures are based on the lists in the *Chicago Directory*. The *City Directory* of 1883 cites forty lodges having their meeting places on the Northwest Side; along with these were eleven church lodges.

42. Schem, *Deutsch-amerikanisches Conversations-Lexicon*, vol. 5, 191.

43. "Bylaws. Article 1: Language;" *Constitution und Nebengesetze der Robert-Blum Loge No. 58 des unabhängigen Ordens der Sonderbaren Brüder des Staates Illinois* . . . (Chicago, 1849).

44. Based on the lodge directory, which lists the names of all members and addresses of most of them. The occupations were looked up in the Chicago city directories for 1882–84;

in addition, members were checked in the manuscript schedules of the U.S. Census on Population, which contain occupational and social data. Of the seven lodges' total 549 members, 34.9 percent were found only in the address books, 5.8 percent only in the census lists, and 36.4 percent in both sources. Thus data on occupation and class can be obtained for more than three-quarters of the members. The remaining data refer only to members living on the Northwest Side, for whom additional information was found in the sources.

45. The corresponding proportion of people having lived longer in Enumeration Districts 143 and 144 was 68.2 percent; manuscript schedules, *U.S. Census on Population 1880*.

46. The saloon keepers, above all, were members in various lodges that met on their premises; they may also have been active in recruiting new members because they came in contact with so many people.

47. For instance, following the terrible floods on the Rhine and Danube in Germany and Austria in the winter of 1882–83; *ChAZ*, 28 and 31 Jan., 9 and 11 Feb. 1883.

48. *ChAZ*, 28 March 1883, 19 Jan. 1884.

49. Cf. Jentz and Keil, "From Immigrants."

50. Alfred Kolb, *Als Arbeiter in Amerika. Unter deutsch-amerikanischen Großstadt-Proletariern* (Berlin, 5th ed., 1909), 133ff.

51. For the notion of public space, see Perry Duis, *The Saloon: Public Drinking in Chicago and Boston, 1800–1920* (Urbana, IL, 1983).

52. Cf. Klaus Ensslen, "German-American Working-Class Saloons in Chicago: Their Social Function in an Ethnic and Class-Specific Cultural Context," in this volume.

53. "Nachtwirthschaften an den Rolling Mills," *Illinois Staatszeitung*, 20 Jan. 1886, quoted in Ensslen, "German-American Working-Class Saloons."

54. The Socialists on the Northwest Side held their meetings in Nutzhorn's Hall on Milwaukee Avenue, the Second Company of the *Lehr- und Wehr-Verein* in Bodecker's Hall on Chicago Avenue, and the 1821 Gerber Assembly of the Knights of Labor in Straub's Hall, also on Milwaukee Avenue.

55. "Despite bad weather" numerous "comrades and their families" showed up for the evening entertainment and ball sponsored by the International Working People's Association of the Northwest Side, *ChAZ*, 18 Feb. 1884.

56. Thus 17 March 1884 in Nutzhorn's Hall, *ChAZ*, 16 March 1884; for the various forms of German popular and working-class theater in Chicago see Christine Heiß, "Popular and Working-Class Theater in Chicago, 1870 to 1910," in this volume.

57. Analysis of the notices and reports of meetings in *ChAZ* from 1 Sept. 1883 to 30 July 1884.

58. *Chicago City Directory* 1881.

59. For an example of the analysis of alternative cultural systems in a large nineteenth-century American city, see Richard J. Oestreicher, "Industrialization, Class, and Competing

Cultural Systems: Detroit Workers, 1875–1900," in *German Workers,* Keil and Jentz, eds., 52–69.

60. The following data were taken from Kalvelage, *Annals,* and Bürgler, *Geschichte.*

61. Schools were sponsored not only by Catholic parishes, but by Lutheran congregations as well (though not as extensively). The largest was the Polish-Catholic St. Stanislaus Church school in the Fourteenth Ward.

62. See for instance the reform suggestions proposed to the Citizens' Association by the Fourteenth Ward's Socialist alderman, Frank Stauber; *ChAZ,* 27 March 1880. By contrast, free-thought Sunday schools were founded primarily as a means of counterbalancing church schools, see among others the report: "Die socialistischen Sonntagsschulen in Chicago. Ihre Entstehung. Ihr Lehrplan. Ihre Wirksamkeit," *New Yorker Volks-Zeitung,* 7 July 1889. For the German labor movement and working-class culture in Chicago also see Hartmut Keil, "The German Immigrant Working Class of Chicago, 1875–1890: Workers, Leaders, and the Labor Movement," in *American Labor and Immigration History, 1877– 1920s: Recent European Research,* Dirk Hoerder, ed. (Urbana, IL, 1983), 156–76; Hartmut Keil, "The Knights of Labor, the Trade Unions, and German Socialists in Chicago, 1870– 1890," in *Impressions,* Chénetier and Kroes, eds., 301–23.

63. *ChAZ,* 31 Aug. and 27 Sept. 1886. Cf. also "Der Aurora Turnverein," *Westen.*

64. *ChAZ,* 14 Nov. 1887.

65. Chicago Project, Geographic Distribution of the German Population, Representative Sample of 1,532 German Households in Chicago for the Year 1900, *U.S. Census on Population 1900;* cf. also Keil, "Chicago's German Working Class in 1900," 30f.

66. Analysis of Enumeration District 520, manuscript schedules, *U.S. Census on Population 1900.*

67. By contrast, only 39.6 percent of all German heads of household living in Chicago in 1900 had immigrated prior to 1800; Chicago Project, Analysis of 1,532 German Households in 1900.

68. Cf. David M. Gordon, Richard Edwards, and Michael Reich, *Segmented Work, Divided Workers: The Historical Transformation of Labor in the United States* (Cambridge, 1982).

CHAPTER 3

Artisan Culture and the Organization of Chicago's German Workers in the Gilded Age, 1860 to 1890

JOHN B. JENTZ

S ince the 1960s, Anglo-American social and labor historians have expended considerable effort in studying artisans and their culture, particularly in the period from the late eighteenth through the mid-nineteenth centuries.[1] Artisans are seen as critically important in the formation of the nineteenth-century working class as they built its institutions and shaped its culture using their strong preindustrial traditions. Not as much attention has been given to artisans in the second half of the nineteenth century, in part because of the assumption that artisan culture by then had been significantly weakened by the impact of industrialization. Yet artisans played a critical role in the formation of the American working class, at least through the 1880s, and their contribution was particularly strong in America's new, booming, industrial cities, which commonly imported most of their workers from Europe. These workers brought with them traditions that formed a resource for building modern working-class institutions when native American ones were either weak or unappealing to the great numbers of foreign-born workers. Chicago's German artisans in the Gilded Age offer the opportunity to study the nature and transformation of these imported traditions at a critical point in the American industrial revolution, when production was being systematically mechanized in a broad range of industries.

In a recently published theory of American economic development, economists David M. Gordon, Richard Edwards, and Michael Reich see the first stage of the American Industrial Revolution beginning around

1820 and running into the later nineteenth century.[2] In this phase, manufacturers consolidated traditional methods of production and the workers involved in them into larger units and marketed the increased output. Machines were introduced, but the production process was not typically organized around them. Although artisans lost considerable independence, they retained some skills as well as significant influence over production. The basic methods of labor were not, therefore, fundamentally transformed, although the context in which labor was performed had been reorganized. The 1870s to the 1890s marked a transitional period when this older industrial order began to be undermined: "Relying primarily on new methods of mechanization, industrial capitalists began in the early 1880s to explore and increasingly to implement new production techniques that typically eliminated skilled workers, reduced required skills to the barest minimum, provided more and more regulation over the pace of production, and generated a spreading homogeneity in the work tasks and working conditions of industrial employees."[3] A new industrial era began in the 1890s and flowered after the turn of the century, based on the transformation of labor through the mechanization and systematic rationalization of production. Unusually skilled, German immigrant workers were in a critical position to experience these changes in the transitional decades between 1860 and 1890, as one era ended and another began.

Chicago expanded from a regional commercial and manufacturing center in 1860 to the second most important industrial city in the country in 1890.[4] Its population grew accordingly, leaping in the same period from one hundred thousand to more than one million.[5] Most of the immigrants who fueled this growth and worked in the city's booming factories came from northern Europe. In 1880, for example, 65.4 percent of those employed in the manufacturing branch of the economy were foreign born, and of these 82 percent were from Germany, Ireland, Great Britain, and Scandinavia.[6] This was, then, the era of the "old immigration," before the massive arrivals from southern and central Europe after the turn of the century. Germans made up a disproportionate share of Chicago's industrial work force—26.3 percent in 1880, when the German-born constituted 15.2 percent of the city's population.[7] The representation of German artisans in the city's skilled trades was often even more pronounced. Table 3.1 summarizes the most important skilled occupations for German men at the end of the period.

TABLE 3.1

The Top Ten Skilled Occupations for German Males in Chicago in 1890

Occupation	Number German-born	Percent of Trade
Carpenters and joiners	4,739	23.6
Tailors	2,439	27.7
Painters, glaziers, and varnishers	1,936	20.1
Masons, brick and stone	1,655	32.3
Butchers	1,609	33.9
Machinists	1,484	18.9
Bakers	1,263	47.8
Cabinetmakers	1,178	39.8
Boot and shoe makers	1,164	32.6
Blacksmiths and wheelwrights	1,057	22.8

Source: *U.S. Eleventh Census, 1890, Statistics of Population: Occupations,* 650–51.

The sheer existence of large numbers of Germans with strong craft traditions was not, however, a guarantee of successful labor institutions.[8] The structure and development of any particular industry, as well as the character of its work force, were equally or more important. The history of particular industries is, however, beyond the scope of this essay. Its purpose is rather to analyze the nature and transformation of artisan culture as German workers used it to organize in Gilded-Age Chicago. This analysis will also contribute to the understanding of other questions, such as why German workers provided such a large constituency for radical politics.

Artisan culture is defined broadly here to include the social practices and political ideas brought to America by German artisans as well as the traditions and values of particular crafts. Three extensive examples have been selected to illustrate German artisan culture and the institutions that represented it—the workers' associations that derived from the German Revolution of 1848–49, the mutual benefit society of Chicago's German bakers, and the tradition of tool ownership among Chicago's skilled furniture workers. Each will be analyzed in an effort to illuminate not only the group in question but also a larger field within the culture of German artisans.

WORKERS' ASSOCIATIONS

The *Arbeitervereine* (workers' associations) founded in Chicago were examples of a type of organization common in Germany, particularly since the 1840s. The Prussian government, for example, tolerated some workers' organizations as replacements for moribund guild institutions, as long as they did not become politically dangerous and kept to moral and intellectual improvement. One of the most important of these, according to P. H. Noyes, was the Berlin Artisans' Union, whose aim was "'to further the popular development of the spiritual, moral, social, industrial and civic life of the workers through teaching and action.' The club held lectures and discussion periods for its members, which included in 1846 some 94 master craftsmen and 1,984 journeymen." Appealing mainly to artisans, such associations spread throughout Germany in the revolutionary 1840s, serving, despite their declared purpose, "to develop a spirit of unity among the working-class members, a sense of common cause which was to carry over into the revolution."[9]

The tradition of workers' associations continued in Germany after the failure of the Revolution of 1848–49. In the 1860s, the Englishman James Samuelson visited the General Improvement Association of Elberfeld in Germany and reported:

> Although extremely plain, this hall is very cheerful and attractive. At one end stands the rostrum, or lecturer's desk, from which lectures and addresses are delivered by the professors at the higher schools, the principals of factories, and by the workingmen themselves. The lectures are on subjects of literary, social, and economical interests, as well as on political questions affecting the welfare of the whole nation, but strictly party politics are wisely excluded. Lectures are also delivered on science applied to the arts. Discussions follow the lectures. During the lecture beer, coffee, and tobacco are allowed, and in order to enable the members to partake of these with comfort, the hall is supplied, not with rows of uncomferaable [sic] benches, as with us, but with a great number of small oblong tables. . . . Ladies are often present at the lectures, . . . and in one [room] there is accommodation for an excellent library.[10]

The institution in Elberfeld promoted a culture of educational enlightenment, entertainment, and general uplift that was common among artisans in Europe and America in the late eighteenth and early nineteenth centuries. The German variety was probably distinctive for its stress on sociability, mixing of the sexes, and use of beer and tobacco. Despite national differences, this international artisan culture supported a tradition of popular republicanism that made artisans a common force in the democratic politics of several countries.[11] German artisans played a large role in founding and sustaining this popular and politically significant culture in Chicago.

Chicago Germans formed the Workers' Association and its related benefit society in an effort to meet their needs during the financial crisis of 1857–58.[12] The people mentioned in accounts of the association in the *Illinois Staats-Zeitung* give an indication of its mixed membership. Of twenty officials in the association in 1861, ten could be found in the city directories—a chairmaker, tailor, shoemaker, blacksmith, clerk, school teacher, city inspector and gauger, grocer, flour and seed store owner, and soap manufacturer. In the early 1860s, the most active secretary of the association was the blacksmith; the most active president, the school teacher. Thus the association united artisans, proprietors, and lower-level professionals; the acceptance of members of higher status—like lawyers and editors—prompted discussions in the association's debating society.[13] Notably, two of the ten officials found in the directories, including the blacksmith, lived in boardinghouses, which functioned as temporary quarters, often for newcomers. The Workers' Association was certainly among the institutions that newcomers found congenial for fellowship and status in a foreign land. It obviously met important needs, for by the early 1860s every geographic section of the city—that is, the North, West, and South Sides—had its own German workers' association built on the model of the central organization. The one on the West Side was by far the most active of these, building its own hall even before the central organization. A description of the new hall opened on the West Side in 1864 gives an idea of the association's functions and purposes:

The building is 40 by 70 feet long and two stories high. On the first floor two stores have been set up, which are to be rented. . . . Behind the stores is a spacious room that is to serve as meeting space for the association. The actual hall on the second floor is 40 by 44 feet long with a high ceiling and beautiful large windows going down to the floor, which make the room bright and airy.

The association enjoys a membership of approximately 130, made up exclusively of workers. They are intensely dedicated to the goals they have set for themselves, namely the social and political education of the members and the strict defense of their rights, in order to guarantee for themselves and their posterity life, freedom, and the pursuit of happiness. . . .

On Sunday evenings the hall is to be used for holding concerts, which are to begin next Sunday, and on Monday evening, the hall is to be dedicated with a splendid ball.[14]

The activities of the central Workers' Association reflected the basic purposes of fellowship, education, and general uplift. In 1861, it had 250 members, five hundred dollars in the bank, a good library, a piano for the new singing club, and a debating society. It also offered free English and drawing classes and sponsored picnics.[15]

By the summer of 1863, the association had more than one thousand members and a library of 740 volumes, which grew to 3,000 books within two years.[16] The source of the association's prosperity was its promotion of entertainment open to the public, usually on Sunday evenings in its meeting hall on the corner of Randolph and Wells Streets, in the center of the city.[17] On October 19, 1861, the program of the evening's entertainment included: a lecture by Dr. Ernst Schmidt, a liberal Forty-Eighter, on the "Prejudices and Errors in the Popular Home Remedies"; an overture; a declamation about the American national union; a concert piece; a song by the singing society; a violin solo; another declamation, "The Song of the Bell"; a humorous talk; a song by the singing society; and another concert piece.[18]

Politics were absent from the program on October 19, 1861, but not from the history of the association. During the Civil War era, it was intimately involved in the politics of the Republican party's left wing, sending, for example, delegates to an 1864 convention of radical Republicans and opponents of Lincoln held in Cleveland, a decision that split the organization.[19] The association also actively supported sending German-American military companies to the war and provided aid to the soldiers' dependents.[20] Afterwards, during the debates prompted by the eight-hour movement in 1867, the association proposed the establishment of workers' cooperatives as the true answer to the labor question, since they would abolish "hired" labor; it expected little from the eight-hour day itself.[21] In 1869, the central Workers' Association began to build its own hall, which, however, tragically burned down soon after completion, along with its entire library.[22]

The association regrouped and continued its work after the Great Fire of 1871, but by then it no longer played such a significant role in the organized life of Chicago's skilled German workers. Founded in the late

1860s and early 1870s, institutions like unions and labor papers became the organizational centers of Chicago's German labor movement. Nevertheless, before these institutions were established, the workers' associations stood out as centers of organized social and political life for Chicago's German workers. They taught the organizational skills, self-discipline, and ideals needed to found labor organizations and participate in politics. In addition, the political culture of popular republicanism that they fostered made the ideals of the American political system congenial to German workers, even when these ideals were severely contradicted by the realities of life in Gilded-Age Chicago.

THE BAKERS' MUTUAL BENEFIT SOCIETY

Mutual benefit societies flowered among artisans in nineteenth-century America as they organized to provide an elementary level of insurance against sickness and death. Commonly organized by trades, the benefit societies also often had secret fraternal features, which make them extremely difficult to trace. In addition, considerable numbers of artisans simply joined one of the popular secret fraternal orders, which also provided insurance. United by a common purpose, appealing to artisans who could afford to pay the dues, and providing tangible returns, the mutual benefit societies frequently predated labor unions and often proved more stable. They also competed with unions when the unions tried to provide their own benefit features, and at the same time they served as models for those very efforts of the unions. The history of Chicago's bakers provides a good example of how a union grew out of a German mutual benefit society in the mid-1880s. Constituting by far the largest national group among the city's bakers, Germans took the lead in organizing the industry.[23]

From the perspective of successful unionists of the progressive era, the benefit societies belonged to a kind of prehistory. John Schudel, a Chicagoan and the historian of the national union, wrote that in the late 1870s and early 1880s "an agitation was going on among the bakers throughout the country with the object of forming open organizations among themselves. To this must be ascribed the existence of those bakers' associations, loose trade union organizations and sick and death benefit associations we meet with at the inception of the National Union of bakery workmen, and wherefrom it took its rise. These associations sprung into life within the years 1880–1885."[24] Although he found these organizations "temporary" and "devoid of clear aim and definite principles," sometimes being mere "pleasure clubs," they were nonetheless the origin of the national union. A closer look at the Chicago bakers reveals the nature and critical role of these early institutions well before the 1880s.

Like so many other trades, Chicago's bakers began to organize in earnest during the Civil War, profiting from the demand for labor produced in part by large military contracts for bread.[25] Journeyman bakers organized in March 1864, but their union disappeared after losing a strike that summer.[26] One of the reasons the journeyman bakers could not sustain themselves was the still-common craft practice of having bakery workers lodge with their bosses.[27] Yet a permanent organization did emerge in this period, when the *Bäcker Unterstützungsverein* (Bakers' Mutual Benefit Society) was founded in 1867, the year that culminated in the city's first eight-hour movement. Uniting masters and journeymen, the society concentrated on providing both insurance and entertainment. These functions sustained it at least until 1917, when it celebrated its fiftieth anniversary.[28] In 1899, it had six hundred members and an insurance fund of ten thousand dollars.[29] For whole periods, the society's annual balls and picnics were the only signs of organized life among Chicago's bakers.

The society closely reflected the craft world of Chicago's German bakers. In the late 1860s, the treasurer, Frank Heuschkel, was also proprietor of a boardinghouse catering especially to German bakers,[30] and he advertised not only his rooms and food but also his ability to find jobs for the unemployed and workers for masters. Through boardinghouses like his, the city had an early institutionalized labor market for German bakery workers, a market controlled by the numerous small masters so prominent in the industry. One of the first objectives of union organizers in the 1880s was to break this control by founding their own hiring bureau.[31] Such conflicts were made especially bitter by the intimacy between masters and the journeymen who boarded with them. The masters also still presumed to speak for the common interests of the trade, as indicated in the unusual career of Mathias Schmiedinger.

Schmiedinger was repeatedly president of the Bakers' Mutual Benefit Society in the 1880s. He had been in Chicago at least since the mid-1870s, when he was part of a circle congregating around the *Vorbote*, a Chicago Socialist paper founded in 1874 with the aid of the most organized German trades, particularly the furniture workers and printers.[32] He was familiar therefore with the other elements of the Chicago German Left and played a controversial part in it. Yet, despite his radical politics, he was a master baker in the 1880s. The fact that he played so central a role in the history of Chicago's bakers' unions is an indication of the craft tradition's strength in the industry, for Schmiedinger saw no difference between his interests and radical ideals and those of the journeymen. The same holds true for those who followed him. The fact that he was ultimately pushed aside by Chicago's German bakery workers is part of the history of the emergence of modern unions from a craft.

After the depression of the 1870s, the first serious efforts to found a bakers' union in Chicago took place in late 1879 and 1880. At an organizational meeting in January 1880, Mathias Schmiedinger gave the opening speech in German, noting the past achievements of the society in providing insurance but emphasizing that the time had come to found a union in order to shorten the workday and raise wages.[33] Schmiedinger was elected chairman of the new body.[34] Yet after apparently successful meetings between German, English-speaking, and Bohemian bakers, the union disappeared.[35] A more successful organizational effort took place the next year, led by the Socialists associated with the *Chicagoer Arbeiter-Zeitung*; the society played a minor role in it, if any at all.[36] After losing a major strike in the summer, this bakers' union also disappeared. The next year, 1882, the Knights of Labor were the main instigators of organization among Chicago bakers, forming German Bakers Assembly No. 1801.[37] Although Schmiedinger appeared prominently in at least one meeting of Assembly No. 1801,[38] it is unclear to what extent the society was involved. Assembly No. 1801 led a shadowy existence for a few years, as did a German Bakers Union, probably formed in 1882.[39] By the middle of the decade, however, little, if anything, remained but the society.[40]

The bakers' union movement revived in Chicago and nationwide when a national bakers' paper, the *Deutsch-Amerikanische Bäcker-Zeitung*, was founded in 1885 under the impetus of the New York journeyman bakers. An international union was organized in January 1886 at a convention in Pittsburgh. Chicago's bakers were represented by the Bakers' Mutual Benefit Society, which was accepted into the international union as Local No. 10.[41] In the spring of 1886, Local No. 10 had 814 members constituting 85 percent of the organized bakers in Chicago.[42] The wholesale acceptance of the society as a union immediately caused deep divisions in the local and problems with the international, in part because masters— including Mathias Schmiedinger—were members and officers. These conflicts were compounded by Schmiedinger's dominating personality and the heated atmosphere of Chicago labor politics during the eight-hour movement and Haymarket affair.

The complicated factional fights among Chicago's baker unionists in the mid-1880s are only worth following in outline, but the stakes were nonetheless high, both for individual members and for the character of the Chicago bakers' unions. The core of the matter was the relationship of the union to the society. In 1886 and 1887, all members of the society had to be union members, which meant conversely that if someone left the union they left the society and lost the benefits due them and the contributions they had made.[43] The relationship between the union and the society was so close that, typically, the society would meet, settle its business, and then declare itself a union and take up labor matters.[44] Members complained that there was often not enough time for the union meeting,[45] and the two meetings were finally separated in late 1886.[46]

Politics entered this festering situation early, when the anarchistically inclined *Chicagoer Arbeiter-Zeitung* was closed down by the police after the Haymarket bomb exploded. Under the leadership of individuals like Schmiedinger, Local No. 10 imposed a one-dollar tax on all members to help the paper get started again.[47] Appealing to the international union for support, a minority opposed this tax and the politics it implied. Schmiedinger was also attacked for being a master baker, a problem the union had tried to solve by making him an honorary member.[48] The international sided with the minority, which left to form its own local. By early 1887, tensions between Local No. 10 and the international were so heated that Local No. 10 withdrew from the larger body.[49] Led by Schmiedinger and others, about three hundred members formed two independent Chicago locals, which strongly supported the left wing of the Chicago labor movement.[50] And, amidst all this factional fighting, members of the Bakers' Mutual Benefit Society were still supposed to be union members—but of which local? At the same time, Schmiedinger used the society to support the independent unions, despite the fact that many of its members belonged to the other locals. At a climactic meeting of the society in March 1887, the members rejected Schmiedinger's leadership and voted to separate the society and its funds from the unions.[51]

The story of these bitter disputes illustrates the ambiguous heritage that craft traditions provided for modern unions. Neither the character of its membership, the nature of its leaders, nor its intended purposes allowed the society to function as a union, and yet it was the only stable organization among Chicago's bakers before 1886. It is thus not surprising that it was the basis for the unions that did emerge. Within it were the people who had learned how to form and run an organization, and it had taught its numerous members the value of uniting for common goals. In addition, although it was not an educational institution like the workers' associations, its regular meetings, picnics, and balls provided occasions for Chicago's German bakers to meet, discuss, and learn from one another's experiences. Without the network of communication and trust built up on such occasions, it probably would have been impossible to organize Chicago's German bakery workers. On the other hand, the society institutionalized outmoded relationships between masters and journeymen, who had become instead employers and workers. The unions could not allow a master, no matter how radical, to speak for them. They later spent immense amounts of time and effort fighting the heritage of craft practices, like the boarding system. It is little wonder that the birth of the Chicago bakers' unions was difficult.

TOOL OWNERSHIP AND CHICAGO'S FURNITURE WORKERS

As a significant force in the Chicago labor movement, the bakers were rather late in arriving, compared, for example, with the woodworkers. Chicago cabinetmakers and joiners, largely German, struck for higher wages in 1852.[52] German cabinetmakers had an association incorporated by the state in 1855, most likely so that it could function better as a benefit society selling insurance and handling funds.[53] Several woodworkers' unions with strong German representation were organized during the Civil War, and woodworkers were the predominant group in the German section of the demonstration for an eight-hour day in 1867.[54] In the early 1870s, Chicago's German cabinetmakers led the movement for a national furniture workers' union, becoming Local No. 1 of that body in recognition of their efforts. The furniture workers were also one of the strongest forces behind the founding of the Chicago *Vorbote* in 1874, the city's first long-lasting German labor paper. Later they were one of the main elements in the eight-hour movement that revived in the mid-1870s, and they promoted the issue strenuously through the 1880s and beyond.

Chicago's German woodworkers, and particularly the furniture workers, obviously had an easier time organizing than the bakers—but why? The furniture workers had an especially strong sense of craft tradition, while they worked in an industry that was a prototype of Gilded-Age mechanization.[55] Beginning in the 1860s, Chicago's furniture entrepreneurs introduced the new machines—planers, circular saws, jigsaws, joiners—that were becoming available to them. With the machines came the subdivision of labor and the employment of unskilled labor, particularly children. And yet the mechanization of the furniture plants was a

Figure 3.1. Furniture workers of the Tonk factory on 30 April 1886. The majority of these workers were probably German immigrants, since the factory was located in a German neighborhood and was owned by a German immigrant.

process under way in the Gilded Age and not an accomplished fact. In 1875, one of the larger Chicago firms employed 150 workers, half of them skilled furniture makers and the other half machinehands and day laborers.[56] Almost as high a proportion of skilled workers was employed in 1880 at a Chicago chairmaking factory with a work force of 160.[57]

The transformation of Chicago's furniture factories deeply affected a group of workers with a special sense of the traditions of their craft and the value of their skills. This pride was supported by the furniture workers' ownership of their tools. The furniture workers literally owned some of the means of production, and, if one includes their skill within that concept, they owned even more. The tools that a skilled woodworker had to have were numerous and costly. A guide for German immigrants to the United States published in 1850 listed more than forty kinds of tools that a carpenter was expected to have in his tool chest in America, and at that time these tools would have cost 20 percent of a year's salary.[58] After a fire destroyed a New York furniture plant in 1888, the *Möbel-Arbeiter-Journal* calculated that the workers had lost a capital investment in the factory worth seven thousand dollars.[59] The tradition of tool ownership among furniture workers was even enforced by the employers. In the early 1880s, the work force of Koenig and Gainer's large furniture plant in Chicago was divided into foremen, engineers, cabinetmakers, turners, carvers, varnishers, finishers, machinehands, packers, and laborers. Among these, the cabinetmakers were the only ones required to supply their own tools. This craft tradition within the factory remained despite the fact that Koenig and Gainer had introduced "labor-saving machinery."[60] Their company was, therefore, a good example of the hybrid character of Gilded-Age manufacturing plants in which machines were used, though the production process had not been mechanized, and yet in which traditional artisans were still essential.

Tool ownership—which helped define these workers as traditional artisans—also shaped the public rituals of the craft. A standard part of the furniture strikes of the period was the return of the skilled workers to the plant to take back their possessions, often accompanied by a noisy crowd of supporters.[61] But why did the strikers have to return to the plants at all? A Chicago chairmakers' strike in 1880 offers a clue: Thirty-six workers returned to the factory to get their tools, including their workbenches.[62] In contrast to English and French workers—and to the custom in Germany—it was standard practice for German furniture workers in America to own both their "large" and their "small" tools.[63] The large ones included workbenches, c clamps, bar clamps, and miter boxes.[64] The quantity and size of the tools required that the strikers return to the plant with friends and wagons to get their tools instead of simply walking out with them at the beginning of the strike. The employers, in turn, used the tools remaining in their factories to blackmail or at least embarrass the strikers.[65] In 1885, the Brunswick and Balke Billiard Table Company in Chicago made the strikers take their tools from the hands of the scabs.[66]

The value of the tools and their indispensability for the livelihood of the workers made their loss a personal and family tragedy. The frequent fires in furniture plants, probably caused by the boilers needed to drive the steam engines, were thus a nightmare to furniture workers. A fire at Stotz and Voltz's plant in Chicago in 1877 was the occasion for considerable discussion in both the labor and popular press. The major German dailies were appalled by the fact that skilled and industrious furniture workers, of long standing in the firm, were unable to buy new tools and were forced to go on to public charity.[67] The furniture workers' union seized the occasion to advertise its tool insurance fund as one of the major benefits of union membership.[68] It noted that New York's furniture workers had had a tool insurance fund since the mid-1860s, and the fund had recently been made available to the national furniture workers' union.[69] Tool insurance remained one of the main concerns and attractions of the Chicago furniture workers' union.[70]

By the end of the 1880s, however, discussion began to appear in the *Möbel-Arbeiter-Journal* about the practice of tool ownership, particularly of large tools. The New York local considered itself sufficiently strong to broach the delicate subject in the paper and lead a movement for the elimination of the custom.[71] According to the New Yorkers, the issue had arisen among the membership because employers increasingly used the tools to blackmail the workers and because employment had become more unstable. Frequent changing of jobs required expensive transporting of the tools, which also increased the likelihood of their loss. What had once been the pride of the furniture workers now limited their freedom of movement and supplied their employers with a weapon against them. The paper concluded that "it's time for a change in this matter. The cabinetmaker—whose prospects for becoming his own boss are exactly zero—should free himself from this drag on his own existence in the form of a wagon full of tools. He should let the boss be responsible for them."[72] It is important to note that this suggestion concerned only the big tools, not the small ones; the furniture workers were not ready to give them all up. Nonetheless, there is no better point at which to mark both the decline of craft traditions among German furniture workers and the growing consciousness that they were modern wage workers.

Both the ownership of tools and the skill they possessed in using them gave German furniture workers in the Gilded Age a special sense of independence and pride in themselves and in their craft. This mentality made it easier for them to act together and oppose their employers in a way that distinguished them from other workers and made them forerunners of the Chicago labor movement. Their union organizers did not have to persistently fight the submissiveness and lethargy that were the constant enemies of the baker unionists. This independence and self-respect among the furniture workers survived for so long because artisans were indispensable to furniture production in the Gilded Age, even in the biggest plants. As the state of mechanization and rationalization of production increased toward the end of the century, this was no longer the case, and craft practices and culture declined, especially in the larger shops. Before these changes took place, however, the craft traditions of the German furniture makers had helped place them among the most organized and progressive groups of workers in America.

CONCLUSION

Artisan culture was indispensable to the organization of Chicago's German workers in the Gilded Age. It gave them the standards by which to judge the changes taking place in their lives, the associational forms and models they could use to begin to organize, and the personal skills and sense of integrity they needed for the task. The workers' associations, the Bakers' Mutual Benefit Society, and the furniture workers' tradition of tool ownership all helped promote a cultural environment that fostered personal independence, a sense of common interest, and intellectual growth. This critical significance of artisan culture for the modern labor movement in Chicago corresponds to that in other countries. Studying the origins of German labor institutions in the 1870s, Wolfgang Renzsch found that "craft values and norms not only provided the framework for judging new social conditions but also helped with the articulation of protest and the formation of organizations. . . . Without artisanal preconceptions about social and labor relations, on the one hand, and the awareness of craft models of organization, on the other, the organized labor movement would not have emerged in the forms described here."[73] Similarly, evaluating the significance of artisans in the labor movements in Western Europe and North America, Bryan Palmer concluded that "it has become a standard axiom of an emerging social history of the working class that the artisan, not the debased proletarian, fathered the labour movement," and he did this using all the resources of artisan culture at his disposal.[74] The case of the German artisans in Gilded-Age Chicago corroborates these general findings while emphasizing the critical importance of the specific period and place.

German artisan culture in Chicago at that time was shaped significantly by the speed and depth of economic change. The simple translation of craft ideals and organizational forms into modern labor institutions was never possible, as the history of the journeymen's unions as early as the Jacksonian era shows.[75] On the other hand, by the late nineteenth century, economic development had put an unusual strain on artisan culture, making large parts of it anachronistic. Practices that had been pillars of strength for the craft became weapons against the artisans in their new role as industrial workers. The clearest example of the strain on artisan culture is the bakers' ill-fated effort to make a traditional benefit society into a modern union. The society was torn apart by the new and conflicting demands placed upon it. The local unions that developed out of the society occupied themselves not only with the annual contracts, but also with fighting the heritage of the craft—like the practice of boarding with the bosses, which had become a means for exploiting the journeymen. In the case of the bakers, the anachronistic character of artisan heritage was probably increased by the importation of German practices that may still have had some relevance in the Old Country but that were practically outdated in Chicago.

The furniture workers offer a fascinating contrast since, according to the *Möbel-Arbeiter-Journal*, the practice of owning the big tools was not typical in Germany but, rather, became common among German furniture workers in several foreign countries. Far from an anachronism for most of the period, tool ownership was encouraged by the manufacturers themselves. Yet by the mid-1880s, it was clear that ownership of at least the big tools was a mixed blessing. The systematic mechanization of production was eliminating the hybrid character of the older manufacturing system, in which traditional production techniques had been integrated into larger units. This transformation destroyed the niches in the factories where craft practices had prospered and turned the tradition of owning the big tools against the furniture workers themselves.

Similarly, the workers' associations showed the limitations of their origins in an earlier era. They performed a vital function in the formative years of the 1860s, when Chicago's first labor movement emerged. They helped train leaders, promoted education and the development of intellectual skills, fostered ideals of mutuality and common effort, and initiated German workers into American politics on the basis of a popular republicanism shared with the larger political culture. They were limited, however, in their usefulness by their cross-class membership and by the tension in their goals between education and entertainment on one hand and political action on the other. When Chicago's German workers founded strong unions and a substantial labor press in the 1870s, the workers' associations declined in significance, and these newer institutions took over their former educational and organizational roles.

To live in Chicago—one of the country's most advanced and rapidly expanding industrial cities during the Gilded Age—meant, for German artisans, to be faced with the anachronistic character of their own culture, and this forced them to make special efforts to adapt and transform their heritage to meet their contemporary needs. One result was a group of workers unusually disposed to radical solutions to social and economic problems. The reputation of the city's German workers for being radical was widespread. Testifying before a congressional committee in 1883, P. H. McLogan, a representative of the Chicago Trades Assembly, said: "In Chicago, three or four years ago, the socialistic labor party polled 13,000 votes. . . . The socialistic party in Chicago, almost without exception, I would say . . . is composed of foreigners, and the great mass of them are Germans."[76] A simple ethnic explanation for this phenomenon is inadequate because there were times before and after the Gilded Age when German workers in Chicago were not radical.

Chicago's large German working class of the period contained a distinctive and volatile mixture of radical emigrés and disaffected artisans severely affected by the changes in their crafts during the peak of the American Industrial Revolution. Between 1878 and 1890, Bismarck's Anti-Socialist Law sent numerous radical labor leaders to America and Chicago who were talented, experienced, and ideologically committed. Yet such emigrés had also arrived earlier, though not in such great numbers, and they had built a small but significant Socialist labor movement even before Bismarck inadvertently aided their efforts. The presence of these radical emigrés does not explain, however, why they had such a large audience among Chicago's German workers in the 1870s and 1880s. More numerous and disproportionately skilled compared to workers of most other nationalities, Chicago's German workers were in a critical position within the work force from which to experience the rapid and fundamental economic changes taking place.[77] By directly threatening traditional skilled workers—who in Gilded-Age Chicago were so frequently German—these changes aroused the artisans who had always been the leaders of the modern labor movement, and they used their craft traditions as best they could to address their plight. As seen here, these traditions were both indispensable and inadequate in themselves, an inadequacy accentuated by Chicago's dynamic and advanced industrial capitalist economy. When the city's German craftsmen looked around for aid in their predicament, they found Marxist and Lassallean emigrés propounding answers in their own language.

NOTES

1. Good reviews of the scholarly literature pertaining to artisans are Bryan D. Palmer, "Most Uncommon Common Men: Craft and Culture in Historical Perspective," *Labour/Le*

Travailleur I No. 1 (1976), 5–31; and Sean Wilentz, "Artisan Origins of the American Work-ing Class," *International Labor and Working Class History* 19 (Spring 1981), 1–22. For an ex-cellent German study in the field see Wolfgang Renzsch, *Handwerker und Lohnarbeiter in der frühen Arbeiterbewegung: Zur sozialen Basis von Gewerkschaften und Sozialdemokratie im Reichsgründungsjahrzehnt,* Kritische Studien zur Geschichtswissenschaft, vol. 43 (Göttingen, 1980).

2. David M. Gordon, Richard Edwards, and Michael Reich, *Segmented Work, Divided Workers: The Historical Transformation of Labor in the United States* (Cambridge, 1982).

3. Gordon, Edwards, Reich, *Segmented Work,* 113.

4. This as judged by the gross value of industrial product. The first city in the country was New York; the third, Philadelphia; Bureau of the Census, *U.S. Eleventh Census, 1890: Report on Manufacturing Industries,* pt. 2: *Statistics of Cities* (Washington, DC, 1895), xxxii.

5. John B. Jentz and Hartmut Keil, "From Immigrants to Urban Workers: Chicago's German Poor in the Gilded Age and Progressive Era, 1883–1908," *Vierteljahrschrift für Sozial- und Wirtschaftsgeschichte* 68 No. 1 (1981), 61.

6. Bessie Louise Pierce, *A History of Chicago,* vol. III (New York, 1957), 517.

7. Pierce, *History,* 517; Jentz and Keil, "From Immigrants," 61.

8. Chicago's German tailors and shoemakers, for example, had large numbers and strong craft traditions to build upon but failed to found unions of comparable strength to those of the furniture workers, building carpenters, masons, metalworkers, bakers, cigarmakers, or brewery workers. The explanation lies primarily in the structure and devel-opment of the industries in which they worked. Between 1860 and 1890, when the German workers in these other trades were organizing, the Chicago clothing and shoemaking indus-tries were decentralizing into sweatshops and putting out more and more work to individu-als and families working at home. The dispersion of these industries and consequent isolation of their workers made them especially hard to organize. At the same time these in-dustries, particularly clothing, were used by new immigrant groups to gain a first foothold in the local economy, making the ethnic turnover of the work force unusually strong. Both in-dustries also faced particularly fierce national competition from other industrial centers. See Pierce, *History,* 171–75.

9. P. H. Noyes, *Organization and Revolution: Working-Class Associations in the Ger-man Revolutions of 1848–1849* (Princeton, NJ, 1966), 48f.

10. As cited in *Workingman's Advocate* (Chicago), 25 Dec. 1869.

11. Palmer, "Most Uncommon Common Men," 11.

12. Gaps in German-language sources created by the Great Fire of 1871 make the early history of the association difficult to follow; surviving issues of the *Illinois Staats-Zeitung* in the early 1860s do make it possible to trace the association in those years. The following sources refer to the founding of the Workers' Association: *Jahres-Bericht der Beamten der Deutschen Gesellschaft in Chicago, für das Jahr, – April 1857–1858* (Chicago, 1858), 12; Hermann Schlüter, *Die Internationale in Amerika. Ein Beitrag zur Geschichte der Arbeiter-*

Bewegung in den Vereinigten Staaten (Chicago, 1918), 307; Bessie Louise Pierce, *A History of Chicago,* vol. II (New York, 1940), 166f.

13. *Illinois Staats-Zeitung (ISZ),* 4 Sept. 1861.

14. *ISZ,* 13 Oct. 1864.

15. *ISZ,* 28 March and 12 June 1861.

16. *ISZ,* 31 Aug. and 10 June 1863; Pierce, *History,* vol. II, 167.

17. *ISZ,* 5 Dec. 1861.

18. *ISZ,* 19 Oct. 1861.

19. *ISZ,* 9 Oct. 1863; 16 March, 11 June, 28 July, and 1 Aug. 1864. On the politics of the Workers' Association during the Civil War, see Bruce Carlan Levine, "Free Soil, Free Labor, and *Freimänner:* German Chicago in the Civil War Era," in *German Workers in Industrial Chicago, 1850–1910: A Comparative Perspective,* Hartmut Keil and John B. Jentz, eds. (DeKalb, IL, 1983), 175–77.

20. *ISZ,* 19 June and 6 Nov. 1861; 13 Aug. 1862.

21. *Chicago Tribune,* 11 April 1867.

22. *ISZ,* 16 April 1869; *Westen* (Sunday edition of the *ISZ*), 28 March 1869; *Deutsche Arbeiter* (Chicago), 28 May 1870.

23. See Table 3.1

24. *The Bakers' Journal and Deutsch-Amerikanische Bäcker-Zeitung (BJ and DABZ),* 6 April 1901.

25. *ISZ,* 10 Dec. 1862.

26. *ISZ,* 7 March and 4 April 1864; 7, 9, 14, 15 June 1864; 4 and 16 July 1864.

27. In a sample of German bakers taken by the Chicago Project at the America Institute, University of Munich, from the federal manuscript census, over half the bakers lived with their bosses, who were also German.

28. *ISZ,* 17 Jan. and 24 Aug. 1867; on the occasion of its fiftieth anniversary, the Bakers' Mutual Benefit Society produced its own pamphlet, "Fünfzig-Jähriges Jubiläum des Chicago Bäcker Unterstützungs Vereins, Samstag den 3. Februar 1917, Nordseite Turn Halle, Chicago."

29. *Fackel* (Chicago; Sunday edition of the *Chicagoer Arbeiter-Zeitung*), 5 Nov. 1899.

30. *Deutsche Arbeiter,* 28. Aug. 1869; 9 June 1870.

31. See, for example, *Chicagoer Arbeiter-Zeitung (ChAZ),* 19 June 1881.

32. *Vorbote* (Chicago), 4 May 1887; Renate Kiesewetter, "Die Institution der deutsch-amerikanischen Arbeiterpresse in Chicago. Zur Geschichte des *Vorboten* und der *Chicagoer Arbeiterzeitung,* 1874–1886" (M.A. thesis, University of Munich, 1982), 75f.

33. *ChAZ*, 3 Jan. 1880.

34. *Fackel*, 4 Jan. 1880.

35. *ChAZ*, 18 Jan. 1880; *ISZ*, 18 Jan. 1880.

36. See the *ChAZ* from April through August, 1881.

37. *ChAZ*, 2 and 28 Aug. 1882.

38. *ChAZ*, 28 Aug. 1882.

39. *ChAZ*, 2 Feb. 1882. In 1886, there were 976 organized bakers in the whole state of Illinois, the overwhelming majority in Chicago; only 16 of these were in the Knights of Labor—the rest were in labor unions; Illinois Bureau of Labor Statistics, *Fourth Biennial Report* (Springfield, IL, 1886), 234.

40. There was a note in the *ChAZ*, 30 Dec. 1884, about a Bohemian Bakers Association.

41. *ChAZ*, 11 Jan. 1887; *BJ and DABZ*, 14 Jan. 1911.

42. Illinois Bureau of Labor Statistics, *Fourth Biennial Report*, 224.

43. *Deutsch-Amerikanische Bäcker-Zeitung* (*DABZ*; the title changed to the *BJ and DABZ* in 1895), 7 July 1886.

44. *DABZ*, 27 Oct. 1886; 22 Dec. 1886.

45. *DABZ*, 27 Oct. 1886.

46. *DABZ*, 23 Nov. 1886.

47. *DABZ*, 9 Feb. 1887; *BJ and DABZ*, 14 Jan. 1911.

48. *DABZ*, 7 July 1886.

49. *ChAZ*, 3 and 4 Feb. 1887.

50. *ChAZ*, 18 Feb. 1887.

51. *DABZ*, 23 March 1887.

52. Bessie Pierce Papers, Chicago Historical Society, citing the *Chicago Daily Democrat*, 15 May 1852.

53. Pierce, *History*, vol. II, 166.

54. *ISZ*, 3 May 1867.

55. U.S. Congress, Senate Committee on Education and Labor, *Report on Relations between Labor and Capital*, vol. I, 47th Cong., 1st Sess., Washington, DC, 1885, 568.

56. *Vorbote*, 22 May 1875.

57. *ChAZ*, 24 March 1880, and the manuscript schedules of the federal manufacturing census for 1880.

58. C. L. Fleischmann, *Erwerbszweige, Fabrikwesen und Handel der Vereinigten Staaten*

von Nordamerika. Mit besonderer Rücksicht auf Deutsche Auswanderer (Stuttgart, 1850), 223–25. The proportion of a year's salary was calculated on the basis of a wage of $1.63 per day, the middle of the range of wages given in this book.

59. *Möbel-Arbeiter-Journal (MAJ)*, 10 March 1888.

60. Bureau of the Census, *U.S. Tenth Census, 1880,* Vol. XX: *Report on the Statistics of Wages in Manufacturing Industries* (Washington, DC, 1886), 440.

61. An especially good example was the strike at the Bruschke factory in Chicago; *Vorbote,* 31 March, 7 and 14 April 1886.

62. *ChAZ,* 20 March 1880.

63. *MAJ,* 7 Dec. 1889.

64. *MAJ,* 7 Dec. 1889; 26 Sept. 1884.

65. *ChAZ,* 26 March 1880; *MAJ,* 7 Dec. 1889.

66. *ChAZ,* 2 June 1885.

67. *Vorbote,* 7 April 1877.

68. *Vorbote,* 31 March and 7 April 1877.

69. *Vorbote,* 7 April 1877.

70. A descendant of Local No. 1 still exists in Chicago today—Local No. 1784 of the United Brotherhood of Carpenters and Joiners of America—and it maintained the sick benefit and tool insurance funds started by Local No. 1 at least through the 1960s; "96th Anniversary of Local Union No. 1784," 4.

71. *MAJ,* 10 March 1888; 7 Dec. 1889.

72. *MAJ,* 10 March 1888.

73. Renzsch, *Handwerker,* 20.

74. Palmer, "Most Uncommon Common Men," 14.

75. The tension between the journeymen's unions and the trade societies organized to represent the whole craft is one of the main themes of the antebellum labor movement. See John R. Commons et al., *History of Labour in the United States,* vol. I (New York, 1981), 185–423.

76. U.S. Congress, Senate Committee on Education and Labor, *Report on Relations between Labor and Capital,* 585.

77. In an extensive sample of the 1880 federal manuscript population census taken by the Chicago Project, over 37 percent of the employed German males were skilled.

CHAPTER 4

Elements of German Working-Class Culture in Chicago, 1880 to 1890

HARTMUT KEIL AND HEINZ ICKSTADT

O n Easter Sunday, 1886, just a few days before the culmination of the eight-hour movement, Chicago witnessed the largest workers' demonstration in its history up to that time. It was sponsored by the Central Labor Union, the organization of trade unions in Chicago composed primarily of German members. Two miles long and made up of an estimated fifteen thousand demonstrators, the procession moved past fifty thousand people on its way through the damp, cold North Side streets to the lake shore. The demonstrating workers carried red flags and banners with slogans evoking the class struggle in various languages; they also drove wagons decorated with symbolic portrayals of the conflict between capital and labor. When they arrived at Lake Michigan, the crowd—grown now to some twenty-five thousand people—listened to speeches by Albert R. Parsons, August Spies, Samuel Fielden, Michael Schwab, and Randa, representatives of the International Working People's Association. Addressing their audience in English, German, and Czech, they called for more effective organization and solidarity of purpose and action. Then Schwab praised the resurgence of Chicago's working class in terms of Easter imagery. "Our fathers and grandfathers," he said, "have been celebrating this day of Nature's, of the Redeemer's, resurrection since ancient times. Today the workers of Chicago are also celebrating their resurrection. They have risen from their long indolence and indifference, they have seen what they can achieve if they walk hand in hand." The rally ended with the singing of the Marseillaise and three cheers for liberty, equality, and fraternity.[1]

The demonstration's origin, range, and manner all reflect essential characteristics of German working-class culture in Chicago between 1880 and 1890. German workers made up the bulk of the demonstrators; they were also in a majority in most of the participating unions, most of which had been founded by Germans. But other groups also took part—Poles, Czechs, Anglo-Americans. Although German workers were well aware—sometimes arrogantly—of their numerical strength and leading intellectual role in Chicago's labor movement, they nevertheless tried to induce workers from all ethnic groups to act in unison. Thus the speeches at the beginning of the demonstration were in English, but the content, symbolism, and rhetoric were also meant to address international traditions. In an American context, references to Jacobin radicalism—singing the Marseillaise and evoking the ideals of the French (and, by implication, the American) Revolution—and to notions of Christian salvation took on heightened meaning. The interconnection of unions and political organizations as reflected in the multiple functions of the speakers—they were at the same time leaders of the International Working People's Association, union organizers, and editors of labor publications—is indicative of the institutional basis for the self-assured behavior of the city's working class in the spring of 1886.

Chicago's labor movement had shifted its orientation in the mid-1870s. Supported by the trade unions, priority had been given initially to political organization, a tactic that led to considerable success in the 1878 and 1879 elections; after 1880, endeavors toward political agitation and trade union organization were predominant.[2] The result was rapid union growth, which lent the demands of the labor movement decisive weight. The demonstration, which took place one week before the Haymarket bombing, documents labor's strengthened position.

Only a brief sketch can be given here of the historical and political context informing German working-class culture in Chicago. Rather, our interest will focus on the following questions: Why did German workers constitute the essential element in the city's labor movement? What was the relationship between their social situation and the labor movement's gathering momentum after 1884? And, what were the characteristics of German working-class culture in Chicago, and in which areas was it effective? Until recently, there have been no studies specifically concerned with these questions. However, this culture's links to working-class culture in Germany, to an ethnic culture imported by German immigrants, and to Chicago's labor movement in general are worth investigating.[3] "Working-class culture" will be understood as the reservoir of traditional patterns of thought, behavior, and representation available to German workers in their encounter with the processes of industrialization and in their efforts at integration into American society.[4] We will attempt to show how working-class culture was inextricably linked to these social and economic processes, what traditions it drew on, and how it changed.

THE SOCIAL AND ECONOMIC CONDITION
OF CHICAGO'S GERMAN WORKERS

As a result of rapid industrialization and continuing mass immigration in the latter half of the nineteenth century, Chicago grew from a medium-sized city to the undisputed metropolis of the Midwest. Rapid advances in mechanization and the introduction of new technology favored expansion and structural change in the industrial sector; in 1890, the most important industries were meat-processing, iron and steel, building and construction, clothing and furniture, printing and publishing, metalworking, and brewing. By that year, Chicago was challenging Philadelphia as the second-largest industrial center (after New York) in the United States; it became the prototype of the American big city and the symbol of industrial expansion at all levels of society.

As early as 1850, reports of Chicago's vast economic potential and its fluid social structure had made their way to regions of emigration in Europe. When German immigrants flooded the Midwest around the middle of the century, Chicago became the region's center for German settlement. In 1850, 5 percent of all the Germans living in Illinois, Wisconsin, Iowa, and Minnesota were in Chicago; by 1880, the number had jumped to 13 percent. The absolute figures give a clearer picture of the enormous growth of Chicago's overall population and its German component: In 1850, Germans accounted for more than 5,000 of the city's 30,000 residents; around 1890, when the population had passed the million mark, 161,000 were German. Representing more than one-third of all the foreign born, Germans were the largest ethnic immigrant group.[5]

Changes that took place from 1880 to 1890 made this decade, in many respects, one of the most important for the development of the German working class in Chicago. Not only did the city's population double (the German population alone rose from 75,000 to 161,000), but there was also a correspondingly spectacular leap in the number of industrial workers (from 92,000 to 208,000). At the same time, technical innovation transformed the industrial sector, where more and more unskilled labor, largely recruited among the immigrants, was employed. The result was a decline in the crafts and small shops, the displacement of skilled labor, and a drop in wages.

Figure 4.1. Caricature with the caption, "How to reach the goal. How workers go about it at the present time. How they should go about it."

In 1890, the ethnic composition of Chicago's working class and the occupational structure among Germans in particular were as follows: Only one-third of the city's workers had been born in America; the remaining two-thirds had been born abroad (as compared with 41 percent foreign born of Chicago's population).[6] Germans represented 22.5 percent of the industrial labor force (47,000). Hence they were the largest immigrant group within the working class, and the majority of all Germans gainfully employed in Chicago (more than 55 percent) worked as skilled or unskilled laborers in trade and industry.

What were conditions like in the working class at this time? Detailed statistical information—sometimes compared with conditions in small- and medium-sized Illinois towns—can be computed from the Illinois Labor Bureau reports for 1884 and 1886.[7] The general wage increases following the economic crisis of 1873–77 did not last long; because of another depression in 1883 (even though it was not as severe), wages fell by 5.7 percent in the period from 1882 to 1886. But structural causes as well as cyclical fluctuations were responsible for this decline.[8] It affected unskilled workers in large factories as well as skilled workers, like cabinetmakers or shoemakers, whose wages were depressed by the introduction of new machines. Skilled German workers, especially, were affected by mechanization. Wages for workers such as bakers, brickmakers, butchers, cabinetmakers, carpenters, carriage and wagon makers, coopers, metalworkers, passementerie makers, and toolmakers, where Germans were strongly represented, fell below the annual average of $569. To make matters worse, the drop in wages was accompanied by high unemployment. In October of the slack year 1884, approximately thirty thousand people in Chicago were unemployed, a burden that exhausted municipal and private welfare institutions. In "normal" years, some 15 percent of the work force was unemployed.[9] Seasonal unemployment proved even more devastating. Only 20 percent of Chicago's workers had full-time employment, whereas one-third were idle for more than six months. The annual average length of employment was thirty-seven weeks. Seasonal employment affected workers organized in trade unions (i.e., primarily skilled German workers) more than members of the Knights of Labor, where unskilled workers made up a relatively higher percentage. It played a more influential role in determining actual annual wages than did wage reductions. Taken together, this precarious employment situation meant that many working-class families were forced to go into debt. Of the seventy-eight German households surveyed in 1884, 40 percent reported higher expenses than earnings, despite the fact that in one-third of the households, several members worked and contributed to the family income (the comparable figure for German working-class families in other parts of Illinois was 18 percent).

Whereas in the rest of Illinois more than one-third of the trade union members owned their own houses, only a few workers were able to realize this dream in Chicago.[10] For German workers as well as others, the purchase of a house depended upon the size of one's income, degree of skill, and type of work. Accordingly, there were substantial differences within the working class. Far more artisans and skilled workers, as well as workers earning more than just average wages, owned a house; but among this group of artisans and skilled workers, those employed in building and construction outnumbered all the others.

In the Illinois Labor Bureau's 1884 report, none of the German working-class families whose living conditions were described in detail and viewed as typical examples owned their own houses. A few artisans and skilled workers (one trunkmaker, two upholsterers, one cigarmaker) rented well-furnished houses, some of them in a "healthy location"; the families were described as being well dressed and "intelligent." The fathers were union members. In one case, the report even went so far as to say that "on the whole, they are a happy family." But the economic and social situation of all the other families was worse. A blacksmith lived with his wife and five children in orderly and clean surroundings, but in a four-room apartment in a tenement house; he only had twenty-five weeks' work that year, and it was reported that "they are not satisfied with their condition." A cigarmaker's family of eight lived in a house with three rooms and paid the exorbitant rent of twenty dollars a month. The house was described as "scantily and poorly furnished, no carpets, and the furniture being of the cheapest kind." It was located in an unhealthy neighborhood and kept in filthy condition; the children were sick "at all times." The father belonged to the union but could only find work occasionally, so the family was dependent on the additional earnings of the wife and the oldest son. A laborer's family was even worse off: Living in "filthy condition, in a block of miserable frame tenements," the family members were poorly clothed and undernourished, sick, and "exceedingly illiterate." Due to his long workdays, a streetcar driver only saw his children when they were already asleep. A conductor, hardly better off, was employed full time but, because of his sixteen-hour workday, did not even have time to look at a newspaper; he complained that "the company is grinding [me] and all the others to the starvation point."[11] Similar complaints about increasing mechanization, the pace of work, the strict work discipline, and the fines imposed for singing or talking on the job were frequently reported in the labor press.

These poor or even wretched living conditions invited comparison with life in Germany. In the winter of 1883, Paul Grottkau, editor of the

Chicagoer Arbeiter-Zeitung, accompanied a committee of the Citizens' Association on its inspection tours of Chicago's tenement districts. Before immigrating to Chicago in 1878, Grottkau had been active in trade unions and in the German Social Democracy in Berlin for several years. Michael Schwab, one of the sentenced Haymarket anarchists, described Grottkau's reaction upon his return to the office in his autobiography: "By his friends, G. is considered a cynic. When he came back he was deadly pale, greatly excited, he was not feeling well. He said that he never would go out to see such terrible things again. He knew a good deal of Berlin and her misery, but such a condition of affairs did not exist there, not even in the poorest quarters."[12] Schwab went out in Grottkau's place and confirmed the latter's impressions. In their autobiographies, all of the Haymarket anarchists who had immigrated from Germany referred to their own experiences. Having failed in Germany as a small businessman, Georg Engel sought economic success in America, that "free and glorious country." Like Schwab and Oskar Neebe (who was born in New York, the son of German parents, though he was apprenticed in Germany), Engel soon realized that the displacement of artisans and skilled workers in America's industrial centers had reached the same stage as in Germany. In comparison with the cost of living, wages for bookbinders, observed Schwab, who had learned the bookbinder's trade, tended to be lower in Chicago than in Germany. August Spies found conditions comparable, but added: "I never saw there such real suffering from want as I have seen in this country. And there is more protection for women and children in Germany than here."[13] The discrepancy between the immigrants' optimistic expectations and their actual circumstances in Chicago was a motif that recurred constantly in the German labor press, especially as a means of promoting union and political organization.

Was this argument appealing? The extent of union organization among Chicago's workers indicates both their awareness of the need for common action and also the degree of existing solidarity. In the 1880s, the trade union movement in the United States received an extraordinary stimulus, primarily from several large railroad strikes and the 1886 eight-hour movement. Chicago was the center of organizational activities. Of the 352,000 workers who took part in the eight-hour movement in the United States, almost one-third lived in Chicago. In June 1886, Chicago's unions reported a membership of 60,191, the trade unions comprising about twice as many members (41,800) as the Knights of Labor (18,350).[14] Measured against their proportion of Chicago's total working class (about

Figure 4.2. Title page of the Pionier, *1902. This symbolic presentation of the worker as the pioneer of social progress refers to basically the same images and artisan traditions as evoked in Figure 4.3.*

22.5 percent), the number of organized German workers was high: They constituted almost one-third of the membership of all Chicago labor organizations. Whereas only 20 percent of the Knights of Labor members were German (Anglo-Americans made up 34 percent), the figure for the trade unions was 35.8 percent (14,910). Germans were the largest ethnic group, even before Anglo-Americans. In twenty-seven of one hundred unions, the proportion of German workers was above this average, sometimes considerably so.[15] It was not only in absolute numbers that German workers were so important within the Chicago labor movement; they also played a decisive role in shaping its political and cultural life, which was institutionally supported by the unions and the International Working People's Association.

Accordingly, German working-class culture in Chicago was founded on the following conditions:

(1) As an important American industrial center, Chicago needed and employed a quickly growing number of workers. Two-thirds of this labor force was composed of immigrants, Germans representing the largest number.

(2) The objective condition of German workers in Chicago between 1880 and 1890 was comparable to that in German industrial centers. When comparing these conditions subjectively, however, the experience of confronting optimistic anticipations with a sobering reality often resulted in disappointment and disillusionment.

(3) To the extent that it was structurally determined, unemployment in the 1880s also affected skilled workers and artisans. We assume a connection between the growing radicalism, especially among German workers, and the structurally conditioned decline of traditional crafts where they were dominant.

(4) The increasing awareness among German workers of their own class situation manifested itself in a high degree of trade union organization. The institutional requisites for a German working-class culture in Chicago were furnished by the trade unions, by labor parties that worked closely with them, and, above all, by the labor press that was supported by both types of organization.

(5) German working-class culture in Chicago developed under the pressure of socioeconomic changes in parts of the ethnic subculture, but it also drew on the forms and traditions of a working-class culture that had emerged during the industrial revolution in Germany.

Figure 4.3. Like Figure 4.2, this illustration depicts American artisans as the source of strident social and industrial progress.

GERMAN WORKING-CLASS CULTURE—LOYALTY TO CLASS OR ETHNIC GROUP?

Traditional acculturation models are inadequate when trying to situate German immigrant workers within the crosscurrents of cultural and class conflict, of ethnic and class-specific solidarity.[16] Since these models assume a cultural homogeneity of ethnic group beyond the category of class, they tend to ignore the fact that immigrants encountered the dominant patterns of Victorian America's middle-class and largely Anglo-Saxon culture in all areas of their work and everyday lives, and that hence cultural conflicts were also—or perhaps above all—class conflicts. It is true that on certain ethnic issues, Germans in Chicago occasionally still acted as a community of interest; but in the course of the 1870s, because of growing social differentiation, the geographical, social, and ideological cohesion of German immigrants began to wane. Interaction across class boundaries within the immigrant group was replaced increasingly by interaction across ethnic boundaries within the same class. (See, for instance, the demonstration described at the beginning of this chapter on the occasion of the founding of the Central Labor Union.) The organization of German workers as an institutionally and culturally independent group within the German immigrant community went hand in hand with their organizational integration into the American working class.

Moreover, these acculturation models imply a unilateral evolutionary direction that does not do justice to the complexity of historical processes. Within this framework, the only legitimate function of an ethnic subculture is to help an ethnic group become integrated smoothly into the mainstream of American society. This understanding of acculturation as the inevitable surrender of the subculture to the historically sanctioned authority of the hegemonial system tends to cloud the actual meaning of subcultural patterns of experience and interpretation. Beyond compensating for disappointed hopes or mediating between expectations and experience, between the familiar and the new, the immigrant culture can become an instrument of heightened social awareness, exposing the deficiencies of its new cultural environment and projecting, in its different life-style, elements of an alternative social existence.

German working-class culture in Chicago was based on the cultural tradition of the petite bourgeoisie (of artisans and journeymen) that found its earliest institutional expression after the wave of immigration in the 1850s. As German immigrants continued to flow into the city, it was influenced by the emerging labor movement and working-class culture in Germany. At the same time, its traditions and institutions were gradually affected by the pressures and potentialities of the new social context, as group specific concerns were identified with those of an ethnically het erogeneous working class (especially when other forms of access to American society did not seem possible). The following will attempt to outline the function of working-class culture, the forms it assumed, and the ways it developed. Looking at normative values, demonstrations of solidarity, and organized leisure-time activities, our discussion will turn first to those areas that permitted the participation of other groups; it will then investigate the written culture, which was ethnically limited by the use of the German language.

Interethnic Cooperation—Common Values and Ideological Differences

The Chicago labor movement was a loose, ideologically fluid alliance comprising diverse groups, ranging from the cautious Knights of Labor to the radical International Working People's Association around Albert R.

Parsons and August Spies. The extensive participation in labor demonstrations and festivities in 1885–86 bears witness to the possibility of pragmatic coalitions (for instance, for demanding the eight-hour day), which, because of common needs, interests, and convictions, was easy to activate, regardless of deep-seated ethnic and ideological differences. If one compares radical newspapers as diverse as the English-language *Journal of the Knights of Labor* and the *Chicagoer Arbeiter-Zeitung* (the organ of German Socialists and anarchists), it is remarkable, despite all the polemics on both sides, how much their political and social positions in fact overlap. Significant differences between the social and historical developments in Germany and the United States notwithstanding, the comparable heritage of bourgeois Enlightenment and the common experience of the Industrial Revolution formed the ideological framework for a working-class culture that, although expressing itself primarily in ethnic terms, also permitted demonstrations of solidarity outside the ethnic group.

As the ensemble of common patterns of interpretation and social behavior, this culture was an alternative to, as well as a projection of, the dominant culture. The working class embraced the dominant culture's system of ethical norms but saw it being undermined by the economic egoism of the rising class society; it believed that the continuity of bourgeois ethics could only be safeguarded in its own subculture. The Knights of Labor, above all, advocated the principles of an "industrial morality," which not only marked and legitimized early industrial capitalism but also provided the moral basis for the American workers' radical insistence on social and economic equality. A proximity to the dominant norms of the Protestant work ethic is self-evident. But it should not be forgotten that cultural traditions change, even if they appear to be identical in substance, with their use in different experiential and communicative contexts. The Knights of Labor's normative catalog—industry, honesty, moderation, family responsibility, domesticity, respect for women—was not only an indication that Anglo-Saxon American workers were rooted in the cultural system of American Victorianism; it also motivated American workers' often violent resistance to a threatening proletarian existence.[17]

Comparable is the German Socialists' affinity to the ethic values of the German petite bourgeoisie. Numerous short stories of the period portray the bourgeoisie as morally corrupt and the worker as the legitimate heir of middle-class virtues. But German working-class culture differed from puritanical attitudes characteristic of the Knights of Labor when it came to sensual experience. Here the Germans were much less constrained, holding fast to early industrial habits of work (like drinking beer on the job) and traditional forms of sociability (dancing and the consumption of beer were found at all German working-class festivities). Given the conflicting claims of dominant culture and ethnic subculture, this different cultural orientation took on a critical edge since German working-class culture in Chicago had a sensual freedom that American Victorianism aimed to repress.

The ideological dispute with the dominant culture was carried out in both the English- and German-language press as a rhetorical battle over the right interpretation of a common social and cultural heritage: the tradition of enlightenment in America. This becomes clear on various levels, as in the satirical reinterpretation of culturally sanctioned texts (such as the Declaration of Independence). While middle-class recourse to the liberal values of early industrial societies (like the ideology of the self-made man) supported existent power structures, both the Knights of Labor and the Socialists reinterpreted the tradition of the American Revolution in terms of a radical, usable past, founded in Christian *communitas*, bourgeois enlightenment, and constitutionally guaranteed equality. "The moral of capital," an editorial in the *Sozialist* maintains, "was imported from the Old World and has just been around for a few decades. It stands in contradiction to all of America's original institutions, to the beliefs of the Fathers of the Republic and all their successors since Thomas Jefferson. . . , 'the worker is worth his wages', 'those who do not work shall not eat', and similar sayings are truly American and still very alive in the people's spirit. Let the exploiters take note of it!"[18]

In their reference to the tradition of the American Revolution, the labor movement and such lower middle-class reform movements as the Greenbacks and Populists seemed to merge, at least rhetorically, even though their interests were fundamentally different. (Thus the frequent, but ultimately unsuccessful, attempts to form a political alliance.) Moreover, American and German-immigrant Socialists aligned themselves with the European heritage of revolutionary class struggle (above all the Paris Commune), while the Knights of Labor held to the notion of a universal middle class comprising small producers and thus to a vision of social harmony where capital and labor ultimately shared the same interests.[19]

In the same vein, radical dissidents of various persuasions, discovered in America's past elements of an alternative society, which would, after going through the historically necessary process from individualism to collectivism, end in the realization of a truly cooperative social organization. Although such conviction was commonly shared, the Socialists failed to furnish any concrete anticipations of its ultimate shape. This may explain why images of middle-class Utopias (primarily Edward Bellamy's *Looking Backward*, but also Ignatius Donnelly's *Caesar's Column*) were so widely and well received among workers.

In anticipation of and practical preparation for this Utopian development, the Knights of Labor and the German Socialists went their separate ways. Among the Knights of Labor, the ideal of a cooperative society led to a number of economic and social experiments (some of them in Chicago). On the one hand, production and consumer cooperatives were established—short-lived, though apparently successful—the range and effectiveness of which have not yet been sufficiently researched. On the other hand, "colonies" were founded that sought to realize alternative organizational forms also in terms of communal life-styles.[20]

The Socialists rejected these cooperative experiments because they felt that the constraints imposed by the existing economic system would necessarily also turn cooperative ventures into capitalistic ones. Instead, they formed institutions such as trade unions, old-age and sickness societies, social and cultural associations, and schools, which were to represent workers' interests in their conflict with organized capital, satisfy their elementary economic needs, and organize their cultural solidarity. They especially hoped that the establishment of "free Sunday schools" would undermine the curricula of parochial schools, "demythologize" the teaching of history and biology, preserve ethnic traditions, and encourage the emergence of a proletarian consciousness at an early stage.[21]

All these different organizational experiments did not only aim at solving practical problems: They anticipated, in their partial realizations, the coming of a Socialist society. As orientation toward the future became less emphatic, the Utopian and alternative character of these institutions was deemphasized in favor of more pragmatic considerations and a concentration of more immediate goals. However, they gave new impulses both to organizational endeavors among America's workers and to emerging industrial reforms.

Working-Class Culture as a Culture of Performance

German working-class culture was above all performed culture. The reason for this can be found in its twofold function: to organize the needs for relaxation and sociability suppressed in the workplace and in everyday life; and to strengthen solidarity within the group through rituals that underlined communality and a consciousness of political and cultural

Figure 4.4. Announcement of the celebration of the Paris Commune in Chicago in 1883 by the German sections of the International Working People's Association. The program included a new song, "The Red Banner," and a new play, The Daughter of the Proletariat, *which was performed by a professional company.*

difference. Workers' festivities—parades, picnics, celebrations—were momentary transfigurations of everyday life, the shabbiness of which could hardly be compensated by its brief spells of leisure. The double task of offering relaxation as well as political education was a structural element of all these events, whose character of popular festival was symbolically heightened by the group's understanding of itself and of its role within the context of secular redemption:

The workers celebrate festivals [a commentary in the German labor press maintained]: Because once in a while, together with their comrades suffering from everyday proletarian existence, they are driven to forget the sorrows of the present...; because feelings of solidarity among workers as a class have to be strengthened...; because festivities give workers the opportunity to playfully procure, as it were, the ammunition which will later be so very necessary for their difficult, enduring struggle.[22]

Most of the workers' big parades were demonstrations of power for some specific, political occasion, but often they took place for no visible reason. On June 30, 1884, under the heading "Vive la Commune," the *Chicagoer Arbeiter-Zeitung* reported on one of these parades; in much the same way as the demonstration described at the beginning of this chapter, it moved through the working-class quarters but then ended with a big picnic on Lake Michigan. The parade's formation recalls the traditional carnival parades and, like them, echoes the public self-presentations of the various guilds in preindustrial societies. Delegations from trade unions and workers' associations (with banners, flags, and bands) were grouped around several floats (*Tableauwagen*), which offered satirical commentaries on everyday political events and middle-class society. (The best were later awarded American flags.) The following description shows clearly how pictorial and stereotypical representations attempted to link antifeudal European and American traditions and to integrate the Jacobin radicalism of America's lower middle class within a proletarian interpretative context:

> 1. Division: Meinken's Band, Custom Taylors Union; Banners: "Private Capital is Stolen Income"; "All Workmen Have Identical Interests"; then came the Typographia No. 9 with red and organization flags, as well as the banner: "Workers of all Countries Unite." There followed the first float, portraying the Rule of Throne, Altar and Moneybags. On top, way up on the throne, there sat a decrepit glutton and idiot, representing God's Grace, at his side stood a mistress as *Rex de facto*. One level lower stood two monks, depicting the Rule of the Church; to the great dismay of our pious citizens, they proclaimed the "Word of Redemption" and distributed "God's Plague" and the "Pestilence of Priests." The two actors played their roles wonderfully. On yet another level sat the Jay Goulds, Vanderbilts, Grants, and others representing the Rule of Money, while below them were the enslaved people, writhing under the policeman's club in work, want, and misery.[23]

The picnic on Lake Michigan that followed continued late into the evening and—with ball games, shooting contests, dancing, and plenty of beer—was in tune with the popular festive nature of the whole day. But even here, the political speeches held by labor leaders were obligatory and played a central role; they were to add a dimension of class consciousness to the general entertainment.

March 18, the day commemorating the Paris Commune, had a special status among labor festivities. Because of its seasonal proximity to Easter, it was celebrated as a festival of proletarian resurrection.[24] Festivities began—often early in the afternoon—with a longer musical perform- ance, generally followed by a gymnastic exhibition put on by the various Turner teams. Next were poetry recitals, men's choirs, and political speeches. Central to the second part was a series of *tableaux vivants* por- traying the end of the Paris Commune (1878), the presentation of a politi- cal play written for the occasion (1882 and 1883), or, as in 1883, the performance of the "great American popular play in four acts and eight tableaus: *The Poor of New York*." Without exception, these events ended with a large ball, where the "sixteen-man orchestra of the Progressive- Musicians Union" played. Admission cost twenty-five cents; women ac- companying men could partake free of charge.

The three or four popular and working-class theaters in the German neighborhood performed in a similar setting, with beer and dancing, though without political instruction. If the plays presented at Commune celebrations were decidedly political and often the joint product of the working-class elite—in 1882, for instance, Michael Schwab, August Spies, and Oscar Neebe played the main roles in *Die Nihilisten* (The Ni- hilists), a play written by Wilhelm Ludwig Rosenberg—these working- class theaters document the unchallenged dominance of ethnic culture in the area of pure entertainment. For the most part, they presented robust plays about traveling journeymen, poor students, and honest artisans; the audiences they attracted were ethnically—but not necessarily socially— homogeneous. There are indications that German workers, in their search for entertainment, also participated in vaudeville and other, pre- dominantly nonverbal, forms of American popular culture at a compara- tively early date. By the beginning of the 1880s, German working-class newspapers were announcing, along with German farces and popular plays, American vaudeville and minstrel shows.[25]

The Literary Culture of the German Working Class

Similar to the way the free schools were to remove education, at least to some degree, from the control of the dominant culture, German workers—by establishing their own publishing companies, bookshops, and libraries—tried to anchor their written culture in alternative institu-

tions. By offering a wide variety of educational, enlightening, and entertaining literature, attempts were made to change the reading habits of the
working class. In 1883, the library of the Socialist Club of Chicago boasted
more than 120 titles and obviously aimed at offering an alternative to the
whole spectrum of middle-class education, but it clearly emphasized the
areas of economic, social, and natural history, and even the majority of fictional works were plainly didactic.[26]

As in Germany, the institutional vehicles—and at the same time the
most important media of working-class culture and literature—were the
labor newspapers. The Socialistic Publishing Society, which printed the
Vorbote, the *Chicagoer Arbeiter-Zeitung*, and the *Fackel*, was a cooperative
publishing company based on German models.[27] As a rule, the editors had
already written for labor publications in Germany, often making use of
their experience immediately after arriving in America; the editor in chief
functioned as a commentator of public life and as an agitator at union and
party meetings. He frequently also wrote poems, plays or dramatic
sketches, satires, short stories, and, in rare cases, even novels.

Nevertheless, the attitude of the labor press toward fiction was
rather ambivalent. An editorial in the *Chicagoer Arbeiter-Zeitung* claimed
that the paper would long ago have renounced printing fictional texts,
"but we are obligated to take into account the general practice of German newspapers and also to satisfy the women's wishes for products of
the imagination."[28]

When choosing texts for publication, the editors' decisions seem to
have been based on the following considerations:

(1) The acceptance of a need for distraction—not held in high es-
teem but recognized as indispensable given the pressures of work—
explains the massive serialization of popular sentimental, regional,
detective, and adventure novels (ranging from works by Ludwig
Ganghofer to Friedrich Gerstäcker).

(2) At the same time, the majority of the German-American Socialist
papers insisted that light reading also be instructive. Acknowledging the
fact that the working class had not yet produced any writers comparable
to, for instance, Harriet Beecher Stowe, they tried to establish a literary
tradition by reprinting socially critical masterpieces from among bourgeois novels. Between 1880 and 1890, works printed in the *Fackel* and the
Chicagoer Arbeiter-Zeitung included Eugène Sue's *Mysteries of Paris* and
Victor Hugo's *Les Misérables*, novels and stories by Alphonse Daudet and
Ivan Turgenev, and Emile Zola's *Germinal*.

(3) Fiction was not, however, of central importance to German

working-class literature in America; much more so were poetry, song, and drama, genres that drew on oral traditions and depended on recital or performance. Here the press functioned as the most important intermediary between the written word and its communicative use in confrontations and festivities. The majority of these texts (political and didactic poems, as well as one-act plays and sketches) were disseminated by the press. They sought to establish solidarity, beyond the communicative act of collective recitation, either by satirically attacking the ideological enemy or by reinforcing communal values and beliefs.

The actual literature of German immigrant workers was therefore pragmatic and functional: a literature of purpose. It was written for a clearly defined audience, addressed itself to a specific political situation or event, and had generally didactic or propagandistic intentions (such as the explanation and illustration of ideological positions, or the promotion of group consciousness). By contrast, literary attempts to express subjective experiences were practically nonexistent. (In this respect, German-American working-class poetry is considerably different from that of Jewish immigrant workers.)[29] By the ritual repetition of symbolic gestures of threat, admonition, or encouragement, and by stereotyping proletarian life and proletarian consciousness, this literature displays its interest not in subjective expression or objective representation but in collective appeal. Accordingly, the lyric persona of working-class poetry and song does not refer to an individualized speaker but is always the representative of a class. In a similar way, the evident predilection for allegory can be understood as an attempt at a symbolic reading of proletarian experience and history.

Nevertheless, working-class literature in Chicago must be seen both as a continuation of bourgeois traditions and as their radical reinterpretation. Having grown up with German classical and Vormärz literature, authors like Gustav Lyser—whose father was a friend of Heinrich Heine's and belonged to the Vormärz circle[30]—employed the literary conventions, with which they were so thoroughly familiar, to their own pragmatic purposes. This is not so much a matter of literary influence, but the conscious cultural appropriation (by reinvention, parody, and travesty) of the well-known classical texts.

In all this, the literature of German workers in the United States differed only slightly from the literature of the early labor movement in Germany.[31] One reason for this was that its leading representatives, fleeing to the United States because of Bismarck's anti-Socialist legislation, continued their work in the new country while remaining in contact with

Germany. In this respect, German-American working-class literature was less an epigonic offshoot of German working-class literature than its living continuation in a phase of rigorous oppression. In addition, the functional character of this literature lent itself to geographical transplantation: its strong conventionalization, the ideologically founded internationalism of its topics, the emphasis on the argumentative as opposed to the experiential—these elements made it independent of specifically local contexts.

Yet even so, the new social and cultural environment exerted a traceable influence. The predilection of American workers for satirizing such culturally sanctioned texts as the Decalogue and the catechism gradually made itself felt in the conventions of German working-class literature.[32] An interest in the American context is reflected more clearly in references to current political events, especially in satirical plays. Gustav Lyser's one-act satire, *Congress zur Verwirrung der Arbeiterfrage in New York* (Congress for the Muddling Up of the Labor Question in New York), printed in the Chicago *Vorbote*, takes to task the hearings of the Hewitt Committee, which had been appointed by Congress to investigate the labor unrest during and following the large railroad strike in 1877.[33]

The play illustrates all the characteristics of German working-class literature outlined above. At the same time, by referring to the myth of an Arcadian America, it treats the German immigrant worker's experience in a specific American context of Utopian expectation and bitter disillusionment:

> When climbing to the mountain's highest peak
> And looking down on roaming fields and meadows,
> And feasting on the view's magnificence,
> Your heart will overflow with joys of heaven,
> Then—like the German giant spirit, Faust,
> Whom Bayard Taylor has revealed to you so splendidly—
> You may exclaim, quite overcome with feeling:
> "An earthly paradise lies at my feet!"
> Oh yes, a paradise indeed! How happy God's own images
> Could be, who now live in it,
> If greed and fury and if jealousy,
> If all these would not poison even children's hearts![34]

Lyser's use of forms borrowed from German classicism almost seems to anticipate Brechtian techniques of travesty and critical distancing (Brecht's famous *Verfremdung*). For Abram S. Hewitt's prologue, not quoted here, he employs the *Knittelvers* (four-stress couplet), the heavy regularity of which lends itself wonderfully to persiflage. The banality of meter and rhyme schemes cast Hewitt's idealistic rhetoric and his concern for social injustice and corruption in an ironic light. By contrast, Lyser grants his idealized labor leader the heroic possibilities of the blank verse, which Friedrich von Schiller, especially, had invested with the humanistic pathos of bourgeois enlightenment. The play is teeming with quotes from *Faust I* and *II*, from Schiller's *Kabale und Liebe* and *Wilhelm Tell*, and from Heine's *Wintermärchen*. And yet Lyser was so familiar with the classical tradition that he also seems to be quoting when, in fact, he is not. It brings to mind the imprisoned German Haymarket anarchists, who exchanged poems à la Heine about the quality of prison food, and it seems to be more characteristic of the German labor leaders than of their American counterparts, for whom literature tended to be an upper-class concern.

From the perspective of an aesthetic of work autonomy, it seems safe to say that such variation of traditional literary forms is merely epigonic. But one should not dispose of the phenomenon of working-class literature so easily. Aesthetic forms are not only either used up or original and new; they also change with their usage in new social and communicative contexts. The use of these forms in the process of cultural redefinition, whereby German workers interpreted and shaped their new social environment, was in itself innovative and creative—especially in a society where, until late into the nineteenth century, the established authors were hardly capable of seeing, let alone addressing, the lower classes.

CONCLUSION

The following theses will summarize our observations about the function of German working-class culture in Chicago; it is also hoped that they will point to further areas of inquiry:

(1) The model of social mobility does not adequately explain the acculturation of German workers. Their integration into American society was part of their integration into the American working class, whose or-

ganizational forms and political strategies were shaped and altered in such processes of cultural interaction.

(2) German working-class culture in Chicago emerged in response to constraints posed by cultural and socioeconomic integration into the capitalist industrial society that was unfolding in America during the latter part of the nineteenth century. Its alternative model of interpretation and its system of alternative institutions offered individuals an option to understand and master these constraints, and thus to maintain self-respect against the cultural and economic pressures of their new environment.

(3) Because of the ethnic diversity found in America's working class, the conditions for German working-class culture in the United States were different from those in Germany. Wanting to sustain its claim to a class culture, it therefore had to transcend the ethnic group.

(4) Nevertheless, between 1880 and 1890 working-class culture in Chicago had to be based on an ethnic subculture, and the culture of German immigrant workers necessarily drew on the traditional values and cultural forms of the ethnic group. At the same time, it must be understood as an attempt to reinterpret the resources of ethnic culture within the contexts of work and everyday life in America.

(5) Elements of ethnic subculture assumed different relevance for the working-class culture. In the context of political practice and politically motivated festivities, ethnic culture was subordinated to the demands of political culture and class consciousness; conversely, when it came to pure entertainment and sociability, ethnic elements were dominant.

(6) German working-class culture (especially its literary manifestations), sought to attain autonomy by reinterpreting the content of the prevalent bourgeois culture. At the same time, it continued the bourgeois tradition by making use of its artistic conventions.

(7) German working-class culture was of special importance for the organization and self-interpretation of Chicago's working class because German workers were numerically the largest segment of Chicago's labor force; because they were radicalized, at least during the 1880s, in the course of structurally determined processes of displacement; and because they would make use of the reservoir of organizational forms and interpretative models provided by a working-class culture that had already come into existence back in Germany.

NOTES

1. See "Prometheus reckt sich," *Chicagoer Arbeiter-Zeitung* (*ChAZ*), 28 April 1886; John R. Commons et al., *History of Labour in the United States,* vol. *2* (New York, 1918), 392; Philip Foner, *History of the Labor Movement in the United States,* vol. 2 (New York, 1975), 102; Henry David, *History of the Haymarket Affair* (New York, 1958), 183.

2. For the history of the labor movement in Chicago, see the above-mentioned titles by Commons, Foner, and David as well as Bessie Louise Pierce, *A History of Chicago,* vol. 3 (Chicago, 1957); Friedrich Adolph Sorge, "Die Arbeiterbewegung in den Vereinigten Staaten," series of articles in *Neue Zeit* 9–14 (1890–95); Barbara Newell, *Chicago and the Labor Movement* (Urbana, IL, 1961); "The Eight-Hour Movement," in Illinois Bureau of Labor Statistics, *Fourth Biennial Report* (Springfield, 1886), 466–98; "Der erste Mai: die Entwicklungsgeschichte der Arbeiterbewegung in Chicago," *Vorbote,* 1 May–15 June 1887.

3. Although recent American scholarship in social history has emphasized the necessity of investigating the relationship between the processes of immigration and industrialization—especially Herbert Gutman in *Culture & Society in Industrializing America* (New York, 1977)—studies on immigrant German workers have been rare. In her examination of Milwaukee, *Immigrant Milwaukee, 1836–60; Accommodation and Community in a Frontier City* (Cambridge, MA, 1976), Kathleen Neils Conzen adopts a social-historical perspective, but refers to the whole immigrant community and does not include the later period of intensive industrialization. The two existing studies on Germans in Chicago, A. Townsend, *The Germans of Chicago* (Chicago, 1927), and Rudolph Hofmeister, *The Germans of Chicago* (Champaign, IL, 1976), consider the whole ethnic group in the light of its contribution to Chicago's development.

4. Here problems arise with respect to defining the limits between a "working-class culture" and the attitudes and life-styles of a lower-middle-class, ethnic, or class-specific subculture, where there are often no apparent differences. Our definition emphasizes the intentionality of this sort of culture and its function within the group's changing experiential and communicative framework. That is why the way this culture was used, in a specific situation with a specific intention, seems to outweigh questions of ideological origins or of the radicality of its contents. Thus the following will emphasize the character of working-class culture as an enacted culture, as an "answer" to the conscious and unconscious needs of those who not only created it, but who, by taking part in its communicative processes, defined themselves and actualized a coherence within the group.

5. Figures were taken from the *U.S. Census on Population* for 1870, 1880, and 1890, as well as from Bessie Louise Pierce, *A History of Chicago,* vol. 2 (New York, 1940), 482–500; vol. 3 (New York, 1957), 516–18; Ulf Beijbom, *Swedes of Chicago* (Växjö, 1971), 116; Thomas Bullard, "Distribution of Chicago's Germans, 1850–1914" (Ms. in the Chicago Historical Society, April 1969).

6. The ethnic character of Chicago's work force becomes clearer if one considers that even 63.5 percent of the city's "American" workers (a category used by the census) were second-generation immigrants. The following table classifies the work force in the trade and industrial sectors according to ethnic criteria:

Americans	34.5%
"Native Parents"	12.5%
"Foreign Parents"	22.0%
Germans	22.5%
Irish	9.8%
British	5.0%
Swedes/Norwegians	11.3%
Others (esp. Poles,	
Italians, Czechs)	13.8%

The table does not take blacks, Canadians, and Danes into account. Source: Bureau of the Census, *U.S. Eleventh Census, 1890: Statistics on Population*, 650f.

7. "Earnings, Expenses and Condition of Workingmen and Their Families," in Illinois Bureau of Labor Statistics, *Third Biennial Report* (Springfield, 1884), 135–414; "Trade and Labor Organizations," in *Fourth Biennial Report*, 145–463. If not otherwise stated, the following figures were also taken from these sources.

8. The available figures do not permit a simple evaluation of structural causes and those resulting from business cycles. Woytinsky ascertains a substantial rise in wages for the 1880s, but this was above all true for the second half of the decade. This fact points to cyclical causes; W. S. Woytinsky et al., *Employment and Wages in the United States* (New York, 1953), 47f. On the other hand, Illinois Labor Bureau figures from 1886 for the development of wages from 1882 to 1886 are very differentiated. Figures were registered for 114 different occupations and businesses, according to which 17 percent of the wages had remained the same, 20 percent had risen and 63 percent had declined. The analysis of the occupations with an above-average decline in wages showed that aside from large production units like coat, shoe, and clock factories (here the decline was above all the result of a shift to female workers) as well as steelworks, those who were affected were workers in the traditional trades and skilled workers, like bakers, carpenters, cabinetmakers, molders, woodworkers, smiths, coopers, machinists, patternmakers, shoemakers; "Wages for a Series of Years," in *Fourth Biennial Report*, 335–61. The comparison with figures for wage fluctuations over at least two decades—from 1871 to 1891 in U.S. Department of Labor, Bureau of Labor Statistics, ed., *History of Wages in the United States from Colonial Times to 1918*, Bulletin No. 604, Washington, DC, 1934—confirms that in these occupations it is in fact a question of long-term structural developments. Bruce Laurie et al. discerned similar developments in cities including Philadelphia for the period from 1850 to 1880; see "Immigrants and Industry: The Philadelphia Experience, 1850–1880," *Journal of Social History* 9 (1975–76), 219–46.

9. The number 30,000 is the mean of the figures given by Pierce, *A History*, vol. 3, 269 and of the *ChAZ* on 27 Oct. 1884 (25,000 and 35,000 respectively). The Illinois Labor Bureau's *Fourth Biennial Report* for the spring and summer of 1886 cites 15 percent as the average quota (193). This percentage refers to 104,000 trade union members in Illinois, 85 percent of whom were listed by their unions as "employed." After careful consideration of the various possible sources of error, the report concludes that these figures accurately reflect the situation for all of Illinois' work force (193f.).

10. The figures listed in the Illinois Labor Bureau's *Fourth Biennial Report*—42 percent for Illinois and 23 percent for Chicago—are undoubtedly too high. Since they only refer to trade union members, unskilled workers were to a large extent ignored, as were also nonorganized workers in general (whose average annual wages were forty dollars less than trade union members). In addition, the figures were only calculated for married trade union members; the allover projection for all trade union members in Chicago is 11 percent. This number comes close to the figures released by the Illinois Labor Bureau for 1884, when only 7.5 percent of the working-class families questioned said they owned their own home. Home ownership is a problematical indicator when measuring real living conditions and change in social status: A possessory title as sole criterion says nothing about the quality of living, about the burden of mortgages and debts; the questionable equating by mobility studies of home ownership with change in class consciousness unequivocally assumes that home ownership was something for which everyone strove. Nevertheless, the comparison with the figures for the rest of Illinois can at least illustrate Chicago's special situation.

11. The data were taken from the extensive description of individual working-class households in Illinois Bureau of Labor Statistics, *Third Biennial Report*, 358–91.

12. "Autobiography of Michael Schwab," *Chicago Knights of Labor (ChKL)*, 18 Dec. 1886, 3; also see the *ChAZ* report on living conditions, 28 and 31 Jan., 3, 5, 7, 14, 22, and 28 Feb. 1883.

13. "Autobiography of August Spies," *ChKL*, 6 Nov. 1886, 3; the autobiographies of Adolph Fischer, Georg Engel, Michael Schwab, and Oskar Neebe appeared on 20 and 27 Nov., 11 and 18 Dec. 1886, and 30 April 1887 in the *ChKL*. Also see Philip Foner, ed., *The Autobiographies of the Haymarket Martyrs* (New York, 1969), which includes Louis Linggs' autobiography as well (and which originally appeared in *Alarm*, 29 Dec. 1888 and 5 and 12 Jan. 1889).

14. The proportion of organized workers among Chicago's total work force can only be ascertained indirectly. For 1886, our estimation of the number of workers in industry, trade, and transportation is 150,000, and we thus arrive at an organizational level of about 40 percent. We arrived at this figure by adding the Census of 1880 figures for "manufacturing, mechanical and mining industries" to those listed under "laborers" and "transportation." The numerical data found for the corresponding occupations in the Census of 1890 were added up, then the average annual increase from 1880 to 1886 computed. Cf. *U.S. Tenth Census: Statistics on Population*, 870, and *U.S. Eleventh Census: Statistics on Population*, 650. The percentage of organized workers may actually have been higher. The Illinois Labor Bureau's *Fourth Biennial Report* points out that because of the rapid growth of the Knights of Labor in 1886, only half of all the Assemblies of the Knights of Labor organized in Chicago could be accounted for in its statistics (221).

15. The ethnic distribution among Chicago's organized workers was as follows (in percent):

	Trade Unions	Knights of Labor	Total
Americans	16.1	33.9	21.6
Germans	35.8	20.7	31.2
Irish	18.9	14.4	17.5
Scandinavians	13.4	4.9	10.8
English	5.0	6.8	5.5
Czechs	1.8	9.0	4.0
Poles	2.1	4.6	2.8
Scots	1.6	0.2	1.2
Italians	0.8	0.2	0.7

The following table specifies the ten unions in Chicago that had the highest absolute number of German members:

Union	Number of German Members	Proportion of Total
Metalworkers	1,815	60.0%
Lumberyard workers	1,545	80.4%
Furniture workers	1,458	60.0%
Hod carriers	1,200	34.3%
Carpenters	1,160	68.1%
Masons	1,015	25.4%
Bakers	814	84.8%
Butchers	700	58.3%
Brewers and maltsters	600	60.3%
Brickmakers	600	51.1%

All the figures were computed from the tables in the *Fourth Biennial Report,* 172ff., 186ff., 224ff.

16. The best known is the model developed by Milton M. Gordon; cf. his *Assimilation in American Life* (New York, 1964), which Kathleen Neils Conzen refined for her study on Milwaukee.

17. For the emergence of "industrial morality" and its significance for American workers, see Paul Faler, "Cultural Aspects of the Industrial Revolution: Lynn, Massachusetts, Shoemakers and Industrial Morality, 1826–1860," *Labor History* 15 (1974), 367–94; also Bruce Laurie, "Nothing on Compulsion: Life Styles of Philadelphia Artisans, 1820–1850," *Labor History* 15 (1974), 337–66. For the ethical code of the Knights of Labor see "True Knights of Labor," *ChKL,* 14 Aug. 1886, and "The True Knight of Labor," *ChKL,* 28 Aug. 1886.

18. "Was ist amerikanisch?" *Sozialist,* 22 Jan. 1887.

19. See the six-part series "Industrial Ideals," *Journal of United Labor,* 10 June 1886 and following issues, which clearly summarizes this position.

20. In newspapers of the Knights of Labor, advertisements and reviews frequently refer to the founding of these cooperative ventures. See "Cooperation," Illinois Bureau of Labor Statistics, *Fourth Biennial Report,* 454–63, for a compilation of cooperative undertakings in Chicago.

21. The movement to found free schools was only part of an alternative educational concept that dealt with kindergarten models as well as adult education. It was successful as early as 1878 and revived again in the late 1880s after a period of stagnation; among others, see *ChAZ,* 16 Oct. 1889 and 8 July 1881.

22. *Sozialist,* 5 July 1890.

23. *ChAZ,* 30 June 1884.

24. "Just as Christianity jubilantly celebrates the resurrection of its idealized Redeemer after weeks of fasting and suffering, so too does humanity, conscious of its bondage, exult in the day when a new savior will arise—the 18th of March. What drastic allegory! And what inner affinity, an affinity of inner essence, these two celebrations have—Easter and the Commune Celebration!" *Fackel,* 5 March 1882. The transferral of Christian allegory to the history of the labor movement (apparent in Michael Schwab's speech quoted at the beginning of this chapter) was not only a frequently used means of proletarian rhetoric, but rather also a common convention of working-class literature; cf. for instance the allegorical Christmas play by Ludwig Geißler, which was staged in New Orleans in 1879 and published in the *Fackel* on 11 Jan. 1880. For allegory as the basic form of working-class poetry, see Gerd Stieg and Bernd Witte, *Abriß einer Geschichte der deutschen Arbeiterliteratur* (Stuttgart, 1973), 26ff.

25. For the development of workers' theater, see Christine Heiß, "Popular and Working-Class German Theater in Chicago, 1870 to 1910" in this volume.

26. The library catalog was regularly printed in *ChAZ.*

27. As to the circulation of the above-mentioned newspapers: In 1880 the weekly *Vorbote* had a circulation of 5,000 copies, in 1885 of 8,000; in 1880 *ChAZ,* a daily, had a circulation of 3,000 and in 1886 of 5,780. *Fackel,* a Sunday paper, was most popular: It has a circulation of 5,000 copies in 1880, of 12,200 in 1886, and of 16,000 in 1890.

28. *ChAZ,* 5 May 1890.

29. Here we are referring to the group of New York "Sweatshop Poets," esp. Morris Rosenfeld, David Edelstadt, and Eliakum Zunser; see R. Sanders, *The Downtown Jews* (New York, 1969).

30. For the biography of Gustav Lyser, see the editorial remarks to the English translation of the Lyser satire: Heinz Ickstadt and Hartmut Keil, "A Forgotten Piece of Working-Class Literature: Gustav Lyser's Satire of the Hewitt Hearing of 1878," *Labor History* 20 (Winter 1979).

31. See Stieg and Witte, *Abriß*, 7–64; also the anthology: Bernd Witte, ed., *Deutsche Arbeiterliteratur von den Anfängen bis 1914* (Stuttgart, 1977).

32. "1. Thou shalt have no other Bosses before me . . . 10. Thou shalt not covet thy Boss's money, nor His ease, nor His conveniences, nor anything which is His. Thou shalt not covet thy Foreman's wages, though he earn three dollars each day to thy one. Thou shalt object to nothing, for I shall rule over thee and order thee, and I shall keep thee in servitude all the days of thy life till thy death, and then, for all I care, thou canst go to Sheol." Quoted from "Zehn Gebote für Arbeiter," *Möbel-Arbeiter Journal,* 25 Sept. 1885. To an increasing extent, the numerous catechisms printed in the American labor press (cf. "Catechism for the Working People," *Alarm,* 24 April 1886) can also be found in German-American newspapers (for instance "Sozialistenkatechismus," *Fackel,* 27 July 1884).

33. There were hearings in all the larger industrial centers. Lyser was referring to the hearing that took place on 2 Aug. 1878 in New York, to which Hewitt had also invited representatives of the Socialistic Labor party.

34. *Vorbote,* 17 and 24 Aug. 1878. Conrad Conzett proceeds in much the same way: His satire about politicians and corrupt voting practices ("The Robbers, A Local Tragedy in 1 Act," *Vorbote,* 5 Feb. 1876) is based on Friedrich von Schiller's *Die Räuber.*

CHAPTER 5

The Portrayal of Women
in the German-American Labor Movement

RUTH SEIFERT

We women are subjected to a twofold slavery; to liberate ourselves, we're thus faced with a twofold task. First, along with the men, we suffer the common yoke of the ruling powers. Having shed this, there's that special yoke which the male sex has placed on us. In a man, only the person is repressed and liberated, in a woman, there's also the sex.

On February 3, 1901, these words appeared in a column the *New Yorker Volks-Zeitung* had just established in its Sunday edition, "For Women." Many women more closely linked to the Socialist movement reacted enthusiastically to the new column. The editorial staff received letters not only from readers in New York, but from all parts of the country—from Illinois to West Virginia, from New Jersey to California. The above quotation, for instance, was written by a woman in Chicago. Although this column was indeed perceived as an opportunity for Socialist public discourse, it soon became evident that women were above all interested in establishing a public discourse focusing specifically on women's issues. In the way they show how women experienced their situation, what kinds of problems they perceived, and how they tried to analytically resolve them, the letters—written by female readers to the female editors—are exemplary. More and more, however, it also became clear that there were often contradictions between the way the woman issue was represented by official socialist theory and the way it was developed by women themselves.

The *New Yorker Volks-Zeitung* initiated the woman's column to offer Social Democratic women a forum for discussion and above all to tie them more closely to the Socialist movement. In the 1890s, it was recognized that the scanty participation by women was a constant hindrance to the Socialist movement, a view shared by the Social Democrats in Germany.[1] The purpose of the woman's page was to inform and agitate, and to make women aware of their vital interests in the Socialist movement. The German-American labor movement thus adopted the same position as its parent party in Germany. The woman question was understood as part of the social question, and the Socialist revolution was seen as both a necessary and a sufficient condition for the liberation of women. Indeed, the woman from Chicago who wrote the letter quoted above felt that a social revolution was necessary to eliminate wage labor; however, as a separate task, she additionally advocated the liberation of the female sex. By assuming two different repressive mechanisms, which affected women and men differently, she touched upon a sore spot in socialist emancipation theory. The question as to whether, and in what way, socialist change in society could be equated with the liberation of women is a problem that still—or again—represents an object of intense controversy between Socialists and feminists today.[2] But this was not the only controversial issue in the Socialist movement. The following pages will show that within German Social Democracy there was by no means agreement as to the tenor of woman's emancipation; on the contrary, there was a clash of the most varied images of woman. This is especially evident if one moves down from the level of pure theory and includes publications from the labor press in the analysis. Here one sees that the constraints imposed by a purely theoretical approach for the sake of veracity are forced aside by a variety of needs, all of which enter into the respective images of woman that were being propagated.

Before going into a detailed analysis of the images of woman found in the German-American labor press, socialist emancipation theory will be recalled briefly. When Socialist women first introduced the question of the emancipation of women into the labor movement, they had little theoretical material to fall back on.[3] To be sure, Karl Marx had dealt sporadically with the woman question and, at least in public remarks, strongly attacked the reduction of women to certain roles and areas of activity. Thus he was of the opinion that bourgeois marriage was a form of private property and regarded the degree of woman's emancipation as a yardstick for society's overall development.[4] At a time when the reduction and fixation of woman to her assigned areas—children, kitchen, church[5]—was at a high point in the hegemonial culture, the progressive nature of these remarks must not be underestimated. But within the system of his class theory, Marx's statements were only of marginal importance. For Marx, the historical subject was the class of wage laborers, that is, the class that, by liberating itself, would bring about the liberation of all other repressed groups. Woman's work consisted primarily of unpaid labor in the family and household, and—even if women also worked for wages—these areas were considered more suitable and of primary significance. Ultimately, however, these primary spheres for women were the private spheres for men and were thus excluded from official politics and history.

To the labor movement in the mid-nineteenth century, the budding woman's movement was initially a phenomenon that did not require close attention. Moreover, the woman's movement—both in Europe and the United States—was almost exclusively composed of privileged middle-class women, and many of their goals at first seemed alien to proletarian women directly affected by exploitative conditions.[6]

Similar to the Social Democrats in Germany, the German-American labor movement exercised some self-restraint well into the 1870s when it came to the woman question. At best, "a few back columns" were dedicated to the problem of woman's position in society.[7] Whereas German Socialists maintained that there was "antagonism between the sexes" in American families, they viewed themselves as representatives of a family idyll, where husband and wife lived together "naturally" and harmoniously.[8] Even when August Bebel's book, *Woman and Socialism*, appeared in the United States, it did not at first, apparently, provoke any substantial discussion among German-American Socialists. On December 4, 1883, the book—which first appeared in Germany in 1879 and would be a pioneering work within Social Democracy—was announced in the *Chicagoer Arbeiter-Zeitung* with a longer article stating that the book dealt almost exhaustively with that social problem known as the woman question. The book was said to be one of the best and most important publications of the time. The *Arbeiter-Zeitung* recommended it primarily to male readers: "The men of said species, for whom, as we know, there is no longer anything new under the sky, will find an opportunity to remember a large part of the wisdom, which in the meantime they allegedly have forgotten again. They will see their allegedly 'outmoded point of view' in a completely new light."[9]

"Bebel's Woman," as the book was soon and tersely to be called, was the first attempt to explicitly write the liberation of women into Marxism. The Social Democratic party was thus offered a detailed position on the woman question. In Socialist circles in Germany, the book quickly became a bestseller. In Social Democratic libraries, *Woman and Socialism* was lent out more than any other work on social issues.[10] Why was Bebel's book so popular? In contrast to Marxist texts, Bebel ventured into social spheres that had received little notice in class theory. Since Marx had focused on social production as the central issue of society, the private sphere per se was excluded. Bebel superseded this dualism between the social and the private, one that runs all through Marxist theory. He was interested in social structures outside of purely economic relationships, such as gender and family relations and the gender-specific separation of social spheres. To be sure, Bebel's analysis was explicitly grounded in socialism. Thus he claimed that the woman question was "only one side of the general social problem, [and can] only be solved by suspending social oppositions and hence eliminating the ills resulting from them."[11] Bebel, too, was of the opinion that the liberation of the working class was necessary as well as sufficient for the emancipation of women. However, he also described phenomena that did not readily accommodate themselves to the slick formula equating the emancipation of workers and women. Thus he saw women as a "sex which is dominated and placed at a disadvantage by the world of men, one which suffers not only from being dependent on economic conditions, but also on the social and political world of men."[12] His estimation of the family was similarly contradictory. Although he perceived the increasing divorce rate as an indication "that a growing number of women have decided to throw off what they see as an unbearable yoke,"[13] he did not manage to arrive at a theoretically founded renunciation of this social form. An existence as wife and mother seemed to him a natural one for a woman, "who—truly heroic, sacrificing herself for her child, or taking care of her family and tending it in sickness—shows herself in the most beautiful light."[14] The "woman of the new society" should be "completely independent, socially and economically," and was to be employed according to the same conditions as men.[15] But for "the other part of the day," Bebel envisioned her in the traditional manner, as "mother, teacher, nurse," thus referring her again to her special abilities, that is, the alleged consequence of her biological functions. Lending himself to a variety of interpretations, Bebel could be cited by conservative men as well as progressive Socialist women. Notwithstanding, "Bebel's Woman" represented an instrument for judging the everyday and immediate experiences of women and men in the labor movement. If Marx's class theory was an interpretive model, which made their position within the structure of society's production relationships plausible, Bebel offered them an explanation for everyday life, for the experience of the sexes, and for real-life relationships. Thus while Bebel was able to attract a large audience by dealing with the sensitive topics of love, feelings, and sexuality, as well as the role of woman, there was a tension in his work that would persistently accompany Social Democratic attitudes toward the woman question.

Figure 5.1. The picture entitled "Roguish Face" portrays the flirtatious maiden combining sweet innocence and teasing seductiveness that was typical of the lower-class ideal of woman of the time.

The gender relations that German immigrants encountered in the United States were, however, quite different from those they had known in Europe. In America, "the 1880s and 1890s saw the emergence of a novel social and political phenomenon—the New Woman." This type, "inconceivable in Europe,"[16] was generally wealthy, "young and unmarried," and "rejected social conventions, especially those imposed on women."[17] But this challenge did not spur the German Socialists on to a further development of their emancipation theory. As late as 1883, the following remark appeared in the *Fackel*, incontestably confirming woman's role as wife and housewife: "The man is the head of the family, its protector, its representative outside the home; the woman is the soul of the family, its guardian angel, its inner compass."[18] Whereas large numbers of young women began to awaken earlier in America than in Europe, the *Fackel*, by defining the woman in these terms, is borrowing from conservative romantic thought. The exclusion of the woman from society's public life and production process is seen as desirable and morally well founded. Because, it was argued, "love is the beginning and end of human bliss," and "true love can only be understood in terms of marriage," it was primarily a question of establishing marriage and family as a culturally elevated and moral institution. However, the article continues to point out that the main responsibility for this lies with the housewife, who should function as the "source of morality" and effuse "order, peace, cheerfulness." Her "innate ability" to bring up children and the assumption that she was less capable outside the house seemed to further legitimize the dominant separation of the spheres. Although the woman should "be able to support herself by means of independent work," this must not occur "at the expense of family life."[19] At a time when working women had in fact gone far beyond the limited sphere of marriage and family and were integrated into all areas of the production process, the romantic attribution to women of specific traits—and, derived from that, specific social spheres—remained a decisive element in the Socialist concept of women. The capitalist disintegration of traditional family relationships and allocation of roles did not lead to the "passing away of illusions and old legitimations"[20]—and this held true for the working class as well. Where it was needed, where it had individual psychological significance, the traditional norm of the feminine was preserved and continued to be valid in everyday life.[21] A letter to the editor from a Swabian woman living in New York shows that despite the romanticization of these norms, they were linked to a contempt for the feminine, even in the labor movement: "But it's always the men who are putting a spoke in our wheels! For any one hundred socialist men there are one or two who consider women their equals, the others all look down on us contemptuously."[22]

In the German-American working class, the interplay of various developments began to unsettle the image of woman. While the emergence of the "New Woman" tended to evoke resistance, reconsiderations among Social Democrats in Germany had more effect. Given the conditions, the labor movement could no longer totally integrate the bourgeois ideal. The bourgeois woman's movement in Germany had gathered momentum and brought forth a radical wing, which was making efforts to establish contact with the Social Democrats.[23] In the United States, in addition to the middle-class woman's movement, an anarchist tendency had also emerged, which was sharply questioning woman's position in all social spheres. This tendency never included a large number of working women, but nevertheless it seems to have been attractive to some, thus forcing the German-American Socialist movement to at least comment on its revolutionary ideas concerning gender relations, even though these comments were anything but sympathetic.[24]

A theoretical treatment by Friedrich Engels addressed the altered circumstances in Germany. In 1884, in the wake of Bebel, he had also published an essay on the relationship between the sexes and socialism. In a more pronounced form than Bebel, he argued that the emancipation of women was unconditionally contingent upon economic independence and integration into society's process of production.[25] But what Lise Vogel says about Bebel is also true of Engels: "He conceptualized the so-called woman question as an issue pertaining to woman's situation as an individual, on the one hand, and to social conditions in general, on the other, but he was unable to construct a reliable bridge between the two levels of analysis."[26] These two texts—Bebel's *Woman* and Engels' *Origin of the Family, Private Property and the State*—uniting both emancipatory content and analytical inconsistency, also became a sort of manual for the German-American labor movement in its attempt to interpret these problems, problems that had entered the social consciousness.

The most extensive change in gender relations, however, was brought about by the massive and continually growing number of women involved in the production process. In spite of the romantic ideal of the family prevalent in the labor movement, conditions had forced more and more women into the work force. In the 1880s, the female worker was an everyday occurrence.[27] It would nevertheless have been possible for German-American Socialists (who, culturally speaking, represented a relatively closed group) to ignore these developments, or at least keep them away from home and family, since they did not affect German workers' wives—whose work capacity tended to be geared toward home and the reproduction of male workers[28]—to the same extent as other ethnic groups. Just the same, the concept of woman's role and place could not remain unchanged by these theoretical and practical developments.

WOMAN AS WAGE EARNER

Woman as wage earner now became an important official model for the labor movement. Two objectives were united in this model: On one hand, women were to be made aware of the necessary connection between emancipation and socialist theory and practice. On the other hand, there was the imperative that women, like men, should join labor organizations. The *Chicagoer Arbeiter-Zeitung* claimed that entry into the social work sphere would free women "from the disparaging influence of household slavery."[29] "By being forced to enter into the battle for bread, the woman—due to her greater economic independence—is simultaneously cutting through the chains of male patronage." Female employment produces a woman who no longer need "play the role of a doll," a woman who can become "independent and stand on her own and possibly free herself from his despotism, for she is in a position to take care of herself."[30] This also seems to have pretty much wrapped up the problem of gender-specific repression for the figurehead of the German-American Socialist woman's movement, Johanna Greie-Cramer: "The capitalist replaced the man as ruler over the woman, and his rule is vastly more ruthless and arbitrary than the man's ever was; that profit-seeking enterprise watched with delight as the woman entered rabid industry, so very willing to embrace this new work force."[31]

By thus reducing female activity to wage labor and, no less simplistically, by confining the socially relevant female experience to just this area, Greie-Cramer also merged the interests of workers and women: "The signature of the women's struggle must not read against the men, but rather with the men, for the same forces which repress and tyrannize the man are those which keep the woman in slavery's chains."[32] It was also noted that "in the struggle over wages, women workers illustrate an exemplary heroism, an extraordinary perseverance," since "in the working class's great struggle for emancipation, one can by no means do without the active participation of women."[33]

Developments in the area of production—forcing more and more women into exhaustingly hard jobs in industry and trade—as well as Socialist demands in the German and American movements, resulted in a loud cry for the "free woman," who unites the "revolutionary spirit," feelings of solidarity, and perseverance in organizational activities. In this context, complaints continually arose as to women's lack of training in and understanding of political necessities. Greie-Cramer lamented how notoriously difficult it was to organize women, seeing the reason "mainly in the ignorance, apathy, and dullness of the large majority of women."[34] The confirmation of their backwardness was linked with the challenge: "Women should grab the chance wherever they are offered the opportunity to learn, they should exploit it, for 'knowledge is power'. Use your free time to read and learn, get to know your rights and obligations as human beings!"[35]

Criticism was not limited to a lack of political awareness, however, but also extended to women's behavior inside labor organizations. Women in individual "branches" were said to behave "wrong," they were "too personal" in their political activity, "they abandon themselves to exaggerated sensitivity" instead of—like men—"occasionally biting their tongues."[36] Having been immersed almost exclusively in the so-called private sphere, women, once in the organizations, were supposed to behave "publicly." Even though female experience and realms of life were completely different from what was going on in the male public (and this held true for working-class as well as bourgeois women), woman's situation was essentially defined in terms of male experience in the production process. To find themselves in these explanations, women had to negate their genuinely female experience and define themselves in relation to men: as wives, daughters, and relatives of working-class men. To be sure, this was also part of their experience. Working-class women's experiences of domination were not completely detached from the sphere of production. However, there were other areas of human activity that proved highly problematic for women and that were interlocked in a complex way with their class experience. This is revealed in a discussion conducted via letters to the editor in the *New Yorker Volks-Zeitung* in March 1902. In this debate, one can see the kind of pressure that family and household work represented in their class position, and how it was intertwined with their gender position.

The occasion for the epistolary discussion was a request for advice on March 9, 1902, by a Mrs. Marie, who could no longer keep house on a worker's budget.[37] She asks her "dear sister comrades" to advise her how to feed a family of five on a household allowance of five dollars. Her husband, she writes, "frequently reproaches" her by arguing "that other people with larger families manage to make do with even less." Although she "knows how to go about it thriftily," she has experienced "not only extremely unpleasant remarks, but even serious quarrels." The following Sunday, Mrs. B. explains how working-class women can manage on their money. After having worked several years in a hotel, she now knows more about the thrift of some housewives and the fidelity of some men. "Some men would be better off asking: Who pays for the things you need that I don't give you? . . . I've found that some men, if they're not too lazy to think, must have figured out that their wives couldn't possibly come up with what they do every day on the few dollars they get, but it's so nice not to have to think. One consoles oneself, saying: I just have a very thrifty wife." On March 23, 1902, Mrs. E. V., from Chicago, writes: "Now I'll say what I think: (1) It is impossible to make do on five dollars a week for five people; (2) your husband has no right to treat you like that. We're not maids who earn wages every week! . . . The men should treat us like women and not like maids! I think it's so horrible the way the men are oppressed by the Herr bosses, and it is an outrage the way our husbands want to oppress us." One woman claims to manage on four dollars, though only by drastically reducing meals and regularly accepting "little handouts" from her husband's boss. Her suggestions are met with vehement opposition. For the other women, the problem lies in the relationship between man and woman, whereby it is not simply a question of the pressure brought on by meager wages, but rather of a dependent relationship in its own right.[38] "Women have four to five dollars to support themselves and their families," Mrs. J. D. remarks on March 30; "what in the world are the men doing with the rest?" And on the same day, Mrs. L. G. issues a challenge: "It's high time women wake up and organize, and leave that kind of man to his own sort."

For the women, the burden of these conditions often led to conflict with the men, who not only passed on the problems resulting from their limited financial means, but also used them as an instrument for disciplining their wives. Nevertheless, many women recognized that economic upheaval represented the first step toward their liberation. Among others, Greie-Cramer saw to it that these experiences were understood in an ideologically correct manner. She pointed out to her readers that many women were "very wrong to reproach the men with being stingy" instead of actively setting out to change the relationships of production.[39] Of course, for many workers' wives the pressure that their class situation entailed was more immediate than the resulting tension between the sexes. It was obvious that many problems would disappear with a larger monthly budget; one needed but to look at other social classes to see what relief there was with more financial latitude. But as to women being gendered beings, the situation was not radically different in other classes. The wealthy housewife belonging to the propertied classes was no less subject to her husband's disposal than was the worker's wife. To be sure, the party's demand that women be revolutionary Socialists clearly struck a vital nerve with many working-class women. "Really, women, it's high time to overthrow this unworthy social order," wrote a member of Branch Four of the Socialist Labor party to the *New Yorker Volks-Zeitung*. "So pick yourselves up, show that you're sick and tired of oppression, decide once and for all to cast off your yoke. Organize, demonstrate, show yourselves in public. Like in the May Day Parade, side by side with the men. That draws attention, not only in the bourgeoisie, but also among workers' wives. They'll be forced to tell themselves that woman's participation in politics isn't just an empty phrase any more."[40]

While women were being challenged to participate in the class struggle and show themselves in the public light of bourgeois society, an ideology of womanhood was also emerging, both in Europe and the United States, propagating a feminine ideal that had an enormous influence within the labor movement. In the United States, this feminine ideal was closely linked to Darwinist views, which, around the end of the nineteenth century, had found a foothold in almost all sectors of American society.[41] Cloaked partly in scientific terms, a "cult of true womanhood" appeared.[42] By assigning to women a specific conception of their role, a "truly feminine standard of conduct," it sought to repress egalitarian demands.[43] It was exactly these scientific trimmings that posed a challenge to the Socialist movement, which claimed to offer the only scientific interpretation of social relationships. But views concerning "respectable femininity" did not pose only a theoretical problem. On a psychological and emotional level, too, this interpretation of the feminine role was quite attractive for male workers.[44]

WOMAN AS A NATURAL AND EMOTIONAL BEING

Notions of woman's natural role and of a "respectable femininity" were at odds with the demand for social equality for women and their active participation in the Socialist movement. Notwithstanding, the labor movement was far from completely disavowing these ideas, which reduced women to a few well-defined social areas. Articles dealing with this problem in German Socialist newspapers reveal no single, unequivocal line. When it was a question of "woman's destiny" or "woman's nature," there was much theoretical confusion. Thus one finds articles vehemently advocating the complete emancipation of women from all ideological and social restrictions and refuting the so-called scientific standpoint, and next to them articles taken from, for instance, the *Häusliche Rathgeber* (Domestic Advice) where the following can be found: "You must give in, you must submit, you must subjugate your own views and opinions to the better judgment of your husband." This recommendation was explained by observing that "it is easier for women to submit" and "in little matters, cleverness often dictates giving in."[45]

Perhaps more than any other, the question pertaining to "woman's nature" was battled over on the relevant pages in Socialist newspapers for years without final agreement. It was clear to many authors that a materialistic approach was irreconcilable with statements about an alleged natural determination of the female sex. The reduction of woman to her "natural qualities" and the recommendation "that it is best to refer her to those spheres, for that is where, according to her disposition, she belongs" reminded one woman author "of the zoologist's classification of insects."[46] The observation that there were radical differences in the socialization and training of boys and girls was also linked to the demand: "All of this must be fundamentally changed and done away with."[47] But in the labor movement, the reinforced demand for a basic change in woman's role led to deep anxiety over the 'loss of femininity"; it was only with a great deal of effort that this was made compatible with the conviction of clearing new ground that the socialist emancipation theory spread. The following "apt remarks by a female correspondent versed in the emancipation of women," were praised by the *Chicagoer Arbeiter-Zeitung*: "Women are making a great mistake if they believe they can emancipate themselves by casting off their femininity, by imitating men, by violating their own I." Instead, the article continued, the woman should recognize "the natural grace and delicacy which continually lend new charm to all things, the rich life of feeling;" she should take advantage of these qualities while trying to liberate her husband and herself.[48] This, however, was not to occur through direct participation in the class struggle, but rather through a consciousness of her "feminine qualities." Since the woman, "because of her nervous system, is much more easily excited" and therefore exceeds the man "in hate as in love," she can utilize her emotions most effectively by manipulating the man: "Once enraptured by the ideal of freedom, she embraced it with all the passion of her being, and could only love the man who payed homage to her ideal. A man who had not at some point taken up weapons or in some way worked for liberation would have a hard time winning the love of a girl."[49]

The Socialist woman, therefore, could best serve the revolution in the role of lover, who should only bestow her favors on a truly revolutionary man. It was hardly possible to make these notions—which were emphatically applauded by the *Chicagoer Arbeiter-Zeitung*—compatible with the image of the independent and wage-earning proletarian woman, an image propagated as the fundamental requisite in the official theory. The mediation between the romanticized woman-in-love and the production process remains obscure. But in spite of these inconsistencies, it was this concept of womanhood—reduced to youth, beauty, and passionate love— that enjoyed great popularity in the labor movement.[50] In the labor movement, too, a woman who did not conform to this ideal found little sympathy. On July 15, 1891, the *Chicagoer Arbeiter-Zeitung* reported the suicide of a young man who had been rejected by "a beauty with a marble heart." The "young, exceedingly beautiful blonde, extraordinarily intelligent but almost devoid of feelings, by refusing . . . to marry him, drove Atwood to his death." And if that was not enough, "the beauty [made] no secret of the fact that she fostered no animosity toward pretty, witty men—only toward marriage." For such behavior, the *Arbeiter-Zeitung* could not help but express the hope that "the beauty" would soon return to her true, feminine feelings:

> From everything the pretty lady said one can see that she doesn't have many feelings and, above all, that she hasn't yet met the right man. Let's hope she doesn't one day have the misfortune of meeting some Don Juan comme il faut, for whom she's suddenly all aflame, and who then will put her down as number 1,003 on his list . . . only to forget her in the shortest time.[51]

Perhaps the labor movement could not be expected to have been in a position to subject the problem of human emotions and interrelations to a materialistic analysis. Concerning the organization of these emotions in a larger social context, however, there were certainly alternative models. Both women's and anarchist movements in America had initiated a controversial discussion of this question.[52] Yet that discussion was neither taken up nor carried on by the labor movement. In this question more than in most others, the interests of the male Socialists seemed contradictory and difficult to reconcile; this attitude impeded further theoretical reflection and kept certain concepts within a vicious circle. There was in fact a call for the emancipation of feelings, for the liberation from bourgeois constraints and restrictions. Not only were women explicitly conceded erotic and emotional inclinations; the labor movement was vehemently committed to offering them the possibility of living out these inclinations to the full. This "freed sensuality" was supposed to lead to the ideal "love between the sexes" (*Geschlechterliebe*) already celebrated by Engels, which was to take the needs of both sexes harmoniously into account.[53] The example cited above, however, shows that—as soon as female needs no longer conformed to the emotionality and feeling attributed to them— this ideally construed love between the sexes was quickly subsumed under the dictate of "naturalness."

"NATURALNESS" IN THE RELATIONSHIP BETWEEN THE SEXES

The views expressed in labor movement organs left no doubt that the liberation of feminine feelings would naturally lead women to the same form of gender relations. The gender relations were first subject to the dictate of "naturalness," then to that of "morality." The idea of "natural" modes of behavior between the sexes, which were based on a "fairly simplistic view of instinct," excluded any drastic change in gender relations and tried to establish the given organization of emotions and impulses as "natural."[54] In this, the labor movement was to a large extent in agreement with the hegemonic culture, where sexuality and relationships between the sexes were categorized in scientific and psychiatric terms, a tendency that began in the second half of the nineteenth century and reached its high point in the twentieth.[55] The demand for morality, on the other hand, called for the vehement denunciation of those bonds—understood as amoral by the labor movement—which had arisen out of economic and financial deliberations and which were assumed to be the primary criteria for bourgeois marriage. Because of property considerations, middle-class marriage had "grown inseparable from the capitalistic social order."[56] It was immoral because it did not derive from the dictates of nature, which led to a bond according to "love between the sexes." "Supreme, divine love," the *Arbeiter-Zeitung* proclaimed to its readers, "is found in naturalness. We must admire nature, which has planted such feelings in living beings, and for the simple reason so as not to let her creatures die out."[57] Since erotic feelings and behavioral patterns were interpreted as "having been bestowed by nature," it could be concluded that only "over-civilized cultural apes" would lace themselves up in a "moral straitjacket." By contrast, the natural, healthy person "is not ashamed of feelings, but rather draws health and happiness from them," since "suppressed urges often venge themselves in the most horrible way. Chastity, for instance, sung by moonstruck poets, has driven thousands of people crazy, has driven them to their death."[58]

By referring to nature, the labor movement felt far superior to middle-class views, which were represented as being characterized by "hypocrisy and lies."[59] The gender-specific behavioral patterns derived from nature, however, seem to have turned out differently for men and women. If male behavioral patterns tended to be prescribed by a nature consisting primarily of urges, then the female patterns were prescribed by a nature in which emotionality played the largest role. It is no coincidence that attention was drawn to the fact that it was "the mark of a free *man*" to free himself from moral conventions and to stop repressing the "necessary life functions." But what was the mark of a "free woman"? She was encouraged to unswervingly follow her feelings and impulses, those which would lead her to "true and moral love," to a willingness to sacrifice, and to conformity. This ideal of strong, feminine emotionality—the substance of which was devotion, self-surrender, and a bourgeois life centered around the family—can be found in almost all the novels printed in the labor press toward the end of the nineteenth century.[60] In these texts, woman's nature almost never points toward the ideal of free love. The "free woman" does not follow short-term impulses but, rather, deep-seated emotions. She does not, of course, cling to trite considerations based on bourgeois conventions, such as marriage. Just the same, her feelings lead to a monogamous, marriagelike bond. Most important is that the liberation of woman and her feelings is founded in the eradication of material deliberations while entering into this bond.

The preceding discussion has attempted to show which perspectives were represented primarily in publications of the German-American labor movement dealing with the various roles assigned to woman. Woman as wage earner was a phenomenon that had to be accepted, because of women's massive entry into the work force and the economic necessity that forced them into factories. The resulting tension vis-à-vis the role of the housewife was a problem the Social Democrats could not solve. That women were subjected to a massive double burden was evidently seen as an unfortunate, but inevitable, fate. It did not occur to Socialist men that this additional pressure on women could be eased if men would, for instance, do some of the housework.[61] But it was conceded that housework could no longer be the only area of female occupation and that woman's intellectual capacity—in principle, equal—would continue to move her beyond this sphere. Recourse to a "feminine nature" was stronger when woman's relationship to man was at issue, that is, when woman was dealt with in her capacity as lover and wife.

WOMAN AS MOTHER

The preceding discussion leads one to conclude that Socialist men tended to be less supportive of emancipation if that led to woman's self-determination. A willingness to treat the position of woman on the grounds of historical materialism and emancipatory theory was even less apparent when she was considered in the role of mother. The notion of the "free woman" was completely abandoned when it came to the female body. This can be seen most clearly when looking at an essential and encompassing portrayal of woman, notably that of woman as mother.

Figure 5.2. The epitome of the "true woman": The self-sacrificing mother, heroic but in need of protection. Depicted as a working-class mother, she also serves to portray the plight of the proletariat. The picture is entitled "In Snow and Ice."

Richard Evans has pointed out that, in Germany, liberals as well as conservatives were convinced that the working class practiced birth control and that the German Social Democracy was advocating contraception.[62] The amorality of birth control and the threat to the family that it entailed constituted one of the most important and presumably ideologically effective arguments in the battle against the Social Democrats.

Most women in the United States who knew of the possibility of birth control and abortion came from the upper middle class, and they made use of this knowledge.[63] Interestingly, the German-American labor movement did not use this as a reason to demand the same privileges for women of their class. Instead, the labor movement adopted the argument of immorality and directed it against the ruling class. While middle-class ideologues in Germany accused working-class women of limiting the number of their children because they craved pleasure and strove to look beautiful,[64] one also finds articles in the German-American labor press castigating middle-class women for their unwillingness to bear children. It is "a well-established fact," wrote the *Chicagoer Arbeiter-Zeitung*, "that women of the so-called upper classes don't want to be bothered with bringing up their children, that some of them even view motherhood as a necessary evil."[65] The middle class, in its decadence, did not even shy away from "a little murder—namely of the unborn child".[66]

Willingness to bear children was seen by both the middle class and the labor movement as a sign of true and natural femininity, as the incontestable consequence of feminine love, and above all as woman's natural capacity. Thus the *New Yorker Volks-Zeitung* promised that "only that woman, who by loving also acknowledges love's original law—the woman who wants to become a mother—will find consolation and true love."[67]

The accusations surrounding birth control and contraception illustrate the extent to which women themselves were excluded from voicing an opinion about which image of woman would win out. The power of determination over the female body and its functions became an essential point in the class dispute, whereby men from both classes reproached one another for losing control over female corporeality. It was clear that this might result in the loss of power not only over the definition of women, but also over the possibilities of demographic control. This fear was met ideologically by a romantic elevation of woman as mother, a role also made romantic and desirable for women, in the hegemonial as well as the working-class culture.[68]

Finally, all the ideas about woman's nature and destiny crystallized in the image of "woman as mother." When considering motherhood, female emancipatory interests are explicitly revoked, and a historical, materialistic manner of perception definitely yields to a biological:

> What good does it do a woman, all this emancipation . . . the possibility . . . to dispose of herself freely, as long as this free right of disposal is limited by the female physiological functions in such a way that, in a certain respect and under certain circumstances, it amounts to its own temporary nullification? As long as we're just dealing with woman who is economically and legally equal to man, then pray let the pretty phrases about the right to self-determination, about woman's economic, intellectual, moral, and even sexual freedom, about "free love," etc., be sufficient and fill their—shall we say—agitational purpose. But as soon as we're dealing with the "mother," we're talking about factors which must be taken seriously.[69]

For when speaking of woman as mother, it is possible that "elements enter into the matter which cast this freedom into an extremely questionable light." According to this argument, motherhood subjects the woman to emotional determinations more than anything else. Mentally, above all, motherhood puts her at the mercy of man, for it is known "that generally the mother yearns for the father of her child, that she is extremely unhappy when her yearning is not fulfilled" and "that passionate affection can even brave brutal mistreatment."[70] Biological notions to the effect that woman, in marriage, must bend to "her condition as wife and mother" went hand in hand with an elevation of motherhood, which was not only typical of the patriarchal culture of the period but was also partly supported by Socialist women as well.[71] Motherhood, being "woman's deepest basic instinct," leads to a situation whereby "emotional motherhood arises . . . out of physical motherhood. It is this emotional motherhood . . . which causes the woman, in a purely intellectual sense, to remain behind the man. But she becomes more and more conscious of the fact that this inferiority is at the same time her triumph, that this painful conflict also represents her greatest wealth."[72] From this, in turn, emerges woman's special capacity to sacrifice, for "without a doubt, the greatest sacrifices have always been demanded from women, as will also be the case in the future."[73]

Karin Hausen has pointed out that, in the long run, investigations by social historians dealing with gender relations cannot get along without sociopsychological resources.[74] This is also evident in the case of Socialist men. Torn between their interests as Socialists, which entailed a stronger inclusion of women, both practically and theoretically, and the "dark forces," which stirred their interests as men in a patriarchal society, they finally gave in to these "fears and longings" and let their emancipatory claims slide. This was especially apparent in the stealthy exclusion of women on the practical, organizational level.[75]

But it also meant that Socialist women were continually subject to unreasonable expectations for their conduct. The conflicting images of woman, from an emancipatory role to one obviously meant to satisfy specific male needs, resulted in demands on women that could not possibly be met.

For their middle-class sisters, the problem of the ideological struggle was comparatively easier. Privileged by belonging to the middle class, they were not subject to the imponderables and disadvantages of a working-class existence. Their immediate ideological struggle could hence focus on the specific constraints created by a patriarchal discourse, and the direction of the struggle was more or less clear. By contrast, for Socialist women, the reality of the oppressed classes was a physical element of their lives, which they experienced just as acutely as that of belonging to the oppressed sex. In certain respects, their struggle took place on two fronts: on that of class and of gender. The ideological framework they had to deal with was twofold and therefore more complex.

WOMEN'S VOICES IN THE *NEW YORKER VOLKS-ZEITUNG*

Johanna Greie-Cramer was responsible for the woman's column in the *New Yorker Volks-Zeitung*. She continually reminded her readers of the integral relationship between the emancipation of women and the Socialist revolution. In complete agreement with the Socialist party's official position, she stereotypically denied that there was a special woman question. She defined woman as either a wage earner or a wife.[76] In either case, it was a question of eliminating capitalist production. Women's concerns going beyond that were basically characterized by Greie-Cramer as a "middle-class sideshow." Greie-Cramer's primary objective was to organize Socialist women's associations and see to it that they functioned smoothly. The fact that women exhibited organizational conduct different from men's—that they were more emotional and spontaneous—was continually referred to in Greie-Cramer's discussion as a "mistake" on the women's part. Sought out as representatives of feeling and sensitivity outside the organization, women were nevertheless advised to be "less personal" in the party branches. But, over the years, a change can be seen in Greie-Cramer's attitude—that is, in the views of the Women's Agitational Committee of the *New Yorker Volks-Zeitung*. Initially, there were precise ideas as to how women were supposed to organize and what the ideal forms and topics should be. Later, though, one can see a willingness to consider women's own special situation, and, above all, a concession that the conduct of male comrades in the organization might be a continuous hindrance to women.[77]

As far as the women who contributed letters were concerned, the hierarchy of concerns as prescribed by the Agitational Committee was unacceptable from the very outset. They were, of course, aware that their lives were deeply influenced by capitalist production. But what they tried to introduce into the woman's corner was an experience not explicitly provided for in Marxist theory. Their lives transpired in places that—at least in theory—were not conceded any historical relevance, and which were thus relegated to the shadows. The women's letters cast some light on this dim area of female experience. Their letters dealt essentially with everyday experience, the "place of individual reproduction,"[78] that is, "the place of the production and reproduction of human beings including their actual capacity for work."[79] This was the primary sphere of female work, and it was characterized for women by a "sense of responsibility for moods, needs, and relationships, which—together with their femininity—was warmly recommended to them."[80] Shortly after the column appeared, the women's letters began to deal consistently with the relationship they found most important and most laden with consequences: marriage. The epistolary discussion, which came under the heading "Marriage and Free Love," extended from the end of 1900 to April 1901. Reforming relationships, wrote one woman on February 3, 1901, belonged "to socialism to the same extent as politics, and is no less necessary." The emotional, deep, and harmonious gender relations put forward by official propaganda as a Socialist model were very different from the women's experience. In their individual attitudes toward men, wrote Mrs. A. H. to the *New Yorker Volks-Zeitung* on March 3, 1901, every woman has felt "how humiliating it is to be dependent, in every respect, on a husband's goodwill; . . . to have to give in on most things because after all, you're bound together . . . it would be good if marriage wasn't so binding, but rather if two people who liked each other lived together, and, if love lasted, they stayed together, but in the other case both partners would be better off if they could separate more easily." Whereas almost all of the women taking part in the discussion spoke in terms of more liberality in questions of gender relations, "one comrade" also pointed out that the structures of contemporary feminine emotionality, as well as the ideological organization of gender relations, precluded this:

> How often do you find that a woman grapples about with some slob, often even has to earn the bread money and still doesn't split up. Just think of poor Eleanor Marx, who wasn't bound legally or through children. I once read that the progenitive act was the stamp of love. Well, how come the men seldom marry the girls who have gotten mixed up with them, and if they do, then only because they're forced to. How often does a woman like that have to duck; if she opens her mouth, her offense is flung right back at her. If you just listen in on the men when they're talking about their loves, how derogatorily they speak about those girls! And then the supporters of free love want to trick me into believing that's love! I say pure love can stand the test, sensual never.[81]

Mrs. A. N. also saw that—given the ruling ideological conditions—the demand for free love just referred to women anyway, for "who says it's improper when a man looks for pleasure outside his marriage!" She was not prepared to accept marriage as a "necessary evil": "I think women should ignore all prejudices and shouldn't bind themselves to one person for the rest of their lives, a person who can generally only make them happy for a short time. . . . If that were the case, I don't believe there'd be so many unhappy women." In spite of the anonymity of the letters, she would like to "apologize . . . if I haven't expressed myself well, and hope I won't be thought of poorly for that."[82] This timidity can be seen as an indication that, as Mrs. A. B. pointed out on March 31, 1901, the theory "hasn't yet seeped into our flesh and blood. Thus the contradictions in almost all our women and men, both in thought and action." In the social spheres of sexuality and procreation, women were confronted with contradictions consistently.

Thus Mrs. A. B. wanted to "pose the question in the woman's corner if it is right or not that here in Paterson a twenty-three-year-old girl was acquitted of murdering her baby?" Mrs. B. welcomed the acquittal on November 4, 1900, and asked the readers: "And why let the man go free? I think he should receive the same punishment as a girl who is charged." "I would have acquitted the girl, too," answered Mrs. M. B. on November 11, 1900. "But it really is terrible that the man can't be called to account, because the girl probably acted out of a sense of abandonment. According to the dominant conditions it is considered shameful for a single girl to have a child. But if the man turns away from her, too, the girl is really in an unfortunate position. At the very least, the man should be branded as a coward."

Attempts like these to advance a female social ethic and create a female public for topics that were suppressed throughout the classes in the patriarchal society were important not only for working-class women. A "letter from a middle-class woman" sent to the *New Yorker Volks-Zeitung* is documentary evidence that these problems concerned women of all classes, and that middle-class women also felt that the Socialist labor press offered them more of a forum for specifically female concerns than other papers. The middle-class woman who contributed a letter on April 13, 1900, did so because "the truly sincere interest you show us [women deserves] public recognition." She was, however, fully aware that here, too, she "will most probably receive your fierce censure," since her attack was directed against the myth of the female attitude toward motherhood. Considering intellectual contempt, her sharpest experience of female oppression, she viewed her letter to the *New Yorker Volks-Zeitung* as a contribution so that "now, with deeper insight into the life of our feelings and thoughts, you will have a better understanding of those women whom you have so strongly condemned up till now." Letters from working-class women also indicate that they experienced the warmth of the household and family life much less sentimentally than the ideology claimed. "Among 100 marriages," wrote Mrs. J. W. to her sisters on January 25, 1900, "there's hardly one which could be called truly happy . . . by happy I don't just mean that two people like each other, but that there's real harmony between them, that one complements the other. This is rarely the case—as I have often had the opportunity to witness—in forced marriages."

It seems that this discussion of the specifically female areas of marriage and family was more or less forced upon the woman's column by the readers. Whereas Greie-Cramer repeatedly stressed economic relationships, one article in the woman's column summarized the letters' general thrust as follows: "The woman of the future will no longer be dependent on a man's good grace. The home, the family, which are based on sacrifices on the part of the woman, will give way to newer and better conditions, conditions which will be based on individual rights and personal freedom."[83]

Economic relationships were not the only factors opposing a realization of these ideas. The women's letters permit a glimpse of working-class practices and of the conduct of Socialist men. "There are even a lot of enlightened men for whom the emancipation of women is a thorn in the flesh, in fact, they even work against it with all their might." This was written by "Mrs. Bertha" on January 12, 1902. She was reporting from a family where "the husband maintains that he's a zealous and good Social Democrat," but when his wife joined a women's association he broke out "in a real rage and didn't exchange a word with his wife for weeks." Even in the working class, confirmed Mrs. E. G., a husband "still assumes the right to treat his wife's thoughts as though they came from a child."[84] Comrade G. R. spoke of attempts to exclude women from appearing in public, and thus from participation in the political decision-making process; "You're not making any progress and don't know anything about the cause," was often the reaction of male comrades at Socialist women's associations. Only "sometimes will you meet one who takes the time and explains this or that, but you have to hunt for them, high and low. It's easier to just make fun of the women, and sometimes it covers up the fact that they [the men] themselves don't know what they want."[85] That there were "lots of men calling themselves Socialists, who even get up and preach socialism, and who say that their wives aren't members of the Social Democracy, who even forbid their wives to join a women's association," was discussed by "a sister comrade" in terms of its function for the men and the incompatability with Socialist ideas. "The woman as mother, the woman who brings up her children, is she supposed to be kept in the dark, supposed to serve the man like a maid? How does that fit in with socialism?"[86] From these experiences, many women came to the conclusion: "Yes, we have a twofold struggle. As workers, I think, it's easier to free ourselves, by joining or founding associations, we often receive the men's support because it's to their advantage, and because the people interested in the cause join the struggle."[87]

It was more difficult, they claimed, to assert themselves as women because this involved ideology; attempts to do so were opposed and subtly sabotaged by the men. Thus the woman who wrote the above passage complained that "quite good suggestions are disregarded because they come from a woman. . . . If one wants to pick oneself up and somehow forge on ahead, it's no good, because the charitable person on one's side condemns it." Along with the problems stemming from the women's husbands and male comrades—which also bear witness to the unconscious contempt of women brought to light in action and word, an everyday occurrence even among Socialists—there was another aspect, which could be characterized as the subjective side of the question: the psychic mark these conditions left on the women. The obstacles embodied in men as well as in the female identity, which was castigated in a male-dominated organization, led to widespread contempt and exclusion of women from social participation, with dire results for their efforts toward self-determination.

CONCLUSION

A constant question for the Socialist movement in Germany and the United States had to do with the lack of political participation by women. The reasons for this were readily sought in women's shortcomings and incompetence. Even many women, once they had advanced and received acknowledgment within the male party structures, had but little empathy for their sisters. This can be seen in the conduct of Klara Zetkin and Rosa Luxemburg in Germany and Johanna Greie-Cramer in the United States. In the course of time, the latter's articles did gradually reveal some understanding for the fact that Socialist working-class women were acting in structures that restricted their mobility at every step. If one looks at the ideological relationships Socialist women were exposed to—both in theory and in practice—the contradictory character of the situation stands out in clear relief. On the one hand, it could no longer be denied that a revolutionary stance on the part of women was absolutely necessary for the class struggle. In addition, a materialist standpoint obviously had to oppose rigid notions of femininity. But on the other hand, there was an unwillingness to do away with those myths of femininity that ensured firm control over women. Women's practical experiences showed that, in this respect, one could not speak in terms of unity in emancipatory endeavors; though they struggled on with the men as class subjects, as women they could not count on much support from their male comrades. In view of such relationships, the question under discussion must be posed in a different way: It is not why so few women organized that needs to be clarified, but rather how it was possible that, despite such resistance and adversity, so many women managed to overcome the obstacles that had been set up in their paths and, in spite of them, arrive at emancipatory thoughts and actions.

NOTES

1. On March 8, 1903, the *New Yorker Volks-Zeitung* (*NYVZ*) reported that at the last conference of the women's societies it was ascertained that an overwhelming majority of society members was composed of party members, while there was a complete lack of working-class women. The situation was similar in the German Reich; cf. Birgit Köhn et al., " 'Verläßliche Frauenpersonen' und 'Luxusdamen'. Anknüpfungspunkte für eine emanzipatorische Frauenpolitik," in Projekt sozialistischer Feminismus, *Geschlechterverhältnisse und Frauenpolitik, Argument Sonderband* 110 (Berlin, 1984), 168ff. Given the growing number of women taking part in the industrial production process, this must have been an important consideration for the German Social Democracy.

2. Cf. for instance Nancy Hartsock, *Money, Sex and Power: Outlines of a Feminist Historical Materialism* (New York, 1984), and Michelle Barrett, *Das unterstellte Geschlecht. Umrisse eines materialistischen Feminismus* (Berlin, 1983).

3. Marx's early writings, upon which later attempts to form a socialist theory of women's liberation were based, were not at the disposal of the nineteenth century Socialist movement. For an example of more recent attempts, see Lise Vogel, *Marxism and the Oppression of Women* (New Brunswick, NJ, 1983).

4. "Manifest der Kommunistischen Partei," in *Ausgewählte Werke*, Karl Marx and Friedrich Engels (Moscow, 1971), 49f.

5. In the nineteenth century, patriarchal German ideology invented as a household word that women were responsible for the three "Ks"—*Kinder, Küche, Kirche,* meaning children, kitchen, church.

6. According to Margaret M. Marsh, "Communist-anarchism drew much of its strength from the men and women who held the dirtiest, worst-paid jobs in America's urban centers," i.e., "working-class immigrants or daughters of immigrants" who "began their working lives in the sweatshops of New York's Lower Eastside or similarly dismal circumstances," but also from middle-class women; *Anarchist Women 1870–1920* (Philadelphia, 1981), 20f.

7. Mary Jo Buhle, *Women and American Socialism* (Urbana, IL, 1981), 19.

8. Buhle, *Women,* 9.

9. *Chicagoer Arbeiter-Zeitung (ChAZ),* 4 Dec. 1883.

10. Cf. Richard Evans, *Sozialdemokratie und Frauenemanzipation im Deutschen Kaiserreich* (Berlin, 1979), 40.

11. August Bebel, *Die Frau und der Sozialismus* (Berlin/East, 1974), 25.

12. Bebel, *Die Frau,* 29.

13. Bebel, *Die Frau,* 155.

14. Bebel, *Die Frau,* 180.

15. Bebel, *Die Frau,* 515.

16. Carroll Smith-Rosenberg, *Disorderly Conduct: Visions of Gender in Victorian America* (New York, 1985), 176.

17. Smith-Rosenberg, *Disorderly Conduct,* 176.

18. *Fackel,* 25 Nov. 1883.

19. This and preceding quotations *ibid.*

20. Ulrike Prokop, *Weiblicher Lebenszusammenhang. Von der Beschränktheit der Strategien und der Unangemessenheit der Wünsche* (Frankfurt, 1977), 197.

21. *Ibid.*

22. *NYVZ,* 22 April 1900.

23. See for instance the activities of the bourgeois feminist Lily Braun in the German Social Democracy; Lily Braun, *Memoiren einer Sozialistin. Kampfjahre* (Munich, 1922).

24. Cf. Margaret Marsh, "The Anarchist-Feminist Response to the 'Woman Question' in Late Nineteenth-Century America." *American Quarterly* XXX (Fall 1978): 533–47; cf. also the discussion on "free love" in the women's column of the *NYVZ* beginning in March 1901; also Margaret Marsh, *Anarchist Women 1870–1920* (Philadelphia, 1981).

25. Engels here refers to Lewis H. Morgan's *Ancient Society;* Friedrich Engels, *Der*

Ursprung der Familie, des Privateigentums und des Staates, Marx-Engels-Werke, *Ausgewählte Schriften* (Berlin/East, 1976), 155f.

26. Vogel, *Marxism,* 103.

27. Cf. Buhle, *Women,* 33.

28. Christiane Harzig, "Chicago's German North Side, 1880–1900: The Structure of a Gilded Age Ethnic Neighborhood," in *German Workers in Industrial Chicago 1850–1910: A Comparative Perspective,* Hartmut Keil and John B. Jentz, eds. (DeKalb, IL, 1983), 137f.

29. *ChAZ,* 26 June 1895.

30. *ChAZ,* 9 Sept. 1895.

31. *NYVZ,* 19 Jan. 1902.

32. *NYVZ,* 16 March 1902.

33. *NYVZ,* 15 March 1903.

34. *NYVZ,* 8 June 1902.

35. *NYVZ,* 25 March 1903.

36. *NYVZ,* 26 Jan. 1902.

37. Referring to a discussion of the family budget conducted in the *NYVZ* in the early 1880s, Dorothee Schneider shows how German working-class families adjusted their standard of living to the general level of their environs. See Dorothee Schneider, "For Whom Are All the Good Things in Life? German-American Housewives Discuss Their Budgets," in *German Workers,* Keil and Jentz, 145f.

38. Cf. also Schneider's observation, referring to the early 1880s, "how dependent [women] were on their husband's voluntary cooperation when it came to saving money and how little they could do to curb the amount the men decided to spend on themselves." "For Whom," 155.

39. *NYVZ,* 6 April 1902.

40. *NYVZ,* 3 May 1900.

41. Cf. Smith-Rosenberg, *Disorderly Conduct,* 178 and 181.

42. The term is taken from Barbara Welter's *The Cult of True Womanhood;* quoted in Smith-Rosenberg, *Disorderly Conduct,* 178.

43. Cf. Sarah Eisenstein, *Give Us Bread but Give Us Roses: Working Women's Consciousness in the United States, 1890 to the First World War* (London, 1981). Eisenstein shows how working-class women tried, despite their "unfeminine" wage work, to maintain a female identity. See p. 5.

44. Cf. Barbara Taylor, *Eve and the New Jerusalem: Socialism and Feminism in the 19th Century* (New York, 1982), 222: "Women's family-centered, nurturing culture came to be seen as a desirable alternative to the masculine, work-centered competitive culture."

45. *NYVZ*, 14 Sept. 1903.

46. *NYVZ*, 7 June 1903.

47. *ChAZ*, 8 July 1890.

48. *ChAZ*, 6 Jan. 1890.

49. *ChAZ*, 6 Jan. 1890.

50. Cf. Gerda Weiler, *Der enteignete Mythos. Eine notwendige Revision der Archetypenlehre C. G. Jungs und Erich Neumanns* (Munich, 1985), 64f.

51. *ChAZ*, 15 July 1891.

52. *ChAZ*, 19 March 1896.

53. Cf. Engels, *Der Ursprung*, 155ff.

54. Vogel, *Marxism*, 101.

55. Cf. Michel Foucault, *Sexualität und Wahrheit* (Frankfurt, 1983.).

56. *NYVZ*, 26 April 1903.

57. *ChAZ*, 16 Dec. 1895.

58. *ChAZ*, 3 Oct. 1895.

59. *ChAZ*, 28 Nov. 1895.

60. Cf. for instance "Frauenliebe," a short story appearing in the *NYVZ* on 17 Sept. 1899, for a good example of the way these feminine qualities were portrayed.

61. The *NYVZ* tends rather to refer to the way electricity will "deliver women from the stove," it representing no less than "a complete revolution in woman's social position," making an "independently thinking, mobile being" out of the "slave of the stove." *NYVZ*, 19 May 1896.

62. Evans, *Sozialdemokratie*, 244f.

63. Cf. Smith-Rosenberg, *Disorderly Conduct*, 220ff.; Catherine Clinton, *The Other Civil War: American Women in the 19th Century* (New York, 1984), 147ff.; Nancy Woloch, *Women and the American Experience* (New York, 1984), 316ff. and 363ff.

64. Evans, *Sozialdemokratie*, 244.

65. *ChAZ*, 30 March 1891.

66. *ChAZ*, 18 June 1890.

67. *NYVZ*, 15 Oct. 1899.

68. Barbara Ketelhut et al. discuss the situation in the German Kaiserreich, where the German Social Democracy rejected all forms of birth control as a form of "self-help leading to reformism." The authors come to the conclusion that this position reveals "the inner conservatism which cast women in the role of procreative machines, as the producers of the

masses"; "Die Familie als Brutstätte der Revolution. Familienpolitik in der Arbeiterbewegung," in *Projekt sozialistischer Feminismus*, 176.

69. *ChAZ*, 14 May 1893.

70. *ChAZ*, 14 May 1893.

71. *ChAZ*, 25 March 1891.

72. *NYVZ*, 31 Aug. 1903.

73. Helen Stöcker, quoted in "Mutterschaft und geistige Arbeit," *NYVZ*, 31 Aug. 1903.

74. Karin Hausen, "Mothers, Sons and the Sale of Symbols and Goods: The German Mother's Day 1923–1933," in *Interest and Emotion: Essays on the Study of Family and Kinship*, Hans Medick and David W. Sabean, eds. (Cambridge, MA, 1984). She points out that the culturally and historically important cult of the mother demanded this sort of interpretation, since "what men hoped for in a mother became the object of celebration. This hope united the longing to be caught up once more in 'unquestioning love'. . . . The cult of the mother was probably also an attempt to exercise some form of control over these socially incalculable fears and longings felt by men"; 403ff.

75. Cf. Willi Albrecht et al., "Frauenfrage und deutsche Sozialdemokratie vom Ende des 19. Jahrhunderts bis zum Beginn der zwanziger Jahre," *Archiv für Sozialgeschichte* XIX (1979): 459–510. The following quotes from letters written by women to the *NYVZ* offer telling testimony of the situation in the United States.

76. *NYVZ*, 8 March 1903; 28 April 1896; cf. also Köhn et al., " 'Verläßliche Frauenpersonen'," 160–202.

77. See letters in *NYVZ*, 13 April 1900; 22 June 1902; and article 8 March 1903.

78. Cf. Agnes Heller, *Das Alltagsleben. Versuch einer Erklärung der individuellen Reproduktion* (Frankfurt, 1978).

79. Brigitte Nölleke, *In alle Richtungen zugleich. Denkstrukturen von Frauen* (Munich, 1985), 241.

80. Nölleke, *In alle Richtungen*, 242.

81. *NYVZ*, 23 Dec. 1900.

82. *NYVZ*, 3 March 1901.

83. *NYVZ*, 7 June 1903.

84. *NYVZ*, 20 Oct. 1901.

85. *NYVZ*, 13 April 1900.

86. *NYVZ*, 3 March 1901.

87. *NYVZ*, 3 March 1901.

German-American Labor Press
The *Vorbote* and the *Chicagoer Arbeiter-Zeitung*

RENATE KIESEWETTER

M ost important of the many cultural institutions belonging to the German-American working-class movement in Chicago (as well as in other North American cities that had drawn great numbers of German immigrant workers) was its own press. By founding the weekly *Vorbote* (Herald) in 1874 and the *Chicagoer Arbeiter-Zeitung* (Chicago Labor Paper) in 1877, German-American workers created a journalistic medium that represented their political interests and, at the same time, in its function as party organ, was a significant organizational factor in the German-American labor movement.[1]

In this sense, these newspapers were in keeping with the German tradition of the political press, "the most essential journalistic phenomenon of the nineteenth century."[2] Unlike in the United States, where it already existed, freedom of the press did not come without a struggle in Germany. Despite attempts to limit its freedom, the press became increasingly significant. A variety of factors contributed to this development, such as the rise of the middle class and its participation in the political process, the introduction of a constitutional monarchy and parliamentary system, and the German Revolution of 1848. As an important element of public opinion, the press also acquired a "social mission,"[3] as is evinced by the changing character of the newspapers themselves: After 1848, "opinion papers" emerged, "founded to advocate certain intellectual and political goals."[4] This development affected all social groups. There were newspapers representing conservative and liberal political parties, and with the coming of the Socialist movement, Socialist papers emerged as well. These publications were party papers in a double sense:

On the one hand they "took part, took sides, were partial," and on the other "they were linked to a party organization."[5]

Both characteristics also hold true for German-American labor papers, which were founded by Germans who had already been active in the labor movement in Germany. There, in 1863, the Lassallean General German Workingmen's Association was established; the Social Democratic Labor party, in 1869. In the same year, German-American Socialists in New York joined the International Workingmen's Association, which had been founded by Karl Marx and Friedrich Engels in 1864. Thus immigrants brought traditions along with them to America, where, in comparison to European—and particularly German—standards, there was more freedom. In North America, for instance, there were no governmental regulations, controls, bans, or censorship standing in the way of journalistic impetus, so newspapers could be founded at any time.

The boom in ethnic newspapers in the United States was naturally linked to phases in immigration. In the first phase of north and west European immigration, many German immigrants came to America; from 1850 to 1890 they outnumbered other groups. In 1854 and 1873, German immigration was especially heavy, and it peaked in 1882 with 250,000 immigrants.[6]

Germans who had settled in American cities formed the readership for urban German-language newspapers. The need to read a newspaper in one's familiar language led to a demand for an ethnic press among all immigrant groups. With 80 percent, German-American newspapers held the lion's share of this foreign-language press.[7] Prior to the Civil War, radical papers were often founded by immigrant Forty-Eighters. After the war, when rapid industrialization in America's quickly expanding industrial centers accommodated increasing numbers of artisans and workers, especially in the East and Midwest, and when the labor movement became stronger, industrial workers also created their own press. Between 1863 and 1873, 120 German-American daily, weekly, and monthly newspapers were founded.[8]

After the depression of the 1870s, and in the course of the large railroad strikes and ensuing labor unrest in 1877, the labor movement once again attracted many new followers, among them a large share of German immigrants who, in turn, formed the basis for a fresh impetus in the German-American labor press. Cities with large numbers of German workers witnessed the emergence of papers such as the *Socialist* (Milwaukee, 1875), the *Ohio Volks-Zeitung* (Cincinnati, 1876), the *Volksstimme des Westens* (St. Louis, 1877), the *Neue Zeit* (Louisville, 1877), the *Philadelphia Tageblatt* (1877–78), the *New Yorker Volks-Zeitung* (1878), and the *Chicagoer Arbeiter-Zeitung.*[9]

It was no accident that a labor newspaper was also founded in Chicago. After the Civil War, Chicago emerged as the Midwest's largest industrial center, including meatpacking, iron and steel, textile, furniture, machine-building, and brewing industries. In the second half of the nineteenth century, German immigrants made up a considerable portion of the city's working-class population. In 1850, five thousand of Chicago's thirty thousand inhabitants were German. By 1884, one-third of the total population was composed of first- and second-generation German immigrants. From the 1850s onward, there was a large German community comprising primarily artisans and skilled workers. They created their own "core press,"[10] a press that was the focal center of the German labor movement in the city.

As was shown in a comparative analysis of the *Illinois Staats-Zeitung* and the *Chicagoer Arbeiter-Zeitung*,[11] German-American newspapers did not really seek "legitimization primarily by referring back to the old homeland."[12] Instead, they tended to report on life in Chicago's German community and to provide information and helpful tips to German-speaking immigrants who suddenly had to fend for themselves in a North American industrial center. In this context, the *Vorbote* and the *Arbeiter-Zeitung* assumed the function of important social institutions; lending organization impetus to the German-American radical labor movement, these two newspapers also served as a cultural vehicle for German-American working-class life in Chicago.

FOUNDING OF THE *VORBOTE* AND *CHICAGOER ARBEITER-ZEITUNG*

The *Vorbote* was founded in 1874, shortly after the Labor party of Illinois was formed in Chicago on the initiative of German Socialists. The party united Chicago's workers to act against the widespread misery in the wake of the economic depression of 1873. The middle-class press did all it could to denounce the endeavors of the Labor party and issued sensational warnings of impending revolution.[13] The newly founded party needed its own press to oppose these assaults, and it therefore established the *Vorbote*: the first issue appeared on February 14, 1874. A party organ, the *Vorbote* was to offer thorough information, convert critical consciousness into active engagement, and recruit new members for the party while continually publicizing strategy and tactics (which, however, often prompted

controversial discussions). As a party paper, it was to spread socialist principles via the written word. In this sense, the *Vorbote* was in keeping with
the tradition of German labor newspapers such as the *Volksstaat*, published in Leipzig, which the Social Democratic Labor party recognized as
its party organ in 1869.[14] In 1871, the Lassalleans also appropriated the
Neuer Social-Demokrat for the party.[15]

Both the *Vorbote*'s name and staff reflect the influence of European
models. The European namesake of the Chicago-based *Vorbote* was edited by Johann Philipp Becker in Geneva from 1866 to 1871. The old
Vorbote was the central organ of the German-language section of the International Workingmen's Association in Switzerland. It was also distributed in the United States; F. A. Sorge (who would later be general
secretary of the International Workingmen's Association in America)
carried out sales from New York. Becker also knew Carl Klings from a
prior period of opposition to Lassalle in 1862 and 1863. Klings, a cutler
from Solingen who had come to the United States in 1865, was the first
editor of the Chicago *Vorbote*.

The specimen issue of the *Arbeiter-Zeitung* appeared in May 1877,
three years after the founding of the *Vorbote*. By June 1877, the *Arbeiter-
Zeitung* was appearing three times a week; two years later it began appearing every day, and continued until 1919. It was established at a time when
the Socialist movement was on the rise; the Workingmen's party of the
United States was formed in 1876, one year after its German counterpart,
and there was "a veritable fever among German-speaking Socialist workers to found German-language labor papers."[16] In fact, of the twenty-four
Socialist papers appearing in 1876 and 1877, fourteen were German-
language publications.[17]

But these new papers also represented competition for the *Vorbote*,
which was distributed nationwide. In May 1877, it found itself in severe
financial trouble. Conrad Conzett, having succeeded Carl Klings to become the *Vorbote*'s second editor, founded the *Arbeiter-Zeitung* as a means
of supporting the weekly. Above all, the *Arbeiter-Zeitung* was to cover the
Chicago area, recruit new readers, and "satisfy the needs of the local labor
movement."[18] It was also hoped that this would counterbalance the
Lassallean political wing of the party in Chicago, which—under Carl
Klings and Jacob Winnen—was pushing for participation in elections and
had been editing its own paper, the *Chicagoer Volks-Zeitung*, since February 1877. The *Arbeiter-Zeitung*, by contrast, was meant to strengthen the
Marxist trade union wing to which Conrad Conzett belonged.

The establishment of the *Arbeiter-Zeitung* also marked the shift from a party organ to an alternative daily newspaper. This was possible because the labor movement was by this time already quite widespread, thus laying the foundation for the favorable reception of a Socialist-oriented daily. Conzett hoped that a daily would enable him to reach a larger public not yet connected with the Socialist movement.

CHARACTERISTICS OF THE PAPERS AS LABOR ORGANS

The *Vorbote* had been appearing every Saturday since February 14, 1874, as a four-page paper. On May 22, 1875, it was enlarged to eight pages. Initially, the *Vorbote* was the party organ of the Labor party of Illinois; when the Workingmen's party of the United States was founded and the *Vorbote* recognized as its organ, it adopted the subtitle "Organ of the Workingmen's Party of the United States." When it was deprived of this capacity in 1877, it referred to itself as the "Independent Organ for the True Interests of the Proletariat."

For the editors, 1879 was a very productive year. The Socialistic Publishing Society's[19] Commune celebration yielded a considerable surplus, making it possible to print the *Arbeiter-Zeitung* on a daily basis; the eight-page *Fackel* (Torch) also began appearing as a Sunday paper. Chicago's workers were now supplied with reading material every day of the week.

What claim did editors make for their newspapers? And how was this claim fulfilled in the conveyance of subject matter? "To bring about a moral elevation of the working class, as well as the recognition of its human dignity"[20] was the stated purpose of the labor press. It intended to achieve its ends via the "dissemination of social and economic knowledge" and the "discussion of relevant current issues from a social and economic sciences perspective."[21] Both newspapers considered it their task to stand up for workers and their class. But the *Arbeiter-Zeitung* sought—as much as, if not more than, the *Vorbote*—to inform instead of to teach, in keeping with its character as a daily newspaper. "Its own financial interests should only be secondary, should just be a means to an end, never the end in itself."[22] In a narrower sense, it was also the purpose of the opinion press to take sides and, as a party newspaper, "to defend socialist principles and to protect the Socialist program from bourgeois narrow-mindedness."[23]

The *Arbeiter-Zeitung* contained reportage and advertisements.[24] Articles accounted for four-fifths of the paper's four pages, business advertisements for one-fifth; there were thus fewer ads than in a middle-class newspaper, but more than in other Socialist papers. Approximately 44 percent of the advertisements—for small stores, specific products, or working-class saloons—were placed on page 1. The smallest number of ads was found on page 2, the editorial page; on page 4, the local section, there were only slightly more. Some two hundred articles appeared each day, most of which were written in a concise manner; two-thirds were no longer than fifteen lines. The daily editorial on page 2 was among the three texts that took up more than one column. This was a characteristic of German party newspapers preserved in German-American newspapers in America, whereas in Anglo-American journalism, the 1870s saw a movement away from opinion papers toward business papers.[25] The feuilleton and serial novel were also foreign to American newspapers. And if these were unique to German journalism, it had to do with the *Arbeiter-Zeitung*'s wanting "to satisfy women's need for products of the imagination."[26] The sixteen notices, most of them located on page 4, were also a part of the reportage. Every second notice announced an association meeting or festivity, and the rest were allotted to announcements by the Socialist Labor party and to trade union information.

What topics did the *Arbeiter-Zeitung* address? Among the main topics (quite surprisingly for a Socialist daily newspaper) were various sensational reports and gossip stories, constituting about 40 percent of all the material. In keeping with its aims and its target group, the *Arbeiter-Zeitung* reported extensively on social events, on working and living conditions, as well as on labor disputes and strikes. This can also be gathered from the extent of information conveyed. The social sphere was dealt with in short notices of up to fifteen lines (55 percent), in medium-length reports (36 percent), and in longer articles of more than half a column (8 percent). By contrast, cultural reports, the feuilleton, and sensational and miscellaneous stories were all treated in short accounts.

Since the area of circulation for the *Arbeiter-Zeitung* was Chicago, half the articles dealt with local events. Just about one-third of the articles reported on national matters, and reports on Germany were rare, accounting for about 4 percent of the total. Again, in keeping with the paper's readers, concentration was focused primarily on local Socialist groups, associations, and federations. One other factor is worth noting in this context: Just about one-third of the articles printed in the *Arbeiter-Zeitung* were commentaries. There was an emphasis on making explicit editorial judgments, thus accentuating the character of the *Arbeiter-Zeitung* as an opinion paper.

INSTITUTIONAL ORGANIZATION

The ideological orientation of the *Vorbote* and the *Arbeiter-Zeitung* was reflected in the way they were organized. The form of business organization, inner structure of the administration, financing, sales, and technical production—all these elements were closely linked to socialist principles. In addition, it also becomes apparent how firmly the labor papers were anchored in Chicago's working-class neighborhoods.

The editorship, administration, and production of the *Vorbote* and later the *Arbeiter-Zeitung* transpired within a cooperative business organization, which united all members of the publishing house and political party in collective ownership. From 1874 to 1876, the Vorbote Society (*Verein Vorbote*) functioned as a publishing society. Later, when the Socialists convened in Philadelphia to form the Workingmen's party of the United States and the *Vorbote* became its party organ, the party's executive committee took over newspaper matters until 1878. From 1879 onward, the publishing company was called the Socialistic Publishing Society. From 1876 to 1878, the papers were published by the party directly, without an intermediary publishing society. Administrative functions were assumed and carried out by actual party officials, the national executive committee, and the supervisory board. The degree of centralization was more pronounced. Newspaper matters were not determined by all members of the publishing society directly, but rather by one of the delegates selected by section members to represent them at the national convention. All told, however, the structure of the publishing business was not essentially different. A description of the Vorbote Society will serve as an example of a cooperative newspaper publishing company.

Represented by its members, the Labor party of Illinois was the owner of the newspaper.[27] The general assembly, comprising all members entitled to vote (i.e., party members having purchased five-dollar share certificates), administered the newspaper business through a six-member press committee and three trustees. All members elected these nine people; they also elected a manager, who was subordinate to the trustees, an editor in chief, and an assistant editor. The press committee—three of whose six members were replaced every six months—acted as a go-between for the editor and the party and was responsible to the "Society for the contents of the *Vorbote*."[28] Ultimately, this was a way of checking the editor, who otherwise had a virtual monopoly. The press committee had other functions, too, such as accepting and excluding members, going over the semiannual inventory, giving notice of the general assemblies in the *Vorbote*, and—should the editor become ill—hiring a substitute. Together with the Vorbote Society's manager, the committee could also found new sales agencies. The trustees' main task was to take inventory twice a year. They also wrote reports on the society, which were then published in the *Vorbote*. In 1877 and 1878, the seven-member national executive committee of the Socialist Labor party (then located in Chicago) took over the responsibilities of the former press committee; the responsibilities of the three trustees were taken over by a five-member administrative board, which was elected on the spot by section delegates.[29]

In the way it was set up, the Socialistic Publishing Society, founded by members of the German-language section of the Socialist Labor party in 1879, was similar to the Vorbote Society. The Social Democratic Cooperative Printing Society, where the *Vorbote* and the *Arbeiter-Zeitung* were printed, also adhered to the organizational models of the other societies.

These administrative and publishing structures were customary in the German Social Democratic labor press, especially in the press institutions of its Eisenach wing. At its 1869 Eisenach Congress, the Social Democratic Labor party recognized the *Volksstaat* as party property and party organ. The administrative conditions (according to which editors, sales agents, and printers were hired by the congress or by the party executive committee, which was controlled by the supervisory committee)[30] were similar to those laid down by the Vorbote Society and later by the Socialist Labor party. If one compares the remarks about the party press made at the 1875 Gotha Unity Congress and at the Philadelphia Congress in 1876, there are hardly any differences. The cooperative organizational form in publishing and printing, which also brought out pamphlets and other publications, emerged in Germany at the beginning of the 1870s. At its Stuttgart Congress in 1870, the Social Democratic Labor party resolved to found a shareholder enterprise; this was realized two years later with the Leipzig Cooperative Printing Company.[31]

With shares of five dollars in the Chicago publishing company and annual dividends of 6 percent, members were interested in seeing the enterprise flourish. But there were also countless party comrades who, committed to the cause, answered the newspapers' calls to find new readers and worked zealously at selling subscriptions. By 1876, readers in eighteen cities could obtain the *Vorbote* via more than twenty-four agents. In Chicago, readers received the newspapers in the German neighborhoods. Saloons frequented by Socialists often subscribed, as was the case in Klings's

saloon in 1874, located on the first floor at 94–96 South Market Street
(the editorial staff used the same house). In 1877, Charles Zepf promoted
his "Wine and Lager Beer Saloon" at 130 West Lake Street by advertising
that clients would find copies of the *Vorbote*, the Milwaukee *Socialist*, and
the *Arbeiter-Stimme* of New York.[32] Whoever sold a subscription could
keep twenty-five of the sixty-five cents the *Vorbote* charged per quarter.
Readers could subscribe to the *Arbeiter-Zeitung* at nine branch offices as
well as at the main office at 87 Fifth Avenue.[33] Most of the branches were
on Chicago's Southwest Side, the Socialist stronghold in the city, with its
large working-class neighborhoods. The other branch offices were on the
Northwest Side, where German-speaking workers and members of the
middle class lived.

In the middle of 1879, the *Arbeiter-Zeitung* had some 4,000 subscribers and was printing editions of 7,000–9,000 copies. In the spring
of 1881, when the newspapers were affected by a financial crisis, subscriptions dropped to 2,800. This decline doubtless also reflects the
split in the Chicago labor movement, when the radical wing of
Chicago's trade unions broke with the Socialist Labor party. In 1886, in
the course of the eight-hour movement, the *Arbeiter-Zeitung*'s subscriptions climbed again, to 5,780. The readers—and there were surely two to
three times as many as copies sold—were not confined to party members; they primarily comprised workers who were organized in trade unions, such as the furniture workers (whose union organ was the *Vorbote*),
printers, joiners, and masons.[34]

Support of labor newspapers also constituted a financial necessity.
The cooperative enterprise did not make much profit and would have
shown a loss in the first four years if Conrad Conzett had not given a loan.
The *Vorbote* and the *Arbeiter-Zeitung* were financed by five financial
sources. These were (in the order of magnitude): newspaper money (subscriptions and street sales); advertisements; certificates of indebtedness
and loans from members; party funds and extra taxes; and proceeds from
working-class festivities. Revenue from ads was limited; in 1875 and 1876,
it accounted for one-fourth of the paper's income; in 1876, for only one-
tenth; and in 1879, one-fifth. But the bulk of the revenue (two-thirds to
three-fourths) came from newspaper sales. And in this sense it is also clear
who constituted the newspaper's main backers: the readers.

The rest of the revenue came from other sources, and it must be
pointed out that the proceeds from workers' festivities were sometimes
considerable. In 1879, the Paris Commune celebration, organized by the
Socialistic Publishing Society, yielded a surplus of $4,461.43,[35] allowing

the editors to turn the *Arbeiter-Zeitung* into a daily and to found the Sunday paper, the *Fackel*. New Year's Eve festivities, autumn and carnival balls, excursions, and picnics—all helped finance the papers.

Material and production costs for paper, typesetting, and printing were generally the highest, accounting for some 60–70 percent.[36] Expenditures for the editorial staff amounted to one-fifth of the total in 1879.[37]

MEMBERSHIP IN THE PUBLISHING SOCIETY

Committed party members ceaselessly agitated for and saw to the distribution of the papers and helped guide them through their financial crises. They were essential for the successful organization and administration of the publishing business, which would hardly have been possible without the support of workers who were already well organized in their trades. Indeed, most members of the newspaper publishing society also held positions in their trade unions.

Of the eighty-two people whose names could be gathered from the *Vorbote* and the *Arbeiter-Zeitung*, most worked in traditionally German crafts. In the Vorbote Society and the Socialistic Publishing Society, the largest group of skilled workers were involved in furniture making. Chicago was a center of furniture production; the International Furniture Workers' Unions of North America was founded in 1873 on the initiative of the radical furniture workers' union from Chicago. The fifteen printers in the publishing society were all members of the German-American Typographical Union No. 9 (among them several presidents, vice presidents, and corresponding secretaries). Conrad Conzett and Gustav Lyser, who were on the newspapers' editorial staffs, also had important posts in the Typographical Union. For its production process, the *Arbeiter-Zeitung* hired only union members.

EDITORIAL STAFF

The heart of the institution was the editorial staff. From the founding of the *Vorbote* in 1874 until the Haymarket tragedy in 1886, there were primarily five editors who determined newspaper policy: Carl Klings (1874–75), Conrad Conzett (1875–78), Paul Grottkau (1878–79, 1880–84), Gustav Lyser (1878–79), and August Spies (1884–86).[38] None of them

Figure 6.1. Paul Grottkau, editor of the Chicagoer Arbeiter-Zeitung, *1879–84. (Photo Courtesy of Milwaukee County Historical Society).*

were professional journalists; they all had worked in traditional trades before. Klings was a cutler, Grottkau a mason, Spies an upholsterer, and Conzett and Lyser printers. With the exception of Spies, who claimed to have known nothing about socialism before coming to America,[39] all of them had had contact with the labor movement in Germany. Some of them had been actively involved, and they brought their experience to the United States. In 1863, Klings was elected to the executive board of the Lassallean General German Workers' Association, but he later turned against Ferdinand Lassalle and was finally expelled from the organization. Lyser had been active in the Social Democratic Labor party before emigrating. In 1867, Conzett received "initial impetus for the sociopolitical movement" while a member of a printers' union in Leipzig. In 1871, Grottkau became president of the General German Masons' and Stonecutters' Union in Berlin. Both he and Lyser had been active in the German movement as journalists.[40] Within about one month of his arrival in Chicago in January 1878, Grottkau was already writing rousing articles for the *Vorbote* and the *Arbeiter-Zeitung*. By March 1878, the party sent him as

Figure 6.2. August Spies, editor of the Chicagoer Arbeiter-Zeitung, *1884–86.*

a speaker at public meetings, describing him in the *Vorbote* as a "first-rate agitator."[41] Here one can see that the editors of labor papers assumed functions beyond their main duties. They were speakers at party and union events, labor leaders, and organizers. Whoever had done the party a great service or, like Grottkau, had already been active in Germany, had a chance of becoming an editor: "To be editor of one of the large party papers . . . was an indication that one had already achieved an influential position within the party and, at the same time, it was a springboard to the highest ranking party posts."[42]

An editor who wrote the daily editorial could play a considerable role in shaping political opinion. At the same time, new editors had to accommodate themselves to the situation in Chicago. Thus Lyser abandoned his antiunion stance in Chicago; here the credo was to further the Socialist movement via trade union support. Or, for instance, when Grottkau opposed the anarchist convictions of the social revolutionary groups, he was forced to make way for Spies.

Figure 6.3. Joseph Dietzgen, editor of the Chicagoer Arbeiter-Zeitung, *1886–87.*

Just as the labor newspaper's office was the headquarters of the movement (where election committees gathered during election campaigns), the editors were labor leaders and agitators. In the *Arbeiter-Zeitung*, for instance, letters appeared in columns like "Newsbox" asking the editors for advice in a variety of areas; apparently the editors were considered especially knowledgeable and informed.

CONCLUSION

In the 1870s and 1880s, the *Vorbote* and *Arbeiter-Zeitung* represented the most important labor press institutions in Chicago's German immigrant community. By conveying information and agitating vigorously, they helped build up a radical labor movement closely linked to the city's trade unions.

Figure 6.4. Advertisement of the Chicagoer Arbeiter-Zeitung, Vorbote, *and* Fackel.

Both newspapers served the Socialist cause. On the one hand, they were committed to conveying information and agitating from a Socialist perspective. As a party organ, the *Vorbote* represented a forum for inner-party discussion about the development of the movement. After the weekly had helped create a substantial following, the *Arbeiter-Zeitung* could join in as an alternative daily and also address unorganized workers.

Figure 6.5. Calendar for the year 1893 in commemoration of the Haymarket anarchists, with "dedication by the newspaper carriers for the Chicagoer Arbeiter-Zeitung, Fackel, *and* Vorbote."

On the other hand, they were organized according to Socialist principles. The newspaper business was based on a cooperative form with capital stock from individual members and supporters. The newspapers were not financed by customers paying for ads, but rather by the readers. This necessitated the commitment of supporters and readers, since there was never much financial latitude. Members of the publishing society, who concurrently belonged to trade unions, established cross-connections to the party and to trade unions, thus facilitating the circulation of the newspapers.

The editors were the outstanding figures: By writing the daily editorials, they exercised great influence on the political bent of the newspapers. Whoever became editor had already served the movement; the strength of his position as editor made him an even more prominent labor leader. Editors appeared as speakers and agitators at workers' festivities, parades, and demonstrations.

The 1870s and 1880s represented the flowering of both German-language newspapers. Although the *Arbeiter-Zeitung* continued to appear until 1919 and the *Vorbote* until 1924, their influence steadily declined after 1890. Their base was the German immigrant community, which, over the course of time, accommodated itself to the language and culture of the new country. When Bismarck's anti-Socialist legislation was retracted in Germany in 1890, there was also a steep decline in the number of party members immigrating to Chicago, and thus a decline in the number of people who could have contributed to the newspapers' editorial staffs.

NOTES

1. This essay is based on my M.A. thesis, "Die Institution der deutsch-amerikanischen Arbeiterpresse in Chicago: Zur Geschichte des *Vorboten* und der *Chicagoer Arbeiterzeitung*, 1874–1876," America Institute, University of Munich, October 1982. It was published in the series, Labor Newspaper Preservation Project, University of Bremen, Dirk Hoerder, series ed., *Glimpses of the German-American Radical Press*, Publications of the Labor Newspaper Preservation Project (Bremen, 1985): 179–214.

2. Kurt Koszyk, *Deutsche Presse im 19. Jahrhundert* (Berlin, 1966), 10.

3. Emil Löbl, *Kultur und Presse* (Leipzig, 1903), 202, quoted in Elisabeth Pitzer, "Bürgerliche Presse und Arbeiterpresse im Wandel" (M.A. thesis, University of Munich, 1980), 38.

4. Emil Dovifat, *Die Zeitungen* (Gotha, 1925), 9, quoted in Pitzer, "Bürgerliche Presse," 38.

5. Koszyk, *Deutsche Presse*, 130.

6. On German immigration, see *Die Vereinigten Staaten von Amerika*, Willi Paul Adams et al., Fischer Weltgeschichte, vol. 30 (Frankfurt, 1977), 184ff; Harry A. Carman and C. Syrett, *A History of the American People* (New York, 1957), 154; Kathleen Neils Conzen, "Germans," in *Harvard Encyclopedia of American Ethnic Groups*, Stephan Thernstrom et al., eds. (Cambridge, MA, 1980), 405–25; Wolfgang Köllman and Peter Marschalck, "German Emigration to the United States," *Perspectives in American History* 7 (1973): 499–554; Mack Walker, *Germany and the Emigration, 1816–1885* (Cambridge, MA, 1964).

7. Carl Wittke, *The German-Language Press in America* (Lexington, KY, 1957), 14.

8. Pitzer, "Bürgerliche Presse," 32ff; John R. Commons et al., *History of Labour in the United States*, 6th ed. (New York, 1951), 15; William F. Kamman, *Socialism in German-American Literature* (Philadelphia, 1917), 44; Hermann Schlüter, *Die Internationale in Amerika* (Chicago, 1918), 308ff.

9. Schlüter, *Die Internationale*, 308ff.

10. Dirk Hoerder, "'Why did you come?' The Proletarian Mass Migration: Research Report 1980–1985," Labor Migration Project, Labor Newspaper Preservation Project, University of Bremen 1986: 68.

11. Cf. Pitzer, "Bürgerliche Presse."

12. Pitzer, "Bürgerliche Presse," 190.

13. Zonita Stewart Jefferys, *The Attitude of the Chicago Press Toward the Local Labor Movement 1873 to 1879* (Chicago, 1936), 50.

14. Wilhelm Schröder, *Handbuch der sozialdemokratischen Parteitage von 1863 bis 1909*, vol. 1 (Munich, 1910), 358.

15. Koszyk, *Deutsche Presse*, part II, 195.

16. Friedrich A. Sorge, "Die Arbeiterbewegung in den Vereinigten Staaten," *Neue Zeit*, vol. 10 part II (1892) 456.

17. Morris Hillquit, *History of Socialism in the United States*, 2d ed. (New York, 1971), 204.

18. *Vorbote*, 2 June 1877.

19. *Chicagoer Arbeiter-Zeitung (ChAZ)*, 16 June 1879.

20. *ChAZ*, 3 Oct. 1874.

21. Leaflet, "Subscription Invitation for New York and Environs."

22. *ChAZ*, 25 June 1879.

23. *ChAZ*, 1 May 1879.

24. The following refers to Pitzer, "Bürgerliche Presse," 97ff.

25. Pitzer, "Bürgerliche Presse," 97ff.

26. *ChAZ*, 5 May 1890, quoted in Hartmut Keil and Heinz Ickstadt, "Elements of German Working-Class Culture in Chicago, 1880 to 1890," in this volume.

27. *Vorbote*, 1 April 1876.

28. *Vorbote*, 10 June 1876.

29. *Vorbote*, 5 Aug. 1876.

30. Schröder, *Handbuch*, 358.

31. Dieter Fricke, *Die deutsche Arbeiterbewegung 1869–1914. Ein Handbuch über ihre Organisation und Tätigkeit im Klassenkampf* (Berlin/East, 1976), 364.

32. *Vorbote*, 20 Jan. 1877.

33. Party members and businesspeople connected with the movement sold newspaper subscriptions and accepted ads. The addresses were: August Frank Pharmacy, 361 Blue Island Avenue; A. Kußmann Pharmacy, 302 South Halsted Street; A. Kußmann Pharmacy, 1491 South Halsted Street; A. Lanfermann Book Shop, 74 Clybourne Avenue; J. G. Schaar Pharmacy, 6671 Blue Island Avenue; Chas. A. Hartwig, 476 Milwaukee Avenue; H. Martin Pharmacy, 717 Milwaukee Avenue; Emil Selle, 237 North Avenue; L. H. Neebe Magazines.

34. *Vorbote*, 13 May 1876.

35. *Vorbote*, 16 June 1879.

36. *Vorbote*, 25 Feb. and 9 Sept. 1876.

37. *ChAZ*, 13 Sept. 1879.

38. In 1879, following Grottkau's resignation, Dr. Ed. Liebig was in charge of the newspapers' editorial staff for about a year, more or less as a stopgap. W. L. Rosenberg was in charge of the *Fackel* (the Sunday edition of the *Chicagoer Arbeiter-Zeitung*, which was founded in 1879) from 1881 to 1884.

39. Philip S. Foner, ed., *The Autobiographies of the Haymarket Martyrs* (New York, 1969), 66.

40. *Vorbote*, 13 May 1876. For additional biographical information about Carl Klings, see *Geschichte der deutschen Arbeiterbewegung. Biographisches Lexikon* (Berlin/East, 1970), 241f.; Samuel Bernstein, *The First International in America* (New York, 1965), 244; Heinz Hümmler, *Opposition gegen Lassalle* (Berlin, 1963), 26f.; Schlüter, *Die Internationale*, 318f.; *Neues Leben*, 27 June 1908. On Paul Grottkau, see Hartmut Keil, "The German Immigrant Working Class of Chicago, 1875–1890: Workers, Leaders, and the Labor Movement," in *American Labor and Immigration History, 1877–1920s: Recent European Research*, Dirk Hoerder, ed. (Urbana, IL, 1983), 156–76; Kiesewetter, "Die Institution der deutsch-amerikanischen Arbeiterpresse," 56ff. On Conrad Conzett, see Kiesewetter, "Die Institution der deutsch-amerikanischen Arbeiterpresse," 53ff. On Gustav Lyser, see Heinz Ickstadt and Hartmut Keil, "A Forgotten Piece of Working-Class Literature: Gustav Lyser's Satire

of the Hewitt Hearing of 1878," *Labor History* 20 (Winter 1979): 127ff; Schlüter, *Die Internationale,* 339; Kiesewetter, "Die Institution der deutsch-amerikanischen Arbeiterpresse," 58ff.

41. *Vobote,* 9 March 1878.

42. Gerhard A. Ritter, *Die Arbeiterbewegung im Wilhelminischen Reich* (Berlin, 1959), 62f.

CHAPTER 7

German-American Working-Class Saloons in Chicago
Their Social Function in an Ethnic and Class-Specific Cultural Context

KLAUS ENSSLEN

The social history of public drinking and the collective attitudes that motivate and inform it offer not only an apt reflection of a culture's work and leisure, but also valuable insight into the normative and practical controls exercised over work and leisure time— some of society's fundamental goods. In nineteenth-century America, the practice of drinking and the public images pertaining to it crystallized economic and moral forces that mark the transition from an agrarian-commercial society to an increasingly industrialized and urbanized one. Among the main catalysts for the widespread changes in the economic and social structures following the political disruption of the Civil War was a growing labor force, which emerged from the rapidly swelling ranks of immigrants in the latter half of the nineteenth century. These minority groups—most of them non-English-speaking—played a significant role in the cities where they tended to concentrate. The Germans and Italians, for instance, brought along recreational and drinking habits so different from those of the Irish that they could not be simply reconciled with American traditions. This importation of an unfamiliar way of life underscored class-specific and ideological discrepancies that, in the long run, would lead to an enrichment of trades and consumer expectations in an increasingly differentiated ethnic society. But in the last thirty years of the nineteenth century, cultural differences tended to reinforce a general feeling of social insecurity brought about by the painful restructuring process of rapid industrialization, and as a consequence they added to the demand for social control as well as ethical and conceptual order. In a society characterized by such change and unrest, the abolitionist reform movement, culminating around the middle of the century, found eager successors in the subsequent nativist and moral-reform movements.

In this context, the temperance movement is of central importance. Together with other social reform endeavors, it was a substantial movement by the 1860s; growing steadily stronger, it broadened its basis and merged into the more radical form of prohibitionism eventually codified in 1920 on a nationwide scale. As is stressed in more recent literature on the temperance question and other contemporary reform movements, the increasing demand for the regulation, and finally complete prohibition, of public drinking was intricately linked to powerful interests and groups in a society undergoing industrialization.[1] The psychodynamic equivalents of rationalization and maximum profit in factory production could be found in the social stereotypes of success and "upward mobility." Thus sobriety and industry not only expressed a certain work discipline but also represented important prerequisites for mass production. It is true that remnants of a puritan work ethic can be detected here. It seems more important, however, that this work ethic was now cast in terms of a dynamic concept of production geared toward efficiency and expansion—a concept based not only on individual competence, but on the competitive, capitalistic principles of a modern social ethic that transcended local differences and was perceived as fitting right in with altered notions of the times for positive change. Temperance advocates considered it their task to push for the acceptance of social virtues that were production (not consumer) oriented.[2] The recreational and drinking habits introduced by various immigrant groups thus seemed to be the remnants of a traditional, preindustrial work ethic,[3] and they consequently seemed to be in opposition to the efficiency and calculability of modern productive processes.

But one cannot attribute the temperance movement solely to the need for efficiency tailored to the demands of industrial production. It also reflects the deep-seated fears, shared by the middle and upper classes, of losing social control over phenomena like industrialization, urbanization, and immigration. Therefore the temperance movement always opposed expanding branches like alcohol distilleries, breweries, and saloons. In the 1870s—marked by the founding of the Woman's Christian Temperance Union—women assumed the leading role in the temperance movement, introducing family-related, moral, and religious arguments and rituals (e.g., prayer meetings) into the debate. These attitudes reveal anxieties about the preservation of fundamental middle-class values and became symptomatic of a trend equating morality with social position (and, correspondingly, viewing corruption and poverty as congenital social diseases, with alcohol as their common root).[4] There was also a socio-psychological function in singling out distant ethnic and lower social strata as those in need of reform and of being missionized: It tended to veil the differences between employers and employed (i.e., between the workers' struggle and vested economic interests). Interestingly enough, these reformers never realized that drinking habits among certain immigrant groups—where alcohol was not looked down upon morally—tended to solve, rather than aggravate, the alcohol problem in America, since regulations and constraints were already embedded in cultural customs (as was the case among Jews, Italians, and Germans).[5] When it came to drinking habits other than their own, reform advocates were unable to form a differentiated picture of minorities. To put it more bluntly: They were unable to perceive the intrinsic value of minority group culture. As a consequence, the temperance movement of the 1870s—with women as its prime movers—had little success, even though spontaneous civic actions closed saloons, a few breweries were forced out of business, and there was a temporary decline in beer consumption. Ironically, however, the exaggerated emphasis on moral aspects not only played down the cultural and economic context of drinking but ultimately led to consolidation in the brewing industry by strengthening those enterprises which already dominated the market.[6]

From the point of view of German immigrant workers, the preservation of certain drinking and recreational habits was far more important in America than in the country of origin, since it was here, above all, that they furnished a cultural and political means of asserting self and identity. It can be shown that a new industrial work discipline, coupled with attempts to improve efficiency, was to be found in Germany, too, and that until shortly after the turn of the century, the consumption of alcoholic beverages—at least in the workplace—was increasingly restricted and supplanted by other drinks. Thus, after 1900, temperance-related endeavors were no longer directed against a habit of the labor force in general, but rather against the weakness of individual workers. In Germany, however, it was never a question of feeling threatened by what might be seen as an alien life-style; at most, it was a question of certain recreational habits, like weekend drinking, that touched upon the work process by way of shortening work on payday or leading to a missed Monday. Organized labor even took part in efforts to reduce on-the-job alcohol consumption (the result of combined on-the-job and leisure claims stemming from a craft tradition that, in the industrial age, would increasingly represent a burden, if not an outright hazard), hoping that staying sober would help boost the workers' political awareness.[7] In America, on the other hand, the temperance movement—as it manifested itself in, for instance, the antisaloon movement toward the end of the nineteenth century—was directed against the life-styles of foreign immigrants, even in their recreational activities. In an easily recognizable scapegoat syndrome, they were not only held responsible for the social unrest of the drastically changing world of work; they were also accused of being in league with the indigenous demons, whiskey or rum. The dominant culture's consistent deprecation of various immigrant groups' communal and recreational behavior (where saloons and beer gardens were seen as indispensable elements of the cultural tradition) led to an increasingly explicit emphasis on oppositional values in the respective life-styles, so that Kenneth Kann, with pointed oversimplification, can state: "Temperance was a crusade directed against immigrants and workingpeople, and the strongest opposition came from immigrant workingpeople."[8] The subordination of private and recreational behavior to a success-oriented, upwardly mobile mentality was characteristic of the dominant culture, whereas for immigrant workers, the division between work and leisure time remained basic. The emphasis on leisure time as a counterbalance and a recuperative space can be seen not only in the high value placed on picnics and other sorts of communal festivities but also in the fact that they were often charged with political content and activities, as explicit manifestations of cultural and social expectations in clear opposition to the dominant society. If—in keeping with a widespread cliché that comes close to their self-image—the Germans in Chicago distinguished themselves as being gemütlich—emotionally and sociably expansive—then this distinction also embodies an antithetical standard vis-à-vis puritan, Protestant behavioral norms as they have been handed down in the term "WASP culture" to this very day.[9] Public and private interests, current and traditional expectations, practical and ideal values—all intermingle in the social phenomenon of the saloon, in such a way as to make it an exemplary touchstone for the experiences of German workers in America at the end of the nineteenth century.

BREWERIES AND SALOONS IN CHICAGO

In the most thorough study on the American saloon to date, Perry Duis ascertains that the development of breweries and saloons was always caught up in the tension accompanying social reform movements.[10] As an urban labor force emerged, these movements tried to find substitutes for the saloons stemming from various ethnic traditions, substitutes that would make saloons superfluous and thus avert the alleged public and moral dangers associated with the drinking habits of large segments of the population.[11] Since one result of urbanization was the emergence of more social public space, moral-reformist groups became especially interested in the semipublic realm of the saloon, pushing hard for the strict observance of license-related business procedures (like business hours and the illegality of alcoholic beverage sales to minors); indeed, sometimes they themselves helped control these regulations. As we know, these efforts were rewarded with little success. Even Chicago settlements like Hull House certainly had no power to influence drinking customs among the working classes or the spilling over of such habits to middle-class residents.

Instead of leading to a greater degree of public control, however, the introduction of high license fees for saloons in June 1883 tended rather to lead to a greater dependency of the saloon keepers on the breweries. The large breweries in Chicago gained enormous influence when, after the Great Fire of 1871, German lager beer profited from the decline in certain English ales that could not be stored. New technology (like kegs, which could be tapped, instead of bottles) increased initial investments for saloon keepers and gave the breweries a clear advantage when it came to controlling the market. However, the tendency in the brewing industry toward concentration led to increased competition between companies and created growing latitude for the keepers with respect to equipping their saloons. An increasingly competitive pressure among the breweries in Chicago and surrounding areas resulted in some of the special offers certain working-class clientele found in saloons; at the same time, the rapid turnover among saloon keepers also made this field especially attractive for newly arrived immigrants.[12]

Especially as far as the public sale of beer was concerned, the Germans in Chicago were to play an extremely important role. The history of the *Alte Wirths Verein* (Old Saloon Keepers' Association) is indicative of this development. Founded in 1877–78, and thus preceding the corresponding English alliance (Saloon Keepers' Association, founded in 1882) by several years, the association emerged as a result of the reformist zeal of the Citizens' League. The consumption of beer represented an interest uniting all Germans in Chicago and led to one of the few coalitions within this ethnic group to transcend class boundaries. The same united front was in evidence when it came to voting on temperance and blue laws. The Germans' special connection with beer was not, however, reflected only (or primarily) in their contingent among the professional saloon keepers in Chicago. This occupation was extremely attractive to all immigrant groups; in 1880, only 23.1 percent of all saloon keepers were American born. Although at that time Germans represented 42.8 percent of the city's saloon keepers and bartenders, by 1900 this proportion had dropped to 36.3 percent (while the proportion of Germans among the working-class population had concurrently risen).[13]

In the context of this discussion, the German presence in this business is less relevant than the functional role played by saloons and saloon keepers in the daily lives of German immigrant workers. Because of their general status and repute, the saloon keepers were also an important element in the saloons' communicative function. A series of articles entitled "A Study of the Saloon Business and How It Is Practiced," contributed to the *Chicagoer Arbeiter-Zeitung* by a German saloon keeper in 1896,[14] are well suited to briefly illustrate this. Falling back on his own experience in Germany and America, the author compared the status of the tavern keeper in Germany with that of the saloon keeper in Chicago. In Germany, he observed, keepers were much more secure; they had a privileged status, guaranteed by the state and not subject to rapid change. In Chicago, by contrast, saloon keepers were much more directly at the mercy of their clientele and economic and political factors. As for the problems caused by the clientele, one had only to look, on the one hand, at the burdensome habit of treating, which frequently forced the saloon keepers to treat others and to have a drink themselves. On the other hand was the clients' disrespectful attitude toward the saloon keepers, which unfortunately limited the keepers' authority when conflicts occurred and which might explain the keepers' poor showing in cases brought before Chicago's courts. Thus the author claimed that "in dealings with individuals, with that thousand-headed Hydra known as public opinion, or with the cadre of both political parties and administrations," the saloon business "requires more intelligence and physical as well as mental agility" than most other professions.[15] The author pointed out that the saloon keepers in Chicago were at a disadvantage vis-à-vis their counterparts in Germany on the institutional level as well: There was a slew of taxes and penalties, a lack of hygienic and building standards (which, in Germany, were strin-gently checked each time the premises changed hands), and competitive pressure resulting in excesses like free meals and price wars.

The author's disapproval of the free meals common in Chicago's saloons aptly illustrates that the interests of the saloon keepers and those of the clientele were at odds. For this reason, the newspaper has-tened to disassociate itself from the opinions expressed in the articles in a short but definitive statement at the end of the series. The clientele's perspective was determined by considerations other than those of the keeper or owner.

DIFFERENT TYPES OF SALOONS IN CHICAGO

Before discussing the particular interest of the working-class clientele in the saloon, it is perhaps best to take a brief look at the various kinds of sa-loons in Chicago. There were several basic types. Flourishing in the city's main commercial streets were the daytime saloons, which concentrated ei-ther on the stream of clients coming for lunch, or—to the extent that cer-tain saloons were purposely situated at final stops or junctions along streetcar lines, close to bridges, or at other traffic intersections—on the mobile city client. Even in 1900, road conditions in parts of the city were so disastrous that it was impractical to take long walks for a drink—an impor-tant reason why, even in Chicago's business districts, it was common to drink on the spot. As opposed to the daytime saloon, which was located in the business districts and catered to a mixed clientele (and which, from an entrepreneurial point of view, was by far the most lucrative), there was the neighborhood saloon, which fulfilled many practical and social functions. (In certain peripheral areas, there were also saloons that catered to the busi-ness world during the day and also the neighborhood inhabitants at night.) It was relatively easy to obtain a license for densely populated residential areas, but much more difficult for the well-to-do suburbs. This not only in-dicates that the extent of social control corresponded to ownership and so-cial status; it also sheds light on why, especially in working-class areas, saloons frequently changed hands. There is evidence that long strikes or factory shutdowns inevitably brought about the shutdown of saloons, which were completely dependent upon the neighborhood's solvency.[16]

Specific ethnic orientation was the rule among neighborhood sa-loons. Thus the German saloon differed from the Irish, which catered to the second most widespread ethnic group in Chicago. The German saloon was well lighted and family oriented, whereas its Irish counterpart was dimly lit and geared solely toward a male clientele.[17] The German neighborhood saloon was a stabilizing factor with regard to the family; children were welcomed as a matter of principle. This must be seen in relation to the status attributed to the home for working-class as opposed to middle-class families. The rise in social status was accompanied by an emphasis on the private sphere, which tended to absorb both social and intellectual activities.[18] But for the worker, home life tended to be marred by practical problems—among them, especially before passage of the eight-hour day, the limited time that could be spent there. One need not go so far as the contemporary sociologist R. L. Melendy, who—with a condescending, moral-reformist attitude—uses the example of the cheap boardinghouses for single workers to underline his view that the worker's "home" (his quotation marks) represents a deficient social space.[19] But even Chicago's contemporary German-language labor press rarely considered domestic life worthy of description or documentation. We can learn quite a bit about families from accounts of festivities, picnics, and other public occasions, but the worker's living quarters are only revealed when it is a question of documenting psychic and material deprivation—for instance, in reports on indigent mothers, on suicide, or on immigrant families urgently in need. Other sources shed at least occasional light on the living conditions among German working-class families, offering descriptions of desolate streets, back alleys, and the problems of garbage removal. They also point indirectly to the fact that, for workers in Chicago, social activities had to take place either in beer gardens and other public areas set aside for festivities or in the semipublic realm of the bar in saloons or Turner halls.[20]

THE WORKING-CLASS SALOON AS A SOCIAL CENTER

The working-class saloon assumed its most general and extensive function for the neighborhood as a center for communication and personal interaction. A number of specifically practical functions also derived from this, functions that added to the general position of the saloon as the "social and intellectual center of the neighborhood," and as the "clearing-house for the common intelligence."[21] It was precisely this capacity of the saloon, to accommodate itself to the rhythm of everyday neighborhood life, that enabled it to become both a communication center and an "extension of the home."[22]

Practical Functions of the Working-Class Saloon

If one seeks to evaluate the communicative and practical functions of the working-class neighborhood saloon, one must first consider the food:

> For the large floating population of these districts, and for the thousands of men whose only home is in the street or the cheap lodging-house, where they are herded together like cattle, the saloon is practically the basis of food supply. The table shows that 68 per cent. furnish free lunches, and 15 per cent. business lunches. On the free-lunch counters are dishes containing bread, several kinds of meats, vegetables, cheeses, etc., to which the men freely help themselves. Red-hots (Frankfurters), clams, and egg sandwiches are dispensed with equal freedom to those who drink and to those who do not.[23]

This is the way a contemporary observer characterized the German working-class saloon around 1900—an observer whose interests focused on the question of how the saloon's everyday functions of supplying food and distraction could be replaced, for instance, by nonalcoholic institutions in the sense of temperance-oriented reform efforts. Realistic enough to recognize that "all the charity institutions in Chicago put together feed fewer people than do the saloons,"[24] he saw the saloon's attraction as lying not only in free or cheap food, but also in the inviting atmosphere; because the saloon was free of even the slightest trace of charitable motivation, the clients could feel not like "deserving poor," but like sovereign consumers of a product, beer.

The economic base for the food offered in the saloons can be found in the competition among the large beer producers. As licenses became more and more expensive, the beer producers began not only to contest the right to supply saloons, but also to purchase or lease them with ever-increasing frequency. This is the only way to explain how the saloons could underbid even the cheapest restaurants (in the price range from five to thirty-five cents a meal) and why the amazing concentration of so many saloons in a small area did not prove counterproductive. The author quoted above refers to Madison Street, which stretched 4 miles from the lake through the business center to the workers' residential area. For the 8 cheap restaurants that the poor could afford (five and ten cents per lunch) there were 115 saloons, most of which offered, in addition to other saloon attractions, free meals.[25] The author concluded that, with the exception of the saloon, there was no other place where a worker could eat in a pleasant atmosphere for five cents, and that reform efforts would be hard pressed to match this sort of service.[26]

At a time predating factory canteens, the saloon thus represented an important factor in the workers' daily routine, if only for the food it offered. Even if the saloon only contributed beer to a packed lunch brought to the premises, workers were so markedly oriented toward the saloon that an idiom for fetching beer emerged in Chicago slang: "To rush the growler." According to the same contemporary source, this was a familiar pattern in factories, where the workers had their lunch outside (on the street or sitting in the windows), especially in summer. In winter, though, the temptation of a warm meal in a saloon proved too strong to resist for many a worker.[27]

The saloon was also part of the worker's daily rhythm: It could mark the beginning and end of the workday. "During the early morning hours—most places opened at either five or six o'clock A.M.—they served the working men, who sought a morning 'bracer' with the coffee they carried in their lunch pails."[28] For those working the night shift, being able to go to an all-night saloon in the early morning hours apparently represented an important part of their living conditions, as can be gathered from a letter written by a rolling-mill worker in January 1886:

> What would happen to us poor people here in the North Side Rolling Mills if they got rid of the all-night saloons? We have to work all through the night where it's far hotter than it is where you stereotypers are, and when morning comes and it's time to quit, we necessarily need a bracer, especially now in winter, since we often have a long way home, and we don't want to wake the wife and children before it's time for them to get up.[29]

As implied in this commentary, not only did saloons accommodate themselves to the business and everyday rhythms of a variety of urban neighborhoods, they also adapted their services to varying work rhythms of certain industries.[30]

The Working-Class Saloon as a Place of Political Activity

The saloon also functioned in other ways closely related to the political culture of Chicago's working class. The *Chicagoer Arbeiter-Zeitung* and other labor papers (like trade union publications) were available in saloons, making the saloons important distribution points for the labor press. Through recommendations for or against certain saloons, which did or did not allow this sort of literature to be left on the premises, organized labor could, to a certain extent, influence the clientele. In 1884, for instance, the North Side Group of the International Working People's Association, under the direction of Gustav Neef, resolved not to frequent any saloon or business that did not have, or did not advertise in, the *Arbeiter-Zeitung*.[31] Such resolutions were not rare. City officials, on the other hand, repeatedly tried to impose restrictions on those saloon keepers who were known to belong to organized labor and who permitted debates and meetings to take place on their premises. After his license was taken away, for example, the German saloon keeper, Carl Klings, spoke with Mayor Colvin. In the course of the discussion, mention was made of a speech held in the saloon, in which the speaker allegedly called for an armed assault—a charge that Klings answered thus: "It is all a lie—all a lie. There isn't a word of truth in it. There was no such speech made in my saloon. Nobody advised violence. Nobody spoke of getting guns and making an attack. That isn't what we want. We want our rights—food, clothing for our families. That's all."[32]

Carl Klings, who acquired a saloon in 1875, was a Lassallean and cofounder of the *Vorbote* and the Labor party of Illinois. For labor leaders as well as middle-class representatives, it was not unusual to recruit from among former saloon keepers, or for them to combine their political activities with this occupation.[33] Following the Haymarket events in 1886, saloon keepers who were close to the labor movement and who tolerated, or actually encouraged, political activities, found themselves subject to increased repression; the incident, described further below, which took place in Greif's Hall in November 1891, demonstrates this.

With the emergence of organized labor, many saloons situated in Chicago's working-class neighborhoods assumed a dual function: They provided a place both for political meetings and for social drinking. The back rooms, frequently large enough to earn the name "hall" and sometimes found above the saloon itself, were regularly used for political events. Sometimes rent was charged for the use of the hall; or, when the saloon keeper was more closely involved with organized labor, there was no charge but always the tacit agreement that the workers assembled there would also buy beer. Unions or sections of the Labor party with this sort of link to a certain saloon tended to try to obtain the possessory title for its "hall," or—as was frequently the case after Haymarket, when financial means had become more substantial—to build their own halls, and, if possible, to acquire a license. Permanent meeting halls of this sort could then be used not only as business headquarters of organized labor, but also as strike headquarters if it came to an actual struggle.

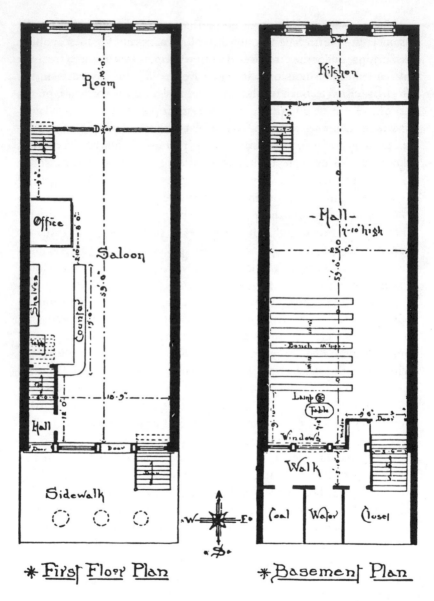

First Floor Plan

Basement Plan

Figure 7.1. Floor plan of Greif's Hall.

Especially in the 1880s, Greif's Hall (54 West Lake Street) represented this kind of political center toward which German organized labor

gravitated; it was used by many Socialist, anarchist, and union groups. Saloons frequently served not only as the focal points for these political gatherings, but also as a kind of infrastructural link between meeting places, business offices of newspapers and groups, and job placement offices (so-called labor bureaus), which, if not located in the saloons themselves, were as closely affiliated with them as possible.

The following passage illustrates how, for a specific occasion, a spontaneous relationship emerged between a saloon with a hall and a group of cloak makers determined to join the workers' struggle:

> One worker, then a boy of about sixteen years participated, and tells the story of the event. . . . One day in April 1886, the mother, who had been shopping in the neighborhood, returned from the butcher's with the information that there was going to be a meeting of the cloak workers the following Saturday afternoon. No official announcements were given of the meeting, and nobody seems to have ever learned how it came to be called. On Saturday the boy went over to the hall where the gathering was supposed to be scheduled, and found a great crowd of men and boys standing around the doorway of a saloon engaged in a heated argument with the saloon keeper who had charge of the hall back of the saloon and who refused to open the door because the hall had not been hired. A collection was taken among the group, and about $2.50 obtained. The saloon keeper agreed to let them have the hall for that amount, with the understanding that some of the boys would buy beer.
>
> The meeting lasted all afternoon and evening, and was not adjourned until two o'clock Sunday morning. It proved very profitable for the saloon, but not very orderly.
>
> The hall which had been so hard to secure for the first meeting now served as headquarters for the strikers. On Tuesday at a meeting attended by about eight hundred men, committees were formed to go to the bosses and ask for better conditions and for conferences, but they met with no success. The strikers began to have frequent meetings and call in speakers. Mr. August Spies, the editor of the *Arbeiter-Zeitung*, a German anarchist paper, made addresses. Members of the Knights of Labor also took an interest and acted as organizers to start a cloak makers' union.[34]

In this example, the workers' relationship to the saloon keeper and renter of the hall was purely commercial. In other halls, however, the opposite was generally true; the saloon keeper had a political interest in the organizations that had chosen the saloon as a meeting place. In the early 1880s, for instance, Zoellner's Hall on Blue Island Avenue on the Southwest Side was the meeting place for the local Socialist Group No. 3. Zoellner himself was among the group's founding members and officials, though this did not prevent him from drawing the greatest possible number of German associations and clubs to his saloon. When Zoellner joined the ranks of the anarchists and another saloon keeper took over the premises, the hall remained the meeting place for the Socialist Labor party, although later it was evidently avoided by the anarchists.[35] An established continuity with respect to meeting places was naturally an organizational advantage for the Socialist Labor party and union groups, an advantage that—as can be gathered from the *Arbeiter-Zeitung*'s "Union Calendar"—was not given up without pressing reasons. If it was necessary to change the meeting place, notice was repeatedly given (sometimes weeks in advance), often in special ads with conspicuous print.

Figure 7.2, a print of Neff's Hall, shows that the back rooms adjoining the saloons were not meeting halls in the strict sense of the word, but rather areas that sought to link political functions with sociability and culture. Apparently set up for some sort of festivity (like a Commune or Lassalle celebration), one sees that tables—not rows of chairs—are predominant; at the front of the speaker's desk is a painted bust. If a meeting hall had a longer tradition (like Greif's Hall and the adjoining rooms), it was furnished primarily with chairs and fewer tables, along with other inventory belonging to a specific union or party. The following description of Greif's Hall was published after the police raided a meeting of the Socialistic Publishing Society in November 1891:

There were some hundred chairs in the room, two tables. There were also several armoires in which various unions kept minutes, flags, and other insignias.

The walls were covered with pictures of Lassalle, Marx, Bebel, and Liebknecht; among many other things, there was a bust of Louis Lingg [one of the Haymarket victims], belonging to the joiners' union, on a pedestal. With the exception of a few chairs and the bust of Lingg, nothing you could see had remained intact. Some eight union flags—among them the Carriage and Waggonmakers' white and red silk banner worth between two hundred and three hundred dollars—and all the property of the various unions worth some thousand dollars were torn to shreds. The pictures lay smashed on the floor, and not one of the large armoires was unscathed.

Figure 7.2. Neff's Hall. This illustration shows a typical meeting hall for organized German workers.

One of the armoires separating a smaller antechamber from the meeting room was smashed apart, and not even the glass panes were spared. The same scene was reenacted with the painters, who had gathered one floor above.[36]

Back rooms and halls were extensions of the saloon. If the back room was linked to political functions, the saloon proper was also affected: Sharing common interests and common topics for conversations, the clientele became more closely bound and homogenized. The distribution of labor's written material, the active role played by the saloon keeper, and the habit of meeting in the same place (especially at critical moments, like during initial organizational activity or strikes)—all these elements contributed to a feeling of commitment among workers that, fostered by saloons, related to them both topographically and politically.

Additional Practical Service Functions

The saloon had other practical functions, which further contributed to its extraordinary adaptability. Prominent among these was the workers' practice, in working-class neighborhoods, of cashing their paychecks at the saloon. Thus the saloon keeper assumed the task of a popular substitute bank, sometimes dealing in considerable sums.[37] (Duis refers to a saloon, not far from the Union Stockyards, that cashed more than forty thousand dollars worth of workers' paychecks each month!) It is evident that this practical function required considerable trust between the saloon keeper and the clientele; or, in other words: This and other kinds of functional relationships—such as receiving and handing out mail for individual workers—were important factors in building a sense of community.[38]

In working-class sections, the saloon served another function, which, if less obviously economic in nature, was all the more practical: Toilets were made available in saloons. Hotels represented the only other possibility in this respect, but they posted warnings prohibiting free use of their facilities.[39] Efforts within the reform movement to see the implementation of public toilets were directed against the saloons (as, among other things, they led to the installation of water fountains in big cities), but it would be a long time before this was realized in Chicago.[40]

Another practical function, which was especially important for members of the working class in a big city like Chicago, had to do with the saloon's role in referring jobs. Originally, this activity was a self-help effort, within individual occupational groups, which transpired when members met at their favorite saloons (sometimes reflected in the saloons' names).[41] In the last two decades of the nineteenth century, however, as the workers' struggle in Chicago intensified, these activities became more closely linked to neighborhood saloons, or in any case they merged into a functionally purposeful rapprochement between commercial job placement agencies and saloons. It was not until around the turn of the century that the commercial labor bureaus felt any real competition from social reformists trying to establish noncommercial job placement agencies as a form of public service. Three such free agencies were opened in 1899. But even a law passed in 1903, explicitly forbidding any connection between labor bureaus and saloons, had little effect: As late as 1908, about half the job placement agencies were found close to saloons.[42] The network of everyday and practical needs, fulfilled by or conglomerated around the working-class saloon, was too close-knit and functioned too well to be simply abolished by decree.

THE WORKING-CLASS SALOON AS A PLACE
OF RECREATION

Up to this point, our attention has been focused primarily on the practical and political functions of the working-class saloon in Chicago. We must not, however, forget that its central function had to do with the worker's leisure time at the end of the workday. All attempts to replace it were doomed to fail, because the saloon guaranteed the preservation of traditional drinking and recreational customs, even though sometimes having to appropriate elements of a new, urban-industrial environment. Being basically family oriented, the German saloon in Chicago also had something to offer by way of evening entertainment. In contrast to the workplace and the limited possibilities workers had to shape their homes, the atmosphere in the saloon was highly attractive—warm, well lit, and cozy, where customers could decide for themselves how much beer they wanted to drink (as opposed to drinking habits in Anglo-American saloons). In addition, the saloon also began to make concerted efforts to include forms of entertainment corresponding to an urban mass culture. In addition to cards and billiards, singers, stand-up comedians, and vaudeville acts became widespread features;[43] and, after 1900, there was an increasing tendency for these forms of entertainment to blend with specific ethnic habits. Thus one finds two opposed factors: an adherence to ethnic, class-specific elements on the one hand, and, on the other, a syncretistic pressure exerted by mass culture in the expanding big city. To what extent did these two elements affect each other, what admixtures or cross-influences resulted from this inevitable clash, and to what extent can these processes of change be analyzed in retrospect? How widespread were vaudeville and stand-up comedy in specifically German working-class saloons? Was their introduction abrupt? How long did at least the language remain intact, and when did English and German start being used side by side within the cultural framework of the saloon? With respect to these questions, sources show but little awareness of such cross-cultural problems; reference to them, if any, is made only in passing. Changes in the culture seem to have entered into the consciousness of its carriers without evoking consternation or reflection.

It seems evident, however, that, especially for the working class, the blending of ethnic traditions was most easily achievable in the area of entertainment. Was the preserving and consolidating character of the working-class saloon maintained with respect to ethnic working-class culture?

Or did the saloon, after 1900, quickly open itself to the influences of mass culture, and—signaling a move away from participatory and toward consumer-oriented attitudes—in this way undermine the particularism and traditional pride of ethnic working-class groups?

Within the specific area of the saloon, changes of this kind cannot be ascertained. They are more likely to surface in descriptions of amusement parks and public events like picnics and folk festivals, where elements of mass culture and specifically ethnic traditions existed side by side. One might almost say that they contaminated each other.

THE BEER GARDEN AS AN EXAMPLE OF ETHNIC AND CULTURAL CONTAMINATION

The beer garden, a specifically German drinking and recreational institution, apparently had the least trouble adapting to the conditions of the big city in America, with its ethnically mixed population, and was the most easily transformed by a new network of relationships. Beer gardens (usually called groves) were found at workers' picnics or at festivities sponsored by Turner societies and other associations. By 1900, beer gardens would crop up at privileged points within the public transport or entertainment infrastructure, such as final stops or junctions on streetcar lines, theaters, and parks.[44] Set up comfortably in full public view, it was not so easy to cast them in the morally questionable light of saloons, and thus they enjoyed a more positive reputation.[45] In beer gardens, the right to drink beer without a bad conscience found public sanction, and the practice spread. One factor that played a considerable role was the family orientation of the beer gardens. Figure 7.3, an illustration of a large beer hall, shows men, women, and children of various ages. The beer mug represents the gravitational center. Another element of German recreational culture, which was inseparable from the organized festivals and which thus found its way into saloons and more specifically into beer halls and beer gardens, was the presence of a band. From the very beginning of the German labor movement, music—mainly in the form of an orchestra or a choir—was an integral part of larger festivities and parades. Around 1900, regular popular concerts were also given in amusement parks (which were by that time quite widespread), though these concerts tended to have an elaborate, middle-class flair.[46] In saloons and halls, wherever entertainment programs had been integrated, music was offered in relatively less lavish forms: singing, vaudeville, or instrumental performances.[47]

Figure 7.3. Beer Hall on the Bowery. The journalist James D. McCabe, Jr., thus de-scribed life in these halls around 1880: "The larger German music halls have the only respectable audiences to be found in the Bowery. To these the children of the Fa-therland resort in great numbers to enjoy their beer and listen to the music. The husband and father takes his wife and family along with him, and the pleasure here is innocent and orderly."

The channeling of certain elements stemming from other ethnic tra-ditions (like vaudeville and stand-up comedy) into the entertainment pro-grams in German saloons, and the expansion of beer gardens into amusement parks with a large variety of entertainment forms,[48] marked an increasing tendency after 1900 to efface distinctions on both the ethnic and the class levels. For instance, in 1910 and 1911, the *Fackel* (the Sunday edition of the *Arbeiter-Zeitung*) recommended and described German sa-loons with clearly middle-class pretensions[49]—something comparable could not have been found in the 1870s and 1880s, unless one counts the lapidary advertisements for establishments that often were too expensive for specifically working-class clients. After 1900, it seems as though even this paper—the German labor movement's most important organ—attributed more importance to ethnically oriented recreation than to class-specific forms of social life among workers in their own neighbor-hoods. For leaders, as well as for the masses of German workers, there was evidently no critical awareness of the transition from a working-class culture to the freely convertible consumerism of the middle class, or to the large-scale homogenization by way of participation in a mass culture. German workers, too, engaged in popular forms of entertainment like team sports (baseball, for instance, in contrast to the traditional gymnastic exercises and competition among the German Turner clubs) and nickelodeons or other forms anticipating the movies. But the records only give indirect answers to certain questions: What they actually thought about these forms, how they integrated them with their traditional recreational expectations, or what sort of defamiliarizing effect mass culture had on their own specific culture.

From discussions, which took place within individual clubs and associations, concerning the new generation of German workers and its attitude toward the German language, one can gather that—with respect to the language, the new medium of film, and recreational penchants—non-German cultural forces were gaining ground. If one wanted the young generation to remain in contact with the life of organized German workers, English would have to be permitted in their associations.[50] And it is obvious that the possibilities of film were recognized by the Socialist party: In 1909, it tried to found a film company to be employed for agitational purposes.[51] Two other changes reflect even more clearly how German culture in Chicago was being penetrated by the demands of mass culture at the beginning of the new century. After 1900, the Aurora Turner Hall—from the mid-1860s to the 1890s the uncontested center for the German labor movement and for German culture and social life on the Northwest Side—was turned into a movie theater. But even more incisive for German working-class culture, and for the value placed on community drinking within it, is the fact that on Chicago's new cultural map, Ogden's Grove—for decades the best known German beer garden and recreational center in the heart of the German North Side neighborhood—had been turned into a baseball park.[52]

NOTES

1. This subject has been written about extensively. Some of the more important works are: David J. Pittman and Charles R. Snyder, *Society, Culture, and Drinking Patterns* (New York, 1962); Joseph R. Gusfield, *Symbolic Crusade: Status Politics and the American Temperance Movement* (Urbana, IL, 1963; Richard Jensen, *The Winning of the Midwest: Social*

Figure 7.4. Members of the German singing society Liederkranz of Wausau, Wisconsin, in a beer garden. The photograph was probably taken in 1913.

and Political Conflict, *1888–1896* (Chicago, 1971); Jack S. Blocker, Jr., ed. *Alcohol, Reform and Society: The Liquor Issue in Social Context* (Westport, CT, 1979); Mark Edward Lender and James Kirby Martin, *Drinking in America: A History* (New York, 1982).

2. Cf. Jan R. Tyrrell, "Temperance and Economic Change in the Antebellum North," in Blocker, Jr., ed., *Alcohol,* 45–67; also see Lender and Martin, *Drinking,* 108–9.

3. Cf. Herbert G. Gutman, "Work, Culture, and Society in Industrializing America, 1815–1919," *American Historical Review* 78 (1973): 531–88.

4. Cf. Ruth Bordin, *Woman and Temperance: The Quest for Power and Liberty, 1873–1900* (Philadelphia, 1981). For equating low moral and social status as caused by alcohol, also see Lender and Martin, *Drinking,* 102–3.

5. See Lender and Martin, *Drinking,* 96–98.

6. Jed Dannenbaum, *Drink and Disorder: Temperance Reform in Cincinnati from the Washingtonian Revival to the WCTU* (Urbana, Chicago, 1984), 219.

7. James B. Roberts, "Drink and Industrial Work Discipline in 19th Century Germany," *Journal of Social History* 15 (Fall 1981): 25–38.

8. Kenneth Lyle Kann, "Working Class Culture and the Labor Movement in Nineteenth Century Chicago" (Ph.D. diss., University of California, Berkeley 1977), 127.

9. For examples of this self-image see *Illinois Staats-Zeitung (ISZ)* of 20 May 1866

("Pfingsten") and 10 March 1867 ("Ein Sonntags-Nachmittag in der Chicago Turnhalle"). Also see note 44 below, and Ernest H. Crosby, "The Saloon in Politics," *Municipal Affairs* 4 (1900): 402–4 ("There is a social kindliness in a German beer garden which is sadly wanting in a dairy lunch-room," 404).

10. Perry R. Duis, *The Saloon. Public Drinking in Chicago and Boston: 1880–1920* (Urbana, Chicago, 1983).

11. An impressive contemporary source for the central reformist interest in discussing substitutes for the saloon is Richard Calkins, *Substitutes for the Saloon . . . An Investigation Made for the Committee of Fifty* (Boston, New York, 1901). Also see Francis Greenwood Peabody, ed., *The Liquor Problem* (Boston, New York, 1905), which contains a substantial chapter by Calkins on substitutes for the saloon.

12. Duis, *The Saloon*, 34–36.

13. Duis, *The Saloon*, 165.

14. *Chicagoer Arbeiter-Zeitung (ChAZ)*, 16–18, 21, and 23 Feb. 1896.

15. *ChAZ*, 23 Feb. 1896.

16. Duis, *The Saloon*, 175; *Chicago Tribune*, 27 Feb. 1886.

17. Jon M. Kingsdale, "The 'Poor Man's Club': Social Functions of the Urban Working-Class Saloon," *American Quarterly* 25 (1973): 472–89. Referring to the Anglo-Saxon saloon, Kingsdale even speaks in terms of a "bachelor subculture," which he feels should be of interest to the social historian. Also see Felix Adler, "The Social Function of the Saloon," *Municipal Affairs* 5 (1901): 876–80.

18. Cf. Richard Sennett, *Families Against the City: Middle-Class Homes of Industrial Chicago, 1872–1890* (Cambridge, MA, 1970).

19. Royal L. Melendy, "The Saloon in Chicago," *American Journal of Sociology* 6 (1900–1901): 289–306 and 433–64, esp. 292.

20. Illinois Bureau of Labor Statistics, *Third Biennial Report* (Springfield, 1884); George Taylor Nesmith, "The Housing of the Wage-earners of the Sixteenth Ward of the City of Chicago" (M.A. thesis, Northwestern University, 1900); Robert Hunter, *Tenement Conditions in Chicago: Report by the Investigating Committee of the City Homes Association* (Chicago, 1901); also see Hartmut Keil, ed., *Deutsche Arbeiterkultur in Chicago von 1850 bis zum Ersten Weltkrieg* (Ostfildern, 1984), esp. 138–225.

21. Melendy, "Saloon," 294. The term "clearing-house for the common intelligence" is borrowed from E. C. Moore, "The Social Function of the Saloon," *American Journal of Sociology* 3 (1897–98): 1–12, though this report is much more superficial and sentimental than Melendy's thorough observations.

22. Duis, *The Saloon*, 105.

23. Melendy, "Saloon," 296.

24. Melendy, "Saloon," 297.

25. Melendy, "Saloon," 455f. Also see R. Calkins, *Substitutes,* 18 (with exact information about daily average amounts of food in a Chicago saloon) and 230. In some respects, Melendy's observations also correspond to those of a Prussian government official, who in 1899 worked temporarily as a laborer in Chicago; Alfred Kolb, *Als Arbeiter in Amerika: Unter deutsch-amerikanischen Großstadt-Proletariern,* 5th rev. ed. (Berlin, 1901).

26. Melendy, "Saloon," 297.

27. Melendy, "Saloon," 456: "One saloon, of which I know, sold ninety gallons every noon to men in a factory and to a railroad gang that was working near."

28. Duis, *The Saloon,* 557.

29. "Nachtwirthschaften in den Rolling Mills," *ISZ,* 20 Jan. 1886.

30. Thus for instance, where Ashland Avenue (also called "Whiskey Row") bordered the packing yards and related industries, there were an average twenty-three daytime saloons per block, while in the surrounding residential areas this number ranged from three to seven; cf. James R. Barrett, "Work Community in 'the Jungle': Chicago's Packing House Workers, 1894–1922" (Ph.D. diss., University of Pittsburgh, 1981), 150. By contrast, Tyrrell, "Temperance," 54, quotes many Pennsylvania laws that prohibited the consumption of alcohol within a radius of 3 miles to certain mines and ironworks—regulations pushed through by entrepreneurs who wanted to make sure industrial work proceeded smoothly. Also see the illuminating fictional representation of the interrelation between saloons and the needs of workers in the meat-processing industry in Upton Sinclair's *The Jungle* (1906).

31. *ChAZ,* 19 Dec. 1884.

32. *Chicago Tribune,* 27 Feb. 1875. The context for the example is the discussion of citizens' militias and a notorious German workers' organization, the "Lehr- und Wehr-Verein'" Cf. Christine Heiß, "German Radicals in Industrial America: The Lehrund Wehr-Verein in Gilded Age Chicago," in *German Workers in Industrial Chicago, 1850–1910: A Comparative Perspective,* Hartmut Keil and John B. Jentz, eds. (DeKalb, IL, 1983), 206–23.

33. Cf. Renate Kiesewetter, "Die Institution der deutsch-amerikanischen Arbeiterpresse in Chicago: Zur Geschichte des *Vorboten* und der *Chicagoer Arbeiterzeitung,* 1874–1886" (M.A. thesis, University of Munich, 1982).

34. Mabel Agnes Magee, "The Women's Clothing Industry of Chicago with Special Reference to Relations Between the Manufacturers and the Union" (Ph.D. diss., University of Chicago, 1927), 92–94.

35. Cf. Theo Fuß, "Arbeitswelt und Nachbarschaft. Die McCormick Harvesting Machine Company und die Arbeiterschaft der Südwestseite Chicagos während des Übergangs zur Massenproduktion, 1873–1886" (M.A. thesis, University of Munich, 1983), 74–77.

36. "Vandalismus," *ChAZ,* 18 Nov. 1891.

37. Duis, *The Saloon,* 182.

38. Calkins, *Substitutes,* 11.

39. Melendy, "Saloon," 299.

40. Duis, *The Saloon*, 191–92.

41. Melendy, "Saloon," 293–94, cites a wide range of such English-language names ("Mechanics' Exchange," "Milkman's Exchange," "Everybody's Exchange"); the first one, however, must have been in close contact to the German working class—the saloon was in the *Chicagoer Arbeiter-Zeitung* building! See the reproduction in *German Workers*, Keil and Jentz, eds., 240.

42. Duis, *The Saloon*, 181f.

43. Melendy, "Saloon," 294–96.

44. Melendy, "Saloon," 304–6.

45. Melendy, "Saloon," 304: "To the German, the word 'beer-garden' carries with it no moral idea whatever; indeed, among them it is a highly creditable feature of their social life."

46. Melendy, 304–5, offers an impressive description of a typical German beer garden and places special emphasis on the music and atmospheric charm. Also see another report in the *ISZ* of 12 June 1886, which addresses the process of contamination seen in various recreational activities: "After having spent six days in a stuffy office or confined shop, German workers and businesspeople simply love to take their wives and children for a walk out of doors and sit down somewhere to a relaxed glass of lager. It is well known that there are many people whose piety is so exaggerated that they would declare this little harmless and innocent pleasure to be sinful; on the other hand, it is encouraging that a large portion of reasonable Americans have gradually come to accept the idea that it is nicer to have a drink out of doors in the company of one's wife and children than to sit in a stuffy room back home and, the secret whisky bottle having been filled on Saturday (because it would be sinful to do so on the 'Sabbath') indulge in the regular Sunday drink."

47. Melendy, "Saloon," 298–99.

48. Melendy, "Saloon," 444–48.

49. *Fackel*, 23 Jan. 1910; 13 March 1910, 15 May 1910; 22 May 1910; 28 May 1911; 25 June 1911; 30 July 1911.

50. Cf. the resolution passed by the German Turner societies in 1908 to permit not only German at their meetings; *ChAZ*, 30 June 1908.

51. A. L. Voorhees to J. Mahlon Barnes, 29 Sept. 1909; Barnes to Voorhees, 6 and 23 Oct. 1909, in Thomas J. Morgan Collection, folder 56, Univ. of Illinois, Urbana.

52. See *Sanborn Fire Insurance Map of Chicago*, vol. 2 (1910).

CHAPTER 8

Popular and Working-Class German Theater in Chicago, 1870 to 1910

CHRISTINE HEISS

T he development of working-class theater in Germany and the various forms it assumed—from its origins in workers' associations to the debate over the *Freie Volksbühne* (Free Popular Stage) in Berlin and the emergence of political theater in the Weimar Republic—have been well documented and described.[1] German theater in the United States (whether middle-class, popular, or working-class) was primarily the theater of a cultural minority constantly struggling to hold its own vis-à-vis the dominant American culture. Although German working-class theater in America drew on experiences and traditions brought from the Old Country, one must nevertheless ask whether the social conditions in the adopted country led to a different, typically German-American form of working-class theater. It could be argued that the absence of meticulous censorship might have allowed the cultural orientation within the North American Socialist Labor party and the International Working People's Association to move in a direction other than that adopted by the Social Democrats in Germany in the 1890s. Unimpeded by legislation directed against the Socialists, the labor movement in the United States may have been able to invest more energy in its cultural policies, whereas the Social Democrats in Germany felt compelled to fight for their political survival.

However, before dealing with the minority status, the ethnic or class-specific ties, or the criteria by which the function of German popular and working-class theater in the United States can be judged, one must first address the larger cultural framework within which German theater in

181

Chicago unfolded. Therefore the first section will deal with the so-called regular theaters. Although they evolved from amateur groups active in German associations in the 1850s, the regular theaters were characterized by steady repertoires and seasons and, above all, by the fact that performances were held in buildings specifically set aside for them, a factor by no means typical of all German theater in Chicago.

In addition to regular theaters, a number of popular theaters emerged in the mid-1870s. Established in association halls, they sometimes supplemented the regular theaters—indeed, there were even years when they replaced them completely. Here one must ask to what extent the popular theaters can be distinguished from the regular theaters, as far as management, programs, and audiences are concerned.[2] On one hand, popular theater was similar to regular theater; on the other, because of a specific working-class audience, it may have anticipated certain functions of working-class theater.

The working-class theater will be dealt with next. Politically motivated, working-class theater was mostly found within the framework of labor-movement festivals and gatherings, or in amateur performances staged by Socialist associations. In addition to describing working-class theater in general, this section will also take a closer look at certain plays that originated within the German-American labor movement and that addressed specific problems and needs of that movement. Since neither the Socialist Labor party nor the International Working People's Association made direct mention of cultural policies,[3] reviews from the labor press have been cited to illustrate the function that was attributed to theater in general, and to working-class theater in particular.

Since both the German-American labor movement and the German-American theater were most important in the years from 1880 to 1910, this discussion will focus primarily on this period.

THE REGULAR THEATER

Initiated by the German Men's Singing Society, the first German theatrical performances in Chicago were presented as early as 1852–53. Initially, the conditions for these performances were quite crude; they took place in halls with neither stage nor curtain. In 1856, however, when growing cultural interest among Germans led to the building of a German cultural center called *Deutsches Haus* (German House), a permanent spot was reserved for German stage presentations. Sunday performances were held there regularly until 1870 (as opposed, for instance, to American theaters, which did not offer Sunday performances). But these uninterrupted fourteen years of German theater in the same house represent something of an exception in Chicago's theatrical history, which was often shaken by crises. After 1870, both management and house changed with relative frequency; there was no other proper German theater until the opening of the Schiller Theater in 1892, which closed, however, after two seasons. In other years, German theaters were forced to rent space in American theaters, and following the last season in the Schiller Theater (1893–94), no regular theater performances took place.[4]

Although attempts were made in the early years to stage more serious plays,[5] the repertoire became increasingly shallow in the 1870s and 1880s, until eventually light social drama came to prevail. This is understandable if one considers that German theater in the United States had to assert itself as a commercial enterprise as soon as it went beyond the amateur stage. Although individual contributions from the German middle class, which emerged in the 1860s, may have helped to compensate for some deficits, there were never sufficient funds for the German theater. The main portion of the costs had to be covered by ticket sales, which meant that German theater was dependent upon the business acumen of individual theater managers; and, to ensure a full house, the latter often opted for plays that they felt would draw large audiences. A lack of sufficient funds was not, however, the only problem; the quality of the acting in the steady ensembles also left much to be desired. As a consequence, the repertoire was restricted to third-class plays, and guest performances often presented the only possibility of seeing more ambitious theater.[6]

And yet the predominance of comedies, farces, burlesques, and light social dramas, whereby theater managers may have counted on the audience's greater tolerance, was not simply due to a lack of talent and insufficient funds. Time and again, the press emphasized that audiences favored this kind of theater. "It seems that today's theater director," wrote the *Illinois Staats-Zeitung* after a disappointing season in the late 1880s, "is merely a speculator, busily counting the dollars in the till and the heads in the hall."[7] Audience expectation in the 1870s and 1880s was reflected in the trivialization of the repertoire. By contrast, the 1850s and 1860s had seen relatively frequent attempts to stage more serious plays. This can be explained by the fact that German cultural life in Chicago in these years was largely determined by a liberal group of intellectuals still oriented toward Vormärz ideals.[8] In the 1870s, however, the newly emerged German middle class, which had other cultural interests, became more influential.

And though it may be questionable to equate middle-class theater audiences in Chicago and Germany, it is nevertheless difficult to ignore parallel developments with respect to the stagnation of theater under Bismarck. Even in America, where liberal German-Americans were so proud of the democratic Constitution of the United States, there was a sense of euphoria accompanying the founding of the Reich. This may partially explain why the theater repertoire current in Germany was adopted in such an uncritical manner, especially in the 1870s; the stereotypes "huge success in Berlin" or "over one hundred performances in Berlin" kept recurring in the preview announcements. Of course, theater in Germany had to serve as a model for a German minority trying to assert its cultural identity in a foreign country; even so it must be asked whether theatrical trends of the German Reich would have been adopted with so little reservation if the liberal tradition so clearly felt in the theater repertoire of the 1850s had not been weakened by the gradual absorption into the middle class of a large part of the older, fully established German immigrants. By the time it had become clear that German-Americans felt alienated from the cultural developments of the German Reich (i.e., in the 1880s and 1890s), plays tailored to audience expectation in Germany began to meet with criticism. A new demand arose for plays dealing with German-American reality.[9] But it was not until German naturalist works in uncensored form were taken up in America that Chicago's stagnating German theater began to revive.

THE COMMERCIAL POPULAR THEATER

The 1870–71 season was decisive for German theater in Chicago, not only because of a budding national consciousness among German citizens. Following the Great Fire of 1871, a wave of German workers started coming to Chicago. By 1890, the German-American population had multiplied by a factor of five. Even if one disregards the cultural and ideological contribution made by the political refugees of 1878, it is evident that this demographic development played a large role in shaping cultural events, which now had to accommodate themselves to a variety of levels of acculturation among Chicago's German population. How did the cultural needs of the newly arrived immigrants differ from those of the Germans who were already established? Can these differences be discerned in the area of theater?

Beginning in the 1880s, as the German population continued to grow, several German theaters in Chicago were able to maintain themselves. The press referred to these as popular theaters. In the 1870s, the main difference between popular and regular theaters, which also incorporated popular elements in some years, was that the former did not stage performances in buildings specifically set aside for theater, but rather in the halls of popular associations and clubs. As the German population grew, these halls, most frequently the gymnasium of one of Chicago's numerous Turner associations, increasingly assumed communication and entertainment functions. Housing all sorts of meetings, rooms in Turner halls were sought not only by the union and labor movements but by the lodges catering to businesspeople as well. Provided with liquor licences, the halls also became increasingly important as saloons. They were used by theater companies not so much because they were well-suited for theatrical events,[10] but rather because they represented the only possibility of renting a large room without incurring excessive expenses. If they provided an actual stage, it was frequently a makeshift construction;[11] in addition, most of the halls had poor ventilation.

Despite these unfavorable conditions, a few theater companies succeeded in establishing steady theaters, which not only played to full houses but also occasionally staged serious plays.[12] Almost all the managers of popular theaters who would attain some degree of notoriety in the coming years had previously been associated with the theater company of the former *Deutsches Haus*. In keeping with the American model,[13] the theater manager was also the lead actor who filled the program with a repertoire tailored to his own talents. Especially during the initial years, this system did German theater more harm than good, since sooner or later most of the well-known actors tried to free themselves from the predominance of the theater director by founding their own theater. This explains why, even from 1860 to 1870, many of the newly founded popular theaters soon had to close because of poor attendance.[14]

A good example of how the popular theater was coming into its own in the 1870s can be seen in Alexander Wurster's career. After having acted in the *Deutsches Haus*, Wurster opened a theater in Baum's Hall in 1873. A year later, he moved to the Aurora Turner Hall, where he enjoyed such success that he also started giving performances during the week in the North Side Turner Hall in 1874. Although the latter were poorly attended,[15] the huge success of the Sunday performances encouraged Wurster to open a theater in the downtown Grand Opera House in 1875.

Alexander Wurster's theater illustrates an overlapping of the regular German theater, with representative buildings in the center of the city, and the popular theater, which, though not necessarily less sophisticated as far as performances were concerned, had to make do with less representative accommodations and more technical imperfections. Wurster's initiative also reflects the attempt to reach an audience who either did not want or did not have the means to make the long trip to the city's center. As opposed to regular theaters, popular theaters were found in German residential areas. It was expensive to attend the theater as a social event in the city center, and this activity tended to correspond with the life-styles of those people who were already established. But walking to a popular theater in a hall just around the corner, which was already familiar to a large part of the population from other events, represented a possibility, on financial and other practical grounds, for members of all social classes. If one takes into account that Chicago's streetcar and elevated railway systems were not expanded into an extensive network until the 1890s, it becomes evident that a trip downtown to the theater was out of the question for a large portion of the immigrants living in German neighborhoods with modest incomes. The founding of several popular theaters in different neighborhoods by the same company illustrates an attempt on the managers' part to exploit this situation commercially. In the 1880s, the character of the neighborhoods became a determining factor for the popular theater's commercial success. The largest companies frequently ran one or two indoor theaters in different parts of the city, though the program was the same. Smaller entrepreneurs sometimes staged their plays as guest performances in popular theaters located in other parts of the city.

In the season of 1881–82, five of these theaters were already flourishing; by 1896–97, the popular theaters had reached the peak of their popularity. On the North and Northwest Sides—where the two largest German neighborhoods were found—there were eight popular indoor theaters in addition to the *Chicagoer Stadttheater* (which had been built that year). On the South and Southwest Sides, in addition to two popular theaters housed in rooms set aside for them, there were three indoor popular theaters.[16] The conspicuous increase in the number of popular theaters in areas where the majority of inhabitants belonged to the working class seems to indicate that a large percentage of the audience was composed of workers.

Figure 8.1. Title page of the song "Home Beach," from the play Corner Grocer, *produced by the New York Germania Theater. Probably written in a Frisian dialect and interspersed with musical numbers, it represented a particular version of popular German traditions. The transition from this to American vaudeville must have been easy.*

What sort of plays were staged in the popular theaters? Why were they so popular, despite the fact that the labor press continually bemoaned poor sets and costumes and faulty performances?[17] With few exceptions, the popular theaters mainly offered light entertainment. Comedies, farces, burlesques, and musical sketches from everyday life made up the programs; better established theaters, like those under the direction of Minna Ostermann (Müller's Hall and the Vorwärts Turner Hall), also staged longer popular plays. In others, like the Theater in Workers' Hall under the direction of Alfred Roland, the program comprised primarily one-act plays, some of which were written by the director. As an additional attraction, dances or balls were held after the performance in all popular theaters; thus, even if they disliked the performance, members of the audience could still "have a good time dancing into the morning hours."[18]

On the average, reserved seats cost fifty cents (the price for the cheapest seats in the regular theaters), unreserved seats thirty-five cents, and balcony seats twenty-five cents. Some theaters offered special children's prices of fifteen cents. Most performances were staged on Sunday evenings, at half past seven or eight o'clock; matinees or Sunday afternoon presentations were rare. Because they did not draw large enough audiences, weekday performances were not feasible. The Southwest Side Workers' Hall offered an especially inexpensive form of entertainment: "family tickets" enabled five people to get in for one dollar; toward the end of 1882, the price of single tickets dropped to as little as fifteen cents.[19]

An evening at the Theater in Workers' Hall included various forms of entertainment: In the spring of 1882, the management enriched its program by adding circus and magic acts.[20] Workers' Hall resembled what the *Illinois Staats-Zeitung* referred to as the numerous *Schmierentheater* (sham theaters)—theaters that, although not announced in the newspapers, were an integral part of the entertainment offered in German neighborhoods:

> In perhaps more than fifteen of these other [small] theaters [housed in halls] . . . the ratio of hapless actors to most hapless amateurs is just the opposite. . . . But the managers of these small theaters choose to renounce support by the press. By giving out generous numbers of free tickets—the manager often sees to it himself—to small merchants and businessmen, the theater can count on the recipients to encourage their customers to attend performances. Good beer consumers will not have to pay for the whole season. But tickets are so cheap that even workers with large families and not so much money can afford to attend performances, frequently "with Mother and all the little children.". . .
>
> The temperature is oppressive in the poorly ventilated and low, narrow halls, where art and beer are on tap. . . . By the end of the first act the audience has developed a burning thirst. Naturally, the intermissions are at least a quarter of an hour, sometimes longer. . . . Spectators, tormented by thirst, gather in the tap-room directly adjacent to the theater. . . . After the performance there is some "leg shaking", for to write that "there will be a ball"—as the program claims—would be doing the greatest injustice to the pleasure of real dancing. And once again money is taken in on beer and other beverages, this time primarily from the young people eager to dance.[21]

If one considers Alexander Pellissier's theater in the Aurora Turner Hall, it becomes clear that the term "popular theater" encompassed a wide range of activity in Chicago. In contrast to presentations in the "back-alley theaters" mentioned above, or to the monotonous one-act plays staged in Workers' Hall (performances that came close to variety or vaudeville shows), Pellissier, seeking to offer a diversified program, staged plays by Johann Nestroy, Friedrich von Schiller, Friedrich Hebbel, and Heinrich von Kleist. The success enjoyed by all these theaters—for Pellissier was still playing to a full house in July[22]—was based on two things: the large demand for German-language entertainment and the appeal of German habits (like the dances held after the performance), which must have reminded a working-class audience of evenings at the theater organized by the Social Democrats in Germany.[23] It is no accident that these theaters had completely disappeared by the turn of the century. The "cultural industry" in America, with its vaudeville theaters—structurally similar to performances found in some popular theaters—and up-and-coming forms of entertainment like the nickelodeons and movies,[24] had been taking over the function of the popular theaters. With regard to recreational activity, a large proportion of the Germans had evidently become Americanized.

Although it could be argued that the popular theaters constituted a kind of entertainment industry for the German masses in Chicago, this does not mean that audiences accepted whatever was offered them uncritically. It was, in fact, just this commercial character of the popular theater that indirectly gave the audience the chance of influencing the program. To avoid financial losses, the theaters housed in halls had to consider audience tastes and wishes. Thus the programs also reflect audience expectations. In this sense, programs in the 1880s and 1890s reveal two tendencies. Local farces from Berlin and Viennese comedies were met with increasing disinterest. At the same time, there was a rising demand for plays dealing with German-American reality. As early as 1882, Pellissier was forced to stage several repeat performances of a play entitled *Von Deutschland nach Chicago* (From Germany to Chicago); in Charlotte Birch-Pfeiffer's play, *Der Leiermann und sein Pflegekind* (The Organ Grinder and His Foster Child), the first act—bearing the title "In the Harbor, or the Immigrants"—seemed to be especially interesting to audiences. In 1896, *Die Straßen von New York* (The Streets of New York), a "German-American popular play," was staged time and again in all the popular theaters.[25] There was also an increasing demand for German adaptations of American plays. *East Lynne, A Famous Courtcase, Two Orphans*, and above all *Rip van Winkle* drew full houses.[26]

The programs of the popular theaters and the construction of the *Chicagoer Stadttheater* illustrate that the emergence of a German-American consciousness was a process that transcended class differences, one that comprised the German middle class as well as small businesspeople and workers. The desire to see German-American reality represented on stage even tended to outweigh class differences or differing political attitudes. One can assume that the audience attending the first play staged in the *Stadttheater*, Wiechers van Gogh's *Chicagoer Leben* (Life in Chicago), comprised primarily middle-class spectators. Although the author sympathized with the labor movement, the middle-class press nevertheless reacted positively, quickly reducing the play to a contrast between "German culture in America" and the "native element," and viewing the critique of "corruption and boodle" as an attack on the dominant American culture, against which "the German song, the emotional depth and soul of Germany" stands out in brilliant relief.[27] In the reverse case, the *Chicagoer Arbeiter-Zeitung*'s critical review approached a middle-class position. *Graf Reckenhorst*, a social drama that had been prohibited in Germany, was deemed just as irrelevant for American conditions as the "ridiculous Berlin farces"; after all, "Everyone knows that Bismarck is a tyrant."[28] One can hardly miss the national pride German-Americans took in a more democratic social order.

At this point it must be asked to what extent audiences frequenting popular theaters were made up of German workers. At first glance, the repertoires of the popular theaters seem to indicate anything but political topics. The majority of spectators, including organized workers, went to the theater for distraction.[29] Nevertheless, the programs offered by the popular theaters as well as the reviews that appeared in the *Arbeiter-Zeitung* illustrate that class consciousness is indirectly reflected in the preference given to plays that, rather than dealing with abstract issues, depicted the living conditions among workers or portrayed everyday problems, thus offering the spectators the opportunity to identify with what they saw. It mattered little that these problems were present only as picturesque backdrops in musical comedies and farces; the spectators interpreted the play according to their own existential interests. The apparently superficial program offered by the popular theaters points to a preference for plays where—even in the title—a familiarity with the workers' day-to-day life and problems is suggested. Due to audience demand, plays such as *Arm aber Ehrlich* (Poor but Honest), *Das Schloß oder die Revolution der Arbeiter* (The Castle, or the Workers' Revolution) or *Der reiche John von Lake View* (Rich John from Lake View) were repeated in various theaters and played to full houses. The fact that a play like Ludwig Fulda's *Kapital und Arbeit oder Das verlorene Paradies* (Capital and Labor, or: Paradise Lost) was staged by a commercial theater can be seen as a reflection of audience expectations.[30]

Vorläufige Anzeige!

Auf vielseitiges Verlangen:

Populäre Theater-Vorstellung

„Die Weber"

Hinzureichsrealistisches Schauspiel in 5 Akten
von Gerhart Hauptmann

aufgeführt am

Samstag, den 2. April

Abends 8 Uhr

im

Bronx Casino

2904—2958 Tremo Ave.-
Hochbahn-Station 156. Str., New York

Eintritt ---- 25 Cents

Nach der Vorstellung:

Grosser Ball!

JOHN MOST ALS DER ALTE BAUMERT

Figure 8.2. Announcement in the Freiheit *for a "popular theater" performance of Gerhart Hauptmann's* Die Weber *(The Weavers) in the Bronx Casino, including John Most, who is depicted in his favorite role of the old Baumert.*

The purely commercial nature of the popular theater's repertoire sometimes left room for working-class performances. In 1895, for instance, John (Johann) Most's Free Theater from New York, an amateur theater group aligned with the Social Revolutionary movement, toured Chicago with their rendition of Gerhart Hauptmann's *Die Weber* (The Weavers). Most was not invited to Chicago by his supporters, but rather by the manager of a popular theater who engaged the group for nine performances within a single week.[31] It was well known that Most's staging of *Die Weber* was purposely agitational; the text had been expanded in certain essential passages.[32] A performance in Newark the year before had been prohibited, the police fearing that the Most production would incite the striking workers there to further unrest.[33] And though the financial success of the weekday performances in Chicago was limited, general requests led Most to rent three of the largest popular theaters in the city for one performance in each. All three performances were well attended and ended with the dancing typical of the popular theaters.[34]

The controversy surrounding the play *Ausgewiesen* (Exiled), presented in the Schiller Theater in 1893, illustrates that audiences composed of workers were not limited to the popular theaters alone, and that a trip to a regular theater was not shunned when promising plays were staged.[35] *Ausgewiesen* deals with the Anti-Socialist Law enacted under Bismarck and was prohibited in Germany. The author, Karl Böttcher, was covering the World's Fair in Chicago for German newspapers and his presence was the main reason for staging the play. Although the play's message can hardly be considered Socialist—the main character is a philanthropic factory owner who is unjustly denounced as being a Socialist—after the premiere the middle-class *Illinois Staats-Zeitung* altered the positive attitude it had expressed toward the play and author in an earlier preview. The play's subject, centering around a law that had been "repealed long ago," was found thoroughly unfitting for a German-American audience; fault was also found with its literary quality. But the real reason for the editor's sudden change of mind seems to have been the audience's reaction: a negative attitude in the "upper circles," applause in "Olympus."[36] Having turned out in great numbers, the workers had altered the function of the theater, using it as a base from which to voice their political attitudes. Understandably, the problems surrounding Socialist legislation were a current topic for Chicago's workers. Many of the Socialists expelled from Germany in 1878 had sought refuge in the United States and found a foothold in the labor movement. In Chicago, several refugees were working on the editorial staff of the *Arbeiter-Zeitung*. Although the labor press also attacked *Ausgewiesen* for presenting the Anti-Socialist Law from a bourgeois point of view, it nevertheless took advantage of the opportunity to stress the pedagogic function of the commercial theater:

> Without doubt, the management of the German Theater Society will have come to the conclusion—if for no other reason than that of the clinking proof in the cash register—that plays of yesterday's genre (though not of its weakness) are the most appealing. Today, the "social question" is a question of such general interest that performances which address it, in whatever way, excite audience curiosity from the very outset, and lead to serious discussion of said question. Discussion must always contribute to enlightenment; thus—by way of exception—in the theater the interests of the cash register and those of enlightening the minds of the masses can occasionally be identical.[37]

Coming from the *Arbeiter-Zeitung*, this positive evaluation of the popular theater's cultural and political function for the workers may come as a surprise, especially when one considers that, at the same time, a debate concerning the *Freie Volksbühnen* (Free Popular Stages) was under way in the German labor movement. Some had proposed that they become separate institutions, completely independent of commercial interests, and that personal contact be established with members of the *Neue Freie Volksbühne* (New Free Popular Theater) in Berlin.[38] The history of the *Freie Volksbühne* (Free Theater) in Berlin shows that the more radical segment of the German labor movement, the segment interested in questions pertaining to culture, found that working-class theater could only be realized by moving away from middle-class, commercially oriented cultural institutions. But in Chicago, the boundaries between commercial and working-class theater seemed to have become more fluid. Although the passage cited above does not reveal which position was to be attributed to middle-class culture, it is nevertheless evident that the intention was to use, or even influence, its established manifestations.

WORKING-CLASS THEATER

What attempts were made within the Chicago labor movement itself to use the theater as a didactic instrument? Was Socialist theater seen as an alternative to commercially oriented cultural activities? What kind of plays were staged? To what extent were workers' obvious needs for leisure time and recreation taken into account at cultural events organized by the Socialist Labor party or the International Working People's Association?

Working-class theater in Chicago was primarily festive. From the outset in the 1870s, attempts were made within the labor movement to combine the workers' needs for entertainment with political education in organizing picnics in the summer, balls, union parties, and—for those belonging to the Socialist movement—club festivities. Celebrations commemorating the anniversary of the Paris Commune, annually held in Turners' and workers' halls, played a special role. During the labor movement's prime in the 1880s, these commemorative celebrations often drew as many as ten thousand people. In the 1890s, the May Day festivities rounded out the picture, though of course they were not as politically charged as the Commune festivities. At these events, a light program geared toward the whole family was offered for twenty-five cents: Speeches with Socialist content were cloaked in musical presentations, poems were recited, games were played, beer was consumed. The high point of the event was marked by the presentation of a *tableau vivant*, usually depicting an event from the French people's struggle for liberty, or a theatrical performance. One of the main attractions was the ensuing ball, a must at each event.

Most of the thesis plays staged for these occasions were written specifically for the event by members of the labor movement. Thesis plays were especially predominant as the Social Revolutionary movement in Chicago approached its peak in the early 1880s, as strikes and unrest brought the political situation to a head. After the late 1880s, aside from the *tableaux vivants*—incontestably the favorite pictorial form for political statements—farces and comedies could also be seen, like those staged in the popular theaters.[39] It is remarkable that, despite personal contacts with the labor movement in Germany, no German thesis plays were staged in Chicago. Plays specifically portraying the situation of the German-American labor movement or reflecting the worker's lot in the United States were also rare.[40] One of the most successful plays, staged for the Commune celebration in 1882 as well as in 1884, was Wilhelm Ludwig Rosenberg's *Die Nihilisten* (The Nihilists).[41] It deals with the legal proceedings against a group of Nihilists in Russia, who are sentenced, banished to Siberia, and finally freed by their followers after the czar has been deposed. Another play by Rosenberg, *Die Tochter des Proletariers* (The Proletarian's Daughter), presented at the Commune celebration in 1883, deals with a working-class girl—as the title suggests—who falls in love with a factory owner's son and is then repudiated by her class-conscious father. *Im Frühroth* (Dawn), written by Martin Drescher for the 1907 Commune celebration, places a melodramatic love story within the events of the Paris Commune: The hero is a freedom fighter who, having been jailed by reactionary forces, manages to return in time to continue the people's fight for liberty.

The staging of *Die Nihilisten* in the North Side Turner Hall on March 18, 1882, is a typical example of class-conscious proletarian theater in Chicago. The actors were amateur performers within the Social Revolutionary movement; even August Spies played a part.[42] In the last act, the liberators were portrayed by members of the *Lehr- und Wehr-Verein* (Education and Defense Society), the largest armed group in Chicago's labor movement. Thus the cast in itself lent the play a special relevance for the situation in Chicago. *Die Nihilisten* was so successful that, upon the request of people from the West Side—who, because of insufficient public transportation, had not been able to take part in the Commune celebration—it was performed again in a popular theater.[43]

The Proletarian's Daughter, however, could the following year boast a cast comprising none other than the ensemble of Chicago's premier theater, McVicker's.[44] Rather than going into the play's content, the review in the *Arbeiter-Zeitung* concentrated on the natural and unaffected portrayal of the workers' character, which continually drew enthusiastic applause. The review stressed that the "staging of similar thesis plays would be highly recommendable as a means of agitation."[45]

Having professionals arrange the artistic parts of the 1883 Commune celebration was not a singular event: More than once, theater managers Moritz Hahn and Robert Hepner were requested to compose the *tableaux vivants* for Commune celebrations.[46] Thus the boundaries between Chicago's working-class theater and commercial theater seem to have been quite flexible. In any case, it was possible for Chicago's labor movement to use commercially oriented cultural activities for its own events. If in addition one considers that all labor movement festivities also sought to raise funds for or to lend financial assistance to Socialist associations, the importance of a professionally conducted theatrical performance becomes self-evident.

Amateur performances staged by Socialist theater groups outside the framework of labor festivities played a subordinate role in Chicago.[47] John Most, editor of the anarchist magazine, *Freiheit*, and prominent advocate of a "propaganda of deed," undertook one of the most systematic attempts to employ theater as a means of agitation. While on a propaganda tour through the United States in 1900, he again staged *Die Weber* in various towns, using local amateur performers belonging to the Social Revolutionary movement in the town of presentation. In Chicago, three presentations in different halls were announced.[48] Unlike the case in Most's 1895 tour, this time the invitation came from party members. One of the main attractions was naturally John Most himself, in the role of the old Baumert; in order to be as authentic as possible, all the roles were cast with performers who could speak the Silesian dialect. At the end of the presentation, there was, as usual, an "extremely genial little dance."

In its discussion of the performances, the *Arbeiter-Zeitung* emphasized that *Die Weber*, with its "life-like" characters "right out of the life of the people," was especially suitable for amateur working-class theater. Just the same, the reviewer alludes to the excellent performances of *Die Weber* staged in New York's Irving Place Theater in 1895; at that time the play ran for four weeks to a full house. The realistic nature of the earlier performance is once again discussed in detail before pointing out "how much can be accomplished when the means and persons required for bringing propaganda into the theater are available."[49] This clearly implies that the presentation of a suitable play on the commercial stage is of greater agitational value than an amateur performance. A similar suggestion was already seen to hold true for the popular theater: Theater for workers was also possible in commercially oriented middle-class cultural institutions.

This emphasis on quality also came to the fore in Chicago in 1896. Based on the format of the *Freie Bühne* (Free Theater) in Berlin, an attempt was made to found a Chicago Free Theater in Schoenhofen's Hall. Enthusiastic previews were printed in both the *Arbeiter-Zeitung* and the *Illinois Staats-Zeitung*. While the latter anticipated a theater that would lean primarily toward a naturalistic avant-garde, the *Arbeiter-Zeitung* stressed the link between the Free Theater and the Socialist movement, since the bulk of its repertoire was to be composed of "Socialist plays prohibited in Germany."[50] It recommended that "progressive workers, having realized that the theater can be an educational institution only as long as artistic interests prevail," should be encouraged to attend.[51] According to the *Arbeiter-Zeitung*, the questionable artistic performances in the premiere were above all responsible for the failure of Wiechers van Gogh's play, *Die Ehe* (Marriage). Without trained personnel, the newspaper continued, an experiment of this sort was doomed to fail.[52]

The examples cited above are not the only evidence of the *Arbeiter-Zeitung*'s conviction that German theater should be used as an educational institution, even if it meant delivering the production of German culture into the hands of the middle class; every week there were also long reports dealing with the regular theater. In part, this interest naturally stemmed from efforts to preserve German culture in Chicago, and German theater in Chicago being the theater of a minority, this was well within the interests of a marginal group. What role was attributed to the workers in this context?

In an article written in 1888—in which, as was so often the case in Chicago's theater criticism, emphasis was placed on the importance of a uniquely German theater for the preservation of the German language and German culture in Chicago—the *Arbeiter-Zeitung* turned against middle-class Germans, finding that they had neglected the theater as an institution for the education of the people. It pointed to the German workers as the actual carriers of the German cultural heritage:

> Since for a certain class of prominent people best characterized as "affluent domestics," there is nothing more repulsive, nothing which instills more loathing and fear than the thought that the masses, who have

been cheated and oppressed by these prominent people, come to realize the causes for their misery and oppressed situation. And the theater is just the place where all the light and dark sides of human existence are faithfully exposed to the audience, and true acting is an extremely important factor for the education of humanity. But, to preserve the full value of the theater to educate the people; to keep the theater pure of detrimental influences; to prevent it from coming under the control of a clique opposed to the people—for all these reasons we are not only appealing to the prominent old foggies, but we are rather of the opinion that all Germans with a feeling for art, whether rich or poor, man for man, each according to his strengths, should stand up for an enterprise which is not only one of the strongest bases for the preservation of the German language and literature in this country, but, if conducted properly, moreover a powerful instrument for educating the masses. That is why we hope that the workers, too, with word and deed, will contribute to this sort of endeavor.[53]

Friedrich von Schiller's concept of the theater as a moral institution is echoed in this passage. It is a claim the labor movement appropriated for itself and which, it felt, it was called upon to defend from the "shallow culture" of the middle class. This claim would continue long after German commercially oriented mass cultural institutions had fallen victim to the American entertainment industry, long after the German theater had been pushed aside by the American theater. As late as 1919, when most of the German-language theaters in America had closed, the call for support sought for a New Free Popular Stage was once again directed to the German-speaking workers of Chicago.[54]

NOTES

1. Cf. Friedrich Knilli and Ursula Münchow, *Frühes deutsches Arbeitertheater 1874 bis 1918. Eine Dokumentation* (Munich, 1970); Ursula Münchow, ed., *Aus den Anfängen der sozialistischen Dramatik*, III, Texausgaben zur frühen sozialistischen Literatur in Deutschland, vol. 11 (Berlin/East, 1972); Ursula Münchow, ed., *Aus den Anfängen der sozialistischen Dramatik*, I–II, Texausgaben zur frühen sozialistischen Literatur in Deutschland, vols. 3 and 5 (Berlin/East, 1973); Peter von Rüden, *Sozialdemokratisches Arbeitertheater (1848–1914). Ein Beitrag zur Geschichte des politischen Theaters* (Frankfurt, 1973); Gustav Schröder, "Das sozialistische deutsche Bühnenstück von den 60er Jahren des 19. Jahrhunderts bis zum Zusammenbruch der II. sozialistischen Internationale" (Habilitation thesis, Potsdam, 1965); Dietmar Trempenau, *Frühe sozialdemokratische und sozialistische Arbeiterdramatik (1890–1914). Entstehungsbedingungen – Entwicklungslinien –*

Ziele – Funktion (Stuttgart, 1979); Ludwig Hoffmann and Daniel Hoffmann-Ostwald, *Deutsches Arbeitertheater 1918–1933*, 2 vols. (Berlin, 1977).

2. The term "popular theater"—like that of "regular theater"—is taken from the contemporary press and does not imply a specific genre.

3. Cf. Carol J. Poore, *German-American Socialist Literature 1865–1900* (Bern, 1982), 77.

4. For an extensive history of German theater in Chicago, see Esther M. Olson, "The German Theater in Chicago," *Deutsch-Amerikanische Geschichtsblätter. Jahrbuch der Deutsch-Amerikanischen Historischen Gesellschaft von Illinois* 33 (1937).

5. In addition to Schiller, individual plays by Heinrich Laube, Karl Gutzkow, Grillparzer and Kotzebue could also be seen. Cf. Olson, "The German Theater," 73–82.

6. The German regular theater had close contacts with the municipal theater in Milwaukee. There were years when both had the same managers. In addition, there were guest performances staged by German thespians from New York, and well-known performers from Germany touring America often stopped in Chicago. Cf. Olson, "The German Theater," 92ff.

7. *Illinois Staats-Zeitung (ISZ)*, 13 Feb. 1888; quoted in Olson, "The German Theater," 96.

8. In 1856, Laube's *Die Karlsschüler* was performed; the lead actor, Alexander Pfeiffer, who had acted at the Royal Theater in Mannheim during the German Vormärz, was so successful that he decided to remain in Chicago. Cf. Olson, "The German Theater," 75.

9. For instance, for the opening of Chicago's municipal theater. Cf. *ISZ*, 6 Sept. 1896.

10. See the *Chicagoer Arbeiter-Zeitung (ChAZ)* on the North Side Turner Hall: "Die Volksbühne," *ChAZ*, 22 May 1882.

11. Some of the larger popular theaters tried to alleviate this deplorable state of affairs in the 1880s and 1890s.

12. Alexander Pellissier, from the theater in the Aurora Turner Hall, had dedicated himself to studying classical plays and tried to introduce them into his theater. Cf. Olson, "The German Theater," 85.

13. Wilhelm Müller, "Die Bühne in den Vereinigten Staaten," in *Amerika*, Armin Tenner, ed. (Berlin, 1886), 106.

14. The West Side Theater Society staged plays from 1863 to 1865; from 1865 to 1869 they were performed in the hall of the Social Workers' Association; in 1867 there was a theater in the Union Turner Hall. Cf. Olson, "The German Theater," 83.

15. Throughout the history of German theater in Chicago, attempts to stage performances on weekdays—whether by regular or popular theaters—were unsuccessful. That was also one of the reasons why the Schiller Theater had to close. Cf. "Verdienter Tadel für das Chicagoer Deutschthum," *Westen* (the Sunday edition of the *ISZ*), 23 Oct. 1892.

16. Popular theaters in 1881 and 1882 on the North and Northwest Sides were: Theater

in Müller's Hall, Sedgwick St. and North Ave.; Theater in the Aurora Turner Hall, Milwaukee Ave. and Huron St.; Theater in the Arbeiterhalle, W. 12th and Waller Sts.; Theater in the Vorwärts Turner Hall, 12th and Halsted Sts. The theaters in Müller's Hall and in the Vorwärts Turner Hall—the two largest popular theaters until the mid-1880s—were both managed by Minna Ostermann. Popular theaters in 1896 and 1897 on the North and Northwest Sides were: Chicagoer Stadttheater, Wicker Park Hall, 501–7 W. North Ave.; Theater in Wolf's Hall, Milwaukee Ave. and Noble and Emma Sts.; Theater in the Fortschritt Turner Hall, 1842 Milwaukee Ave.; Criterion Theater, Sedgwick and Division Sts.; Theater in the Social Turner Hall, Fullerton and Burling Sts.; Theater in the New Aurora Turner Hall, Ashland Ave. and Division St.; Chicagoer Freie Bühne in Schoenhofen's Hall, Division St. and Ashland Ave. On the South and Southwest Sides: Theater in the New Vorwärts Turner Hall, 251–55 Western Ave. and 12th St.; Apollo Theater, Blue Island Ave. and 12th St.; Theater in Hoerber's Hall, 710–14 East 22th St.; Wendel's Opera House, address unknown. With the exception of the Theater in the Arbeiterhalle, all of the theaters listed for 1881 and 1882 were still in existence. The theaters in Müller's Hall and the Vorwärts Turner Hall were managed by Minna Ostermann. By contrast, during the 1906–07 season, the only existing popular theaters were those in the Social Turner Hall and the Vorwärts Turner Hall.

17. Cf. "Theater und Musik," *Fackel* (the Sunday edition of the *ChAZ*), 25 Sept. 1881.

18. "Die Volksbühne," *ChAZ*, 6 March 1882.

19. As a rule, even at performances sponsored by the labor movement, there was a twenty-five cent admission charge.

20. Guest performance by acrobats from the Berlin-based Renz Circus and by the Viennese magician, Prof. Gerhardi, *ChAZ*, 22 Jan. 1882; 5 Feb. 1882.

21. "Chicagoer Schmierentheater," *Westen*, 23 Oct. 1892.

22. "Die Volksbühne," *ChAZ*, 26 June 1882.

23. Cf. Rüden, *Sozialdemokratisches Arbeitertheater*, 37.

24. In most cases, after 1900 one finds a cinema instead of German theater.

25. "Die Volksbühne," *ChAZ*, 20 March 1882.

26. In the season of 1896, these titles constantly recur in announcements and theater reviews in the *ChAZ* and the *ISZ*.

27. "Chicagoer Stadttheater," *ISZ*, 6 Sept. 1896.

28. "Das reguläre Theater," *ChAZ*, 9 May 1882.

29. Social Democratic performances in Germany took this need into account and offered entertaining interludes. Cf. Rüden, *Sozialdemokratisches Arbeitertheater*, 89ff.

30. On 18 Oct. 1896 in Freiberg's Opera House.

31. "Miese Massematten," *ChAZ*, 14 Jan. 1895.

32. See *New Yorker Volks-Zeitung*, *(NYVZ)* 9 Oct 1894; also see John C. Blankenagel,

"The Early Reception of Hauptmann's *Die Weber* in the United States," *Modern Language Notes* 68 (1953): 337.

33. Blankenagel, "The Early Reception," 338; also see Poore, *German-American Socialist Literature*, 103.

34. Preliminary notice for *Die Weber, ChAZ,* 2 Jan. 1895 and 6 Jan. 1895. "Miese Massematten," *ChAZ,* 14 Jan. 1895.

35. As a rule, the cheapest seats in the regular theaters cost the same as the most expensive in popular theaters or reserved seats for specific working-class festivities, namely fifty cents (approximately one-third of an unskilled worker's daily wages, one-fifth of a skilled worker's wages). Cf. "Earnings, Expenses and Conditions of Workingmen and Their Families," Illinois Bureau of Labor Statistics, *Third Biennial Report* (Springfield, IL, 1884), 135–414; Karl Böttcher. *Ausgewiesen! Soziales Drama aus den achtziger Jahren in vier Aufzügen* (Munich, 1906).

36. "Schillertheater. *Ausgewiesen,*" *ISZ,* 9 Jan. 1893.

37. "*Ausgewiesen*. Die gestrige Vorstellung im Schillertheater," *ChAZ,* 9 Jan. 1893.

38. In 1894, Max Baginski—who belonged to the group around the New Free Popular Theater (which opposed official social democratic cultural policy)—became a member of the *ChAZ* editorial staff. Cf. Manfred Brauneck, *Literatur und Öffentlichkeit im ausgehenden 19. Jahrhundert. Studien zur Rezeption des naturalistischen Theaters in Deutschland* (Stuttgart, 1974), 42; also Karl J. R. Arndt and May E. Olson, *German-American Newspapers and Periodicals 1732–1955, History and Bibliography* (Heidelberg, 1961), 58. Arndt and Olson erroneously list him under the name of "Gaginski."

39. For example: "*Ein weißer Othello*" by W. Friedrich (1896 Commune celebration); "*Abu Seid*" by Oskar Blumenthal (1901 Commune celebration); "*Am Rande des Glücks*" by Heinrich Bartel (*ChAZ* festival in 1908).

40. Cf. Poore, *German-American Socialist Literature,* 102.

41. The play was first attributed to August Spies. But an article in the *NYVZ* demonstrates that Rosenberg was the author. Cf. W. L. Rosenberg, "Erinnerungen aus der Frühzeit der socialistischen Bewegung in den Ver. Staaten," *Sonntagsblatt der New Yorker Volks-Zeitung,* V, 29 Jan. 1928.

42. See the announcement for the Commune celebration, *ChAZ,* 20 March 1882.

43. "Unsere Commune-Feier," *ChAZ,* 20 March 1882.

44. See the announcement for the Commune celebration, *ChAZ,* 17 March 1883.

45. "Die Commune-Feier," *Fackel,* 18 March 1883.

46. At the Commune celebrations in 1893, 1896, and 1897.

47. Because of the sporadic notices for amateur theater evenings, only a few examples could be found; in these cases, however, entertainment seems to have been given preference to agitational activity. See for instance Poore, *German-American Socialist Literature,* 101f.

One of the most impressive attempts was the staging of Ibsen's *The Pillars of Society* by the dramatic section of the Social Turner Society. Cf. *ChAZ,* 24 April 1896.

48. On 21 Feb. 1900, in the Aurora Turner Hall; on 25 Feb. 1900, in the Social Turner Hall; and on 28 Feb. 1900, in Hoerber's Hall. *ChAZ,* 21, 25 and 28 Feb. 1900.

49. "*Die Weber* von G. Hauptmann unter Mitwirkung von John Most," *ChAZ,* 22 Feb. 1900.

50. "Freie Bühne Chicago," *ISZ,* 6 Dec. 1896; "Freie Bühne," *ChAZ,* 8 Nov. 1896.

51. "Freie Bühne Chicago," *ChAZ,* 5 Dec. 1896.

52. *ChAZ,* 7 Dec. 1896. It is unclear whether the *Fackel*'s having previously printed the play—it is set in a middle-class milieu and attacks the institution of marriage—may have thwarted expectations. The *ChAZ* emphasized that success would have been certain if there had already been a repertoire of naturalistic plays. Although there were reviews in the *ChAZ* that reflected Mehring's critique of naturalism, the main tendency—at least as far as the anarchist group is concerned—seems to have advocated the new artistic direction as a mouthpiece for the "social question." Cf. "Freie Bühne Chicago," *ChAZ,* 5 Dec. 1896, as well as the positive reaction of Hermann Sudermann, *ChAZ,* 8 Feb. 1897.

53. "Unser deutsches Theater," *Fackel,* 18 Jan. 1888.

54. "Freie Volksbühne," *Fackel,* 13 April 1919.

German Workers' Literature in Chicago —Old Forms in New Contexts

HEINZ ICKSTADT

L iterary texts recently discovered in German-American working-class papers of the late nineteenth century do not, perhaps, constitute a treasure of unknown masterpieces, but they do testify to the intention of German immigrant workers to create a specific proletarian art—an art at once aesthetic and political.[1] The songs, ballads, morality plays, satires, and dramatic sketches published in the *Chicagoer Arbeiter-Zeitung*, its Sunday edition, the *Fackel*, and its weekly edition, the *Vorbote*, from the 1870s until the First World War were written for a purpose—to be used for a variety of occasions, in a variety of contexts. They were written for a well-defined audience of politically conscious or politically active workers, by authors who, in most cases, belonged to the editorial staff of German working-class papers and were, at the same time, political agitators who organized unions, gave innumerable political speeches, and were engaged in establishing a network of interethnic and innerethnic working-class communication.

It is a literature that is, perhaps surprisingly, nonrepresentational; that is, one finds little realistic treatment of everyday life, of the experience of immigration, or of the tensions and conflicts that are part of the difficult process of becoming an American. German working-class literature in America did not produce an Abraham Cahan, who sought literary rank and place in American literature and—in novels like *Yekl* and *The Rise of David Levinsky*—attempted to convey to an English-speaking audience the psychological price immigrants paid for Americanization. None of the authors and editors of the *Arbeiter-Zeitung* saw themselves in Cahan's role as mediator between dominant culture and ethnic subculture. Their liter-

ary production aimed at creating political consciousness within their ethnic group or class (at the same time that their political activism aimed at
mediating between the different ethnic groups of Chicago's labor force.)
Accordingly, the novel—not only the representational genre par excellence but also a literary product made for private consumption—played a
minor part: With the single exception of August Otto-Walster's classic
working-class novel, *Am Webstuhl der Zeit* (At the Loom of Time, a work
written and published in Germany in 1873 and reprinted, during Otto-
Walster's political exile in the United States, in St. Louis in 1877–78; Chicago, 1889; and Cincinnati, 1890),[2] the editors of Chicago's German labor
press confined themselves to reprinting the most important texts of the
realist and naturalist tradition (Victor Hugo, Emile Zola, Alphonse
Daudet, Ivan Sergeyevich Turgenev, Maksim Gorky, William Dean
Howells, Frank Norris) in addition to its usual fare of sentimental fiction.
Apart from a possible shortage of narrative talent, the novel simply did not
figure in a working-class literature that was essentially made for communal use and was public even when it addressed the private reader.[3] It was
used to create political awareness and class consciousness and to enforce
confidence in the inevitable process of history. It was recited, performed,
or sung together, and consequently song, ballad, didactic poem
(*Lehrgedicht*), poetic allegory, pageant, and dramatic sketch were its most
favored genres. In short, the literature of German workers in Chicago was
part of a political culture that celebrated and ritualized, in a series of iden-
tically patterned festivities and commemorations, working-class community and ethnic and political identity.

   In this respect, it was not essentially different from the literary forms
and traditions that the writers and editors of the German working-class
press—people like Conrad Conzett, Gustav Lyser, Wilhelm Ludwig
Rosenberg, August Spies, Martin Drescher, and Heinrich Bartel—had
brought with them from Germany.[4] There, the early working-class movement had produced at least elements of an autonomous literature, which
had adapted to its own political purposes the literary traditions of revolutionary and prerevolutionary Germany: of the Sturm und Drang (the early
plays of Johann Wolfgang von Goethe and Friedrich von Schiller, especially *Faust I* and *Die Räuber*), of romantic poetry (its artful folksongs and
Wanderlieder), and of the Vormärz (e.g., the poetry of Ferdinand
Freiligrath, Georg Herwegh, and, most conspicuously, the songs and ballads of Heinrich Heine).[5] This amounted generally to an appropriation of
form and tone—Heine's "voice" is present in German working-class poetry until the turn of the century. But appropriation could also become

conscious literary strategy when the well-known texts of the classical tradition or songs of the popular culture were rewritten from the perspective of the working class. Such rewriting became parody and travesty when the canonized texts of the dominant bourgeois culture were mercilessly "debunked" and their ideology turned upside down. With comparable countercultural intention, working-class theater, as it first developed in the late 1870s, combined didactic purpose with satire and parody. These one-act plays, produced and performed by amateur groups, enacted and explained Socialist doctrine and ridiculed the rhetoric of the class enemy. Plays like Jean Baptist von Schweitzer's *Ein Schlingel* (A Rascal) and *Eine Gans* (A Goose) relied heavily on dialogue; others, like Josef Schiller's *Selbstbefreiung* (Self-Liberation) and Friedrich Bosses's *Die Alten und die Neuen* (The Old Ones and the New Ones) added music and special light effects. The presence of the classical tradition is noticeable in style and near-quotation, but there is also an affinity to agrarian-artisan adaptations of the highly allegorical mode of religious theater with its Easter and Nativity pageants or morality plays.

The beginnings of German working-class literature can be traced back to the 1830s and 1840s, but it fully emerged some thirty years later, together with its most important medium: the labor press. Influential papers of the Social Democratic party like the *Socialdemokrat*, the *Volksstaat*, its sequel *Vorwärts*, and the weekly *Neue Welt* were founded during the 1860s and 1870s and continued until 1878, when Bismarck's Anti-Socialist Law forbade—until it was revoked twelve years later by act of parliament—all Socialist political activities. During this time, however, the *Socialdemokrat*, founded in 1879, was published first from Switzerland, later from London. The great satirical magazines *Der wahre Jakob* and *Süddeutscher Postillon* were brought out in the early 1880s despite the severe restrictions imposed by Bismarck's law.[6] It is important to remember that the writers and editors of the *Arbeiter-Zeitung* were in their twenties or early thirties when they fled Germany and that they left a budding working-class culture, which they hoped to transplant and continue in the United States. Not only did they keep their eyes on what was going on in Germany, they also published or reprinted poems and essays that had been written in the homeland (pieces by Andreas Scheu, August Geib, Otto Krille, Ernst Preszang, and many others). Founding the *Vorbote* and the *Arbeiter-Zeitung* as a medium to create a "counterpublic" and as an instrument of group communication meant for these writers to apply organizational skills learned in Germany to a situation marked by social instability and growing labor unrest. Yet, at the same time, it seemed a first step toward an autonomous political culture in exile and a vanguard venture spearheading the advance of socialism in America.

Apart from the many examples of political *Gelegenheitsdichtung* (that is, poetry written for a specific occasion and therefore of a rather improvisational character, such as an editorial that abruptly turns into verse), German working-class literature in Chicago can be differentiated according to its form, content, and intention. There are the ballads, satirical poems, and one-act plays that attack an ideological and political enemy "out there," and there are the songs, the didactic and allegorical poems, and the mystery or morality plays directed "inward" to enact the solidarity and collective identity of an ethnic and political community.

The satires (verse or dramatic sketch) were written in most cases in connection with actual political events. Thus an election fraud in 1875 inspired Conrad Conzett to write his one-act satire, *Die Räuber* (The Robbers, a burlesque version of Schiller's radical drama).[7] In a similar manner, Gustav Lyser attacked the congressional hearings on the violent strikes and labor rebellions of 1877 in his satire, *Congress for the Muddling Up of the Labor Question in New York: A Comedy at the Expense of the Proletariat*—a play that, like Conzett's, makes abundant use of classical quotations (from Goethe, Schiller, Heine), and which evidently fills the "new wine" of socialism and working-class consciousness into the "old bottles" of German classical theater.[8] Satires such as these, which attack and make fun of the class enemy, or poems condemning the inhumanity of the capitalist system (e.g., poems on the strike of the Colorado mine workers in 1903–04, or on the trial of Big Bill Haywood) grew out of, and took part in, everyday working-class struggle, and thus were forms of an aggressively political literature.

The holidays and memorial days of the working-class movement (such as the Day of the Paris Commune on March 18, or May Day) generated poems, songs, and plays meant to enforce and celebrate working-class solidarity and Socialist *communitas*. In addition, the Christian holidays (especially Christmas, Easter, and Pentecost) gave rise to a great number of poems, allegories, or mystery plays that translate the Christian cycle of death and resurrection into Socialist sacred history. Ludwig Geissler's *Allegorisches Weihnachtsfestspiel* (Allegorical Christmas Play), which identifies the birth of Christ with the birth of socialism,[9] and Martin Drescher's Easter and Pentecost poems (in which Christ's Resurrection and the revelation of tongues are adapted to the new Socialist gospel) are good examples.[10] A similar combination of quasi-religious celebration and didactic enlightenment is evident in Josef Schiller's allegorical plays, *Selbstbefreiung* and *Die Wahrheit im Kampfe mit Lüge und Unverstand* (The Battle of Truth Against Folly and Deceit), both written and performed in Austria but printed by the *Arbeiter-Zeitung* for the May Day and the Paris Commune commemorations of 1908 and 1909,[11] or in Martin Drescher's one-act plays, *Die Weihe der Kraft. Ein Festspiel zum 1. Mai* (The Consecration of Strength: A Pageant for the First of May), a ceremonial and didactic consecration of youth to a life of socialism, written in celebration of May 1, 1904, and *Im Frühroth* (Dawn, 1907), which—part allegory, part historical drama—translates the short moment of the Paris Commune's seeming success into a symbol of future victory.[12]

The satirical and explicitly political literature, as well as the celebratory or ceremonious poems and plays, relate to the conflicts and confusions of everyday experience yet at the same time seem strangely removed from it. They project a symbolic realm of ideologically and morally ordered history in which the powers of light and darkness, virtue and vice, labor and capital fight for supremacy and eventual victory. Accordingly, caricature on the one hand and allegory on the other are dominant stylistic devices: Misery, Poverty, and Need personified as women; the capitalist exploiter, as idler and glutton thriving on the blessings of the clergy; the workingman, as Prometheus enchained; Human Rights, as an angel from heaven forcing capital to its knees. Figures such as these are part of an iconography of working-class world- and self-interpretation, also to be found in newspaper illustrations, *tableaux vivants*, pageants, or floats at demonstrations and parades.[13] It is an iconography in which traditions and motifs of radical bourgeois or artisan protest survive (yet which, at the same time, echoes the tendency toward emblem and allegorization also noticeable in the public art of the dominant culture).

Emblems and images of a more strictly religious kind reappear in the nature poems of German immigrant working-class literature and with them the signals and motifs of millennial expectations, of a salvation in and through history. In these poems, the Socialist community is cast in the role of a quasi-religious *communitas*, which, in a time of crisis, yearns for the apocalyptic fulfillment of time. I quote from an anonymous poem ("Easter Hope," 1906, presumably written by Martin Drescher), which shows the influence of the consciously simple folksong manner of German romantic poetry and also illustrates the working-class adaptation of religious motifs:

Oh, his slumber still is deep,
Under stones, so dead and cold,
All his faithful, tears untold,
Hoping life's reward to reap—

Crucified each day once more,
Daily to the grave he's sent,
By the people smug, content,
Now as in those days of yore.

Alone the poor they wish and wait,
Yearning that he reappear
Full of longing, full of fear,
Waiting for a better fate.

All this Easter signifies:
Breezes rushing through the heart,
Grievances will then depart,
When the people choose to rise!

Courage growing now, oh dreamer!
Come, oh novel Easter fest,
Come, oh freedom's valiant quest,
Come, the only *true* redeemer![14]

It is important to understand the literature of the German working-class movement in Chicago as part of a political culture that, with its various institutions, organizations, and festivities, consciously set itself against a drab world of everyday experience on the one hand, and the pressures (or attractions) of the dominant culture on the other. Recurring elements of all working-class festivities were entertainment, especially sports (such as gymnastics, rowing, bowling, and running) and dancing; but also political education: It was often a speech that signaled or ensured the political character of the event. Central, however, were artistic activities, such as recitations and performances by choirs and orchestras (or by individual singers, instrumentalists, and recitalists); and theatricals of all kinds, including the *tableau vivant*. Each festivity followed more or less the same pattern by selecting at least one element of each area of the physical, political, and aesthetic education of the worker. With the exception of the Commune and Haymarket commemorations, all such occasions ended with a dance that might last until the morning hours.[15] The aesthetic, or—in the idealist rhetoric of the *Arbeiter-Zeitung*—"the Beautiful," was almost as important as the political speech: The "ennobling effect of art," as much as the political battle, ensured the coming of the "new race." The festivals of the working-class movement were therefore not only a necessary escape from the pressures of everyday life, relaxation from work for more work, but also Utopian anticipation of the "whole human being" and the "liberated society" in which work and creativity, art and life, would become one.[16]

It is therefore not really surprising that, after the turn of the century when Germans—and especially those of the second generation—became more and more integrated into American society, the *Arbeiter-Zeitung* admonished its readers time and again to return to the aesthetic premises of German working-class culture. On the commemoration of the twentieth anniversary of the execution of the Haymarket anarchists, Heinrich Bartel, then editor of the *Arbeiter-Zeitung* and an author of poems and allegorical plays,[17] violently attacked the materialism of American society ("ruled by money and the belly"), and especially the materialism of the American unions ("where everybody dreams of his own little house"). Then he continued:

> The labor question is a cultural question in the widest sense. Untold numbers of the poor, otherwise lost in the grime of their misery, send their prayers to the eternal goddesses, to Aphrodite in her unveiled beauty, and to Athena, the embodiment of wisdom and strength. Here is one of the most ennobling tasks of the working-class movement. Over the fight for our material well-being we may not ever, not for a single moment, forget the reality of the Ideal. To master Beauty and Art and Science: This, too, is a duty of the working class. We want to change the world and to take possession of everything that makes life magnificent. That is how August Spies conceived of the working-class movement.[18]

Bartel's speech illustrates the dilemma that confronted the German working class movement and its elite in the United States: To maintain the Utopian ideal of the "whole human being" as the only true alternative to

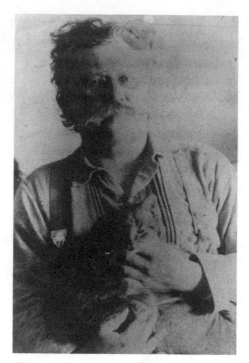

*Figure 9.1. Robert Reitzel, the
founder and editor of the radical
paper,* Der Arme Teufel, *published
in Detroit from 1884 to 1900.*

existing (i.e., American) conditions, implied loyalty to a specific form of
ethnic cultural idealism and the identification of true socialism with German socialism. But the consciousness of cultural superiority (evident in
Bartel's speech as well as in those of many others) is only another aspect of
the growing isolation of this working-class intellectual elite from its constitutional basis. The attack against the philistinism of the Americans
therefore runs parallel to the repeated complaint about the *Verspiesserung*
("embourgeoisement") of the German workers in America. Accordingly,
the Utopian image can be kept alive only by its projection backward into
the past (Haymarket, the 1870s and 1880s, when German workers
founded and dominated Chicago's labor organizations—a past nostalgically transfigured into heroic history and lost greatness.[19]

While the forms and content of German working-class literature and culture stayed almost the same over a period of more than forty years, the needs of those who used them changed—and thus changed the nature of the culture's social and pragmatic function. It had served a vital purpose during the height of German working-class immigration in the early 1880s and within a context of intense labor organization and assertion (during a time, that is, when class conflict could also be defined in ethnic and cultural terms). After Haymarket and after the numerically large second wave of immigration from southern and eastern Europe, German working-class culture gradually lost its former energy and raison d'être. Robert Reitzel's poem on Haymarket obliquely illustrates this change of function during the later period:

> It was as always,
>> Was just the same;
> We all were upright,
>> And very tame.
>
> Courageous we were
>> In saloons well filled;
> And bravely watched,
>> While others were killed.
>
> For now, we said,
>> We must keep cheer!
> And grimly ordered
>> Another beer.
>
> Our advice to the people,
>> Was very exact—
> The hangman, however,
>> Knew how to act.[20]

The poem describes with savage self-depreciation the hangover well-known to participants in a radical movement that failed. In a context of class and cultural conflict, of assimilation and ethnic identity, however, Reitzel's poem also connotes more: If true Socialist identity can be maintained only in acts of resistance (as a quasi-Utopian present of ongoing revolutionary action), then pragmatic adjustment logically must be considered as accommodation, "embourgeoisement"; in short, as Americanization. In such a complex field of cultural tensions (a field of highly unstable individual and collective self-definition), in which the accommodated self nostalgically mourns and transfigures a lost "authentic" self (by which, at the same time, it knows itself condemned), German working-class culture in Chicago, even though still overtly political, became increasingly depoliticized. It offered a largely rhetorical identity that one might nostalgically cling to, but which one might also easily discard like a garment that no longer fits. "The German America," Robert Reitzel wrote shortly before his death in 1898, "which carried in its blood Lessing, Feuerbach, and Börne, dies with us who have lost our home and are strangers in our own house."

This was the problem most of all of the first generation, for whom the idea of an alternative Socialist society was tied to the specific forms and manifestations of an ethnic working-class movement. Its intellectual elite, who had come to the United States mostly in reaction to Bismarck's Anti-Socialist Law, had invested impressive energies in the organization of an interethnic working-class movement on the one hand, and in the establishment of an autonomous German working-class literature and culture on the other. But these working-class intellectuals were more of an initiating than a stabilizing factor: They moved from one working-class paper to another on their organizing mission or were forced out from the editorial staff by either ideological or viciously fought personal conflicts within the local movement.[21] Some never lost the sense of being in exile and went back to Germany as soon as it was politically possible; others left the movement altogether. Wilhelm Liebknecht's report on his trip to the United States in 1886 indicates that the pressures of cultural and political loyalties frequently became a heavy burden after the first few years of fervent commitment: "I found many an old friend there," he wrote in *Ein Blick in die Neue Welt* (A Look into the New World), "some still alive, others already dead, even though alive."[22] Conzett, Lyser, Rosenberg, Drescher, and Bartel all left the *Arbeiter-Zeitung* for various reasons after a comparatively brief period of three or four years. That is why German working-class literature in Chicago was written and performed in a local context but was never really a local product.[23]

As the editors came and went, the editorial policies changed (especially in the case of the Sunday paper, the *Fackel*), most often from an emphasis on literature to one on education and science (and vice versa).[24]

Figure 9.2. Title page of a German workers' songbook published in Chicago in the early 1880s and containing poems and songs by radical German writers, mostly from the Vormärz period.

The writers of the movement used the literary and cultural conventions they had brought with them within a new social and cultural environment, and they occasionally adopted the literary forms of an English-American working-class cultural tradition.[25] They were innovators in that they applied the familiar to what was essentially new and unfamiliar, but all in all they stuck to the literary styles and conventions they had known and practiced in Germany—with the exception, perhaps, of Martin Drescher. Next to Wilhelm Ludwig Rosenberg (who was editor of the *Fackel* in the early 1880s), Drescher was the most accomplished and versatile poet ever to work for the *Arbeiter-Zeitung*. He had come to the United States in 1891, barely lived through years of economic crisis as a tramp and vagabond, became, after Reitzel's death in 1898, editor of the satirical magazine *Der Arme Teufel* (which Reitzel had founded and edited in Detroit), and finally joined the editorial staff of Chicago's German labor press in the first years of the new century.

Drescher, like Gustav Lyser and other poets of the working-class movement, tried (in his life as much as in his work) to negotiate between romantic bohemianism and political commitment (apparently with diminishing success).[26] His poems echo with the voices of German classic and romantic poetry,[27] but he also brought with him the energetic and declamatory manner of new working-class poets like Richard Dehmel. Under his pen names "Flamingo" and "Peter Schlemihl," he wrote in the satirical or bohemian-romantic vein of Heine and Reitzel; and, in his allegorical nature poems, he went back to earlier traditions of working-class poetry. His didactic one-act plays, *Dawn* and *The Consecration of Strength: A Pageant for the First of May* (performed in 1904), apparently attempt to combine the allegorical manner of early working-class theater (suggested in the title) with forms of historical drama on the one hand and the idealizing mode of the German classical tradition on the other (to which he adds a realistic touch by placing his pageant in the "environments of an American metropolis"). Another of his one-act plays, *Maria Magdalena*, is somewhat reminiscent of the early plays of Hugo von Hofmannsthal, even though Drescher manages to mix into his refined brew of religious aestheticism and fin-de-siècle decadence a drop of political commitment (together with oblique references to his state of exile: "Would I have never come here to this country, Never to this bleak and dirty city"). In other words, Drescher was well versed in the established traditions of working-class literature and at the same time tried to reconcile them with the forms and styles of a slowly emerging modernism. Yet despite his penchant for the new[28] and his mild literary experimentalism, one can nevertheless maintain that innovations of literary forms, and the definitions and redefinitions of the value and direction of working-class literature and culture, happened in Germany and were then brought to Chicago. In fact, one may assume with some justification that the old forms, by having become part of an ethnic heritage, survived longer in the American environment than in the homeland where they were slowly crowded out by a new emphasis on a high cultural definition of art, which left the creation of true proletarian literature to a postrevolutionary future.[29] In any case, the life of the literary culture of Chicago's German working class depended on its contacts with the "old home"—most of all, it needed a steady stream of new immigrants who would bring their creative talent and their knowledge of the living tradition with them to America.

However, with German immigration to the United States dwindling after the turn of the century, this creative and regenerative influx into German-American working-class culture diminished, and with it

Figure 9.3. First page of sheet music to the "Workers' Solidarity Song," written and composed by Carl Sahm, the foremost composer of songs for German workers in the United States in the last third of the nineteenth century. Sahm, who was a conductor in New York, wrote several hundred pieces for men's choir and other compositions including operas.

the need for the German language. For the second generation, German and the participation in a specifically German working-class culture became increasingly optional. Accordingly, the meaning of German working-class traditions changed: Inevitably, they played a lesser role in the lives of the children of immigrants than they had played in those of their parents. If the second-generation Germans were politically conscious and active, they were members of American labor organizations or of the Socialist party (both of which their parents had helped to establish). With this realignment of loyalties, German working-class culture lost its vital function of providing its participants with a (transitional) cultural identity. Nevertheless, it did not altogether vanish with its true constituents, the workers and intellectuals of the first generation. Some of the forms and traditions, especially of its organized leisure (such as picnics and *tableaux vivants*), entered the repertoire of a radical political culture that, after the turn of the century, defined itself increasingly as multiethnic and American.

NOTES

1. Carol Poore, *German-American Socialist Literature 1865–1900* (Bern, 1982); Hartmut Keil, ed., *Deutsche Arbeiterkultur in Chicago von 1850 bis zum Ersten Weltkrieg. Eine Anthologie* (Ostfildern, 1984); the (translated) American edition is *German Workers in Chicago: A Documentary History of Working-Class Culture from 1850 to World War I*, Hartmut Keil and John B. Jentz, eds. (Urbana, 1988); Hartmut Keil and Heinz Ickstadt, "Elements of German Working-Class Culture in Chicago, 1880 to 1890," in this volume; and Carol Poore, ed., *Deutsch-amerikanische sozialistische Literatur 1865–1900* (Berlin, 1987).

2. Wolfgang Friedrich, ed., *August Otto-Walster. Leben und Werk* (Berlin, 1966). The *Chicagoer Arbeiter-Zeitung (ChAZ)* started its printing of Otto-Walster's novel (of which Friedrich is not aware) on 12 Aug. 1889 without any comment or introductory remarks. Otto-Walster apparently tried his hand at an American novel, *Der Fürst des Geldes und der König der Tramps: Sozialer Roman aus den neuesten Tagen der grossen Republik*, *Volksstimme des Westens*, St. Louis, 2 Aug. 1879–8 June 1880. He also wrote several "American" short stories for working-class calenders and illustrated magazines in Germany, cf. Friedrich, 241.

3. It was characteristically in the area of the novel that the editors of the *ChAZ* seemed to embrace without reservation a bourgeois aesthetic separating high art from works written for mere entertainment. They printed many of the latter "for the benefit of their women readers" but also insisted, against all opposition, on the worker's right and need to know the master works. (Even then, they did not simply accept the literary canon of the bourgeoisie.)

4. Cf. Bernd Witte, ed., *Deutsche Arbeiterliteratur von den Anfängen bis 1914* (Stuttgart, 1977); Gerd Stieg and Bernd Witte, *Abriss einer Geschichte der deutschen*

Arbeiterliteratur (Stuttgart, 1973), 7–36; Bernd Witte, "Literatur der Opposition. Über Geschichte, Funktion und Wirkmittel der frühen Arbeiterliteratur," in *Handbuch zur deutschen Arbeiterliteratur,* H. L. Arnold, ed. (Munich, 1977); Frank Trommler, *Sozialistische Literatur in Deutschland* (Stuttgart, 1976); Peter von Rüden, *Sozialdemokratisches Arbeitertheater, 1848–1914* (Frankfurt, 1973); Peter von Rüden, ed. *Beiträge zur Kulturgeschichte der deutschen Arbeiterbewegung, 1848–1918* (Frankfurt, 1979); and Vernon L. Lidtke, *The Alternative Culture: Socialist Labor in Imperial Germany* (New York, 1985).

5. However, it is the ironic and not the subjective voice of German romanticism that enters a working-class poetry preoccupied with ideas and collective attitudes. On working-class theater, see von Rüden, *Sozialdemokratisches Arbeitertheater,* and Lidtke, *The Alternative Culture.*

6. On the German working-class press, see Kurt Koszyk, "Kultur und Presse der Arbeiterbewegung," in Rüden, ed., *Beiträge.* 63–78; Reinhard Weisbach, ed., *Das lyrische Feuilleton des "Volkstaat"* (Berlin, 1979); and Norbert Rothe, ed., *Frühe sozialistische satirische Lyrik aus den Zeitschriften "Der wahre Jakob" und "Süddeutscher Postillon"* (Berlin, 1977).

7. Conrad Conzett, *Die Räuber, Lokal-Trauerspiel in 1 Akt frei nach Schiller, Vorbote,* 5 Feb. 1876. Conzett wrote a number of similar political burlesques, such as *Der egoistische General-Rath oder Die schwarzen Kommunisten: Ein Krach-Schwanck mit Gesang in 1 Akt, Vorbote,* 28 Feb. 1874. As to the preceding remarks on *Gelegenheitsdichtung* and editorials abruptly changing into verse, see *Vorbote,* 23 Aug. 1905. The two stanzas on Chicago's "graft" unmistakably echo the tone and versification of Goethe's short poems.

8. Gustav Lyser, *Congress zur Verwirrung der Arbeiterfrage in New York, Vorbote,* 17 and 24 Aug. 1878. See Heinz Ickstadt and Hartmut Keil, "A Forgotten Piece of Working-Class Literature: Gustav Lyser's Satire of the Hewitt Hearing of 1878," *Labor History* 20 No. 1 (1979); 127–140.

9. Ludwig A. Geissler, *Allegorisches Weihnachtsfestspiel, Fackel,* 11 Jan. 1880; reprinted in Keil, ed., *Deutsche Arbeiterkultur,* 326–29.

10. Drescher's poems were regularly published in the *Fackel* from 1904 to 1907. However, only some of these became part of a collection of his poetry, *Gedichte* (n.p., 1909).

11. Josef Schiller (or Schiller Seff) was a Bohemian writer prominent in the Austrian working-class movement. Both allegories were written around 1880 (*Selbst-Befreiung* was performed in 1883). However, it was presumably the publication of *Die Wahrheit im Kampf mit Lüge und Unverstand* that became the reason for one of his several imprisonments. He left Austria for the United States in 1896 but died there one year later. His two allegories were reprinted in the *ChAZ* by his son-in-law, Heinrich Bartel, who was then chief editor of the paper and tried very hard to keep the traditions of the early literature alive. See Norbert Rothe, *Josef Schiller: Auswahl aus seinem Werk* (Berlin, 1982), and Heinrich Bartel, "Autobiographische Notizen," *Solidarität,* July, Sept., Oct. 1946, 127f., 165f., 183f. (I thank Anne Spiess for bringing this rare source to my attention.)

12. Martin Drescher, *Die Weihe der Macht, Vorbote*, 4 May 1904, and *Im Frühroth, Fackel*, 24 March 1907.

13. Cf. Lidtke for similar patterns in the public displays of the German movement: "All *tableaux vivants*"—he writes about a May Day festival of 1898—"were structured to highlight antinomies, for example, freedom versus tyranny and capital versus labor. This dualistic structure and the usual depiction of freedom as a Greek goddess, as well as still other allegorical forms, had been absorbed from older German and European traditions. Here, as with many other aspects of the alternative culture of the labor movement, socialists filled old forms with new content and different meanings," *The Alternative Culture*, 154.

14. "Osterhoffnung," *Vorbote*, 18 April 1906; also Keil, ed., *Deutsche Arbeiterkultur*, 322.

15. See Keil and Ickstadt, "Elemente," 117f.

16. ". . . That the creator of wealth and culture, the workingman, should also receive his share of the riches, joys, and beauties of this world," *ChAZ*, 1 Jan. 1910. This point was made over and over again, especially by Bartel. His position seemed to link an earlier aesthetic anarchism (Spies, Parsons) with an idealism that invested "art" and "education" (*Bildung*) with transcendent and redemptive qualities.

17. Heinrich Bartel, like his father-in-law Josef Schiller, grew up in northern Bohemia. He began writing poems and political songs to "well-known melodies" when he was twenty and published his first volume of poems, *Nordböhmische Klänge*, in 1897. He went to the United States in 1905 and joined the editorial staff of the *ChAZ* and the *Fackel* one year later.

18. *ChAZ*, 12 Nov. 1907.

19. See Klaus Ensslen and Heinz Ickstadt, "German Working-Class Culture in Chicago: Continuity and Changes in the Decade from 1900 to 1910," in *German Workers in Industrial Chicago, 1850–1910: A Comparative Perspective*, Hartmut Keil and John B. Jentz, eds. (DeKalb, IL, 1983), 236–52.

20. *Fackel*, 1 Jan. 1888; cf. Keil, ed., *Deutsche Arbeiterkultur*, 319.

21. There are many examples. Wilhelm Ludwig Rosenberg, who left the *ChAZ* because he could not get along with Paul Grottkau, gave a vivid account of their animosities in his "Erinnerungen aus der Frühzeit der sozialistischen Bewegung in den Ver. Staaten," *New Yorker Volks-Zeitung*, 29 Jan. 1928.

22. Quoted in Friedrich, ed., *August Otto-Walster*, 232.

23. If course one could argue that a political, didactic, and ritualized literature was not dependent on local contexts and tradition. It was easily transplanted and was constantly circulated in the innercontinental and transatlantic network of the German labor press. A lack of continuity in literary production as mediated through Chicago's German labor press is nevertheless noticeable.

24. There obvious slumps in the literary quality of the paper, for example in the 1890s, when the *ChAZ* and the *Fackel* were highly educational in their editorial policy, printed arti-

cles on the arts and sciences and novels of all kinds, but published hardly anything that gave evidence of an original literary production.

25. Such as the travesty of the canonized documents of the American republican tradition (e.g., the Declaration of Independence), or the parodistic inversion of religious texts (e.g., the Decalogue, the catechism, etc.). However, it is often hard to decide where influence begins and traditions overlap. The political rewriting of the catechism, for example, is also an element of the German tradition.

26. The *ChAZ* never comments on the hiring and firing of its editors. Drescher left the paper in 1907 or 1908, and one is tempted to relate editorial remarks on bohemians and unreliable characters to his disappearance from its editorial staff. He left the movement before he left Chicago and died in Canada in 1920.

27. The collection of poems he brought out in 1909 emphasizes the romantic and sentimental aspect of his poetry over the political.

28. Thus he wrote in an article on the twenty-fifth anniversary of the *Fackel*: "The Sunday paper of the workingman should open its pages to the products of modern novelwriting at last," 4 May 1904.

29. This was essentially the position of Franz Mehring, which dominated the theoretical debate on literature and culture within the Social Democratic party from around the turn of the century to the First World War. See von Rüden, ed., *Beiträge*, and Peter von Rüden and Kurt Koszyk, eds., *Dokumente und Materialien zur Kulturgeschichte der deutschen Arbeiterbewegung, 1848–1918* (Frankfurt, 1979); also Litdke, *The Alternative Culture*.

CHAPTER 10

Turner Societies and the Socialist Tradition

RALF WAGNER

The wave of strikes for the eight-hour day in the spring of 1886, culminating in the Haymarket tragedy in Chicago, demonstrations in New York, and the Bay View riots in Milwaukee, represented a decisive turning point in the German-American Turner movement. Both the *Nordamerikanische Turnerbund* (North American Turner Association) and individual societies were forced by these dramatic events to define their attitudes toward socialism and the labor movement. For the first time, ideological differences and tensions that had developed within the course of its thirty-five-year history came to the fore, both within and between individual societies in North America's urban centers. After participation in the fight against slavery, opposition to Reconstruction policies, and the elaboration of remedies for socioeconomic problems brought on by industrialization, the North American Turner Association now was divided into two antithetical groups reflecting the predominant social tensions and economic problems of the period. The relationship between these two political tendencies—the Socialist and the middle-class conservative—deserves special attention; so does the question as to how and why these two groups developed along such uncompromising lines. Symptomatic of ideological and political tendencies within the Turner Association, Haymarket marked the climax of a gradual development, when previously latent conflicts became apparent. More clearly than ever before, the association's reactions to Haymarket shed light on the relationship of the Turners to the labor movement. In order to understand this development, it is first of all necessary to look at the historical origins of the North American Turner movement, especially its radical roots—which can be traced back to the Vormärz period and the German Revolution of 1848–49—and the changes they underwent.[1]

In 1811, Friedrich Ludwig Jahn established his first Turner ground in Berlin; this represented the initial step toward the realization of his ideas, which he had laid down in two major works, *Deutsche Turnkunst* (The Art of German Gymnastics) and *Deutsches Volkstum* (German Folklore).[2] Along with the notion of physical education as a means of creating a people fit to fight, Jahn also elucidated his ideas concerning a transformation of the governmental and social order. The first priority was to free Germany from Napoleonic rule, but after that, Jahn advocated a fundamental change in the political and social structures within the boundaries of the German Bund that was splintered into numerous separate states. On the political level, he envisioned the creation of an all-German empire; on the social level, he favored the transfer of power from the hereditary to the appointed nobility. These conditions, he felt, should be laid down in a people's constitution guaranteeing free transition between the estates. The people were to be the prime movers of the state, and it would come of age as a nation through universal education.

By advancing ideas of this sort, and especially because they were linked to radical democratic *Burschenschaften* (student fraternities), which were then emerging,[3] Jahnian Turners were soon considered subversive. It was not long before the student fraternity movement split. In addition to the student fraternity at the University of Jena, which was quite moderate and propagated Jahn's way of thinking, a radical segment developed, manifesting itself mainly in the Gießen student fraternity, founded in 1815 under the leadership of the brothers Karl and Adolph Follen. Thus it did not take much to evoke repressive measures: When the reactionary writer, August von Kotzebue, was murdered by Carl Sand, a Turner and member of a student fraternity, both organizations were prohibited in the Carlsbad Decrees of 1819.

The ban of student fraternities and Turner societies led to their gradual radicalization. Thus the *Jünglingsbund* (Young Men's Association), founded by Karl Follen, sought to do away with the present constitutions and, for this purpose, called on its members to arm themselves.[4] And the *Burschentag* (Student Fraternity Conference) held at Stuttgart in 1832 passed the resolution: "From this point on, the purpose of student fraternities will be to bring about a revolution so as to liberate and unify Germany."[5]

In a parallel development, the Turner movement became more radical in the German Vormärz, especially after the Hambach Festival in May

1832, which served as a rallying signal for the political opposition.[6] Although the opposition could not agree on specific goals and, above all, the means to attain them, a common denominator was the demand for a unified Germany. When the prohibition of Turner societies was suspended in 1842, allowing members to travel to various regions for Turner festivities, where they could make contact with other groups without drawing much attention, these societies became a matrix of activity for all oppositional groups.

In this period, with new Turner societies springing up everywhere, the main change in the Turner movement manifested itself in the social composition of its members. Until 1819, the Turner movement had comprised primarily academics and secondary-school and university students; but subsequent to the lifting of the ban in 1842, there was a marked democratization of associational life, one that reflected the rise of bourgeois society.[7] It was especially members from the artisan and lower middle classes who rushed to the newly founded Turner societies. And with this, socialist thought found its way into the Turner movement for the first time.

The 1840s were marked by growing dissatisfaction among peasants, agricultural laborers, artisans, and journeymen. Poor harvests had resulted in famine and an increase in food prices; high taxes had brought on the ruin of the small holders, and emerging mechanization and industrialization made crafts increasingly difficult to maintain, so that artisans and journeymen were often forced to seek work in factories. The economic crisis of 1847 eventually turned into a "crisis of the social structure,"[8] showing clearly the inevitability of change of the economic and social order. It is hardly surprising that these years saw the emergence of terms like "the social question" or "socialism."[9] Early socialistic ideas were imported to Germany from foreign countries—mainly France—frequently by wayfaring journeymen. And it was the Turner societies, because they seemed so little deserving of suspicion, that became substitute institutions for political activity. Radical groups founded Turner societies or sought, often successfully, to politicize and influence already existing societies. When Turners from Heidelberg, for instance, came in contact with the neighboring Mannheim Turner Society (which was led by Gustav Struve and outlawed in 1847 because of tendencies felt to be threatening to the state authority), their activities became more and more politically oriented and radical. Struve propagated turning the "Turner societies into nurseries of democracy," and the Mannheim Turner, Karl Blind, elaborated: "The Turners are revolutionary. To achieve their goals, they must employ all means, open and secret, to ensure the good of the people."[10]

On the eve of the Revolution of 1848–49, the Turner movement was split into three factions: the apolitical Turners, who were essentially interested in physical training; the Jahn followers, who wanted to realize his ideas and preserve the monarchy in the way Jahn had advocated; and the republican Turners, who sought a complete overthrow of the existing political conditions.

In April 1848, at the Turner Convention in Hanau, the German Turner Association was founded. Although many societies—especially those from southern Germany—had pushed for a resolution for a democratic republic, the association declined to pass one. When, in July 1848, at the Second Turner Convention in Hanau, a new motion was turned down again, the disappointed republican Turners quit the newly founded association and formed their own Democratic Turner Association. The German Turner Association felt that its main task lay in preserving law and order. By contrast, when the National Assembly convened in St. Paul's Church at Frankfurt to draw up a new German constitution, the republican Turners placed themselves at its disposal to help carry out any resolutions that might be passed.

After the failure of the National Assembly, the armed Turner societies organized into militias. The Jahnian Turners formed citizens' militias for the preservation of order, while the radical southern German Turner societies—and notably the Hanau Turner Guard—armed themselves to take part in the revolution as a volunteer corps. Some of them fought side by side with the Besançon Column, composed primarily of artisans and journeymen and led by August Willich, a member of the *Bund der Kommunisten* (Union of Communists).[11]

When the revolution failed, emigration was the only alternative open to the republicans. Some fled to Switzerland or England; but as the American Constitution had already served as a republican model in St. Paul's Church,[12] most of them chose to emigrate to America, where they once again organized into Turner societies. Earlier attempts to found Turner societies in America had been unsuccessful.[13] By contrast, the Turner societies initiated exclusively by Forty-Eighters and founded up to the mid-1850s attracted a great deal of interest. And since only the radical group within the German Turner movement had emigrated and reunited in America—whereas the German nationalists had stayed at home—the societies were also very homogeneous. The first German-American Turner society was founded in Cincinnati as early as 1848; Friedrich Hecker was active in its creation. At the end of 1848 there followed the *Newark Turngemeinde*—composed of goldsmiths from Pforzheim and Hanau—and the *New York Turngemeinde*. The next Turner societies were formed by Forty-Eighters in Boston, Baltimore, Indianapolis, St. Louis, Chicago, Milwaukee, and a number of other cities. Many southern German Turners who had fought for a republican constitution in the Hanau Turner Guard under August Schärttner gathered in the *Socialistischer Turnverein* (Socialist Turner Society) in New York.[14]

In 1850–51—at the suggestion of the Socialist Turner Society in New York—a national organization, the *Vereinigte Turnvereine Nordamerika's* (United Turner Societies of North America), was established to ensure political effectiveness; at a meeting in Philadelphia in October 1851, its name was changed to *Socialistischer Turnerbund von Nord-Amerika* (North American Socialist Turner Association). Its basic goal was "the advancement of socialism and of the endeavors of the Social Democratic party."[15] By themselves, even the names of individual societies and of the Turner Association point to a specific political tendency in the American Turner movement, even though the frequent equation of "social," "socialistic," "social democratic," "radical democratic," or "communistic" indicates a certain vagueness. The Turner Association's demands included: "A democratic-republican constitution, the guaranteed welfare of 'all', the best possible and free education for all according to the individual's capabilities, the removal of all hierarchic and privileged powers."[16] The Turner Association was also quick to adopt a position favorable to the emerging labor movement. The *Turn-Zeitung* (Turner Newspaper), which first appeared in New York, explained that many Turner societies felt as though they were workers' societies anyway, since the majority of Turners were workers in the narrow sense of the word; thus both movements would have the same goals.[17]

At first, Turner societies oriented themselves back to their home country; they considered themselves a sort of reservoir for political refugees, a basis from which a new German revolution could be organized. During this period the idea of equipping themselves with arms played a major role, and Turners were especially active in taking up collections in support of new revolutionary uprisings, or for the defense of communists facing charges in German courts. In 1851, Gottfried Kinkel and Amand Goegg, representing two competing revolutionary groups, came to America on a fund-raising tour. Because of the competitive nature of the situation, the Turner Association declined to take a stand, but many influential Turners showed up at both their meetings. Kinkel appeared at the

Turner festival of 1851 in Philadelphia; Gustav Struve, Wilhelm Weitling, August Willich, Wilhelm Rothacker, Georg Hillgärtner, Friedrich Hecker, and Fritz Anneke were among those who took part in Kinkel's mass meeting in Cincinnati.[18] In his speech dedicating the new red flag of the New York Socialist Turner Society, Gustav Struve seemed confident that the near future would witness this banner being unfurled in a renewed fight for freedom in Germany.[19]

Not long afterwards, however, hopes of returning to Germany were shattered; at the same time, immigrant Turners became aware of the fact that the enthusiastic notions about America and its Constitution did not correspond to reality. Whereas most of the Germans who had immigrated earlier were drawn into the Democratic party, the Forty-Eighters—and with them the Turners—rushed to the Republican party when it was founded in 1854, because they shared its views on slavery, nativism, and temperance. The question of American slavery was discussed in detail at the 1855 Turner Convention. A vote resulted in sixty-three delegates for, nine against a resolution condemning slavery. In addition, nativism and temperance laws were newly included in the declaration of principles as deplorable social grievances that had to be opposed.[20] Prior to the 1856 elections, the *Turn-Zeitung* came out in support of the Republican candidate for the presidency, Frémont, praising him as a representative of working-class and immigrant interests. Turner conventions lent their official support to the Republican party in succeeding years as well, in the expectation that reciprocal support for Turner demands would be forthcoming.

The homogeneity marking the initial years of the Turner Association soon came to an end, however, as German immigrants who had not taken an active part in the revolution also flowed into Turner societies. As had formerly been the case in Germany, both groups were thus once again represented in the Turner movement. More and more, radical Forty-Eighters found themselves in the presence of apolitical or conservative Turners; the close-knit structure of the societies was lost. This is clearly reflected in changes in the *Turn-Zeitung*, the Turner Association's official organ. Originally, the association selected a society in a different city each year to assume the function of an executive committee and to edit the *Turn-Zeitung*. When it was printed under the auspices of the Socialist Turner Society in New York, the Turner organ assumed a strong Socialist tendency, which soon came under harsh criticism from several Turner societies. The open propaganda for socialist or communist ideas and goals—especially the writings of Joseph Weydemeyer,[21] V. W. Fröhlich, and Harro Harring—was widely condemned and repudiated. The Turner societies in Utica and St. Louis, for instance, approved of the *Turn-Zeitung*'s direction, while the Turner Society in Cleveland was its most outspoken critic; in November 1851, the *Boston Turngemeinde* left the association because of the attribute "Socialist" in its name.[22] When the newspaper moved to Philadelphia as the new seat of the executive committee at the end of 1853, the revolutionary tendency yielded to a more moderate and pragmatic policy, thereby reflecting the increasing conformity to America's political system among the membership. The radicals were thus subdued for a while.

The following years were marked by heightened tension within the Turner Association; several Turner societies accused each other of having betrayed their goals and furtively tried to work together with the Democratic party. These polemics, voiced mainly by the new executive committee in Cincinnati and the New York Socialistic Turner Society and resulting in the latter's suspension, reflect an increasing undermining of radical principles. The dispute was ignited by the Turners' position on slavery. A large portion of the Turners were convinced that the only way to abolish the abominable institution was by forming a solid coalition with the Republican party. It is noteworthy that the most radical of all societies, the New York Socialistic Turner Society, was suspected of having made a pact with the Democrats and joined the proslavery side. While being edited by Otto Reventlow, the *Turn-Zeitung* purposely stirred up the controversy and contributed to the embitterment between the opposing factions. Reventlow was in contact with the Communist Club, founded in 1857 by Forty-Eighters in New York. Its goals were to promote religious freedom and socialist ideas.[23]

As a result of these controversies, in 1856 the Turner Association split into an eastern and a western alliance, both of which pursued the same goals and had almost identical constitutions. But the eastern alliance—contrary to the wishes of Friedrich Hecker—only rejected unequivocal support for the Republicans, calling instead for influencing members through education; however, it did not want to give in to demands of other groups that they stay out of politics altogether.[24] At this time there could be no more doubt that the Turner movement in the United States had assumed the same sort of heterogeneity it had displayed in Germany. Membership was no longer limited mainly to workers and artisans, but rather increasingly tended to reflect the whole social spectrum. The diversified interests represented in the Turner Association now made radical resolutions impossible; the immediate result of these changes was a decline in radical demands in the political program.

Figure 10.1. Milwaukee Turner Hall in 1864. (Photo Courtesy of Milwaukee County Historical Society)

At the outbreak of the Civil War, Turner societies from both alliances formed Turner companies to fight against slavery, benefiting from their experience gained in the revolutionary years in Germany and the sharpshooter sections that already existed in many Turner societies. With the founding of the Socialist Turner Association, societies had been obliged to arm themselves, and later such a move was at least strongly urged. Seeking to help train Turner societies uniformly in regular military discipline, the executive committee published Franz Sigel's "Drill Regulations" in 1852–53.[25] The enthusiastic participation in the Civil War and the coalition with the Republican party opposing slavery indicate an increasing turn to American politics. And the fact that an American issue led to a split in the German-American Turner movement shows that American structures were assuming a far larger role, whereas former ideas and goals were fading into the background. At this point, the Turner movement had lost its original radical nature.

The end of the Civil War marked a new phase in the German- American Turner movement. The Turner associations, which by the end of the war only existed on paper anyway, regrouped and came together again in 1865 as the North American Turner Association. The appellation alone is indication of a deep-seated political change. From the beginning, in the hopes of preventing another split, the association tried to take all the various political views within the Turner movement into account, but at the cost of a loss of determination and clear direction, with increasing exposure to outside influence.

The end of the Civil War also saw the emergence of new conditions that the Turner societies could not ignore. The Turners were highly critical of Republican Reconstruction policies under Andrew Johnson, which left the South's political structure largely unaffected and thus failed to improve conditions among blacks. Losing faith in this party, Turners began to distance themselves from it. As early as 1867, the executive committee of the Turner Association, then located in New York, submitted a plan for the foundation of a party and drew up a "Platform for the National Association of the Independent Progressive Party"; at the time, however, it found little resonance within the North American Turner Association.[26] Although delegates at the 1867 Convention had already decided that the association could not officially endorse a party, links to the Republican party were preserved. It was not until 1874 that the Turner Association decided to withdraw support from both existing political parties. This was due to disappointment over the Republican party's having ignored its suggestions concerning the introduction of equal civil rights, a Reconstruction policy in keeping with the Constitution, general military service, unlimited immigration, and school reform. But the most decisive factor was doubtless the Republican party's stance toward temperance endeavors.[27] Nevertheless, the project of forming their own party—

discussed once more in the same year—was not realized. It was to have been the task of this party to guarantee freedom and oppose corruption.

In addition, rapid industrialization—bringing about extreme changes in political, economic, and social conditions—led to discussion of resulting social problems. As was the case with all ethnic associations and clubs, the Turner societies were influenced by the appearance of a new, rather apolitical generation, and by a new wave of German immigration, which in the 1870s and 1880s included many workers who had come in contact with the Social Democratic party in Germany. This antithetical mixture inevitably led to social and political tensions, again at first only latent, within the Turner Association.

On one hand, Turner societies had become more and more middle class, placing emphasis on their nonpolitical activities. They assumed a much stronger significance as places of relaxation and entertainment. Turner excursions, picnics, balls, and social evenings, as well as concerts and theater performances, came to the fore, while in the larger societies actual gymnastics and, especially, political debates, met with increasing disinterest. The Franco-Prussian War of 1870–71 and the subsequent establishment of the German Reich provided an additional impetus toward middle-class conservatism. The enthusiasm resulting from victory over France and the establishment of an all-German Reich led to a reorientation toward Germany. Even the Forty-Eighters joined in, since the creation of a united Germany corresponded to demands that both Jahn and the republican Turners had made prior to the Revolution of 1848–49. Thus the anti-Socialist legislation passed under Bismarck in 1878 was largely ignored by apolitical and conservative Turners as well as by former Forty-Eighters. Relatively few German-Americans judged this development critically. In 1873, Friedrich Hecker visited Germany and returned disappointed. Adolf Douai was unequivocal in his rejection of the new Germany, as was Karl Heinzen, whose Boston-based *Pionier* subsequently lost a large portion of its subscribers.[28]

On the other hand, there were Turner societies located in large industrial cities and whose membership comprised largely, or almost exclusively, workers. This was especially true in Chicago, where the *Aurora* and *Vorwärts* Turner Societies were opposed to the middle-class, conservative *Chicago Turngemeinde*. New socialist ideas from Germany found their way into the Turner Association via a wave of politically conscious workers, some of whom, forced to flee the anti-Socialist measures in Germany, joined working-class Turner societies upon their arrival in the United States.[29] The development and dissemination of such ideas were especially favored by the depression of 1873, which led to high unemployment, and by the general changes in living and working conditions resulting from industrialization.

Despite the heterogeneity of the Turner Association and the conservative or apolitical orientation of the majority of its members, radical reformist goals were nevertheless included in the platform and declaration of principles of the North American Turner Association. As a rule, the most prominent and politically active members of individual societies were sent to the national conventions as delegates. Most of them ranged from quite progressive to Socialist, and they generally managed to push through their ideas. The Turner Association consequently adopted a radical program; but because it was not absolutely binding, and because its realization was left up to the individual societies, its radical character was not very significant as far as actual activities were concerned. This also explains why the program met with only mild opposition from the conservative, middle-class element in the Turner Association, even though conservatives represented a majority of the members.

In the early 1870s, the discussion of social problems resulting from industrialization and the demand for an eight-hour day became central topics for the association. All subsequent conventions, both national and regional, discussed the association's relationship to the labor movement; within individual societies, this topic led to heated debates carried on by radicals and conservatives alike. Whereas the latter argued mainly in terms of humanity and the improvement of living conditions, the Socialists who had immigrated in the 1880s—among them Victor L. Berger in Milwaukee, Julius Vahlteich in Chicago, and Gustav Schweppendieck in Long Island—wanted to fundamentally change the existing political and economic system. The radical wing was not, however, composed of a homogeneous group; thus, alongside the Socialists, there was also an anarchist and a radical-republican tendency.

Representatives of radical-republican persuasion—among them Karl Heinzen, Heinrich Huhn, and above all the Milwaukee Turner and freethinker, Carl Hermann Boppe (whose influence on the formation of the Turner Association's program was considerable)—still tended to advocate the old ideals of the Forty-Eighters. And though they sympathized strongly with practical Socialist demands, they definitely rejected a socialist, let alone communist, form of government. Despite far-reaching criticism of conditions in America, they held firmly to the existing democratic republic, which, they felt, simply needed to be reformed. The argument that took place at the 1884 national convention between C. H. Boppe and August

Spies (who would be executed in 1887 because of his involvement in the Haymarket affair) is indicative of the republican stance toward socialist, communist, and above all anarchist tendencies. As a member of the Platform and Statute Committee, August Spies—delegate from the Aurora Turner Society in Chicago—had tried to introduce a resolution into the platform of the North American Turner Association calling for the "socialization of the means of production." Boppe opposed Spies, the result being that this question was referred back to the individual societies for discussion.[30] Speaking at the convention, Boppe warned that one-sided communism was not possible, since it impeded all progress; communism, he said, should only be permitted if it existed alongside individualism.[31]

Notwithstanding, republican Turners and Socialists cooperated in many points. This manifested itself both in the Turner Association's reform program, and in coalitions with other groups. Especially noteworthy was the close cooperation between Turner societies and *freie Gemeinden* (free congregations). In the German Vormärz, the negative attitude of the established churches toward republican movements had led to a strong anticlerical stance within the Turner movement, and this tendency continued in the United States. It was clearly seen in 1878, when the Turner Association chose the Milwaukee-based *Freidenker* (Freethinker) as its new organ. But this decision also evoked considerable criticism from within the association, especially since an increasing tendency to cooperate with the Socialists was evident in the *freie Gemeinden*. It was especially in Milwaukee that the *Freidenker* was attacked by middle-class groups in local Turner societies; the opposition was led by Emil Wallber, later the mayor of Milwaukee, who unequivocally repudiated the political direction of the new organ.[32]

Although the freethinkers' programs went too far for a majority of the Turners, the radical wing in the Turner Association felt drawn to the *freie Gemeinden*, primarily because of their call for the restraint of church influence and for the establishment of nonconfessional schools. It was especially on the local level that the two organizations maintained official contacts. This was clearly reflected in the annual celebrations commemorating Thomas Paine, which were sponsored by *freie Gemeinden* and Turner societies in Milwaukee and other cities, and where—especially from the 1870s on—Socialists took part. Smaller associations, like the *Bund der Radikalen* (Union of Radicals), strongly influenced by Karl Heinzen and republican ideals of the Forty-Eighters, were commonly sustained by Turner societies and *freie Gemeinden*.

The Turner Association's collaboration with other groups, including the labor movement, always centered on a practical issue and never led to any long-standing affiliations. When confronting special problems like prohibition, blue laws, and other restrictions, short-term coalitions were sought. In this sense, social class never constituted the link—it was always a question of ethnicity. In 1878, a new basic program was drafted in reaction to urgent socioeconomic problems. Sent back to the individual societies for a vote, the so-called Cleveland Platform made general statements about the association's intentions and listed twenty-three separate political, social, and economic demands meant to eliminate concrete grievances. The platform essentially called for a constitution that would allow for both a referendum and a recall of government representatives who abused their offices, the abolition of all ecclesiastical privileges and all monopolies, reforms in the area of fiscal law and judicial administration, general compulsory education; it also offered suggestions for solving the labor question. Resolutions five to nine read as follows:

> As appropriate means to suspend the state of distress and ameliorate social conditions, the Convention recommends: Protecting workers from exploitation, and safeguarding their real earnings. Sanitary protective measures by governmental controls of factories, foodstuffs, and lodgings. Statistical enquiries into working conditions by the government. The prohibition of exploiting child labor for industrial purposes. The suspension of all further land donations and sales to individuals as well as corporations. Public lands must remain in the inalienable possession of the people, and only allocated to real cultivators under reliable conditions.[33]

With this, the North American Turner Association passed a program almost identical, in essential matters, to the practical demands made by the Social Democrats. Cooperation with radical and Socialist groups was therefore made possible, at least in certain areas.

The Turner Association was also swept up in the eight-hour movement. Turner societies had already begun discussing this question in the early 1880s; at the 1886 national convention, a corresponding demand was included in the association's platform, and was to be submitted to a written inquiry in the same year. Measures were also taken to inform people about this topic. The *Amerikanische Turnzeitung*, the association's official newspaper, which had been appearing in Milwaukee since 1885, printed articles dealing with the eight-hour question, and a pamphlet written by the Social Democrat H. W. Fabian, entitled "The Social Question and the Eight-Hour Movement,"[34] was recommended to Turner societies as a

Figure 10.2. This lithograph by Louis Kurz of Milwaukee from the early 1860s shows the members of the Madison, Wisconsin, Turner Association. It is just one example of numerous similar presentations, which apparently were in vogue from the 1860s to the 1880s.

basis for discussion. In addition, the Turner organ reviewed the "The Eight-Hour Normal Workday," a brochure that the national executive committee of the Socialist Labor party had commissioned Alexander Jonas to write.[35]

At the same time, the votes held on the platform of 1878 and on the eight-hour question in 1886 reveal strong resistance to the association's Socialist inclinations. The societies in small towns and those in the big cities, which tended to be composed of middle-class members, rejected such programs. This, coupled with the indifference to the association's platforms, explains the relatively close vote in favor of these demands.[36] The votes that were decisive for passing the resolutions came on the one hand from the older Turner societies in the East (above all in New York and Boston), which had always leaned strongly toward the Socialists, and on the other hand from those Turner societies in big cities that had high proportions of working-class members (such as the *Aurora* and *Vorwärts* Turner Societies in Chicago). By contrast, most of the small-town Turner societies rejected the proposals.

With the 1886 Haymarket affair, the tensions between middle-class and Socialist Turner societies—reflected in the voting results just discussed—erupted. Especially in Chicago, the positions adopted toward the anarchists by individual Turner societies led to a realignment within the Turner movement. Conservative and progressive Turners, many of whom had until then competed with each other within individual societies, now split apart and organized their own societies,[37] so that confrontations no longer took part within, but rather between, Turner societies. The fact that this did not lead to a split in the national association is an indication that although it set guidelines, the actual activities took place on the local level, and it was also there that battles over policy were conducted. It did, however, lead to a crisis within the association, set off by the Social Democrat Julius Vahlteich. A member of the middle-class *Chicago Turngemeinde*, Vahlteich had always tried, as he wrote in the preface to a published speech held in his society, to explain his ideas to people who were either "indifferent or hostile to socialism."[38] Following a dispute with conservative members, Vahlteich was expelled from the society in 1891; his objection to this measure was sustained by the district executive committee. When the *Chicago Turngemeinde* refused to readmit him, it was expelled from the North American Turner Association. At that point, three more middle-class conservative Turner societies in Chicago—the *Central Turnverein*, the *Südseite Turngemeinde*, and the *Germania Turnverein*—left the association and founded the National Turner Alliance, which did not, however, last very long.[39] Subsequent to the expulsion or resignation of the four Turner societies, the Chicago district assumed a more pronounced Socialist position. Meanwhile the remaining districts in the Turner Association were marked by more or less visible policy struggles.

In Chicago, especially, the period after Haymarket witnessed a close-knit coalition between Turner societies and Socialist organizations opposing repressive measures directed by the authorities against Socialists. Similar to the republicans in the German Vormärz before them, the Socialists first gathered in Turner societies until the organization of their own political party was once again feasible. After Haymarket, Socialists seeking refuge joined Turner societies, but this also led to a dilution of previously held radical views. In 1897, Michael Schwab, one of the anarchists to receive a pardon, complained:

When the police campaigns started, radicals all fled to Turner societies and similar associations. And there they stayed and were turned into good bourgeois. The Turner societies became somewhat more radical, but the price for it—the crippling of socialist associations—was much too high. I myself am on the executive committee in Chicago's largest Turner society and was a delegate to the national convention, I know of what I speak.[40]

In 1901, official delegates from Chicago's Turner district went to Indianapolis to take part in the founding congress of the Socialist party of the United States.[41]

In Milwaukee, there was also a close connection between Turner societies and the Social Democratic party, which was founded in 1897 by Victor Berger, a member of the "South Side Turner Society." Like the city's Turner societies, the Social Democratic party concentrated on municipal reforms and adopted a pragmatic, moderately Socialist course. This coalition reached its short-lived climax in April 1910, when Emil Seidel was elected Milwaukee's first Socialist mayor.[42]

At the beginning of the twentieth century, however, when the Socialists created their own labor and political organizations, the coalition with the Turners lost its close-knit coherency. This became more and more apparent as Turner societies dwindled into purely social organizations. With World War I and the pressure exerted on Socialists and German culture in general, this connection practically ceased to exist. Merging completely with Anglo-American culture, Turner societies gradually abandoned their original ideals.

NOTES

1. Until now, the only extensive work on German-American Turner societies concentrates solely on the institutional and programmatic development of Turner organizations in America without addressing the way these programs were actually realized on the local level: Horst Ueberhorst, *Turner unterm Sternenbanner* (Munich, 1978). Some works on the Turner movement in Germany also describe its emigrant development up to the American Civil War, above all Klemens Wildt, *Auswanderer und Emigranten in der Geschichte der Leibesübungen* (Schorndorf near Stuttgart, 1964), and Hannes Neumann, *Die deutsche Turnbewegung in der Revolution 1848–49 und in der amerikanischen Emigration* (Schorndorf near Stuttgart, 1968). Other short studies address primarily the significance of the Turner movement for the Forty-Eighters in America, above all Augustus J. Prahl, "The Turner," in *The Forty-Eighters: Political Refugees of the German Revolution of 1848*, A. E. Zucker, ed. (New York, 1950), 79–110, and Carl Wittke, "The Turner," in his *Refugees of Revolution* (Philadelphia, 1952), 147–160. For the most important developments within the German-American Turner movement, see Heinrich Metzner, ed., *Jahrbücher der Deutsch-Amerik.*

Turnerei. Dem gesammten Turnwesen mit besonderer Berücksichtigung der Geschichte des Nordamerikanischen Turner-Bundes gewidmet, 3 vols. (New York, 1892–94).

2. Friedrich Ludwig Jahn and Ernst Eiselen, *Die Deutsche Turnkunst* (Berlin, 1816; Friedrich Ludwig Jahn, *Deutsches Volksthum* (1810; repr. Leipzig, 1817).

3. In a sense, the organization of *Burschenschaften* (student fraternities) can also be traced back to Jahn. In 1812, he and his assistants, Karl Friedrich Friesen and the Jena professor, Heinrich Luden, drafted the *Burschenschaftsordnung* (student fraternity regulations). See Wolfgang Meyer, ed., *Die Briefe Friedrich Ludwig Jahns* (Leipzig, 1913), 52. The student fraternities adopted the colors that the Lützow Volunteer Corps had in the German Wars of Liberation, black, red, and gold, the symbol for a unified German Reich.

4. Meyer, ed., *Briefe*, 283; see also Karl-Alexander Hellfaier, "Die politische Funktion der Burschenschaft von ihren Aufängen 1814 bis zum Revolutionsjahr 1848 an der Universität Halle—Wittenberg," *Jahrbuch für die Geschichte Mittel- und Ostdeutschlands* 12 (Berlin, 1963): 128.

5. Karl Obermann, *Deutschland von 1815 bis 1849* (Berlin/East, 1976), 102.

6. In response to a call, representatives of the most varied oppositional movements gathered at Hambach Castle in 1832 to discuss political goals and means of achieving them.

7. For the significance of societies in Germany, cf. Thomas Nipperdey, "Verein als soziale Struktur in Deutschland im späten 18. und frühen 19. Jahrhundert," in *Geschichtswissenschaft und Vereinswesen im 19. Jahrhundert*, H. Boockmann et al., eds. (Göttingen, 1972), 1–44.

8. Wolfram Fischer, "Staat und Gesellschaft Badens im Vormärz," in *Staat und Gesellschaft im deutschen Vormärz 1815–1848*, Werner Conze, ed. (1962; repr. Stuttgart, 1978), 168.

9. Werner Conze, "Das Spannungsverhältnis von Staat und Gesellschaft im Vormärz," in Conze, ed., *Staat und Gesellschaft*, 248.

10. Quoted in Neumann, *Die deutsche Turnbewegung*, 17 and 21.

11. For the volunteer corps, see Karl Geisel, *Die Hanauer Turnerwehr. Ihr Einsatz in der badischen Mairevolution von 1849 und der Turnerprozeß* (Hanau, 1974); Neumann, *Die deutsche Turnbewegung*, 43–49; Karl Obermann, "Zur Zusammensetzung einiger Freischaren in der Revolution von 1848–49, *Jahrbuch für Wirtschaftsgeschichte* IV (Berlin/East, 1973): 125–45.

12. Cf. Eckhardt G. Franz, *Das Amerikabild der deutschen Revolution von 1848–49. Zum Problem der Übertragung gewachsener Verfassungsformen* (Heidelberg, 1958).

13. Karl Beck, Franz Lieber, as well as Karl Follen, who had earlier founded the *Jünglingsbund* (Young Men's Association), all tried to establish Turner organizations in America. For their efforts see esp. Wildt, *Auswanderer*, 49–51; Neumann, *Die deutsche Turnbewegung*, 58ff.; Ueberhorst, *Turner unterm Sternenbanner*, 18–22.

14. See Heinrich Metzner, "Die Turnvereine des Nordamerikanischen Turner-

bundes," *Jahrbücher der deutschamerikanischen Turnerei* 1, No. 2: 87–92; No. 3: 142–44; No. 4: 185–90; No. 5: 225–29; also see Neumann, *Die deutsche Turnbewegung,* 118–36; for information about the founding members, also see Wildt, *Auswanderer,* 106–8.

15. "An die Turnvereine der Vereinigten Staaten Nord-Amerika's," *Turn-Zeitung* (Cincinnati) No. 2 (Feb. 1851): 18f.

16. "Sozialismus und Turnerei," in Metzner, *Jahrbücher* 1, No. 4: 147 (reprint from the *Turn-Zeitung* of 1851–52). The Turner society founded in Milwaukee in 1853 on the initiative of August Willich was first called the "Milwaukee Social Turner Society"; it was renamed "Milwaukee Turner Society" in 1855.

17. "Turner und Arbeiter," *Turn-Zeitung,* April 1, 1853, 185f.

18. Metzner, *Jahrbücher* 1, No. 3: 100–106; Wittke, *Refugees,* 99ff.; Neumann, *Die deutsche Turnbewegung,* 87f; Eitel W. Dobert, "The Radicals," in Zucker, ed., *The Forty-Eighters,* 157–70.

19. *New Yorker Staatszeitung,* 23 Aug. 1851; quoted in Wittke, *Refugees,* 95.

20. "Verhandlungen der Turner-Tagsatzung zu Buffalo, vom 24. bis 27. September 1855. Im Auszuge herausgegeben vom Vorort." Also see Metzner, *Jahrbücher* 1, No. 6: 255–78.

21. For Weydemeyer, see Karl Obermann, *Joseph Weydemeyer. Ein Lebensbild (1818–1866)* (Berlin/East, 1968).

22. Neumann, *Die deutsche Turnbewegung,* 79–81; Metzner, *Jahrbücher* 1, No. 4: 154.

23. William Frederic Kamman, *Socialism in German American Literature* (Philadelphia, 1917), 25. For the dispute within the Turner movement, see among others Heinrich Huhn, "Die Spaltung und die Wiedervereinigung des Turnerbundes," *Amerikanischer Turner-Kalender,* 1890: 24–35.

24. See "Verhandlungen der Turner-Tagsatzung in Bloomingdale, N.Y., am 26. und 27. September 1858, im Auszuge herausgregeben vom Vorort Williamsburgh."

25. Cf. the convention minutes for the corresponding years. For the role played by Turner societies in the American Civil War, see esp. Metzner, *Jahrbücher* 3, No. 2: 62–71.

26. See Metzner, *Jahrbücher* 3: 159–62, 167f., 226, and 244; also see Heinrich Metzner, *Geschichte des Turner-Bundes* (Indianapolis, 1874), 94.

27. See esp. "Offizielles Protokoll der Verhandlungen der 3. Tagsatzung des Nordamerikan. Turner-Bundes. Abgehalten zu Boston, vom 3. bis 6. Mai 1868"; "Der Vorort des Nordamerikanischen Turnerbundes an die Turnvereine Amerika's" (1865); also see Metzner, *Jahrbücher* 3: 148f.

28. Wittke, *Refugees,* 356.

29. For class-conscious workers forced to emigrate because of the Anti-Socialist Law, see Hartmut Keil, "Deutsche sozialistische Einwanderer in den USA im letzten Drittel des 19. Jahrhunderts: Lebensweise und Organisation im Spannungsfeld von Tradition und Integration" (Habilitation thesis, University of Munich, 1985), 126–84.

30. "Elfte Tagsatzung des nordamerikanischen Turnerbundes," *Turn-Zeitung. Beilage zum Freidenker,* 15 June 1884, 11. Cf. also "Autobiography of August Spies," in Philip S. Foner, ed., *The Autobiographies of the Haymarket Martyrs* (New York, 1969), 70f.

31. "Autobiography of August Spies, 70f.; cf. also C. H. Boppe, "Die demokratische Republik im Gegensatze zu Communismus und Anarchismus," *Freidenker-Almanach,* 1889: 99–116; "Sociale Reformpolitik in der Republik," *Amerikanischer Turner-Kalender,* 1894: 92–110.

32. See "14. Bezirks-Tagsatzung des Wisconsin Turn-Bezirks," *Turn-Zeitung. Beilage zum Freidenker,* 21 July 1878: 10f.

33. "Die Platform des Nordamerikanischen Turnerbundes," *Freidenker,* 16 June 1878: 1.

34. Originally it centered around a lecture held at the New York Turner Society, where Fabian was a member, entitled "The Turners and the Eight-Hour Movement." Excerpts were printed in the *Amerikanischen Turnzeitung (AMTZ)* after the speech appeared in pamphlet form. (*AMTZ,* 14 March 1886, 1; reprinted in the *AMTZ* 18 April 1886, 1, and 25 April 1886, 1).

35. *AMTZ,* 28 March 1886, 4; cf. also Keil, "Deutsche sozialistische Einwanderer," 389.

36. For individual voting results on the eight-hour question, see *AMTZ,* 14 Nov. 1886, 8; for the 1878 platform see "Resultat der Urabstimmung über die Platform und die principiellen Beschlüsse der Clevelander Tagsatzung, 1878," *Turn-Zeitung. Beilage zum Freidenker,* 8 Dec. 1878 to 2 Feb. 1879.

37. For splits within organizations and the founding of new ones, see *Chicago und sein Deutschthum,* German-American Biographical Publ. Co., ed. (Cleveland, 1901–02), 90f.

38. *Ein Beitrag zur Lösung der socialen Frage,* Chicago, 1888.

39. Theodor Janssen, *Geschichte der Chicago Turn-Gemeinde* (Chicago, 1897), 75f. In 1892 the four Turner societies were readmitted to the North American Turner Association.

40. Michael Schwab to Hermann Schlüter, 4 June 1897, Kleine Korrespondenz, International Institute of Social History, Amsterdam, quoted in Keil, "Deutsche sozialistische Einwanderer," 394.

41. Keil, "Deutsche sozialistische Einwanderer," 395.

42. See Marvin Wachman, *History of the Social-Democratic Party of Milwaukee 1897–1910* (Urbana, IL, 1945), 41ff.

CHAPTER 11

Radical German-American Freethinkers and the Socialist Labor Movement
The *Freie Gemeinde* in Milwaukee, Wisconsin[1]

BETTINA GOLDBERG

L ocal *freie Gemeinden* (free congregations) and freethinker associations represented one of the organizational forms found among
radical German-Americans in the second half of the nineteenth
century. Founded and shaped by political refugees of the Revolution of
1848–49, these organizations sought above all to counter the influence of
religion and church through education and enlightenment and thus to
work toward the creation of a democratic society that was politically as
well as economically just. Compared with the Turner movement, also
founded by immigrant Forty-Eighters, the freethinkers remained a small
group—but one that maintained its radical character into the twentieth
century and tended increasingly to view the Socialist labor movement as a
political ally.

In this respect, the *Freie Gemeinde* of Milwaukee, founded in 1867 by
intellectuals, artisans, and small-businesspeople, represents a typical example. Politically committed to the ideas of the petit-bourgeois democratic Left of the German Vormärz and organizationally embedded in the
liberal-minded German-American associations in Milwaukee, the
Gemeinde initially looked upon the emerging Socialist organizations with
disapproval. Despite substantial agreement on individual questions, it
strove above all to maintain its ideological distance. But from the late
1880s onward, and increasingly after the turn of the century, there is evidence of a gradual shift on the part of the radical freethinkers toward the
Socialist movement, notably the Social Democratic party in Milwaukee.
On March 31, 1917, commemorating the fiftieth anniversary of the *Freie*

Gemeinde, the *Vorwärts* (the central organ of the Social Democratic party) wrote: "The German Socialists have always maintained good relations with the *Freie Gemeinde*; several of them have been actively involved in it. And now the 'Vorwärts' also salutes the fiftieth anniversary."

This essay will discuss the *Freie Gemeinde* of Milwaukee and its changing relationship to the Socialist labor movement. It will first treat the philosophical basis for and the sociopolitical roots of German-American free thought in Vormärz and revolutionary Germany and the early development of the free-thought movement in pre–Civil War Milwaukee. The main section will focus on the late 1870s and the 1880s, one of the prime periods of German-American free thought. After considering organizational structure and membership trends, as well as the objectives and activities of the *Freie Gemeinde* of Milwaukee, it will analyze how the sociopolitical notions of the freethinkers differed from Socialist positions, and where points of contact between the two movements—which would later allow for their rapprochement—existed. A detailed account of this rapprochement and the practical effects it had, under what circumstances, and for what reason it occurred—these issues are central to the last section, which sketches the development up to World War I.[2]

GERMAN ROOTS OF GERMAN-AMERICAN FREE THOUGHT

German precursors of the German-American freethinker organizations developed in the early 1840s. These forerunners were the Protestant *Lichtfreunde* (Friends of Light), a group that originated as a faction within the church; the free-Protestant congregations, which emerged from this group and were independent of the church; and the "German-catholic" congregations, which were dissident from the outset. They represented the rationalist-oriented theologians' answer to attempts on the part of conservative circles in Protestant as well as Catholic churches, in alliance with the state, to ban theological rationalism from the church and to ensure that neo-orthodox theology was the sole and compulsory dogma, thus hoping to revive religion as a means of social control. Under the alliance of ecclesiastical orthodoxy and a restorative state, oppressive measures were soon directed against dissident religious groups. Contrary to expectations, however, these measures, instead of intimidating dissident groups, tended rather to assist their popularization: In some regions in

Germany, an oppositional movement arose, supported by large portions of the urban middle class, which was no longer satisfied with internal church reforms but increasingly began submitting the political and social conditions to a rationalist critique.[3] In 1847, there were already over 250 local congregations with a membership of well above one hundred thousand; the majority were in Silesia and Saxony, the centers of religious dissent.[4]

Ideologically, rationalism remained the theological basis for most of the free-Protestant congregations; moderate liberalism, the political foundation. However, many of the German-catholic congregations, under the influence of early Hegelian religious critique—especially the writings of Ludwig Feuerbach—broke with Christianity completely. They developed from denominationally independent religious societies committed to religious freedom and the restoration of the Christian church into purely secular associations, which no longer strove for freedom within, but rather freedom from, the Christian religion as a precondition for both individual and social progress. Congregational life was secularized; Christian customs were either entirely eliminated or at least reinterpreted in the sense of secular ethics and replaced or supplemented by forms of petit-bourgeois sociability. Convinced that comprehensive education and enlightenment could free people from ignorance and religious superstition and thus create the conditions for political and social change, the congregations gave priority to educational work.[5]

This group of religious dissenters was in political sympathy with the republican democratic wing of the Vormärz oppositional movement. During the revolutionary years of 1848–49, many congregation members were active in forming democratic and workers' associations and took part in the uprisings in Berlin, Vienna, and southwest Germany. Neither the proletarianized intellectual spokespeople nor the congregation members—the majority of whom were urban artisans and traders threatened by pauperization—felt that sovereignty of the people would be accomplished by the removal of the monarchy and the creation of a parliamentary system. Rather, they advocated a system, modeled after the radical-democratic organization of their congregations and associations, which, incorporating the principle of direct democracy in all social areas, would limit state power by self-government on the part of the citizens.[6] The model developed by Adolf Douai in the *Volkskatechismus der Altenburger Republikaner von 1848* (People's Catechism of the Altenburg Republicans of 1848) can be viewed as representative of the political aspirations of the free-congregation movement's radical wing. Douai pro-

posed an egalitarian society based on petit-bourgeois property relationships, where "as much prosperity, freedom, and education as possible"
would be granted to everyone.[7] Douai's democratic republic "was on the
one hand directed against the old feudal-bureaucratic system, on the other
against capitalist development; it was antihierarchical and anticapitalist, it
excluded vast property as well as lack of property."[8]

As it became increasingly clear that the Revolution was about to fail,
German-catholics and free-Protestants again withdrew into their congregations. Convinced that the people's immaturity—prejudices in religious
attitudes and thought—were primarily responsible for the Revolution's
failure, they considered it their most urgent task to intensify educational
work in the congregations.[9] But the attempt to outlast the restoration period as free religious societies failed. By the mid-1850s at the latest, the
congregations had either been prohibited as political associations or undermined by an ingenious system of police infiltration. Radical intellectual spokespeople found themselves in an especially precarious situation.
In order to escape political persecution, many of them had already left
Germany toward the end of the 1840s. For those who had remained—and,
suspended from their positions as priests, ministers, or teachers, were dependent on the congregations—it became increasingly difficult to earn
their living. Since the greatly weakened congregations found it more and
more difficult to support them, and since the remaining opportunities to
earn a living—by giving private lessons, for instance—had been eliminated by the authorities, they were forced either to enter new occupations
or, like those before them, to emigrate.[10]

THE GERMAN-AMERICAN FREE-THOUGHT MOVEMENT
IN PRE-CIVIL WAR MILWAUKEE

Regarded as the epitome of an ideal democracy by left liberals of the
Vormärz,[11] the United States became the favorite destination for the persecuted representatives of the free congregations as well as other Forty-
Eighters. When confronted with an American reality that corresponded
so little with their expectations, some of these immigrants withdrew from
political and social life altogether. Others, in contrast, did not resign
themselves when confronting American nativism and political corruption, racism, and slavery, as well as the influential position enjoyed by religion and church, but felt challenged to continue the educational work

aimed at restructuring social and political relationships in their new homeland.

As was the case in Germany, the birthplace of this work was the *freie Gemeinde*. In the early 1850s, more than forty free congregations were founded: in New York, Boston, and Philadelphia, and especially in the Midwest, the center of German mass immigration. In addition, so-called *Freimänner-* and *Freifrauenvereine* (Free Men's and Free Women's Societies), initiated by the Austrian Forty-Eighter Friedrich Hassaurek, sprang up in many places; their goals hardly differed from those of the *freie Gemeinden*. Through lectures, debates, and the founding of independent schools, they sought to "stem on the one hand the rising tide of the clergy's ever-increasing interference and its efforts to limit freedom, and on the other indifference and intellectual stagnation."[12]

Milwaukee's first *Freie Gemeinde* was formed in August 1851 on the initiative of Eduard Schroeter, the former speaker of the German-catholic congregation in Worms. Like many others, it evolved from a free-Christian congregation dedicated to theological rationalism. A visible sign of secularization was the replacement of the ministry by a paid speaker, whose task was to hold regular lectures on historical and philosophical topics as well as to give instruction in ethics for children and young people. However, Heinrich Loose, Schroeter's successor as speaker of the *Gemeinde*, resigned from the post in 1853, when it came under strong attack for being a relic of "the priesthood" by the *Verein Freier Männer* (Free Men's Society), which had been founded in 1852. Because it had merged with the local *Arbeiter-Bildungs-und Lese-Gesellschaft* (Workers' Educational and Reading Society), an organization originally founded by artisans and intellectuals to further consumer and production cooperatives, the *Verein Freier Männer* gained more importance. For a time it had several hundred members and was significantly larger than the *Freie Gemeinde*, which numbered approximately one hundred people. After Loose's renunciation of the speaker's post had made cooperation between the two organizations possible, they merged in May 1854 to form the *Verein der Freien* (Association of the Free).[13]

Because of the predominantly local character of American society, but also as a result of the principle of sovereignty among individual congregations, the local organization represented the actual basis of German-American free thought. But from the beginning, there were also endeavors to unite the various congregations, or even all German-American organizations with "free-thought" tendencies, nationally or at least statewide. It is in this context that one should consider the convention organized by the *Freie Gemeinde*, the *Verein Freier Männer*, and the *Sociale Turnverein* (Social Turner Society). Held in Milwaukee in October 1853, sixty-three delegates representing twenty-three associations in Wisconsin met and formed the *Bund freier Menschen* (Union of Free People). Whereas similar conventions in Kentucky and Ohio passed far-reaching social and political reform programs, in Wisconsin the delegates were able to agree only on the demand for complete separation of church and state. Political differences—not limited to the slavery question—broke out between the radical Forty-Eighters and the immigrants of the 1820s and 1830s, who were oriented toward the Democratic party and who were primarily represented through the lodges. As a result, the union—which had gathered around the motto, "Strength through Unity!" —existed solely on paper and, without ever having formally disbanded, disappeared a year later.[14]

The *Verein der Freien* was in desolate straits, too, and finally broke up in the late summer of 1855.[15] This was brought about by various factors. First, internal battles between different factions had prevented the formulation of positive objectives that went beyond the negation of church and religion. Another factor was the founding of the Republican party, which, for a while at least, became the new political home for many Forty-Eighters and freethinkers. A further cause for the decline of organized German-American free thought, observable in other places as well, lay in the fact that in the United States, in contrast to Germany, an antireligious movement did not attract much attention per se, and thus there was "no strong external force, no decided opposition to crystallize the movement."[16] In addition, a differentiated network of German-American clubs and organizations had come into being, especially in the cities, and as they tended to be anticlerical anyway, they were thus well suited to absorb those Germans who might otherwise have turned to the free congregations. The generally friendly relations between these organizations does not obscure the fact that there was also much competition.

RADICAL GERMAN-AMERICAN FREE THOUGHT AND THE SOCIALIST MOVEMENT IN THE LATE 1870S AND 1880S

Free thought received fresh impetus in the second half of the nineteenth century, along with further developments in the natural sciences and their increasing social significance, with the popularization of positivism and empiricism as well as the dissemination of Darwin's and Haeckel's evolutionary theories. It did not evolve into a widespread antichurch movement, and especially the overwhelming majority of German immigrants remained—at least in appearance—linked to religion and church. The altered atmosphere could be felt, however, in a growing religious indifference as well as in a militant anticlericalism reflected both in the Socialist movement and in the founding and revival of independent freethinker organizations.[17]

In Milwaukee, a new *Freie Gemeinde* was formed in April 1867. It was organized as a secular association along radical-democratic lines and, according to the principle of equal rights, accepted men and women who had turned nineteen.[18] In comparison with other German-American organizations like the Turner societies, the *Gemeinde* always remained relatively small. According to the *Freidenker*, there was an average of 176 members from 1877 to 1890, a minute number if one considers that more than half of Milwaukee's population was of German descent. The range of activities of the *Gemeinde* was not, however, limited to the circle of its members. Moreover, though it was small, the *Gemeinde* nevertheless proved stable: It appears to have been the only freethinker organization that—while maintaining its German-American character—existed well into the 1960s.[19]

Owing to a lack of membership lists, the social composition of the *Gemeinde* cannot be reconstructed in detail. But with the help of the *Freidenker* and older city histories it is, in fact, possible to establish the occupations of half the people in the executive body from 1877 to 1890. To draw conclusions about all the members from such a small group would be inadmissible, especially since certain social groups might have been over-represented on the executive level. The strong representation of intellectual or semi-intellectual professions (sixteen of the twenty-five identified executive members) can be traced back to the marked educational self-concept of the *Gemeinde*. Another eight executives were fairly prosperous businesspeople, artisans, and small entrepreneurs, which is not surprising since the *Gemeinde* was eager to involve its more affluent members in official activities. Together, especially in the beginning, these two groups apparently made up a large part of the membership. But it seems that increasing numbers of workers also joined the *Gemeinde*. Among those executive members who could be identified, there was only one worker. But since the biographical sources are generally distorted in favor of the "successful," it is quite possible that some of the other people who were only referred to by name may also have belonged to the working class and that this group was also represented on the official level.[20]

The *Gemeinde* saw itself as a union of freethinkers dedicated to combating all "religious views based on a strong belief in authority" by propagating a "world view and philosophy of life based on reason and science." It believed its main task was to enlighten the public by holding regular Sunday lectures and evening debates, as well as by publishing pamphlets and the weekly newspaper, *Freidenker*.[21] Since the multifaceted educational program of the *Gemeinde* was not directed primarily toward its own members—they had already given proof of their enlightenment by joining—but rather was conceived for a broader German-American audience, all events were open to the public and free of charge. Whereas the lectures covered more fundamental topics, the debates focused on current social, economic, and political issues; to prepare for the debates, seven German and American newspapers were subscribed to by the *Gemeinde* library.[22]

The *Gemeinde* Sunday school was conceived as a corrective to the public school system, which the freethinkers felt was free of church influence in form but not in substance. Nonmembers could also send their children free of charge. Children from six to sixteen years old were to be led, "in progressive steps, from instruction in playing, singing, physical exercise, and visual observation to true ethics," that is, to the scientific and philosophical foundation of free thought. Thus, they would be enabled to participate later in the regular *Gemeinde* events. In the 1880s, the school was attended by an average of 116 pupils.[23]

Education in its narrow sense took up only part of the *Gemeinde* activities. The stabilizing function of the social gatherings can hardly be overestimated; depending on the season, there were "afternoon entertainments," dances and balls in the *Gemeinde* hall, or local excursions, mostly combined with picnics. In addition, most of the members belonged to the Women's Club, the Singing Society, or the Dramatic Reading Section of the *Gemeinde*; the latter two societies saw their activities as a contribution to the cultivation and dissemination of the German *Lied* and of classical and modern German literature. The "Social Advancement Club," an English-speaking section for younger members who were no longer in command of German, was formed relatively late, not until 1923.[24]

The celebrations commemorating "important people and events" functioned as a mediator between the educational and enlightening objectives of the *Gemeinde* and its claims to culture and entertainment. Every year the anniversary of the founding of the *Gemeinde*, the Fourth of July, and George Washington's and Thomas Paine's birthdays were celebrated. The celebrations commemorating Thomas Paine were held within a larger framework; they represented a link between the *Freie Gemeinde* and Milwaukee's other liberal-minded organizations. They were carried out in cooperation with the local *Musikverein* (music society), the Turner societies, and with educators from the German-English Academy and the Teachers' Seminary who were organized in the National German-American Teachers' Association. These educators also supervised the *Gemeinde* Sunday school and often made themselves available for the *Gemeinde* as lecturers. In the late 1870s and 1880s, organizers also included the local Anglo-American freethinker associations, such as the "Liberal League" and the "American Secular Union," with which there seemed to have been only little contact otherwise.[25]

In Thomas Paine, the German and Anglo-American freethinkers saw one of the most important pioneers in the struggle for religious and intellectual freedom, political equality, and economic justice. They honored him as the symbol of a politically and religiously enlightened America. Thus the celebration of his birthday was more than an occasion for biographical and historical reflection: By remembering him, they were also criticizing conditions in the United States and advocating religious, political, and social reforms. Following speeches in German and English and diverse cultural performances, the so-called Declarations of Principles were passed; prepared by a committee consisting of representatives from all participating organizations, they summed up relevant current issues.[26] Sometimes there were disputes between representatives of the *Freie Gemeinde* and members of the Milwaukee section of the "Social Democratic party"—later known as the "Socialist Labor party"—which was also among the sponsors of the Paine celebration for a few years.[27] The controversies reveal basic ideological differences between the radical-democratic wing of the freethinker movement and the Socialist German-American labor movement. The latter could not gain as strong a foothold in the Milwaukee *Gemeinde* as it did, for instance, in the Chicago free-thought congregations, which were formed from the late 1880s onwards. This can be explained partly by the fact that the *Freie Gemeinde* in Milwaukee was founded at a time when the process of industrialization had hardly started and Socialist organizations had only just begun to take shape.[28]

The first public dissociation from Socialist objectives occurred in 1876, when C. H. Doerflinger purchased the free-thought weekly, the *Freidenker*. It had been edited for two years by Joseph Brucker, an ardent Lassallean and member of the Milwaukee section of the International Workingmen's Association, and during this time it had lost many of its subscribers. In his introductory editorial, Doerflinger stated that the goals of the *Freidenker* would remain the same as before—with respect to religion and morals, the insistence on scientific materialism; with respect to politics, the creation of a democratic republic; and "with respect to social problems, the striving toward the greatest possible happiness for the greatest number of the people." As to the means of attaining these goals, however, the newspaper would follow a different course from that of its previous editor. In the future, the notions of eliminating the system of wage work and of nationalizing the means of production would be rejected, "because these hinder the free development of individuality" and "as a consequence would engender an anticultural communism."[29] A similar position was advocated by the Swiss-born C. H. Boppe, who assumed the editorship of the *Freidenker* in 1877 and also belonged to the executive committee of the *Freie Gemeinde* until his death in 1899. Boppe edited the newspaper according to the principles of the *Bund der Radikalen* (Union of Radicals), which, founded in Philadelphia in 1876 through the initiative of Karl Heinzen, considered itself a continuation of the confederations of free Germans of the 1850s.[30]

Boppe and other freethinkers close to the *Bund der Radikalen* complained that the Socialists, by preaching class struggle and asserting the necessity of labor parties, had failed to grasp the character of a republican system. As opposed to an aristocratic or a monarchical system, there was no class antagonism in a republic; everything could be straightened out without violence or revolutionary acts. There was nothing wrong, Boppe felt, if people working in different industrial branches joined together in unions representing their specific interests; but if a separate labor party as such sought to take over the government, that was not acceptable. The worker, too, would have to attain his rights with the people and through the people. Granted, the argument continued, there were some people even in the republic—notably the big "monopolists"—who would try to get rich at the expense of the general public; but the majority of the populace consisted of working people, and they had to see to it that the small minority of social parasites was stopped by the law. As soon as the people freed themselves from the dictates of professional politicians who were only out for themselves, and once they were determined to make use of their rights of self-government, the general welfare would be the ultimate goal of all politics and all legislation, and a free, economically just society—with neither excessive wealth nor crass poverty—would result. Therefore the decisive prerequisite for social change was not class struggle, but rather the development of a political consciousness.[31]

However, to reduce the relationship between radical freethinkers and the Socialist labor movement to basic ideological disputes and differences would not do justice to the facts. When it came to daily political practice, the Socialist parties' ultimate goals—rejected by the freethinkers as "communistic"—were less important than their concrete suggestions for gradual economic and social reform. And to a large degree, the freethinkers could sympathize with such suggestions: progressive taxation and land reform, freedom to organize, protective labor legislation, minimum wages and the eight-hour day. These and similar reform measures seemed appropriate steps to remedy the most basic social grievance that, they felt, was threatening the republic's very existence: the widening gap between rich and poor.[32] They were in agreement in other areas, too, notably municipal educational policy. Here, the German-American freethinkers and Socialists not only promoted their ethnic agenda of German language, gymnastics, and art instruction in the curriculum, but also vehemently demanded strict secularism and the expansion of the public school system, a democratically elected school board, and free textbooks.[33]

All ideological differences notwithstanding, the radical freethinkers were sympathetic toward the Socialist parties. This was primarily because of their programmatic proximity in short- and medium-range reform proposals; but it must also be seen as the consequence of a deepseated disappointment in the policies of the established parties. Both parties, the Democratic and the Republican (the latter still having attracted many radicals in the 1850s), were regarded by the freethinkers as "spoils parties," devoid of principles, corrupt puppets of the monopolies. And in spite of all skepticism, the freethinkers saw the emerging Socialist parties as the embodiment of the people's dissatisfaction with existing power relations and of the claim to realize self-government.[34] Whenever there were attacks from conservatives, the freethinkers supported the Socialists, though they never stopped posing critical questions. They also maintained this stance in 1886, when, after the strikes for an eight-hour day and the Haymarket bombing in Chicago, a campaign was launched against anarchist and Socialist movements. The freethinkers distanced themselves from anarchism; but at the same time, they condemned the repressive measures employed by the state, which reminded them of Bismarck's Anti-Socialist Law in Germany, if not indeed of Russian despotism. Police persecution of labor leaders, the trials, the fines and prison terms, the agitation for the expulsion of those who held other political convictions and for a stiffening of immigration and naturalization regulations—all, according to the freethinkers, amounted to little more than an attempt on the part of the old parties to intimidate the people and thus protect their position of power, which had already begun to crumble. To the freethinkers, it hardly seemed surprising that conservative Germans were supporting the Democratic and Republican parties: "In time, the masses of workers, inspired by Social Democratic ideals will . . . be won over to reasonable progressive policy in the Republic, but worshipers of the Kaiser and venerators of Bismarck will always form a coalition with any and all reactionary forces, even if nativist xenophobia is at the bottom of them!"[35]

FURTHER DEVELOPMENTS UP TO WORLD WAR I

In the late 1890s, and even more in the first two decades of the twentieth century, a further approach is discernible on the part of the *Freie Gemeinde* in Milwaukee toward the Socialist movement, namely the local Social Democracy under Victor Berger. This is clearly illustrated by the *Freidenker*'s generally positive assessment of Social Democratic policies, but it also manifests itself in increased cooperation between the *Freie Gemeinde* and local Socialist sections, especially in the organization and presentations of the celebrations commemorating Thomas Paine, the Paris Commune, and the Haymarket anarchists.

From the mid-1890s onward, these celebrations almost always took place in the *Freie Gemeinde* hall. Even if, at the beginning, the *Gemeinde* was not the official sponsor of the Commune and Haymarket anarchists celebrations, many of its members took part in shaping the accompanying cultural programs. Reciprocally, the *Sozialistische Männerchor* (Socialist Men's Choir) and the *Sozialistische Liedertafel* (Socialist Choral Society) participated in the annual Thomas Paine celebration, as well as in other *Gemeinde* events. A new quality was attained when, in 1917, given the circumstances brought about by World War I, the *Freie Gemeinde* and the local German sections of the Social Democratic party jointly called for the commemoration of the victims of the Chicago labor movement on November 11, and when, two years later, in January 1919, the *Freie Gemeinde* invited Heinrich Bartel—editor of the Social Democratic *Vorwärts*—to hold the German speech at the Thomas Paine commemorative celebration.[36]

Figure 11.1. Freethinkers' Hall in Milwaukee on Fourth Street. (Photo Courtesy of Milwaukee County Historical Society)

Rather than interpreting the movement of the *Freie Gemeinde* toward the Social Democratic party as an ideological reorientation, it should be seen in the context of the comparatively moderate direction of the Social Democracy in Milwaukee, whose policies aimed at limited reforms and tried to attract a broader spectrum of the population. In the spring of 1898, when—just one year after being founded—the Social Democratic party put up candidates to run for local elections in Milwaukee for the first time, the freethinkers had tended to be somewhat skeptical. C. H. Boppe had judged that parties like these came and went; and besides, although the party platform contained reasonable demands, there were also elements far too Utopian to be practicable.[37] As the overwhelming victory of the Social Democrats in the municipal elections of 1910 demonstrates, however, the party had succeeded in the following decade in becoming recognized as a consistent advocate of a reliable and efficient municipal policy, independent of private business interests and oriented toward the needs of the population. The *Freidenker* commented on the election results as a victory for Eduard Bernstein and revisionism and as proof that Milwaukee had taken the right path, one that should serve as an example for Social Democrats in other cities as well. Like the Social Democracy in Germany before it, the commentary continued, the Milwaukee Social Democracy also understood that it was a political reformist and people's party—not a labor party stressing revolution and class struggle—that could lead to a gradual change in social conditions.[38]

More than ever before, the *Freie Gemeinde* was inclined to view the Socialist movement as a potential ally. But this can be only partially explained by the reformist position of the Social Democracy in Milwaukee, which was similar to the freethinkers' own ideology. Just as important was the fact that many of the organizations with which the freethinkers traditionally kept close contact were gradually shedding their radical character, and hence the liberal-minded milieu in which the *Gemeinde* had been situated was being eroded. In February 1912, on the occasion of the inauguration of Engelmann Hall—named after the founder of the German-English Academy—the *Freidenker* criticized the representatives of the National German-American Teachers' Association for having gone out of their way to avoid mentioning the freethought conviction and politically radical stance of the old Forty-Eighter, Peter Engelmann.[39] Shortly thereafter, freethinkers had to deal with the Teutomania in which the Teachers' Association and many of the Turner societies were increasingly caught up.[40] There were repeated complaints that the Turner associations' activities were limited to sociability and physical training, while the republican tradition of "intellectual gymnastics" had become a thing of the past.[41] When the Republicans and Democrats, running on a common ballot, succeeded in preventing another Social Democratic victory in the city elections of 1912, the *Freidenker* attributed this primarily to the unprincipled electoral conduct of a large portion of liberal-minded Germans: The Turners, especially, should have been unanimous in their support for a continuation of Social Democratic power, since Social Democracy had always been in agreement with the principles and resolutions of the Turner Association. Instead, the *Freidenker* continued, many of them decided to slander the most honest government Milwaukee had ever had and to play the role of the executioner for big capital and the Catholic church.[42] In 1919, Heinrich Metzner, one of the pioneers of the North American Turner Association, also expressed his disappointment in the Turner societies. Formerly, he said, the Turner societies had walked hand in hand with the free congregations and stood up frankly for their ideals. By contrast, he felt, they were now tame; though they had their gymnastic successes, these had been attained in a lamentable manner, namely at the expense of progressive ideas.[43]

While the majority of the Turner associations were becoming de-politicized, or were swinging toward the middle-class camp after the turn of the century, the *Freie Gemeinde* in Milwaukee was not only preserving its anticlerical character but was also remaining true to its radical political objectives. A *Freidenker* polemic against the German-American National Alliance reads as follows:

> Does [the National Alliance] ever think . . . if only once in a while, of the working class? The wage-slaves? . . . hundreds of thousands of Germans are among these wage-slaves . . . Why not at least reach out a hand to them when they strike or go to the polls? Because it is afraid of being counted among the Socialists! Well, that wouldn't be such a pity, and a lot more honest than . . . reaching out a hand to re-actionary elements![44]

In its relationship to the labor movement, Milwaukee's *Freie Gemeinde* differed not only from those German-American organizations that had become conservative; it had also developed in different directions from the free congregations and free-thought societies in the German Reich. There they had undergone political polarization, and finally, after the turn of the century, the free-thought movement had split into two different camps: one middle-class and the other proletarian-Socialist. In Milwaukee, the *Freie Gemeinde* neither distanced itself from the Socialists—as was characteristic of the middle-class free-thought socie-ties in Germany—nor did it become—as did Germany's proletarian free-thought associations—a part of the Socialist movement, a cultural organization operating as a front for the Social Democrat or Communist parties.[45] Instead, it had remained an anticlerical society with radical-democratic objectives. Nonetheless, it felt closely bound to the local So-cial Democratic party, and some of its members also belonged to this party. To what degree immigration or the different sociopolitical contexts played a role in the different developments experienced by the German and German-American freethinkers can adequately only be answered by a comparative study.

NOTES

1. The essay is based in part on the author's *Staatsexamen* thesis, "Deutsch-amerikanische Freidenker in Milwaukee 1877–1890: Organisation und gesell-

schaftspolitische Orientierung," submitted to the University of Bochum in 1982. Copies can be found at the Milwaukee County Historical Society and the Max Kade Institute for German-American Studies, Madison, WI.

2. For a long time, the free-thought movement received hardly any attention from historians. By now, however, there are independent studies on the free-thought movement in Vormärz Germany (see note 3); on the proletarian freethinker organizations in Germany since the turn of the century, see especially Jochen-Christoph Kaiser, *Arbeiterbewegung und organisierte Religionskritik. Proletarische Freidenkerverbände in Kaiserreich und Weimarer Republik* (Stuttgart, 1981); and on Anglo-American free thought, see Marshall G. Brown and Gordon Stein, *Freethought in the United States. A Descriptive Bibliography* (Westport, CT, 1978). With the exception of a few articles—see for instance Berenice Cooper, "Die Freie Gemeinde: Freethinkers on the Frontier," *Minnesota History* 41 (1968): 53–60; N. J. Demerath and Victor Thiessen, "On Spitting against the Wind: Organizational Precariousness and American Irreligion," *American Journal of Sociology* 71 (1965–66): 674–87; J. J. Schlicher, "Eduard Schroeter the Humanist," *Wisconsin Magazine of History* 29 (1946): 319–32, 435–56—German-American freethinkers, by contrast, are at best considered within the context of research on the Forty-Eighters, and then mostly only peripherally; see for instance Carl Wittke, *Refugees of Revolution. The German Forty-Eighters in America* (Westport, CT, 1970); A. E. Zucker, ed., *The Forty-Eighters. Political Refugees of the German Revolution of 1848* (New York, 1950); Sr. M. Hedwigis Overmoehle, "The Anti-Clerical Activities of the Forty-Eighters in Wisconsin 1848–1860: A Study in German-American Liberalism" (Ph.D. diss., St. Louis Unversity, 1941). Much of the information on the *Freie Gemeinde* in Milwaukee is based on contemporary material, especially on a systematic evaluation of the *Freidenker*, a weekly that began appearing in Milwaukee in 1872. Since there are neither congregation minutes nor membership lists for the period treated here, the representation is necessarily incomplete.

3. Cf. Jörn Brederlow, *"Lichtfreunde" und "Freie Gemeinden." Religiöser Protest und Freiheitsbewegung im Vormärz und in der Revolution von 1848–49* (Munich, 1976); Friedrich Wilhelm Graf, *Die Politisierung des religiösen Bewußtseins. Die bürgerlichen Religionsparteien im deutschen Vormärz: Das Beispiel des Deutschkatholizismus* (Stuttgart, 1978); Catherine Magill Holden, "A Decade of Dissent in Germany: An Historical Study of The Society of Protestant Friends and the German-catholic Church, 1840–1848" (Ph.D. diss., Yale University, 1954).

4. Brederlow, *"Lichtfreunde,"* 50–62; Helmut Hirsch, "Carl Heinrich Marx als Prediger der Krefelder Deutschkatholiken (1847–1851)," *Archiv für Sozialgeschichte* III (1963): 119–37; the quote is on p. 136.

5. See Holden, "Decade of Dissent," 269–70; Brederlow, *"Lichtfreunde,"* 51, 54, 66–72; Annete Kuhn, "Die Provokation des Friedens und der religiöse Sozialismus der Deutschkatholiken," in *Theorie und Praxis historischer Friedensforschung* (Stuttgart, 1971), 35–104.

6. See Kuhn, "Die Provokation," 68–95; Brederlow, *"Lichtfreunde,"* 76–80, 83–96; Günter Kolbe, "Demokratische Opposition und antikirchliche Bewegung im Königreich Sachsen" (Ph.D. diss., University of Leipzig, 1964), 50–102.

7. Quoted in Brederlow, *"Lichtfreunde,"* 88f. Because his revolutionary writings had led to several prison sentences, Douai (1819–1888) immigrated to the United States in 1852. There he worked as a pedagogue and journalist and was active in the abolitionist movement; after the Civil War he joined the German-American Socialist movement; cf. Zucker, ed., *Forty-Eighters,* 288.

8. Brederlow, *"Lichtfreunde,"* 90.

9. Brederlow, *"Lichtfreunde,"* 99–111.

10. Brederlow, *"Lichtfreunde,"* 112–14; Kolbe, "Demokratische Opposition," 140ff.; for the repression of the free congregation movement, cf. especially Ferdinand Kampe, *Geschichte der religiösen Bewegung der neuern Zeit,* vol. IV (Leipzig, 1860), 206–369.

11. See Eckhart G. Franz, *Das Amerikabild der deutschen Revolution von 1848–49. Zum Problem der Übertragung gewachsener Verfassungsformen* (Heidelberg, 1958), 104–8, 134–38.

12. C. F. Huch, "Die freireligiöse Bewegung unter den Deutschamerikanern," *Mitteilungen des Deutschen Pionier-Vereins von Philadelphia* 11 (1909): 1–33; see especially p. 8ff.

13. See Rudolph A. Koss, *Milwaukee* (Milwaukee, 1871), 314, 336, 366, 399–400; Schlicher, "Eduard Schroeter," 174–75, 181; Kathleen Neils Conzen, *Immigrant Milwaukee, 1836–1860: Accommodation and Community in a Frontier City* (Cambridge, MA, 1976), 178f.

14. Conzen, *Immigrant Milwaukee,* 179f.; Koss, *Milwaukee,* 404f.; the platforms of the various associations are reprinted in Overmoehle, "Anti-Clerical Activities," 303–6, 309–13, and *Jahrbücher der Deutsch-Amerikanischen Turnerei* 1 (1892): 241–48.

15. Conzen, *Immigrant Milwaukee,* 180.

16. William Frederic Kamman, *Socialism in German American Literature* (Philadelphia, 1917), 53f.

17. Freethinker societies and free congregations were formed in cities including San Francisco, Indianapolis, Washington, D.C., and (from 1888 on) in Chicago; cf. *Geschichtliche Mittheilungen über die Deutschen Freien Gemeinden von Nord-Amerika. Ein Gedenkbuch des fünfundzwanzigjährigen Bestehens der Deutschen Freien Gemeinde von Philadelphia* (Philadelphia, 1877), 63–71; see also *Freidenker (FD),* 29 July 1917, 1–2).

18. *Verfassung der Freien Gemeinde von Milwaukee* (Milwaukee, 1878), esp. sec. 4. An evaluation of *Gemeinde* elections based on reports in the *Freidenker* showed that between 1877 and 1890, nine of the forty-nine executive members were nevertheless women; for the printed commitment to equal rights for women in the political sphere, see, for instance, "Männerrechte oder Menschenrechte," *FD,* 12 Dec. 1882.

19. See Paul A. Kaufmann, "The First Hundred Years," *Voice of Freedom/Das Freie Wort,* April 1967 (the successor publication to the *FD* published by the *Gemeinde*). As is the case with all other statistical information, the membership figures were taken from reports in the *FD* on the *Gemeinde* general assembly held each year in May; according to Berenice Cooper, the *Gemeinde* was able to basically maintain its membership figures during succes-

sive decades after 1890: "Die Freien Gemeinden in Wisconsin," typescript, the State Historical Society of Wisconsin, Madison, 19.

20. For particulars see the biographical index of *Gemeinde* executive members in Goldberg, "Deutsch-amerikanische Freidenker," Appendix IIIc.

21. *Verfassung*, sec. 2–3.

22. *Geschichtliche Mittheilungen*, 64ff. In 1877, the lectures and debates, generally announced in the *Freidenker*, were attended by an average of eighty people. Most of the speakers were members of the Milwaukee *Gemeinde* or of other free-thought societies. Typical lecture topics were, for instance, "Knowledge and Faith" and "The School, the Church, and the State"; see Goldberg, "Deutsch-amerikanische Freidenker," Appendices IIId–e.

23. *FD*, 19 Aug. 1877 ("Die Sonntagsschule der Freien Gemeinde"), 7 Jan. 1883 ("Notizen"), 24 April 1887 ("Mahnworte").

24. *FD*, 2 Jan. 1887, 5; *Geschichtliche Mittheilungen*, 66; *Freie Gemeinde of Milwaukee: Dedication Souvenir Jefferson Hall* (Milwaukee, 1928), "*Freie Gemeinde* Collection" of the Milwaukee County Historical Society.

25. For the Paine celebrations, see each year's first February issue of the *FD*. The fact that there was hardly any collaboration between German and Anglo-American freethinkers—despite their internationalist self-image—seems not to have resulted from ideological differences or problems of language, but may rather be interpreted as a consequence of cultural and historical differences. Although the celebrations of Independence Day and Washington's and Paine's birthdays demonstrate that the *Gemeinde* strove to adopt Anglo-American democratic traditions, it was nevertheless much more firmly anchored in the culture of German-American free thought, and it was there that it primarily sought its contacts.

26. See the reports in the *FD*; in addition, Mark O. Kistler, "German-American Liberalism and Thomas Paine," *American Quarterly* XIV (1962): 81–91; Sidney Warren, *American Freethought, 1860–1914* (New York, 1966), 110ff.

27. In 1877, 1881, 1883, and 1885–87; more on the controversies further below in the text; see also "Der 29. Januar," *FD*, 2 Feb. 1877.

28. Thus the Milwaukee section of the International Workingmen's Association was founded in 1874; the Workers' Union and the Labor party, in 1876, i.e., seven and nine years respectively after the founding of the *Freie Gemeinde*; see Thomas W. Gavett, *Development of the Labor Movement in Milwaukee* (Madison, 1965), 27ff.; for the free-thought congregations in Chicago, cf. *FD*, 11 Nov. 1917, 5–6.

29. "An die Leser," *FD*, 5 Nov. 1876; for Doerflinger, see "Chas. H. Doerflinger starb heute früh," *Milwaukee Germania*, 9 Nov. 1911; for Brucker, see Gavett, *Development*, 28ff.; Jos. Brucker, "An die Leser des 'Freidenker'," *FD*, 5 Nov. 1876.

30. See the obituary for C. H. Boppe, *FD*, 22 Jan. 1899, 4–5; for the Union of Radicals: C. F. Huch, "Die Konventionen der Freigesinnten im Jahre 1876," *Mitteilungen des Deutschen Pionier-Vereins von Philadelphia* 23 (1911): 1–18; *Geschichtliche Mittheilungen*, 83–87 (Union platform).

31. Cf. "Gegen Klassenkampf und Klassenbewußtsein," *FD*, 27 Oct. 1878; "Gewaltrevolution und Republik," *FD*, 3 April 1887; "Gesellschaftsretterische Anstrengungen," *FD*, 15 May 1887; "Notizen," *FD*, 15 Jan. 1888.

32. "Individualismus, Socialismus, Communismus," *FD*, 2 May 1886; "Zur Achtstundenbewegung," *FD*, 7 March 1886; see also the platform of the Union of Radicals in *Geschichtliche Mittheilungen*, 83–87.

33. See, for instance, "Die Weltlichkeit unserer Volksschule," *FD*, 23 Nov. 1890 and "Der Kampf um die Schule," *FD*, 6 April 1890 (the controversy centering around the so-called Bennett School Law in Wisconsin); "Der Schulrath in seiner neuen Zusammensetzung," *FD*, 25 April 1897; also Huch, "Konventionen," 4; William J. Reese, "'Partisans of the Proletariat': The Socialist Working Class and the Milwaukee Schools, 1890–1920," *History of Education Quarterly* 21 (Spring 1981): 3–50.

34. "Unsere städtischen Wahlen," *FD*, 28 March 1886; "Die Allianz der alten Parteien," *FD*, 22 May 1887; "Gesellschaftsretterische Anstrengungen," *FD*, 15 May 1887.

35. "Unterthanenseligkeit und Republicanerthum," *FD*, 16 Jan. 1887; see also "'Demokratie' und Anarchie," *FD*, 10 Oct. 1887; "Der 11. November," *FD*, 20 Nov. 1887.

36. See, for instance, "Zu Ehren von Thomas Paine," *FD*, 6 Feb. 1898; "Thomas Paine Feier," *FD*, 6 Feb. 1910; "Herrliche Feier," *FD*, 22 April 1917; "Vive la Commune!" *Vorwärts*, 21 March 1898; "'11. November'-Gedenkfeier," *Vorwärts*, 3 Nov. 1917; "Geistig-gemütlicher Abend in der Freien Gemeinde," *Vorwärts*, 25 Jan. 1919. In 1933 Heinrich Bartel became the editor of the *Freie Wort* (Voice of Freedom), published by the Milwaukee *Gemeinde*; see "Autobiographische Skizzen von Mitgliedern der Krankenkasse. I. Heinrich Bartel," *Solidarität. Offizielles Organ der Arbeiter Kranken- und Sterbe-Kasse der Vereinigten Staaten von Amerika* 41 (1946), 184.

37. "Bereits hat eine 'neue Partei' für die kommenden städtischen Wahlen einen Parteizettel aufgestellt," *FD*, 6 Feb. 1898; see also "Socialdemokratie von Amerika," *FD*, 27 June 1897.

38. "Der sozialdemokratische Sieg in Milwaukee," *FD*, 17 April 1910; for the evaluation of the German Social Democracy: "Und immer noch beschäftigt. . .," *FD*, 6 March 1898; for general works on revisionism and Bernstein, see Peter Gay, *The Dilemma of Democratic Socialism: Eduard Bernstein's Challenge to Marx* (New York, 1952); Carl E. Schorske, *German Social Democracy 1905–1917. The Development of the Great Schism?* (Cambridge, MA, 1955).

39. Otto Soubron, "Des Lehrers höchster Ruhm," *FD*, 25 Feb. 1912.

40. See, for example, "Zum neuen Jahre 1917," *FD*, 1 Jan. 1917; "Unser Standpunkt in der jetzigen Kriegslage," *FD*, 20 May 1917; see also Henry J. Schmidt, "The Rhetoric of Survival: The Germanist in America from 1900 to 1925," in *America and the Germans: An Assessment of a Three-Hundred-Year-History*, vol. II, Frank Trommler and Joseph McVeigh, eds. (Philadelphia, 1985), 204–16.

41. See, for example, "Editorielles," *FD*, 24 Feb. 1918; 17 March 1918.

42. "Zur politischen Lage in Milwaukee," *FD*, 14 April 1912; see also "Glossen zur Milwaukee'r Wahl," *FD*, 21 April 1912.

43. H. Metzner, "Turnerei und Fortschritt," *FD*, 15 June 1919.

44. "Das Protokoll der fünften Nationalbundkonvention," *FD*, 16 Jan. 1910.

45. For the split within the German free-thought movement, see Kaiser, *Arbeiterbewegung*, and Hartmann Wunderer, "Freidenkertum und Arbeiterbewegung. Ein Überblick," *Internationale wissenschaftliche Korrespondenz zur Geschichte der deutschen Arbeiterbewegung* 16 (1980): 1–33.

CHAPTER 12

"The Diluted Second Generation"
German-Americans in Music, 1870 to 1920

BERNDT OSTENDORF

One of the most crucial yet neglected groups in the history of American musical culture is that of second-generation German-Americans.[1] To be sure, there are countless books and articles on the formation of modern American music between the years 1870 and 1920. However, these studies pay little or no attention to the "ethnic factor" or to the bicultural position of its principal agents. American musicologists, with some justified pride, treat second-generation ethnics as Americans pure and simple, whose ethnic ancestry is at best incidental to their achievement.[2] Why should they not, when the agents themselves chose to keep a low ethnic profile: Walter Damrosch, second son of the German immigrant conductor Leopold Damrosch, begins his autobiography "I am an American musician." Perhaps the date of its appearance, 1923, may have triggered this defiant first sentence, but the sentiment is by no means unusual among typical members of this group. Indeed, ethnic traditionalists often took the second generation to task for betraying their parents' heritage. Julius Drachsler, one such ethnic filiopietist, wrote in the twenties: "The fatal disease gnawing at the vitals of the immigrant community is the diluted second generation," and Marcus Lee Hansen, himself the son of immigrants, beat his own breast: "Nothing can absolve the traitors of the second generation who deliberately threw away what had been preserved in the home."[3] To many American natives, this ethnic family quarrel must have seemed irrelevant. Why should proud Americans make anything of the fact that John Philip Sousa, who gave America's imperial era its marching music, is of Portuguese and Bavarian parentage? Is it really important to know that the songwriter

Gus Edwards was born Augustus Eduard Simon in Hohenzollern, Germany, and came to America as an eight-year-old boy? Why should historians drag the ethnics out of closets, which they themselves have chosen to seal? Conversely, is ethnic persistence or loyalty on the part of the second generation, which Drachsler and Hansen so emphatically insist on, the only litmus test of proper ethnicity? Must members of the second generation "think ethnic," openly and recognizably so, in order to be included in histories of ethnic groups? Must we find Bavarian traces in Sousa's music before we may consider him worthy of ethnohistorical attention? Historically more important is the question, what did this second generation do, what choices did it have, what compromises and fusions did it attempt, how did it negotiate between a variety of cultural alternatives? For this generation holds the key to an explanation of modern American musical culture.[4] An important part of the explanation lies in the manner in which its members managed to solve the problem of being a transitional group, both in terms of generational sequence and of American cultural development. They were instrumental in changing the formerly ethnic culture, founded by their parents, into a transethnic and new American culture.[5] Their situation was quite singular: Caught between the moribund old-world culture of their parents, which they may have loved or despised, and an unavailable or as yet unformed modern American culture, these second-generation German-Americans became either the founders of a previously nonexistent tradition or agents of cultural change. To achieve this end, they selected elements and components of a bicultural heritage, and with these they filled out the social space between family (Old World) and society (New World). The nature of their contribution to American music had something to do with the point in history when they entered the American scene. For the evolution of American musical culture unfolded within the framework of immigration, industrialization, and urbanization, in a period of transition and rapid social change. American culture had remained until 1850 relatively unified, but after 1870, due to the cultural consequences of modernization, it became increasingly segmented and fragmented along the lines of race, class, sex, and ethnicity. By the end of the century, there was a bewildering heterogeneity of agents, audiences, and cultural realms. On all levels, from popular to high musical culture, and in all contexts, as managers or creators of music, the second generation participated in shaping the new genres and institutions and in defining what is today considered the quintessentially American modernist musical tradition. Musically speaking, the melting pot worked so well that it has affected our historical memory: Today we would identify the

Figure 12.1. The title of this song by Gus Williams, one of the best-known vaude-ville performers in German dialect comedies, indicates the dialect gags on which this genre thrived.

minstrel show, the musical, Gershwin's music, and jazz as typical products of American culture. What to us today are American traditions would have appeared to the cultural custodians of 1920 as un-American intrusions.[6] In other words, it was the second generation that created the new culture, effected the change in the canon, and hence altered the course of musical history and with it our historical perspective. Indeed, its members ultimately became the new cultural custodians, unseating the older Yankee hegemony.

Between 1870 and 1930, America witnessed a segmentation of culture.[7] As we shall see later, the diverse segments were not, as perhaps in Europe, sealed off from each other along class lines. Not only did members of the upper class participate in vaudeville or workers go to concerts, there were in fact any number of ethnic conduits that perforated the class and cultural divisions in the larger second-generation peer group. But despite these numerous personal contacts, the structural divisions caused by the musical market grew deeper and the territorialization of realms continued: In the 1870s and 1880s, there was a consolidation of symphony orchestras in New York, Boston, and Chicago, effecting what one critic calls the "sacralization" of high culture.[8] In counterpoint, between 1880 and 1900 an unpretentious, low-class leisure industry evolved, a veritable entertainment racket represented by Keith and Albee's vaudeville empires. After 1890, a new type of music publishers entered the scene, who aggressively marketed a new type of sheet music in a symbolic street known as Tin Pan Alley. In that same period occurred a subtle change in the ethnic communities: Ethnic associations, such as singing clubs with names like *Harmonia* or *Liederkranz*, either turned into professional choirs with a transethnic, professional appeal or lost their second-generation clientele. In tune with this change was the founding after 1900 of professional schools of music, catering to both rich and poor, to workers and the middle class, to whites and blacks. Some of these institutions, such as the Institute of Musical Art (later the Juilliard School) or the Mannes College, are still with us. New cultural media emerged: Nickelodeons graduated into films, and the film industry ushered in a secondary network of new institutions; in photography, which had become a mere mass entertainment (made possible by Kodak's new film and the promise "you push the button, we do the rest"), a group of second-generation German-Americans self-consciously presented themselves as avant-garde modernists.[9] The mass entertainment market as well as its high cultural twin was drastically changed by the arrival of the record and the radio in the twenties. Lastly, a new American musical idiom, jazz, was born at this crucial juncture with a number of second-generation Germans officiating as midwives.[10] A large new sector of cultural services developed in all these areas, and at every crucial point we find second-generation German-Americans.

We may draw two conclusions: (1) The evolution of an American musical culture is not sufficiently explained by a number of studies of this or that agent and his or her work. (2) An important part of that history will remain vague if we ignore the ethnic factor. What is needed is an investigation of these transitional generational groups at large and across class lines as part of a process of simultaneous ethnicization and Americanization. Nor will it do to stop the investigation at the ethnic boundary, as does the otherwise useful *Harvard Encyclopedia of American Ethnic Groups*. If we were to take its portrayal of America's ethnic makeup as gospel truth, we would miss the most intriguing part of the story. As the *Encyclopedia* has it, America is made up of 106 discrete ethnic groups, all loyal to their sense of ethnicity and all of them Horatio Alger versions of a dream of pure pluralism.[11] Was there no contact between these groups? What happened to the melting pot? In the Harvard conceptualization of ethnicity, there is no room for the Irishman who takes a German wife, or for their son, who, adopting his mother's maiden name and adding a "Von" for style, becomes an important writer of German-type songs and waltzes—Harry Von Tilzer. No allowance is made for the assimilated German Jew from Baden, who by way of marrying a Bohemian Jew becomes re-Judaized. Their son studies music in Germany, marries an Englishwoman, adopts her cultural ways, and, by merging German operetta and English music hall, becomes a founding father of the American musical—Jerome Kern. Much is made of Victor Herbert's Irishness. No doubt his parents were Irish; yet, when his father died, his mother married a German doctor, and young Victor grew up in Stuttgart immersed in German music. He married a German singer and was brought to New York through the German-American network. There he joined the German music establishment, first as a cellist, later as a composer of American operettas. Eubie Blake, the black pianist, claims Herbert spoke with a thick German "stage accent." Where should he be listed? As Irish? There is no room for these "exceptions" in the storyline of pure ethnic descent, which has in recent years been so popular in ethnic studies. But were these musical ethnics exceptions? It needs to be said emphatically that in the story of American musical culture, these mixers and melters were the rule. They were at the center of the musical action in New York and, though attacked by both the loyal ethnic and the nativist Yankee, they ultimately prevailed. Yet, for all sorts of reasons, these cultural mixers remain outside the ethnic tunnel vision of recent scholarship.[12] Granted, they have contributed to their own invisibility, for often they hid their ethnic profile when facing the nativist public in what I have previously called a playful travesty of Americanization.[13] Granted also, these bicultural, ambivalent Americans often ignored the tacit boundaries between German and American culture; for they were sitting on the fence and were thus invisible to the scholar in search of undivided commitment. We will not find their names in the roster of the New York Schiller Society celebration of 1905 (which is reserved for the ethnic loyalists), and they are less likely to join rabid ethnic lodges, such as the Sons of Herman; they may even avoid the old-fashioned *Turnverein*. They were Americanized traitors indeed, but only of a narrowly defined, nostalgic ethnicity. Does this make them instant Americans? Not for the Yankee establishment, who eyed them with suspicion. Whereas the ethnic loyalists condemned the second generation as traitors, the nativists suspected them to be closet Germans, a distrust that emerged forcefully after 1916. Should we be surprised that the second generation studiously avoided being typecast in either facile category?

This essay is an attempt to reconstruct the musical cultural milieu of German-Americans between 1870 and 1920 in the large urban centers of America, primarily in New York. This is not easy, since the two world wars have become powerful, retroactive censors, which have revised the historical record in the memories of the participants, particularly when it came to writing autobiographies for the popular market. A powerful German musical establishment dominated popular and high culture in New York between 1870 and 1920. It was so powerful, in fact, that it led some people in the music business to change their names from English to German for reasons of marketability (from Clapp to Dockstader, from Gumm to Von Tilzer). Recently there has been a spate of books on many individual artists of this second generation. This essay will try to read these discrete histories back into a general social history of German-American music.

GERMANS WITH A MISSION: "SACRALIZING" THE CLASSICS

Scanning the available life histories and autobiographies of these musical first- and second-generation German-Americans, we notice that they fall into a recognizable pattern and that there are family resemblances. Among the first to enter the musical scene were high cultural Germans, who came to America inspired by a pedagogical mission. Their goal was to educate

America toward accepting a German notion of musical high culture. Often they welcomed American political democracy, but were shocked by its popular culture, and therefore they deplored America's devotion to "Yankee Doodle" or the "minstrel show." This group worked toward "sacralizing" high culture and toward carving out for its protection a sacred sphere far from the marketplace. Toward the end of the nineteenth century, this German musical Utopia found native support in the progressive demand for cultural uplift that caught on in the grant-giving Yankee establishment. Prominent members of this group were Anton Seidl, conductor of the New York Philharmonic, or Karl Muck, who founded and led the Boston Symphony Orchestra, which his benefactor Henry L. Higginson backed financially. Both arrived in America as adults late in the century. They had uncompromising standards and refused to give in to popular taste.

Theodore Thomas may be counted in this group. And yet his biography does not fit neatly into an upper class or high cultural pattern. He was born in 1835 in Esens, East Frisia, as son of the town musician—certainly not an auspicious beginning; Esens was a tiny, poor community and a *Stadtpfeiffer* (town musician) was as low in social status as in pay.[14] But his father put him on a severe training course, and he began playing the violin in public at age six. In 1845, the family emigrated to New York, where Thomas played for dances and weddings to help the family budget. At age sixteen he began touring the country as Master Thomas, offering in his program variations on "Home Sweet Home" or other popular favorites. Since he came from a poor background, he was acquainted with low-class popular styles and could have made a good living in that market. Yet, he yearned for pure, high culture and its music. Back in New York he became a member of the New York Philharmonic Society and in 1862 organized an orchestra for symphony soirees at Irving Hall, later at Steinway Hall, which ran until 1878. Thomas set out to create a proper audience through educational programs in a series of duly famous Central Park Summer Concerts. Although he included popular material in his programs, he did it only as an educational ruse and as a temporary compromise to draw an audience, which he then would educate. Up to the 1880s, he had to leave his base of operations, New York, for periodic national tours, often with small pickup orchestras, for the dual purpose of raising money and expanding his educational mission to elevate taste. Thomas set the foundations for quite a number of institutions, such as the Cincinnati Biennial Festival, which he conducted until his death in 1905, and the Cincinnati College of Music, of which he was president from 1878 to 1880. Before and after this tenure in Cincinnati, he was conductor of the New York Philharmonic Society or of his own symphony orchestra, which he shaped to conform to his own notion of excellence and artistry. Besides orchestral bodies he also conducted choral groups. From 1885 to 1887, he was conductor of the American Opera Company. In 1891, he finally settled in Chicago as conductor of the Chicago Orchestra, which he turned into one of the best American orchestras (next to the Boston Symphony and the New York Symphony under Leopold and Walter Damrosch). He was instrumental in creating, by public subscription, a permanent home for the Chicago Symphony—Orchestra Hall, which was formally opened in 1904, one year before his death. The influence of Thomas on classical music in America has been strong. Thomas favored Wagner, Liszt, and Brahms and was instrumental in changing the American canon and taste from French and Italian to German composers. But he also played for the first time in America works by Pyotr Ilich Tchaikovsky, Antonín Dvorak, Camille Saint-Saens, and C. V. Stanford. His death was caused by what seems to have been a combination of exhaustion and pneumonia. Thomas died without issue.

GERMAN JEWS AND MUSICAL INSTITUTIONS: THE DAMROSCH DYNASTY

In German musical life, there was a relatively prominent group of assimilated Jews without religious ties—high cultural Germans of German-Jewish background, often intermarried with Gentiles. They brought to America a historical memory of being a minority and of having successfully assimilated by joining the forces of modernization, enlightenment, and liberalism. They shared the sense of cultural mission with the aforementioned group but adjusted with greater ease to the priorities of an American political culture and therefore did not shy away from exploring the noisy marketplace. Although fully German in their preference for high culture, they came with a special set of attitudes: (1) a powerful sense of civic and social service and (2) a keen sense of the possibilities in forming secondary associations and institutions in tune with American political culture. In the wider context of Jewish secularization, music had filled the emotional and moral place previously occupied by religion and became a cultural or social gospel. This is the ideological underpinning of the musical heritage the Damrosch family brought to the United States.[15] In the prolific Damrosch dynasty, we find both first-

and second-generation participants sharing one cosmopolitan musical ideology.

The Damrosch family arrived in America at a somewhat later date than Theodore Thomas and on a secure financial basis. Leopold Damrosch was already a distinguished conductor before his emigration. Born of German-Jewish parents in 1832 in Posen, West Prussia, he studied law and medicine according to his parent's wishes but later defected to the world of music. He received an excellent education, which, after time spent in Weimar, allowed him to become conductor in Breslau, the regional capital of Silesia. He had by this time married Helene von Heimburg of Jever (a small town in the Grand Duchy of Oldenburg). The "von" identified her as a member of the regional minor nobility, known for its stern Protestant credentials. Since Leopold Damrosch had become thoroughly assimilated and secularized, the Heimburg heritage—its Northern German, Protestant customs and rituals—became the dominant family tradition. There was little consciousness in the family of being Jewish, and the question of "Jewish descent" arose only in response to a burst of anti-Semitic nativism in the twenties. A fear of professional deadlock and his disgust with the emerging jingoistic spirit following national unification made Leopold Damrosch leave Bismarck's Reich for the United States. He accepted the invitation of the New York Arion Society, one of the many German singing groups in the country. The Arion began in 1854 as an offshoot of the New York *Liederkranz* and, after absorbing the *Teutonia Männerchor*, had reached a point in size and sophisitication of its membership where the final step toward professionalization was in order. Therefore its leadership looked for a truly distinguished musical director. (This is an interesting instance of the inner logic of modernizing change in an ethnic institution.) For Damrosch, the appointment was both a demotion and a challenge: To work for a German *Liederkranz* was a step down in his professional career, yet the willingness of the Arion Society to reach out for professional status meant that he could rise with it. By the time of his resignation from the Arion in 1883, he had turned it into an excellent choir, had also founded the Oratorio Society for more ambitious singing projects, and had been guest conductor at New York orchestras. Damrosch had exhausted the usefulness of this German ethnic institution. For his family, the Arion Society had been a hospitable setting, serving not only as a culture broker but also as a decompression chamber facilitating adjustment to American ways. There were picnics, *Liederabende*, and social gatherings. The Arion, despite its aim for high cultural achievements, continued to be ethnically committed. However, in many ways the larger musical scene of New York had by this time become more German both in taste and composition. The New York Philharmonic had had a series of German conductors and its personnel had, by the end of the century, become Germanized: In 1842, 40 percent; in 1855, 79 percent; and by 1892, 97 percent of its players were of first- or second-generation German ethnic background. Thus by the time of Damrosch's resignation from the Arion Society, the market for German-style classical music had expanded considerably, and a new competitive spirit had arisen between him and Thomas, who saw in Damrosch a potent rival as musical prime force in New York. Typically, Thomas was defensive of his turf and believed New York could only house one truly superb orchestra; Damrosch thought otherwise. Although their taste in music was largely similar—both favored the trend toward Germanizing the canon and bringing Wagner to America—they could hardly have been more different in personality: Damrosch was small and lively, didactic and talkative, given to bursts of enthusiasm. His enthusiasm tended to inspire orchestras but also to make them nervous. Thomas was practical, taciturn, literal, a towering, solid father figure whom the players idolized. In short, Thomas had been first on the block and was Nordic; Damrosch arrived later and was Semitic, an outgoing upstart.

Damrosch scored a victory over Thomas when the New York Metropolitan invited him to introduce an all-German program for the season of 1884–85, thus giving him the chance of introducing Wagner to America. Before the successful season officially ended, Leopold Damrosch died from a combination of exhaustion and pneumonia. Damrosch's second son, Walter, who had assisted him all along, took over the baton without missing a beat and finished the season. Walter was barely twenty-three years old when he assumed his father's place. Born in 1862, he was only nine when the family arrived in the United States. The charge of being an upstart, of being a dilettantish youngster, would accompany him from here on. Walter's older brother Frank, though equally musical, had not wanted to follow in his father's footsteps and had begun a career in business far away in Denver. The sudden death of his father, however, brought him back to New York, and he assumed the directorship of the Metropolitan's choir. After finishing his father's season, Walter was asked by the directors of the Metropolitan to help find a new director and conductor for the New York Met. Walter went on a scouting trip to Germany and brought over Anton Seidl, a first-rate conductor of German opera, who would later become his archrival over the question of who had the right and musical authority (or maturity) to direct Wagner: For the first-generation Seidl, Walter Damrosch was a typical American dilettant. Frank Damrosch joined Walter on this talent hunt to look for new singers familiar with German opera. He found a Stuttgart soprano, Therese Förster, who brought in her wake a cellist husband. Förster would relocate to New York only if her husband was promised a job as well. Hence Walter, on Frank's request, hired Victor Herbert for the orchestra. (This was the entry into America of one of its chief composers of operettas and the beginning of a musical network that connects the Damrosch dynasty with the world of popular music.)

In order to shed the reputation of being an upstart and a dilettant, Walter took a private course in conducting with Hans von Bülow in Germany. On his return, he began a tradition for which he later would be best known in America: music education. To wit, Theodore Thomas had made the first large-scale attempt at elevating taste by improving the canon. But Damrosch went one step further and started a series of lecture recitals on classical masterpieces, which was enormously successful, particularly among young New York ladies who would later become the backbone of the musical world. At this time he began a lifelong friendship with Andrew Carnegie, who became his benefactor and a bit of a father figure. Through Carnegie, Walter met the family and daughter of Secretary of State James Gillespie Blaine. Margaret Blaine would become his wife in 1890.[16] This new access to money and politics gave Walter a type of power that Thomas or any of the other contenders lacked. Many members of the musical establishment found this coalition of old-world high culture and new-world money unsavory, if not disreputable. The *Musical Courier* in particular never let Walter forget that he had more influence than talent.

After the New York Philharmonic had shifted in 1884 from a French-Italian repertoire to a German one, a change for which they had enlisted the services of Leopold Damrosch, there was around 1891 a temporary French-Italian backlash that forced his son Walter to return to the lesser New York Symphony Orchestra and drove Thomas to Chicago. At this time, Damrosch made use of his Carnegie connection to finance the building of a new symphony hall, later to be called Carnegie Hall. By this time the lean years of American classical music, which lasted from 1850 to the 1880s, had become fat years, and the second generation of the Damrosches flourished in this ripe climate. Although Frank had deserted music in order to become a businessman in Denver, he played the organ at a number of local churches or synagogues. After his father's death he returned to his family fold in order to assume—

much in the German fashion—filial duties of support. Frank, much more than Walter, was active in all sorts of civic offices, first in Denver as musical supervisor of the public school system, an office he assumed after his move to New York from 1897 to 1905 as well. Frank was the quieter, but in many ways equally interesting, of the two. An accomplished organist, he played frequently in Dr. Felix Adler's Society for Ethical Culture (the final secular transformation of the synagogue), and in 1892 he founded, with the help of union leaders, a "People's Chorus" for the purpose of educating the working classes in good music. By 1894 he had set up three beginners' and one advanced course numbering three thousand participants. Frank loved this marriage of the German musical tradition with the American social gospel of uplift: "It teaches discipline, obedience, subordination, self-reliance, attention, concentration, precision . . . the larger lessons of unselfishness and cooperation, and points the way to the broader view of human life by its example of fellowship and brotherhood."[17] These eminently successful singing classes continued until 1916, when they abruptly stopped. Frank was often at odds with the political and organizational leadership of the "People's Chorus," whose goals were political whereas his remained primarily musical. They wanted to have more popular, political songs regardless of their quality, he wanted Schubert and Haydn; they wanted only participants with excellent working-class credentials, he welcomed white-collar workers and bookkeepers if they loved music. After 1900, Frank began thinking of founding a more permanent institution for music education, and he enlisted the help of James Loeb, a second-generation business tycoon (to whom credit goes for the Loeb Music Library at Harvard). Around 1905, he founded the Institute of Musical Art, which would later continue as the Juilliard School.

It is interesting to observe a pattern that recurs in the biographies of many second-generation German-Americans who returned to Germany for purposes of "finishing" their musical education. For Walter and Frank (as for Alfred Stieglitz), the sojourn brought out an affirmation of their Americanness. Frank wrote from Germany: "I wish I were home. I am sick of Europe. It is all a delusion and a snare. . . . We have a beautiful, broad, productive country and free institutions and a spirit lives in our people which causes them to strive continually for greater perfection in every way. We do not need Europe." The Damrosch second generation was in tune with this free spirit of America, and the new nationalism and militarism in the Reich may have speeded their assimilation. Moreover, Frank and Walter were convinced that the American musical scene—

through their own innovative services and those of their peers—had become just as good if not better than the German original. A proud sense of personal achievement in having "Germanized" and improved the musical scene emerged as a strengthened American patriotism.

In the late 1920s, Walter Damrosch continued his educational lecture recital programs, but this time for the new medium of radio. Some of the critics considered his "music appreciation hours" a shameless popularization of the classics. Yet, Walter Damrosch made the best high cultural use of a popular medium despised by members of the elite. These programs continued well into the 1940s and made his name a household word.[18] In contrast to Seidl or Muck and in oppositon to the critical establishment, Walter Damrosch supported the new American composers including George Gershwin. He even spoke up, though with some restraint, for indigenous traditions such as jazz, which many of his peers considered the death of musical culture. The price he had to pay, both for reaching out to the masses and for his innovative curiosity, was the constant reproach of dilettantism and of being a trifle too shallow or light.

A third member of the Damrosch second generation was the talented pianist Clara. In the elder Damrosch's enlightened educational scheme, daughters and sons were treated on a par. Clara received excellent instruction in piano and within the family fold had occasion to demonstrate her talent publicly. She married Walter's concertmaster, David Mannes. Mannes was the secularized and therefore disaffected son of an east European Jewish immigrant, and he idolized Walter Damrosch. He had gladly joined the "German" musical scene in New York, a step not untypical for an upwardly mobile east European Jew. Mannes was a child of the ghetto. Within the context of American racial and social relations, it is of interest that he received his first musical instruction from a talented black classical violinist named John Douglas, whose race barred him from public success. Mannes, who never forgot this help, would later found the Music School Settlement for Colored People and would also become a trustee of Fisk University. Mannes, even more than his in-laws, believed in the redemptive function of music; indeed, he called his autobiography *Music Is My Faith*. For his settlement school in Harlem, he won as backers people as far apart as Dr. Felix Adler (the founder of the Society for Ethical Culture) and James Reese Europe (director of the most popular black band). The latter agreed to give a fund-raising concert for the benefit of the Harlem Music School. As director, Mannes hired the black composer J. Rosamond Johnson, the brother of the author and diplomat James Weldon Johnson. Although aware of black musicality and supportive of black talent, he was dismayed at Johnson's exclusive interest in black music. This would in time cause friction between him and the black leadership, and the school folded after a few years. Immediately after the failure of this institution, Mannes set out to find another niche for his talent and his educational drive. In 1916 he founded, on a shoestring budget, the Mannes School of Music as a service for the nonprofessional public.

SCHMALTZ AND WALTZES: PAUL DRESSER AND SENTIMENTAL GERMAN SONGS

Middle- or lower-middle class German families, Gentile or Jewish, with no particular cultural pretensions or missions are also part of the story of American music. Often it was the story of one individual in the second generation making good by leaving home somewhere in the country and entering urban show business, a career described powerfully by a second-generation author, Theodore Dreiser. These individuals partook of and fully adopted the new urban space and its institutions: the bars and pubs, beer gardens, and music halls. They became well versed in the second-generation interethnic discourse as it developed in such forms as popular theater, the joke tradition, advertising, and cartoons. Typical principals were Theodore Dreiser's musical brother Paul Dresser, Harry Von Tilzer, Sam Bernard, Gustav Lüders, or Gus Edwards. All turned the positive stereotype of the gemütlich German culture with its love of wine, women, and song to good use. As members of the second generation they were bilingual, but they used the English language. Still they were beholden in their songs to a German sentimental tradition focusing on themes such as motherhood, a sense of loss, and decline (all sentimental antidotes to the speedy modernization and assimilation of which they were a part). The heyday of these pre–Tin Pan Alley songwriters in the German sentimental tradition ended between 1890 and 1900 when black-derived music entered the scene.

Paul Dresser was born in 1857 or 1858 (his brother Theodore in 1871) and he died in 1906. He was the oldest son of a strong, dour German Catholic father with little or no luck in life, who had earmarked him for the priesthood. Paul ran away with a medicine show (this is a typical pattern in this middling class) and later joined a stock company minstrel troupe. He

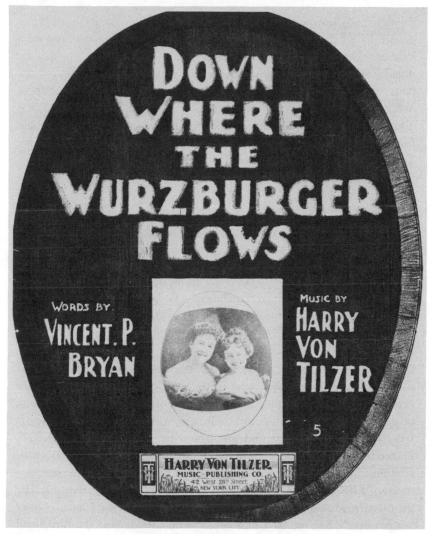

Figure 12.2. One of Harry Von Tilzer's early popular songs, composed in 1905, it brought the performer Nora Bayes fame as the Wurzburger Girl. Second-generation Von Tilzer, who had taken his mother's maiden name and added a "Von," published some 2,000 songs to become one of Tin Pan Alley's most prolific composers.

wrote his first songs for this company, and by the middle of the 1880s began to publish his songs under his own name, which he changed from Dreiser to Dresser. Although in running away he had joined the forces of the devil, his prosperity, unheard of in the Dreiser family, gave him a chance to act the good angel toward his younger siblings and toward a mother whom he idolized. Paul wholeheartedly embraced the world of the popular stage and mixed well with the new urban audience of shop assistants, salespeople, and white collar workers—with that new group of urban dwellers who shared his love of a good time in the inner city. Theodore Dreiser immortalized this world in *Sister Carrie*, whose people inhabit the places that Paul loved. Theodore, whom Paul had lured to New York, wrote with a mixture of adulation and disgust about this brave new world of urban entertainment:

> And what a realm! Rounders and what not were here ensconded at round tables, their backs against the leather-cushioned wall seats, the adjoining windows open to all Broadway. . . . It was wonderful, the loud clothes, the bright straw hats, the canes, the diamonds, the "hot" socks, the air of security and well-being. . . . Among them my dearest brother was at his best. It was "Paul" here and "Paul" there—"Why, hello, Dresser, you're just in time! Come on in. What'll you have? Let me tell you something, Paul, a good one—" More drinks, cigars, tales.[19]

Dresser's talent was not exhausted in writing sentimental and popular songs. To introduce a new song in the preelectronic market, a writer needed the services of a good firm, which in turn had to enlist the interest of singers to adopt the song into their repertoire. Paul combined the offices of writer and plugger and would later be his own publisher as well. Hence under the convivial bonhomie of the urban mixer there was a substratum of commercial shrewdness. Two of his songs achieved some notoriety, "I Believe It for My Mother Told Me So" and a ballad inspired by his own frustrated love affairs, "The Letter that Never Came." Other songs were "The Outcast Unknown," "The Convict and the Bird," and "The Pardon Came Too Late." Dresser's chief claim to fame is the song "By the Banks of the Wabash Far Away," which was adopted as the state song of Indiana. During the 1890s he formed a publishing firm, Howley, Haviland and Dresser, which flourished as long as his songs dominated the market. Although Dresser earned large sums of money with his songs (David Ewen speaks of a total of more than half a million dollars in less than two decades), he spent it all on wine and women and died a pauper. As Ellen Moers tells the story in *The Two Dreisers*, Paul Dresser introduced his brother Theodore to the new commercial, urban world and gave him the inspiration for several of the characters in his novel *Sister Carrie*.

It is interesting to note that Dresser's songs gave hyperbolic expression to a sentimental mood basic to the nineties, a mood stressing motherhood, filial love, death, frustration, loss, and attenuation. In Dresser, the bad conscience of the oldest boy, who deserted his struggling immigrant family, merged with the sentiment of rarified post-Victorian virtues, which had long since become ideological and nostalgic ciphers. Whereas in their daily lives these songsters gladly gave the lie to the sentiments expressed in their ballads (after all they did leave their old-world country kin to live in the modern city), the large urban audience, new to the city and somewhat ambivalent toward modernization, shared and endorsed the tearful nostalgia of these songsters. This sentimental yearning for the older preindustrial world was typical of those who had deserted it to come to the city, not of the newer groups who were born as urbanites. Hence the high time of Dresser or Von Tilzer was over by 1900, when a new audience born in the city demanded a new type of music, inspired in part by a new, urban, black style.

Augustus Eduard Simon was a transitional figure. Born in the realm of the Hohenzollerns in Germany in 1879, he arrived in the United States at age eight with his parents. Young Simon attended night school and worked as a tobacco stripper. Early on, he used to entertain his fellow workers by singing folk songs he had learned in Germany. Through Tony Pastor, one of the first new impresarios of America's emerging cultural industry, he entered show business and at Pastor's suggestion he changed his name to Gus Edwards. Edwards became a popular star in the vaudeville and music hall circuits. With William Cobb, a lyric writer, he wrote an enormously successful tune, "I Can't Tell Why I Love You, But I Do," which earned him the largest advance royalty ever received in the business up to that time. In 1905 he established the Gus Edwards Music Publishing Company and became a bit of a talent scout. He published several musical comedies and later toured the country with his Gus Edwards Song Revue. Edwards moved on to Hollywood and radio, starring in many films and talent scouting for Metro-Goldwyn-Mayer. A prolific songwriter, he composed "By the Light of the Silvery Moon," "Tammany," "School Days," "In My Merry Oldsmobile," and "Look Out for Jimmy Valentine." In 1939, Bing Crosby starred in a film based on his life. Like many of his age group, he became a founding member of the American Society of Authors, Composers and Publishers (ASCAP).[20] Simon stands halfway between the Dressers and their successors who would fully adopt and market the new popular music of Tin Pan Alley.

GERMANS IN TIN PAN ALLEY: THE HOUSE
OF WITMARK

The fourth group was drawn from the same pool as the third yet was appreciably different. This has to do more with their time of entry into the American market than with their social or musical background. These were younger, more aggressive, entirely urban families and individuals who entered the market just as, demographically speaking, the second generation became larger than the first, which happened some time before the 1880 census. They were in tune with the dreams and desires of a new kind of urban second generation, which, totally committed to modernization, participated fully and without nostalgic backward glances in the new urban cultural industry. Hence they became its principal agents by founding the appropriate urban networks, adopting more aggressive marketing styles, and seeking out innovative niches of the market—in short, by creating what became known as Tin Pan Alley. As a rule, its members rushed into assimilation and modernization. These Germans, often of Jewish background, mixed with east European Jews without the qualms of their more fortunate high cultural peers. A prominent example are the Witmark brothers, a quintet of brash city kids, who set up a music publishing business in 1885 to become—after 1900—one of the largest firms in the country.[21]

The Witmarks have, next to the Damrosch family, the most interesting, but also most typically American, story to tell. Perhaps this explains why they, as opposed to the Damrosch dynasty, are virtually ignored by those interested in German immigration. They are true traitors in Oscar Handlin's or Marcus Lee Hansen's sense—and yet, they were in their own way quite as German as any of the others. Marcus Witmark was born in Prussia and emigrated to America in 1853 to join his brothers, who were peddlers in the South. After service in the Civil War under Confederate command, he moved to New York, married Henrietta Peyser, and opened a business in liquor and wine. Neither the Peyser nor Witmark families were devout Jews, but, as opposed to their upper-class peers, they lived close to the ghetto, setting up shop at the border of Hell's Kitchen in New York. Their six children were born in quick succession. A photograph dating from 1886 shows Isidore, aged sixteen, Julian (called Julie), fifteen, Frank, nine, and Adoph (called Eddie), seven, in front of the print shop these mere children set up in their home. The store front advertises a variety of services in both English and German. Of the brothers, Isidore and

Frank played piano, Julie and their sister Frances sang. With their father giving expert advice on the market, the young brothers had an ideal combination of talents: Isidore had the business sense and composed at the piano; Julie and Frances went out and plugged their own songs. These songs were then printed on the fledgling family press.

The Witmarks were true urban children, totally at home in and committed to the urban market place. At the same time, they had an older German-Jewish family sense (the siblings stuck together and stayed in the firm until it merged with Warner Brothers in 1929) and a strong work ethic that grew out of a desire to escape drudgery and become independent and wealthy. In order to break into a rather fickle market, they tried to turn to profit the major events and happenings of the time. On the basis of a rumor of a pending marriage of President Cleveland, Isidore composed a wedding march and when, after initial disclaimers, the event did take place they rushed onto the market with ready copies. Isidore would also write songs to order, as for a German butchers' convention ("Only a Butcher") or for other ceremonial occasions. Soon their home became too small for the growing business and they moved to larger quarters, a pattern that would continue. Until the firm merged with Warner Brothers, the House of Witmark continued to move uptown along with Tin Pan Alley, first from 14th to 18th Streets, then to 34th Street, and finally to 51st and Broadway, thus following the center of the music publishing industry. Typically, these second-generation siblings were devoted to America's favorite entertainment, the minstrel show, and, being themselves adolescents, also made quick use of the craze for "mother songs" or songs involving domestic drama. Julie excelled at this sort of song early on, when in 1884 at the tender age of thirteen he belted out "Always Take Mother's Advice" or "Karl's Lullaby."

When the Witmark brothers started out in the music publishing business, the group of second-generation immigrants was, for the first time, larger than the first generation, and, what is more important, they were in tune with the social changes wrought by industrialization and urbanization.[22] Their interest in the minstrel show and their lack of racial phobia made them champions in the discovery of the emerging black musical talent, just at the time when the audience was growing tired of the German sentimental waltz. Whereas before 1895 the audience delighted in "After the Ball" by Charles Harris, toward the end of the decade they wanted ragtime and the cakewalk. This new demand opened the door for blacks, if only a crack, and the Witmarks were willing doorkeepers to let the new talent in. Ben Harney, who according to Eubie Blake was a Negro passing for white, published his ragtime pieces under the auspices of the Witmark publishers. Harney's song of 1896, "Dat Old Wagon Done Broke Down," is often called the first popular tune with a recognizably black inflection. And the Witmarks liked it. Isidore wrote perceptively in his autobiography of 1939 about the meaning of black music for the urban second-generation immigrant: "The negro has become for us a mask from behind which we speak with less self-consciousness of our own primitive beliefs and emotions." Ernest Hogan, a black who wrote for the Witmark catalog, scored a success with a so-called coon-song "All Coons Look Alike to Me." These were popular songs, which had emerged from the minstrel shows and which gave "humorous" expression to the current racism. Black artists and black audiences had no choice but to participate in this dominant tradition and, for the price of being accepted by the market, took its racism in stride.[23] But this time Hogan had gone too far, and the black audience turned against him. Later in his life Hogan was ashamed of having authored this song. The interesting part of the story is that Isidore Witmark, who considered himself a friend of blacks, had coauthored the lyrics the black audience found so objectionable. Isidore, being white and in love with the minstrel show, had no qualms about indulging in racist ribbing, which he meant in good fun.

The Witmarks continued to invite and publish such blacks who would work in the minstrel idiom. But they also backed and published a more important venture in black culture: the black composer Will Marion Cook, who had studied classical music under A. Dvorak and J. Joachim and teamed up with the black poet Paul Laurence Dunbar to write "Clorindy, or the Origins of the Cakewalk." Isidore Witmark published this important black musical and supported its production. Cook would later be found cooperating with David Mannes's Harlem School. Witmark, like Mannes from his high cultural perch, continued to champion and support black talent, such as the Johnson brothers or Harry Thacker Burleigh, a distinguished classical singer. Yet, Isidore Witmark remained the child of his racist times, a fact expressed in his interest in minstrel shows. But still he was closer to and had more appreciation of black music than his high cultural ethnic peers. Isidore Witmark set up a separate minstrel department within his firm that offered its services to nonprofessionals interested in doing a show. The service included personalized advice, custom-made shows for specific purposes, and any number of gag books and end men's joke books. In 1899, he published *The First Minstrel Encyclopedia.*

A typical instance of the Witmark services occurred in 1897, when an ethnic association, the German-American *Freundschafts* Club, approached Witmark and ordered the production of a minstrel show. Behind this request was a social drama that occurred all over German-America at this time; for this was to be the first dramatic production in English of a club dedicated to the preservation of German culture. The elders had finally bowed to the demands of a vociferous second generation who were tired of Friedrich von Schiller and August von Kotzebue. Needless to say, Isidore Witmark gladly filled that new need and gave them excellent advice on this most American genre of the popular stage. There is some irony in the fact that a second-generation group should solicit the help of their peers to break out of an ethnic horizon and go English using a pseudo-black vehicle. The Witmarks welcomed jazz with considerable interest and appreciation, for they recognized in it merely a paradigm of their own cultural assimilation. "The history of American popular music," wrote Isidore in his autobiography, "represents a strange mixture of racial qualities: white, black, American, Negro, Jewish, Yankee. Jazz, in history, stands for the latest phase (even in the new terminology, "swing" and "jam") of a trend that is to be discovered even in the old minstrel shows." Surely, Witmark believed in the cultural melting pot.

In 1898 the Witmarks became sole publishers of Victor Herbert. At this time, the House of Witmark was located in a neighborhood with any number of German beer gardens, *Hofbräuhäuser,* and *Stammtische* where Herbert, who loved food and fellowship quite as much as Dresser, used to hang out. The proprietor of Janssen's Hofbräu on 30th Street and Broadway, one of the places where the music people would gather, was the father of Werner Janssen, born in 1899, who would later become conductor of the New York Philharmonic under Toscanini and of the Utah and San Diego Symphony Orchestras. When his irate father, who had earmarked him as his successor of the Hofbräuhaus, refused to pay for his musical education, young Janssen survived by composing pop songs for Isidore Witmark's catalog. Thus the musical histories intersect and overlap. We might follow these networks across the racial line and pursue the Eubie Blake subplot: Blake, born in Baltimore's black ghetto, grew into a first-rate composer and pianist. After gaining a foothold in the business, he eventually signed up with the House of Witmark. One of his models and sources of inspiration (next to his own indigenous black tradition) was the music of Victor Herbert, as published by Witmark. When Blake built one of his songs noticeably close on the chords of Herbert's "Gypsy Love Call" and there was talk of plagiarism, Blake approached Herbert. In Al Rose's version as told by Eubie Blake the encounter went like this:

Eubie told Herbert he had stolen nothing from him and Herbert, in his stage-German dialect, asked, "But you *used* mein zong?" Eubie acknowledged that, to the extent described, he had. "Then," said the old man, smiling, "I must be ein pretty goot composer, hah?"[24]

The Witmarks received high ratings in Eubie Blake's catalog of white peers. Apart from publishing a number of black composers, they saw to it that blacks were admitted to ASCAP.

Around 1900 the Witmark brothers honored their parents by buying them a new house. In its basement, the brothers installed a *Bierkeller* with four thousand steins, some bought, some donated by friends. This represents not only an act of filial devotion but is also a typical thinning out of German ethnicity into its folkloric elements, a type of ethnic "fakelore" all ethnic groups or generations would find acceptable and quite in German style. Ultimately, the Witmark version of German culture, not the Thomas or Damrosch version, would prevail in America.[25]

The class difference between the Damrosch and Witmark families played a role in certain choices. The Witmarks conversed with their parents in German and spoke the language fluently. Unlike the Damrosch family, however, they had little investment in, or use for, the culture of the Old World. Yet, like the Damrosch family, they were never narrowly ethnic. All of the Witmarks were members of the Freemasons, which for them was a way of being both loyal Americans and cosmopolitans. The allegiance to a cosmopolitan idea of America can be called a recurrent pattern in the ethnic second generation. Upon opening a London office, Witmark insisted on displaying the American flag—much to the chagrin of his British hosts. Yet, when World War I loomed large in 1911, the Witmarks, Julie in particular, began a "Let Us Have Peace Movement," and Julie sang the song entitled "Let Us Have Peace" written by George Graff and George Ball and dedicated it to William Taft. Loyal Americans, but cosmopolitan; patriotic, but pacifists.

CONCLUSION

What accounts for the remarkable success of the second-generation German-Americans in the field of music? Is there a second-generation family resemblance across class lines and across the musical spectrum? I believe there is. The following categories capture the specific contribution of second-generation German-Americans to American music.

(1) Liberal cosmopolitanism. Although there is a common German background, there is also a tendency toward a cultural cosmopolitanism. In politics, most members are closet liberals reaching out for other groups but rarely coming out with a clear-cut political program. They are enlightened, unconventional believers in modernism.

(2) Transcendent musical culture. Music is a secularized religion, which assumes some of the older functions as social ethics. The modernization and secularization drives go in the direction of creating culture as a transethnic social bond.

(3) Innovation. With the exception of the high cultural first generation, they are apostles of modernization and embrace new genres and media without qualms. They fit in with the avant-garde motto: Make it new.

(4) Social uplift. Most are oblivious of social class divisions and want to transcend the class structure, either by reaching down from above, or by inclusion of hitherto excluded groups. All seem to have in their spiritual baggage Beethoven's *Ninth Symphony*. Marriages are made both up and down socially without so much as a ripple of reaction from the families.

(5) Cultural idealism and political pragmatism. Although remarkably successful in terms of the market, they are more interested in music than in money; they are single-mindedly devoted to making, creating, and publishing music. To achieve this end, they are constantly willing to enter a new field, to improvise the techniques if necessary. They make excellent use of the tradition of voluntarism and of operating in a system of secondary associations.

(6) Founding fathers. They are active in founding associations, institutions, and schools and thus set up the musical infrastructure. They participate in cultural politics with a tendency toward inclusion rather than exclusion.

(7) Ethics. All are sticklers for standards, both in music and ethics and are in constant conflict with those who have different priorities. Music is a transethnic medium; it transcends ethnic descent or social class.

(8) Altruism. There is a pattern of altruism, a willingness to be exploited for the sake of music. All of them worked for a larger transcendent political goal: for a new, American culture of their own.[26]

There is a remarkable family resemblance in the social behavior of second-generation ethnics: the fervent embrace of modernization and sociocultural change. This may have to do with their position in the generational sequence. The first-generation immigrant is asymmetrically bicultural through successive socializations, of which the first is arrested at the time of emigration, and the second incomplete at best. As a consequence, adult immigrants are often defensively static in matters of culture. The bicultural socialization of the second generation, however, occurs in one time frame, but in a variety of spatial subcontexts: It is split between family and street, Old World and New World, school and home. This is a dynamic scenario, for it trains code switching, explains the love for improvisation and for innovation, and encourages the handling of compromises in the negotiation of conflict—in short, it causes that cluster of dispositions and creates that cultural competence that explains the singular success of the Damrosch and Witmark families. Many members of the second generation kept a low ethnic profile, for they had to succeed in a difficult market, which was not necessarily hostile to displays of ethnicity, but yet American enough not to allow too much unalloyed ethnocentrism. Hence mainstream filiopietist scholarship, of the type primarily interested in ethnic persistence, tended to avoid this group unless of course its members were important to high culture. In a typical book on the German tradition in America, we find Theodore Thomas, Leopold, Walter, and Frank Damrosch, and Theodore Dreiser—but not his brother Paul, let alone the Witmark brothers, who marketed his songs. There is a sense of shame that the Dressers and Witmarks betrayed not only *Germanitas*, but German high cultural ideals with it. They sold out to the American market, to Tin Pan Alley, thus vindicating the deepest fear of German traditionalists: that German ethnic decline would be caused by American commercialization. There is some historical irony in the fact that a good part of that commercial music is of solid German-American making. The accepted wisdom in the history of music, which pits high cultural Germans against low cultural, commercial Americans (or other ethnics), clearly needs revision.

NOTES

1. On generational contexts and the unity of generational experience, see Karl Mannheim, "Das Problem der Generationen," *Wissenssoziologie* (Berlin, 1964).

2. A good example is David Ewen, *All The Years of American Popular Music* (Englewood Cliffs, NJ, 1977). See also Charles Hamm's masterly work *Yesterday: Popular Song in America* (New York, 1973).

3. On the bad press the second generation has had in American scholarship, often at the hands of second-generation ethnic scholars with an apparently bad conscience, see Werner Sollors, *Beyond Ethnicity: Consent and Descent in American Culture* (New York, 1986); both quotations on p. 215.

4. Not in music alone does the second generation play a key role. Photography (Alfred Stieglitz, Edward Steichen, Gertrude Käsebier, and others) and film are unthinkable without the contribution of hyphenate Americans. See Sue Davidson Lowe, *Stieglitz: A Memoir/Biography* (New York, 1983).

5. The best book on the role of the second generation in the creation of secondary associations and institutions is Deborah Dash Moore, *At Home in America: Second Generation New York Jews* (New York, 1981).

6. For a review of older, nativist fears in American music, which today have all but disappeared, see McDonald Smith Moore, *Yankee Blues: Musical Culture and American Identity* (Bloomington, IN, 1985).

7. Cf. Gunther Barth, *City People: The Rise of Modern City Culture in Nineteenth-Century America* (New York: 1980), which is disappointing. Also Ewen, *All the Years;* R. W. Fox and T. J. Lears, eds., *The Culture of Consumption* (New York, 1983); and John Kasson, *Amusing the Millions: Coney Island at the Turn of the Century* (New York, 1978).

8. Lawrence Levine argued in a series of public lectures at Harvard University, 14–17 April 1986, entitled "The Fragmentation of American Culture," that American culture became "sacralized" through the single-minded efforts of high-minded German-oriented cultural custodians. This, as I shall argue, is merely one aspect of a many-faceted process of modernization, fragmentation, and territorialization of American culture. American culture becomes realigned in its entirety, and German-Americans were active on all levels including its middle- and low-brow ends.

9. On the rise of film: Larry May, *Screening Out the Past: The Birth of Mass Culture and the Motion Picture Industry* (New York, 1980). On Stieglitz and the avant-garde movement in photography: Lowe, *Stieglitz.* It is striking that so many second-generation ethnics were active in the avant-garde or in cultural innovation. Ethnics were eager to try out new media, appropriate innovations, such as film, radio, and photography for the purpose of setting up their own "creolized" culture. They managed to ethnicize the main stream. The contemporary nativist critics were more than alarmed by this development. See note no. 6.

10. Second-generation German-Americans played an important role as midwives in the birth of jazz. With the exception of Bix Beiderbecke, they did not contribute much artis-

tically to the evolution of jazz. Most of the outstanding white jazz musicians are second-generation Jewish or Italian Americans. See Berndt Ostendorf, "Bebop and the Beat Generation," *Amerikastudien/American Studies* 30 No. 4 (1985).

11. A critique of the ethnic purism practiced by the *Encyclopedia* may be found in Werner Sollor's essay "A Critique of Pure Pluralism," in *Reconstructing American Literary History,* Sacvan Bercovitch, ed. (Cambridge, MA, 1986).

12. To chart the reasons for this studied avoidance, here is a brief phenomenology of repression. The first problem is epistemological: There is a pregeneric myth in storytelling that registers social change primarily as loss or decline of strength, quality, or purity. This nostalgia for the old and fear of the new have given rise to a narratological and typological habit: a deep generational suspicion exacerbated by the act of immigration, which runs from father to son, from mother to son and daughter, namely that the next generation will not be willing or able to preserve the heritage well enough. The second problem has to do with the psychopathology of "mixing." In hermeneutics, politics, religion, and biology there is a preference for the pure, clean text. This preference has created a bad press for all instances of mixing. Decline, degeneracy, and mongrelization are the metaphors of a deep fear. Until recently, racial mixing was said to cause sterility. This concerns the question of American identity. The search for an American identity has excluded paradigms of racial or ethnic ambiguity. Therefore America has had a tradition of practicing the melting pot but preaching against mongrelization. This also explains why second-generation ethnics of mixed parentage kept a low ethnic profile.

13. "Ghetto Literature, or: What Makes Ethnic Literature Ethnic?" in *Le facteur ethnique aux États-Unis et au Canada,* Monique Lecomte and Claudine Thomas, eds. (Lille, 1983).

14. T. Russell, *Theodore Thomas: His Role in the Development of Musical Culture in the U.S.* (Minneapolis, 1969).

15. The information on the Damrosch family is drawn from George Martin's magisterial book, *The Damrosch Dynasty: America's First Family of Music* (Boston, 1983). The book presents an unusually sensitive reading of the ethnic factor and thus is not afflicted by a nativist or ethnic tunnel vision.

16. The Blaines were of part-Catholic, part-Presbyterian background, well established in politics and public life. The young engaged couple, part Lutheran-Jewish, part Catholic-Presbyterian, had an Episcopal wedding. Margaret's sister would marry the heir of the McCormick empire.

17. Martin, *The Damrosch Dynasty,* 153.

18. These educational music appreciation hours by Walter Damrosch were syndicated all over the United States and reached all the way to the plains of South Dakota. George McGovern writes in his autobiography *Grassroots:* "On December 7, 1941, I was at home listening to a radio broadcast by the New York Philharmonic. These listening sessions on Sunday afternoon were required of all students participating in Professor Brown's course in Music Appreciation. . . . I was jotting down a few impressions of the concert when an an-

nouncer suddenly broke in to report that the Japanese had bombed the American naval base at Pearl Harbor" (New York, 1977).

19. Ellen Moers, *Two Dreisers* (New York, 1969), 86. Theodore Dreiser, "My Brother Paul," *Twelve Men* (London, 1930); "Whence the Song," *The Color of a Great City* (New York, 1923).

20. *The National Cyclopedia of American Biography,* vol. 34, 54f.

21. Isidore Witmark and Isaac Goldberg, *The Story of the House of Witmark: From Ragtime to Swingtime* (New York, 1939). A second account by a participant and witness is Edward Bennett Marks, *They All Sang: From Tony Pastor to Rudy Vallee* (New York, 1934). Marks's father, the son of a cantor in Berlin, emigrated to the United States. Edward Marks, born in 1865, became a powerful force in theater and music publishing. First he joined the Joseph W. Stern Company and later took it over. Besides being the head of his own publishing company, Marks was director of the Emerson Phonograph Company and president of ASCAP for many years. See also the breezy chronicle of the American popular music racket, *Tin Pan Alley* by Isaac Goldberg (New York, 1930). Goldberg was a professor of romance languages. From his high cultural perch, he identifies deeply with his subject matter. In the world of vaudeville, the story of the Marx brothers is very similar: Their parents had immigrated from Alsace and Baden, and had joined the vaudeville circuit. See Groucho Marx, *The Grouchophile* (Indianapolis, 1976).

22. E. P. Hutchinson, *Immigrants and Their Children, 1850–1950* (New York, 1956). In the 1880 census, the second generation for the first time outnumbered the first; thereafter the second generation increased in size and reached the proportion 5 to 3 by 1920. Hutchinson notes also that between 1890 and 1920, the median age of the second generation was lower than that of its peer group of American natives. The combination of youth, willingness to embrace urban culture, curiosity, and eagerness to adopt the new made this group so successful.

23. Witmark and Goldberg, *The Story of the House of Witmark,* 131. On this curious tradition see Berndt Ostendorf, "Minstrelsy and Early Jazz," *The Massachusetts Review* XX (Autumn 1979). See also Sam Dennison, *Scandalize My Name: Black Imagery in American Popular Music* (New York, 1982), and the review by Berndt Ostendorf in *Popular Music 3,* Richard Middleton and David Horn, eds. (Cambridge, 1983).

24. Al Rose, *Eubie Blake* (New York, 1979). One ought to note in passing that Schirmer publishers were part of the German musical culture in New York from the beginning.

25. On the attenuation of ethnic culture into American folklore, see Berndt Ostendorf's introduction to *Amerikanische Gettoliterature* (Wiesbaden, 1983), 1–26.

26. This summary was inspired partly by George Martin's preface, *The Damrosch Dynasty.*

CHAPTER 13

A Tale of Two Cities
Culture and Its Social Function in Chicago during the Progressive Period

HEINZ ICKSTADT

C hicago, at the turn of the century, appeared to many of its visiting contemporaries a city of excess—enormous in its energies and its ambitions as well as its corruptions. In this, it also seemed the most American of cities: Here the full power and violence of the industrializing process were played out without the social and cultural impediments of inherited structures and traditions. In Chicago's history, the fundamental change of the United States from a predominantly rural society to an urban one was enacted as an ongoing drama of brutal growth and modernization.[1] Incorporated in 1835—a settlement of barely 350 inhabitants—Chicago, within seventy years, became a metropolis of 2,000,000, in size second only to New York. Boomtown par excellence of the Gilded Age and therefore a magnet for thousands of immigrants from all parts of Europe, it was always changing, always expanding, in a constant process of demolition and construction. Chicago seemed the embodiment of urban ugliness: a city grimy with soot from the smokestacks of hundreds of factories; a city of unbearable stenches, whose streets reminded Frederick C. Howe, even in 1903, of the primitive mud roads of a frontier town. It was excessive also in its social contrasts: While the degrading housing conditions of its working-class sections shocked observers from both sides of the social fence, William Le Baron Jenney, Dankmar Adler, Louis Sullivan, John Wellborn Root, and Daniel Burnham—the avant-garde of modern urban architecture—constructed the first skyscrapers for a small and wealthy clientele. Class conflicts tended to be especially bitter here, as a predominantly Anglo-Saxon economic and cultural elite of quasi-colonialist status struggled to maintain control over a majority of foreign or non-English-speaking citizens. (In fact, 78 percent of Chicago's population were immigrants or the children of immigrants.) Chicago was the city of crime, a cesspool of corruption and of unceasing political scandal; in the eyes of one of its leading novelists, it had become the "cloaca maxima of modern civilization."[2] But it was also the center of radical protest, of working-class organization, of progressive reform (such as the Settlement House, the Playground, and the City Beautiful movements). Finally, it was the city of enlightened patrons who, taking example from the merchant princes of the Italian Renaissance, sought to demonstrate Chicago's civilizing potential (together with their own financial power) by founding a great number of diverse cultural institutions.

A city such as this gave impulse to a variety of interpretations. For a majority of observers, however, Chicago's many contradictions seemed to come together in a dualistic image of two cities: the present Black City of poverty, corruption, and industrial chaos, and the White City of Chicago's aspirations toward civic order and high culture. The ideological implications of this opposition are manifold and obvious: The barbarous mass of ethnic workers is set against the civilized elite, moral looseness against reason and willpower, the wild growth of the industrializing city against the reform spirit of a "civic regeneration." In placing fact against ideal and, implicitly, the present against a possible future, oppositions such as these imply a progressive concept of history, in which chaos is increasingly transformed into an ever more perfect order of civilization. This concept, with its peculiar set of semantic contrasts, is central to the social perception of the dominant culture—it enters Daniel Burnham's city planning and the various reform programs of the progressives, as well as the novels of Henry Blake Fuller, where the order of the old elite is constantly besieged by the surrounding chaos of the raw and barbarous city. Upton Sinclair's attempt at an alternative perception from the bottom up, by inverting the pattern, also reaffirms it: In *The Jungle*, it is the proletarian and ethnic culture that is beleaguered and destroyed by an encroaching capitalist wilderness of profit and corruption. Of all novels of the period, only Theodore Dreiser's *Sister Carrie* abandons the idea of civilized order altogether. Here, Chicago is total sensuous environment, a field of contingency that symbolically embodies and anticipates a new urban culture—a culture, however, that is different, in essence, from the White Cities of Victorian civilization.

Kapitaliſtiſche „Gerechtigkeit".

Figure 13.1. This caricature, entitled "Capitalist 'Justice'," reflects the workers' perspective on the upper class. The caption reads: "The moneybag will prevail until the capitalist robber system will be abolished by the workers."

The historical relevance of literary fiction is, of course, open to debate. However, these novels mark the boundaries of a sociocultural field of forces in which competing cultures, responding to the pressures of a changing environment, acted on or against each other and were themselves changed by such processes of interaction. The following attempt to outline this field in a montage of different cultural perspectives is, as I well know, problematical, since the blurred and limited social and cultural perceptions of each group is part of my own presentation. (Thus, the German working-class subculture did not explicitly become the object of upper-class social observation, since the gentry reformers tended to see the immigrants as an undefined mass of foreigners, or, around the turn of the century, focused their attention on the more conspicuously foreign groups of the second wave of immigration.) Nevertheless, it seems worthwhile and necessary to at least try to place Chicago's German working-class culture within a larger context of change, in which the erosion of cultural hierarchy on one hand and of ethnic autonomy on the other, the expansion of social perception (i.e., of a perception of what society is and who belongs to it), and the rise of an urban mass culture, are only different phases or aspects of the same sociocultural processes. The city as it emerged after the turn of the century was the product of antagonistic groups and forces at the same time that the people themselves increasingly became products of the city. The Americanization of the immigrants was part of a larger process that concerned all groups alike: the adjustment to city life and the formation of city habits—that is, the growth of a specific urban consciousness and culture.

RECONSTRUCTING CHICAGO: THE WHITE CITY AND UPPER-CLASS REFORM

No event had a more profound impact on Chicago's various reform movements than the White City of the World's Columbian Exposition in 1893. In the harmonious design of its boulevards, squares, fountains, and Renaissance palaces, Chicago had, or so it seemed, projected an ideal image of its future.[3] But it was the English journalist and reformer William Stead who first insisted on redeeming the implicit Utopian promise of the city's moral and physical regeneration through practice. The meeting of the city's reform-minded people, which convened on his initiative in Central Music Hall on November 12, 1893, had gained urgency through a worsening economic crisis and its ensuing hardships. "Such a gathering Chicago had never seen before and is not likely to see again," wrote Graham Taylor in his *Pioneering on Social Frontiers*.

> The floor and galleries of the city's greatest forum were thronged by men and women of all grades, races, sects and conditions. . . . On the stage there was such a grouping of people from the extremes of life as no one could have imagined to be possible. Side by side sat leading business men and labor leaders, representatives of the city government and of its exclusive clubs, preachers and saloon keepers, gamblers and theological professors, matrons of distinguished families and notorious "madames" from houses of ill fame, judges of the courts and one of the men convicted in the Haymarket Riot trial [Samuel Fielden] who had just been pardoned from the state prison by Governor Altgeld.[4]

Stead—who had not only seen the White City but also had visited the Chicago slums—called the misery of Chicago's homeless and unemployed, the corruption of the city's politics, and the protection of vice a public scandal and disgrace. What Chicago desperately needed was a "Civic Church or Federation of all good citizens."[5] After a long and passionate debate, the evening ended with the foundation of the Civic Federation of Chicago.

Its first meeting took place, some days later, in the villa of Mrs. Potter Palmer. The prominent banker Lyman Gage (one of the leading organizers of the Columbian Exposition) was elected president; Mrs. Potter Palmer became vice president. Its trustees were (in addition to Jane Addams and some representatives of the unions) the millionaires Franklin MacVeagh, George E. Adams, and Marshall Field—names that appear over and over in the registers of Chicago's most important clubs and social institutions. In other words, the Civic Federation seemed to be one more in a series of organizations that had served a small but active economic and social elite's efforts to control the turbulent development of Chicago during the 1870s and 1880s, through a hot–cold treatment of patronage, repression, and reform. Like the gentry of the East Coast (ancestors of, and examples for, many of them), Chicago's elite did not see in wealth sufficient proof of success. Culture and the manifest care for the commonweal were to legitimize its privileged social position; they became part of a rite of social redemption, through which the rich purged themselves from the opprobrium of mere money-making. In a similar fashion, the cultural idealism of Chicago's social elite aimed at the elevation of a raw and unformed public, which was to learn, by the uplifting presence and experience of art, the denial of its lowest needs. Thus philanthropy in all its forms was a privilege of good society, a public duty that one owed oneself and others.

And yet, the Civic Federation was more than just another manifestation of Chicagoan noblesse oblige. The foundations of the 1880s and 1890s (e.g., the Art Institute, the Crerar and Newberry Libraries, the University of Chicago, the Chicago Symphony Orchestra) had all been objects of prestige and of a consciousness of culture that transcended, and yet depended on, the harsh world of laissez-faire. Faced with the most severe economic crisis of the nineteenth century, the elite, in founding the Civic Federation, seemed willing to redefine the relation of culture and business as well as its own social function. Even though firmly in the hands of the gentry, the Civic Federation conceived of itself as a community of interest for all Chicago citizens and looked—at least in its early phase—for members in all groups and social strata:

> The objects of the Federation shall be. . . . To serve as a medium of acquaintance and sympathy between persons who reside in the different parts of the city, who pursue different vocations, who are by birth of different nationalities, who profess different creeds, or no creed, who for all these reasons are unknown to each other, but who, nevertheless, have similar interests in the well-being of Chicago, and who agree in the desire to promote every kind of municipal welfare.[6]

Albion Small, professor for sociology at the newly founded University of Chicago, a member of the Civic Federation, and its first theoretician, saw in its foundation an additional sign for a social consciousness that became increasingly disaffected with the tenets of laissez-faire and drawn, at the same time, to arguments of social coherence. If society was worth its name only as an organic unity of all its parts, then communication and cooperation between classes ceased to be a question of philanthropy and became a matter of social and economic efficiency. Conciliation and not confrontation was sound economic reasoning: Reform interest was business interest, "society must pick up its own chips or the chips will clog the wheel."[7]

It is therefore not surprising that, with Small as well as with other members of the Civic Federation, the transitions between corporative and cooperative thought were fluid: "You are"—wrote Small quoting Gage—"a shareholder in the cooperative corporation, the business company known as the city." Indeed, the federation itself operated in the manner of a business firm—well organized, determined, and efficient. In this connection it is interesting to note how smoothly Small manages to combine the exalted, almost religious rhetoric of reform ("civic revival," "civic patriotism," "civic salvation") with a cool and calculated view of the pragmatic. The time of well-meaning amateur reformers was coming to an end. The men and women of the Civic Federation were passionately engaged and capable managers of reform—persevering, obsessed with facts, experts of the concrete case.

The Civic Federation ordered and coordinated the various activities of the reform movement throughout the 1890s (the movement's avant-garde, however—people like Jane Addams and Graham Taylor—operated on the "social frontiers" of the tenement districts.) It investigated into social grievances, drafted several reform bills (e.g., the Civil

Service Bill), agitated, with fist and quill, against the forces of vice and corruption, centralized Chicago's welfare organizations to cope more efficiently with the hardships of the severe winter of 1893–94, and, advocating an essential harmony of interest between all social groups, tried to mediate between capital and labor during the Pullman conflict.

Central to an understanding of this many-faceted will to reform (on the part of the Civic Federation as well as a myriad of other reform groups) is the word "organization" in its twofold meaning of "efficient order" and "process or method of achieving order." In an urban wilderness of foreign tongues and races, and of rivaling groups and interests, only organized space was truly social space, because only here was communication (and thus consensus) possible. Organization, systematization, centralization, and the transformation of heterogeneous social fragments into a homogeneous whole created the ideal civic order of civilized (i.e., moral, rational, and efficient) human beings. Urban reform in Chicago, therefore, was neither a purely political nor a purely social reform movement, but the simultaneous and analogous realization of a central cultural paradigm (the creation of order) on several levels of human practice. It treated moral reform as social reform as much as it regarded urban reform and city planning as instruments of moral regeneration.

The cultivation of city environment had been demanded by representatives of the Settlement House Movement long before it became—through the financial backing of the Merchants' Club (the club of the younger millionaires and businesspeople of Chicago)—an essential part of Chicago's reform politics at the turn of the century. Jane Addams, Graham Taylor, and Jacob Riis had frequently insisted on the connection between the crime rate and living conditions and tried to persuade the members of the Merchants' Club—and through them Chicago's politicians—that to establish public parks and playgrounds was "a work of expediency rather than philanthropy. The City is asked to do something not out of the goodness of its heart, but out of the soundness of its head."[8] Between 1899 and 1904, the South Park Commission built ten new parks and recreation areas close to the most infamous tenement districts near the stockyards and the steelmills at the Southern Branch of the Chicago River. They were generously equipped with playgrounds, basketball courts, baseball fields, gymnasiums, swimming pools, washing facilities, and shower rooms. Neighborhood children and adolescents used these facilities—if we may believe the official reports—by the thousands; and under the supervising eyes of educators and social workers, they learned social behavior by learning to play American games according to the rules.

Fresh milk and low-priced food were sold in the field houses of these parks. There, branches of the public library supplied the needs of a lower-class reading public, and rooms were made available to groups and neigh-borhood clubs for dances or other social events (which, in all likelihood, were also supervised). Newspapers were quick to note a drastic decrease in crime in the surrounding neighborhoods (in some cases as much as 40 percent) and glowingly reported on happy workers who, freed from the pressures of their working and living conditions for a few hours, found regeneration in play. "Down in Russell Square"—Ernest Poole wrote in the *Outlook*—"which lies close under the flame-belching towers of the steel mills, the pool has often twelve hundred bathers a day; the night gang of workers coming by day, and the day gang coming at night—Poles, Hun-garians, Germans, and Swedes—swimming and shouting and laughing till late in the evening, with the sky above them lurid and red from the blast-furnace flames."[9]

Therefore these park areas, which had been designed and built by Frederick Law Olmsted and Daniel Burnham, were not only "one of the most notable achievements of any American city"[10] but also good invest-ments for an efficient preservation of the work force. In addition, the park centers were considered to be outposts of civilization, within the wasteland of the industrializing city, which would help shape a faceless and yet unformed mass. In centers like these, "in which social life may be organized and carried on steadily and normally,"[11] the foreign mass could, as Jane Addams believed, learn the forms and possibilities of so-cial communication and therefore the preconditions of a civilized and social existence. Others spoke more directly of "recreation" as, literally, a reconstruction of personality and therefore as a means of assimilation and social control: "All thinking people agree"—said Henry Foreman, president of the South Park Commission, before an audience of poten-tial sponsors—

we must raise the standard of living among them, and they must be-come more rational in their thinking and acting, to make them safe and good citizens. If we can do this we will make our cities more de-sirable for the home-seeker, and a safe place for business enterprise and developments. . . . One finds that muscle exercised on a punching bag or a swinging club, or a turning pole or in a swimming pool, is not apt to be used to bully fellow-workers and lead to struggles against law and order.[12]

The arrogance of these upper-class reformers cannot be separated from their unconditional devotion to their civilizing mission, their duty to social reform, which they fulfilled—often to the point of physical collapse—as instruments of history. Men like Frank MacVeagh, Henry G. Foreman, Daniel Burnham, and many others projected with quasi-religious fervor the ideal image of Chicago as the Venice, Rome, or Athens of a splendid future which they, in their own lifetime, had to model out from the raw material of history. The pragmatic and millennial dimensions of reform ("the spectacle of a city saving itself")[13] are both present in Burnham's *Plan of Chicago*, which—conceived in the spirit of the White City of 1893 and published sixteen years afterwards—marks the time span of the reform movement and, in many ways, can be considered its paradigm.

Burnham's *Plan*, commissioned by the Commercial and Merchants' Clubs, attempted to take into consideration the commmercial needs and the traffic problems of a modern metropolis and to impose on them an overall neoclassical design—which may seem a contradiction from our vantage point but, for Burnham, was the raison d'être of his enterprise.[14] He believed that the time was ripe to heal the wounds of economic laissez-faire, to mitigate the cultural distance toward a new population "of many nationalities without common traditions and habits of life,"[15] and to restore the lost unity of the body politic. If the nineteenth century had been an epoch of blind expansion, the twentieth would be a time of enlightened conservation. In Burnham's *Plan*, the city was to be a space of rediscovered continuities (between past and future, progress and balance, economy and culture), brought about by the subjection of diverse social elements under one controlling idea of order and coherence.

Burnham's organic city, "in which all the functions are related to one another,"[16] consisted of a system of boulevards and transport and traffic ways grouped in semicircles around the city's center. It was intersected by large avenues radiating from the center toward the city's periphery. An interconnected park system, linking the periphery with the downtown area, and broad avenues lined by trees that cut through the residential quarters were to bring air and light also to the tenement districts, eliminating the "unwholesome conditions" of contemporary Chicago.[17] The heart of the Burnham *Plan*, however, and the geographic as well as the aesthetic center of the future city, was to be the civic center. Rising from a group of public buildings (placed symmetrically around a huge central square), rose the city's highest edifice, the city administration building. Modeled after St. Peter's Basilica in the Vatican—its secular replica, in fact—it was to be "a monument to the spirit of civic unity."[18] Evident is the dominance of a quasi-imperial order, which submits the imperfect and barbarous city of the contemporary present to a principle of hierarchy at once social, moral, and aesthetic. Design is everything, human beings—as John Atherton observes—are nowhere to be seen in the accompanying drawings of Jules Guérin.[19] And they are indeed without importance in Burnham's vision of a well-functioning urban organism. Man vanishes, so to speak, in the ideal and monumental order of urban space. Burnham's plan of a well-ordered city, perfect in the efficient coordination of all its elements and functions, and dominated by the central cupola of an ever vigilant civic conscious-ness, is the inner form, projected outward into architectural design, of an ideal "self-less" man, who, in finding transcendence in the higher social order, is blotted out by it.

Chicago took from the plan whatever it needed: parts of its traffic and highway pattern, an extended system of public parks, the reconstruc-tion of the lake front. The civic center was never realized, however—an omission that had a logic of its own, since the reform movement, despite intense efforts, never succeeded in gaining control of the city administra-tion. The gentry had given up its former reluctance and entered the low life of city politics with the foundation of the Municipal Voters' League (initiated in 1896 by the tireless MacVeagh). Within a comparatively brief period of barely six years, it was able to break the local power of corrupt but ethnically loyal bosses, yet its efforts to coordinate and centralize the city's administration were defeated, and its later move toward the center of the city's political power also failed. The bill of a new city charter was rejected in 1907 by a majority of Chicago's population, partly because the reformers had not been able (in spite of frequent "information meetings" in factories and workhalls) to convince Chicago's workers and its various ethnic groups that a victory for the reform movement was not equivalent to "dry Sundays" and an encroachment on ethnic rights and traditions.[20] Four years afterward, Charles Merriam (professor at the University of Chicago and member of the Merchants' Club), seemingly close to the final and long-expected triumph of reform, lost the municipal election of 1911 to Carter Harrison, Jr. The loss broke the momentum of the reform movement, even though it was still strong enough to give the candidate of the Progressive party, Theodore Roosevelt, a local (but nationally unim-portant) victory in the presidential election of 1912.

The dream of philanthropists and patrons during the eighties to civi-lize society, by submitting it to the uplifting influence of "high culture," obviously had to be discarded for more practical responses to social change. However, its pragmatic sequel, the attempt to transform and culti-vate "savage" urban space, proved equally elusive. The proclaimed alli-ance of the spirit of reform with an enlightened economic spirit had to fail when tested against the ultimate economic principle of profit—just as the postulated homogeneity of a rational and efficient society crumbled be-fore the reality of ethnic rights and interests. The dynamics of economy, ethnic diversity, and the sensuous anarchy of the city itself eluded the rigid and static order of Burnham's design—even though the dreamed of "civic order," in these failing and continuously renewed efforts of fulfillment, became increasingly flexible and varied, before it finally dissolved.

ETHNIC CHICAGO: THE GERMAN WORKING CLASS

With the foundation of the Chicago Symphony Orchestra in 1891, Chi-cago acquired a cultural institution, surpassed in social prestige only by its new university. Adding to its fame was Theodore Thomas, at that time the most renowned musician in the United States, whom George E. Adams and Charles Norman Fay had persuaded to come to Chicago as the orches-tra's first conductor. Thomas, who had immigrated from Germany forty-six years earlier, at first reacted skeptically to the offer of his friends and patrons. The concerts he had conducted in the large Exposition Hall each summer since 1877 had, indeed, always been overcrowded with an audi-ence from all social classes, but as long as serious musicians had to play in beer halls to earn a living, the city was not yet ready to support a perma-nent orchestra:

> Chicago is a city of nearly two million inhabitants but the great majority of them belong to the class employed in mills, factories, and at all kinds of manual labor, while the cultivated class is comparatively small. This gives only a limited field of activity for a musician, and offers him little opportunity to add to his income by teaching or private engagements. The consequence is that there is little inducement outside of the orches-tra for men of the ability required for a first-rank orchestra to settle there, and this makes it difficult to procure them . . . and as Chicago could not furnish our leading players, they had to be brought from other parts of the world.[21]

Since German was the language used during rehearsals, one may safely as-sume that the majority of the musicians brought to Chicago came from

Germany. Yet it was also mostly Germans, playing and singing in the city's many orchestras and singing clubs, to whom Chicago owed its reputation as a "music-loving city." These Thomas ignored completely. His rigorous professionalism, his insistence on European standards, and his impatience with everything he considered mediocre made him draw a sharp line between high culture and popular or ethnic culture. It made him also support the orchestra's policy of high admission fees, aimed at maintaining social exclusiveness even at the price of heavy and constant financial losses.[22]

Thomas's is only another example of a culturally conditioned weakness of social vision, endemic to the gentry, which made it incapable of seeing the heterogeneous population of Chicago other than in terms of the low and barbarous. The chasm between the true community and "its million workers"—a revealing phrase of Daniel Burnham's[23]—separated the high from the low, the area of the civilized and socially acceptable from a social and cultural vacuum.

What seemed merely wasteland to the civilized eye, however, was in fact densely organized social space. In recent years, social historians have made abundantly clear that the neighborhoods were small societies in themselves: "Family relations, peer groups, and adaptations to work and living conditions formed the basis of that society."[24] In addition, the pub at the street corner was an institution of everyday life, especially for the Germans. Beer gardens and excursion restaurants in the parks along the city's periphery, or the popular theater situated in one of the many Turner halls, were traditional centers of a leisure culture whose elements of dancing, drinking, and folklore entertainment were distinctly ethnic. Churches, ethnic and professional organizations, or institutions of the working-class movement (e.g., the *Chicagoer Arbeiter-Zeitung*) tried to integrate immigrants beyond such forms of family- or neighborhood-oriented sociability into a larger social network. With mutual aid societies, unions, *Turnvereine*, singing clubs, debating clubs, societies for the education of workers, women's clubs, orchestras of *Turnvereine* and singing clubs, and workers' lodges—each with a yearly cycle of excursions, picnics, dances, commemorations, and other festivities—the German working-class movement in Chicago could claim to reach and organize all aspects and areas of German working-class life. It was political and ethnic and thus a quasi-autonomous counterculture, which defined and organized itself—not unlike the culture of the gentry, if in violent opposition to it—against the chaos of capitalist laissez-faire society.

This claim of cultural completeness and autonomy was lived and propagated especially by the intellectuals around the *Chicagoer Arbeiter-Zeitung*, who founded unions, gave political speeches, produced the newspaper, or wrote poems and plays that were recited or performed at the many festivities of the working-class movement (e.g., the memorial day of the Paris Commune).[25] They considered union organization a prerequisite to fundamental social change; regarded pleasure, play, and leisure necessary to the restoration of human beings worn out by the strains of industrial labor; staged festivities and celebrations as rituals of group solidarity; and propagated the education of the workers in anticipation of a time when culture and the domain of the beautiful would cease to be the privilege of the elect.

The combination of political radicalism with cultural idealism was characteristic of the intellectuals associated with the *Arbeiter-Zeitung*, who considered themselves the vanguard of a new society and the true heirs of the cultural traditions of the Enlightenment. This explains the relatively high intellectual and aesthetic standards of the *Arbeiter-Zeitung* and the *Fackel* which, in addition to the usual fare of novels of adventure and sentiment, reprinted the classic authors of European literary realism and naturalism—at a time when William Dean Howells was still fighting for their recognition in *Harper's New Monthly Magazine*. But it also explains the implicit identification of Americanization with embourgeoisement and the correlation of true class consciousness with a specifically ethnic pride and appreciation of art and culture.[26]

Whether this cultural idealism eventually isolated these intellectuals from a new generation of Germans born in America and from a working class that grew in cultural heterogeneity is open to speculation. The admonitions, in 1910, of its chief editor, Heinrich Bartel, to never forget "the ideal" over "the fight for the material" and his tirade against the "materialism" of the unions, the general "bogging down" of the working-class movement, and the growing philistinism of the Germans[27]—all seem to indicate that the role German workers and their intellectual leaders played in Chicago's working class had changed.

Whereas the forms of the political culture of Chicago's German workers—the ritualistic arrangement of their picnics, celebrations, commemorations—stayed roughly the same over a period of almost forty years, there was a constant turnover in membership and participation. Names and faces—the *Arbeiter-Zeitung* complained—changed at ever shorter intervals. Geographic mobility from the tenement districts to the suburbs, social mobility into the ranks of skilled or white-collar work, or

even mobility within the social and communicative network of the working-class movement itself, made German workers drop out of the circle
and the published notice of the *Arbeiter-Zeitung* after only two or three
years of participation. Therefore, the paper remarked, the survival, "in
the land of the Yankees" of "German life-styles" and the true "revolutionary idea" depended on the continuing flow of immigrants from Germany, "since it has been noted, especially with the Germans, that already
the first generation becomes completely Americanized."[28]

Twenty years before, the Germans had been at the center of
Chicago's working class, which they dominated numerically, organizationally, and ideologically. At the beginning of the new century, with the
coming of age of a second generation of Germans born in America, they
still formed the largest ethnic element within Chicago's working class
(despite the new immigration from southern and eastern Europe) but, if
they were unionized at all, they belonged to the predominantly Anglo-
American Federation of Labor, or, if they pursued more radical political
goals, were members of the German section of the international (i.e.,
multiethnic) Socialist party.[29] Even though the working-class movement
in Chicago grew throughout that period, the German-American working-class movement, it seems, weakened in the process of becoming part
of multiethnic or American organizations. The process is traceable in the
pages of the *Arbeiter-Zeitung* itself as a gradual reduction of ethnic visibil-
ity: first, and most noticeably, in the area of class conflict and organization; last and least, in the area of festivity and leisure, the true domain of
ethnic culture. But even where German workers fought for specific ethnic interests, they learned to defend them—in the heyday of an aggressive
and predominantly Anglo-Saxon reform movement—with the help of organizations transcending class or ethnic group.

In principle, alliances were possible also with the progressive movement (e.g., on issues like housing, labor legislation, or political corruption). In general, however, the *Arbeiter-Zeitung* regarded the organizations of progressive reform as the vanguard of dominant powers and
interests.[30] It called the Civic Federation's concept of social harmony
mere window dressing, made fun of Mrs. Potter Palmer's radical chic, and
identified, in a number of satirical sketches, the fervor of upper-class reformers with the missionary zeal of the Salvation Army.[31] The movement
for a clean and dry Chicago—which must have had its comic highpoint in
the midnight confrontation of a group of hymn-singing evangelists with
Chicago's prostitutes, the latter parading in lines of four through the red-
light district[32]—was barely held in check by a coalition of all ethnic

Figure 13.2. Caricature "The Capitalist's Christmas Presents for the Working Class in 1894."

groups between 1906 and 1911. Even though the *Arbeiter-Zeitung* had some bitter comments on German philistines who showed a greater commitment to the fight for beer than to the fight for their political freedoms, it gave front-page coverage to a parade of eighty thousand Germans, Bohemians, Poles, Irish, Hungarians, Danes, and Norwegians demonstrating against plans for a "dry Sunday," in March 1906, and constantly invoked the solidarity of the foreigners against the impending Anti-Saloon Laws.[33] It supported the Federation of Labor and the United Societies for Local Self-Government (a federation of more than four hundred ethnic organizations) in their resistance against the passing of the new city charter because "almost all regulations of this capital bill"—the pun was surely intended—"are directed against the poor and especially against the workers."[34] Whereas the *Chicago Tribune*, after the overwhelming victory of the opponents of the city charter, commented sadly: "[Chicago] has decided that it does not want uniformity, efficiency, and sanity in city government," the *Arbeiter-Zeitung* jubilantly expressed its pride in a new consciousness of multiethnic solidarity: "The 'foreigners' have brought this off."[35]

The invective that the *Arbeiter-Zeitung* directed persistently against all actions of the Anti-Saloon and Law-and-Order Leagues came from a suspicion that their true target was not alcohol or prostitution but the autonomy of ethnic working-class culture itself. Loss of licence ("15,000 pubs have been closed within one year"),[36] the drastic rise of licence costs, as well as the taxation of "all places of amusement" from the five-cent theaters to the Turner halls (in December 1909), endangered the institutional basis of the various *Vereine* and thus the core of ethnic social life.[37] The *Vereine* organized festivities, concerts, theatrical performances, commemorations, costume balls, and bazaars in the Turner and brewery halls of the city. In the summer, they lured the workers out of their hot tenements with weekend excursions or with picnics in Brand's Park or in Riverview Park. Dancing, music, and the consumption of large quantities of beer were the sine qua non of such events, which were self-confident demonstrations (sometimes to the point of provocation) of ethnic lower-class vitality. One of these was the mass excursion of the *Aurora Turnverein* to Cedar Lake, Indiana, in June 1906, where more than five thousand people (who had come in five special trains) spent their time with racing, rowing, price fishing, gymnastics, and dancing; another, four years later, was the huge festival of German workers' singing societies, which, for three days, demonstrated the continuing presence of German cultural traditions in Chicago with several parades and public concerts.[38]

If on these and similar occasions German working-class culture presented itself as German beyond any doubt, the contours of ethnic leisure-time activities nevertheless became gradually less distinct. There was, for once, growing interaction between ethnic groups. (Thus the *Arbeiter-Zeitung*, commenting on a picnic of the Milwaukee Socialists, noted "a Babylonian multitude of tongues but the structure of the feast was no doubt German.")[39] Yet changes in the urban environment are also relevant in this connection. The history of Riverview Park can be taken as a case in point: As "Schützen-Park," with beer garden and picnic grove, it had been "the most beautiful German recreation area in Chicago" and a favorite spot for weekend excursions. As Riverview Park, it developed from 1906 onward into Chicago's Coney Island, with daring roller coasters and other hair-raising excitements (such as "the Chutes" or "Shooting the Rapids"), with "Old Time Minstrel Shows," monstrosities of all kinds, and such breathtaking spectacles as "War of the Worlds" ("tremendous battle at sea, land, and air"), "Pharao's Daughter" ("from stone to flesh, from flesh back into stone") and the sinking of the Titanic ("the height of realism through technology").[40] In the columns of the *Arbeiter-Zeitung*, its promoters advertised Riverview Park by referring to its German past, but they aimed beyond the single ethnic group to the city's large foreign population. Even the Socialists tried to enhance the attraction of their multiethnic picnics by offering reduced tickets to Riverview's various excitements.

John Kasson called the amusement parks of the turn of the century "laboratories of the rising urban culture"[41] because they made a heterogeneous and as yet unmixed urban population physically mix and touch in ecstasies of pleasure. In a way they corresponded, if obversely, to the integrative organizations of the working class (like the unions or the Socialist party) as well as to the institutions of the Settlement House and Playground movements, which reproduced the ethnic heterogeneity of the city in the name of a higher, quasi-transcendent social coherence. At the same time, it becomes increasingly clear that ethnic culture began to lose its dominant influence in the area of leisure and was slowly drawn into a new culture of consumption and distraction,[42] compensating the loss of ethnic identity with the participation in a more intensive life—a life richer in possibilities, desires, and dreams of their fulfillment.

URBAN REFORM, ETHNIC LIFE, AND URBAN CULTURE

And yet the *Arbeiter-Zeitung* took note of this "new urban culture" in a rather casual fashion and apparently without any sense of danger or of a break in continuity.[43] It advertised for Riverview, defended the nickelodeons against the attacks of the reformers, and its descriptions of working-class festivities show a gradual replacement of older forms (like the *tableaux vivants*) by cinematograph and "moving pictures."[44] The new instruments and institutions of urban amusement seemed much more dangerous to the representatives of progressive reform who saw the saloon, the house of prostitution, vaudeville, burlesque shows, nickelodeons, dance halls, and amusement parks as part of a single network of seduction ("of vicious excitements and trivial amusements.")[45] While the *Arbeiter-Zeitung* still reported patiently on the celebrations of German *Turnvereine* or singing clubs, the *Survey* justified the censorship of movies with the "unsatiable desire" of the masses for "cheap amusements."[46] According to Jane Addams's estimates, one-sixth of Chicago's population spent its Saturday evenings in the theater, mostly to see melodrama, burlesque shows, or vaudeville. On summer weekends, thousands thronged to amusement parks, more than one hundred thousand daily went to the five-cent theaters or to amusements equally inexpensive.[47] In the dim light of the nickelodeons, a predominantly young audience of both sexes—but also, as Sherman Kingsley of the Chicago Relief and Aid Society noticed with some astonishment, the whole family from baby to grandfather—saw a mixed program of "moving pictures, instrumental music, clog dancing, jokes, and sometimes a play with more or less of a plot." The reformers regarded such places of public and uncontrolled amusement with profound distrust; yet they could not deny that "these places . . . answer, imperfectly to be sure, a real need of the community."[48]

These needs were analyzed by Jane Addams in a wonderfully warm, and yet curiously Victorian, book, *The Spirit of Youth and the City Street*. More sensitive than others, she recognized in the rise of the new popular culture the expression of genuine, if grotesquely distorted, creative needs and desires, especially of the children of immigrants who tried to escape the meaningless strictures and values of an imported and rootless ethnic culture. The miseries of adolescence, the despair over the monotony of factory work, the secret desire for a life of personal freedom and fulfillment—all these were intensified and perverted by the sensuous excitements of the large city: "The public dance halls, filled with frivolous and irresponsible young people in a feverish search for pleasure, are but the sorry substitute for the old dances on the village green in which all older people of the village participated." Yet even this trivial world of false fulfillments and appearances pointed toward a hidden "redemptive beauty . . . which these multitudes of young people might supply to our dingy towns." What was missing were more genuine and truthful means and manners to express individual and collective creativity.[49]

The Settlement House movement had originated in comparable needs, as Jane Addams pointed out on several occasions.[50] It sought fulfillment—beyond the confined area of genteel culture and beyond an abstract dedication to the "Spirit of Chicago"—in the creative reconstruction of social space. Hull House and Chicago Commons were to form a neutral territory, a middle ground of communication and interaction between classes, which would help bridge social distance and broaden social perception; in that sense, it was a type and anticipation of the future "unification of all good citizens, capitalist and proletarian in a single, solidary society."[51] If the Hull House reformers indeed aimed at improving the social vision of the gentry—Charles Hutchinson, Walter Fisher, and William Kent (all members of the Merchants' Club) were friends and frequent visitors of Hull House—they also tried to hand down the forms of civilized life to those apparently in need of them. In this respect, the settlement houses were outposts of a civilization that had to be redefined and its order reestablished in a social landscape marked by the decay of traditional forms of social life. Not unlike the editors of the *Arbeiter-Zeitung*, the reformers recognized early that to morally control the urban masses one had to organize its leisure: "Recreation alone can stifle the lust for vice," Jane Addams wrote in the heavy rhetoric of moral fundamentalism. In a similar manner, Luther H. Gulick, president of the Playground Association of America, attempted to convey to the larger public that to balance out the centrifugal dynamics of a heterogeneous society, "the organization of leisure was just as important and technically feasible as the organization of work."[52] Settlement houses, playgrounds, the field houses of the new park areas, public schools, and similar progressive institutions were the germs of a new community and "neighborship," whose forms of organized sociability (such as debating clubs, educational forums, lay theater, respectable dancing, and team sports) were to counter the institutions of the new urban culture at all points and on all levels.[53]

The highest form of organized leisure was the festival, however—and it is only appropriate that William Stead begins his Utopian apotheosis of reformed Chicago in the last chapter of his *If Christ Came to Chicago* with the phrase: "Chicago was en fête."[54] The festival transformed profane society into sacred community—here society's buried creativity found symbolic form and expression. Important, in this connection, is Gulick's distinction between 'festival' as a means of building up community, and 'carnival' as a destructive force."[55] Preindustrial ritual and cer-

tain elements of ethnic culture (its costumes, dances, parades, and cere-
monies) could thus be integrated to form a vital and organic urban culture,
while the orgiastic, carnival-like aspects of ethnic sociability (its "vicious
amusements") would be purged from the body politic as undesirable and
disruptive elements. In the eyes of Gulick or Addams, these "foreign colonies in the hearts of our cities" formed the inexhaustible reservoir of a
future "municipal art," which began to announce itself in ceremonious
Labor Day parades, the campaign "For a Sane Fourth of July," or the play
festivals and pageants enacting episodes or patriotic legends from local or
national history.[56] At the Play Festivals of the Chicago Playground
Association—which started in 1907—ethnic culture was made visible and
its value publicly acknowledged at the same time that the dominant culture, its hierarchies distinctly softened, reconfirmed its dominance by the
integration of the ethnic. The presentations of the Italians, Germans,
Jews, Russians, Poles, and Greeks seemed to outline a new urban community, at once heterogeneous and coherent, which formed itself through
the paternal guidance of the reformers, and which rediscovered, in the
preindustrial heritage of its ethnic minorities, the buried values of its own
agrarian past. "Chicago"—Graham Romney Taylor wrote at the end of
his report on the second Play Festival in 1908—"offers to the nation a pro-
phetic glimpse of that growing spirit which is bringing a new humanity
into city conditions and a new joyousness to all the people who dwell
therein."[57]

THE NEW CHICAGO: ITS POSSIBILITIES AND LIMITS

To what extent the mass of immigrants shared this new consciousness, or
even made use of the programs or organized leisure offered by Hull
House or Commons, cannot be determined with any certainty. Recent
studies see the influence of the settlement houses as limited, confined to
Anglo-Saxon or English-speaking workers of higher social status.[58] The
Arbeiter-Zeitung passed over the pageants and festivals of the reformers
with eloquent silence. To its editors, the official staging of ethnicity must
have seemed as absurd as the moralizing separation of festival and sensuous pleasure. Accordingly, the attack of the reformers on the commercial-
ism of the new popular (or mass) culture—"to commercialize pleasure is
as monstrous as it is to commercialize art"[59]—was of no concern to the
Arbeiter-Zeitung, since the pressures of the dominant culture made solidarity with working people and their amusements practically automatic.[60]

Hull House and Commons were no match for saloon, *Verein*, ball park, nickelodeon, or amusement park. On the contrary, the subversive carnival of a "culture of hilarity" began to undermine the rigid hierarchies of a Victorian "culture of decorum."[61]

In a phase of historic transition, regarded by some as a period of cultural decay, by others as the gestation period of a "new civic order"; in which some hoped to make Illinois "the red Saxony of America" and others to make Chicago the future capital of a democratic empire[62]—in such a phase of competing cultural ideals, the symbolic space of the city extended, became organized and diversified. None of these different models of a new civic order was able to shape "raw" Chicago according to its own image. But the efforts of philanthropists and reformers, of union organizers and Socialists, of churches and ethnic groups, to fill "empty" city space (in each case a different one) with the bare structures of social existence and cultural survival resulted in the complex social and communicative network of a new Chicago—even though its proliferating structures parody the ideal of "order" to which it owes its origins.

This new Chicago opened new margins of cultural participation and thus the possibility of more differentiated social behavior and role play. The German working-class immigrants of the first, or even more so of the second, generation were able to define themselves in different contexts of communication as American workers, as Germans in language and culture, as "foreigners" insisting on their constitutional rights, or as German-American Socialists. They might meet their Bohemian or Italian comrades at the picnic of the Socialists in Riverview Park or might visit the Field Museum or the Union Saloon with some German fellow union members. They and their families might spend Sunday morning at the *Volksgarten*, or go to the Sunday concerts arranged by the Women's Club for the benefit of the general public in one of the city's new parks.[63] Possibly they went not only to the meetings of the German workers' debating club or *Bildungsverein* but, from time to time, also to a lecture at Hull House. Perhaps they even made occasional use of a branch of the public library established in the neighborhood park and, once there, saw the exhibition that Charles Hutchinson—patron of the arts, sponsor of Hull House, and president of the Art Institute—had arranged there for the elevation of popular taste. The horizon of perceived society had broadened, together with the margin of individual choices, especially compared with the socially restricted vision of the 1880s and 1890s. This is evident in the public demonstrations of Chicago's multiethnic character as well as in the Chicago Industrial Exhibition (produced by Hull House and the trade unions), which was to show Chicago's citizens "to what extent the interests and welfare of wage earners are coincident with the interests and welfare of the whole people."[64]

Of course, this new image of Chicago as a cosmopolitan, culturally mixed yet integrated city had some cracks along existing barriers of class and growing barriers of race. They are manifest in a continuous history of strikes and labor conflicts, in the persistence of social misery, and, most of all, in the brutal race riots of 1919, in which class conflict found outlet in a violent discharge of racial hatred. For the majority of Germans, however—as much as for other groups of an earlier wave of immigration—"progressive" Chicago allowed integration into American society on several levels: on the track of social mobility as a rise of skilled work, as a rise into the professions of the old and new middle class, or even as a rise within the hierarchies of union or party. Yet in the growing perception of the city as a diverse and sensuous environment, in the awareness of the new variety of life it offered, in the proud recognition that "the immigrants and their children have contributed much to make Chicago one of the largest and richest cities of the world,"[65] there is evidence, above all, of the lure and assimilative power of the metropolis itself: as a gradual adjustment to, perhaps even a partially repressed affection for, Chicago.

NOTES

1. On Chicago in the Gilded Age, see Ray Ginger, *Altgeld's America* (New York, 1973); Helen L. Horowitz, *Culture and the City: Cultural Philanthropy in Chicago from the 1880s to 1917* (Lexington, KY, 1976); Giorgio Ciucci et al., *The American City: From the Civil War to the New Deal* (London, 1980); also Hartmut Keil and John B. Jentz, eds., *German Workers in Industrial Chicago, 1850–1910: A Comparative Perspective* (DeKalb, IL, 1983).

2. Henry B. Fuller, "The Upward Movement in Chicago," *Atlantic Monthly* 80 (1897): 547. For contemporary views of Chicago, cf. Fuller, "Chicago," *Century* 84 (May 1912): 25–33; Frederick C. Howe, "The Municipal Character and Achievements of Chicago," *World's Work* 5 (March 1903): 3240–44; and George K. Turner, "The City of Chicago: A Study of the Great Immoralities," *McClure's* 28 (April 1907): 575–92.

3. "In building its 'White City,' Chicago rose above itself, above all it had ever been and above all it would become until it had time to grow into the gradual realization of this vision of its future," Graham Taylor, *Pioneering on Social Frontiers* (Chicago, 1930), 3.

4. Taylor, *Pioneering*, 29. For an ironic report of the event, see the *Chicagoer Arbeiter-Zeitung (ChAZ)* of 13 Nov. 1893.

5. William T. Stead, *If Christ Came to Chicago* (London, 1894), 452.

6. Albion W. Small, "The Civic Federation of Chicago: A Study in Social Dynamics," *American Journal of Sociology (AJS)* 1 (1895–96): 97.

7. Small, "Civic Federation," 92.

8. *Daily News*, 13 Nov. 1899, quoted in Michael McCarthy, "Businessmen and Professionals in Municipal Reform: The Chicago Experience, 1877–1920" (Ph. D. diss., Northwestern University, 1970), 89. On Chicago's new parks and on the Playground movement, see Horowitz, *Culture and the City* (especially chapter 3); Graham R. Taylor, "Recreational Developments in Chicago's Parks," *The Annals of the American Academy of Social and Political Science* 35 (March 1910): 304–21; Charles Zueblin, "Municipal Playgrounds in Chicago," *AJS* 4 (1898–99): 145–58; Henry G. Foreman, "Chicago's New Park Service," *Century* 69 (1905): 610–20; Ernest Poole, "Chicago's Public Playgrounds," *Outlook* 87 (1907): 775–81; Jane Addams, "Recreation as a Public Function in Urban Communities," *AJS* 17 (1912–13): 615–19; Robert Lewis, "'Well-Directed Play': Urban Recreation and Urban Reform," in *Impressions of a Gilded Age: The American Fin de Siècle*, Marc Chénetier and Rob Kroes, eds. (Amsterdam, 1983), 183–202; and Dominick Cavallo, *Muscles and Morals: Organized Playground and Urban Reform, 1880–1920* (Philadelphia, 1981).

9. Poole, "Chicago's Public Playgrounds," 777; on the decrease of crime, see Allen Burns, "Relation of Playgrounds to Juvenile Delinquency," *Charities and the Commons* 21 (3 Oct. 1908): 25–31.

10. Theodore Roosevelt, cited by Taylor, "Recreational Developments," 304.

11. Jane Addams, "Recreation as a Public Function," 615ff.

12. Quoted in McCarthy, "Businessmen and Professionals," 93.

13. Taylor, "Recreational Developments," 316.

14. Like Stead and Henry D. Lloyd, Burnham saw in Chicago the future capital of a democratic empire with a population of fifteen million in 1950, *Plan of Chicago, Prepared Under the Direction of the Commercial Club During the Years MXMVI, MCMVII, and MCMVIII by Daniel Burnham and Edward H. Bennett, Architects.* Charles Moore, ed., Chicago Commercial Club, 1909. On the Burnham plan, see Charles Eliot, "A Study of the Plan of Chicago," *Century* 74 (Jan. 1910): 417–31; Thomas Hines, *Burnham of Chicago* (New York, 1974); Ciucci et al., *The American City*, 89–104; Paul Boyer, *Urban Masses and Moral Order in America, 1820–1920* (Cambridge, MA, 1978), 262–76; and John Atherton, "Urban Order and Moral Order: Burnham's *Plan of Chicago*," in *Impressions*, Chénetier and Kroes, eds., 165–82.

15. Burnham, *Plan of Chicago*, 1.

16. Burnham, *Plan of Chicago*, title of drawing no. LXXXV.

17. Critics from the Settlement House movement attacked Burnham for concentrating too much on the reconstruction of the city's center and the lake front, yet leaving the slum areas on the West Side essentially unchanged; see McCarthy, "Businessmen and Professionals," 138.

18. Burnham, *Plan of Chicago*, title of drawing no. CXXX.

19. Atherton, "Urban Order," 171.

20. See McCarthy, "Businessmen and Professionals," 53–80.

21. Theodore Thomas, *A Musical Autobiography*, George P. Upton, ed., with a new introduction by Leon Stein (New York, 1964), 101f.

22. On the antiethnic policies of the orchestra's administration, see Horowitz, *Culture and the City*, 110f. The *ChAZ* was apparently so bitter about its class bias that it did not even mention Thomas's unexpected death in February 1905. In contrast, it regularly reviewed the concerts of the less exclusive Philharmonic Orchestra: "If one compares the program of the Philharmonic Orchestra with that of the Thomas-orchestra, he will come to the conviction that there is no difference as to musical tastes or standards. . . . But whereas the so-called elite orchestra charges high prices for tickets and monopolizes art for the owner class, the Philharmonic Orchestra counts with the people and its tickets are so low that the pleasures of art are available for everyone," *ChAZ*, 15 Nov. 1909. (This and all following quotes from the German were translated by the author).

23. "The community will get more out of its million workers, when their nerves cease to be wrecked by irritating conditions," Burnham, *Plan of Chicago*, 74.

24. Thomas L. Philpott, *The Slum and the Ghetto: Neighborhood Deterioration and Middle-Class Reform, Chicago, 1880–1930* (New York, 1978), 88.

25. See Hartmut Keil and Heinz Ickstadt, "Elements of German Working-Class Culture in Chicago, 1880 to 1890," in this volume; and Klaus Ensslen and H. Ickstadt, "German Working-Class Culture in Chicago: Continuity and Change in the Decade from 1900 to 1910," in *German Workers*, Keil and Jentz, eds., 236–52.

26. "The American, alas, is no German. Even if he is not a complete ignoramus in all matters of art—and 99 from 100 Americans belong to that category—his light and superficial mind finds no interest in German depth"; "The Germans and Art in America," *Fackel*, 27 Feb. 1910.

27. "Chicago Remembers Its Martyrs," *ChAZ*, 12 Nov. 1907; see also Heinz Ickstadt, "German Workers' Literature in Chicago—Old Forms in New Contexts," in this volume.

28. Vorbote, 14 Feb. 1906.

29. Accordingly, the *ChAZ*—which had been the organizational and communicative center of the radical German labor movement in the 1880s—became the German organ of the Socialist party in 1910; see Ensslen and Ickstadt, "German Working-Class Culture."

30. "Chicago's Patchwork of Reform," *ChAZ*, 26 and 27 May 1905.

31. Cf. the comments of the *ChAZ* on the Civic Federation, 13 Nov. 1893 and 24 Jan. 1911, also the report of the *Vorbote* on a reception Mrs. Potter Palmer gave for the National Civic Federation: "Last night, the wolves had invited the sheep to the palace of Mrs. Potter Palmer. . . . It was a touching sight to observe diamond-laden ladies and elegant gentlemen pretending interest in the labor question," 16 Jan. 1907. The event also became the subject of a satiric poem by Flamingo (Martin Drescher's pen name when he wrote in the satiric vein),

Fackel, 20 Jan. 1907, reprinted in *Deutsche Arbeiterkultur in Chicago von 1850 bis zum Ersten Welkrieg. Eine Anthologie,* Hartmut Keil, ed. (Ostfildern, 1984), 347f.

32. Graham Taylor, "The Police and Vice in Chicago," *Survey* 6 (Nov. 1909): 164.

33. "A Demonstration of the People," *ChAZ,* 26 March 1906; also see the proclamation: "No tutelage required. The foreigner is not below the 'American'," *ChAZ,* 10 March 1910.

34. *ChAZ,* 22 July 1907.

35. *Chicago Tribune,* 18 Sept. 1907, cited in McCarthy, "Businessmen and Professionals," 79; and the report in the *ChAZ* of the same day.

36. "The Work of the Philistines," *ChAZ,* 30 Nov. 1909.

37. *ChAZ,* 26 Nov. 1907.

38. *ChAZ,* 25 June 1906; on the festival of the singing societies, see the reports in the *ChAZ* of June 24–26, 1910.

39. *ChAZ,* 18 July 1910.

40. *ChAZ,* 6 June 1914; also the extensive reports in the *Fackel* of 19 Sept. 1906 and 7 July 1907. On Riverview, see Gary Kyriazi, *The Great American Amusement Parks* (Secaugus, NY, 1976), 113f.

41. John Kasson, *Amusing the Millions: Coney Island at the Turn of the Century* (New York, 1978), 8. See Larry May, *Screening Out the Past: The Birth of Mass Culture Industry* (New York, 1980) for a similar interpretation of the social function of the movies. Ballpark, amusement park, nickelodeon, and similar institutions of the rising consumer culture were considered agents of social integration, the democratic loci of a quasi-ritual transgression of class and ethnic lines.

42. I have taken the term "culture of distraction" from Philip Fisher's excellent analysis of the novel as urban space, "Torn Space" (Unpublished ms.); see also his "City Matters: City Minds," in *The World of Victorian Fiction,* Jerome H. Buckley, ed. (Cambridge, MA, 1975), 371–90.

43. This easy cohabitation of ethnic with the new forms of urban culture is apparent in a report of the *New Yorker Volks-Zeitung* on the twenty-fifth commemoration of the *Arbeiter Kranken- und Sterbe-Kasse der Vereinigten Staaten:* the usual concert with old favorites ("overtures and potpourris of Wagner, Suppé and Gounod") on the ground floor, vaudeville in the upper rooms, and, for the children, moving pictures in the Turner hall; *New Yorker Volks-Zeitung,* 6 Nov. 1909.

44. *ChAZ,* 15 March 1909.

45. Jane Addams, "Public Recreation and Social Morality," *Charities and The Commons* 18 (3 Aug. 1907): 492.

46. *Survey,* 3 April 1909, 8ff.

47. Cavallo, *Muscles and Morals,* 46; Jane Addams, *The Spirit of Youth and the City Streets* (Urbana, IL, 1972), 85; and *Survey,* 3 April 1909, 8ff. Also Garth Jowett, "The First

Motion Picture Audiences," *Journal of Popular Film* (Winter 1974): 39–54; Russell Merritt, "The Nickelodeon Theaters 1905–1914," in *The American Film Industry,* Tino Ballio, ed. (Madison, WI, 1976), 59–82; and May, *Screening Out the Past.*

48. Sherman C. Kingsley, "The Penny Arcade and the Cheap Theatre," *Charities and the Commons,* 8 June 1907, 295.

49. Addams, *The Spirit of Youth,* 9 and 13.

50. "The Subjective Necessity for Social Settlement," *Twenty Years at Hull House* (New York, 1961), 90–100; also Mary L. Cree, "The First Year of Hull House, 1889–1890, Letters by Jane Addams and Ellen Gates Starr," *Chicago History* 1 (1970–71): 101–14.

51. See Philpott, *The Slum and the Ghetto,* 76.

52. Addams, *The Spirit of Youth,* 19ff., and Gulick, cited in Cavallo, *Muscles and Morals,* 38.

53. Graham R. Taylor, "Survival and Revival of Neighborship," *Survey* 28 (1912): 226–31 and Jane Addams, "What the Theatre Has Done for the Neighborhood People," *Charities and The Commons* 8 (March 1902): 284.

54. Stead, *If Christ Came to Chicago,* Chapter VI: "In the Twentieth Century," 409.

55. Luther H. Gulick, "The New and More Glorious Fourth of July," *World's Work* (July 1909), 11784–11787; see Kasson, *Amusing the Millions,* 56, for a similar argument.

56. Boyer, *Urban Masses,* 253–60; David Glassberg, "Restoring a 'Forgotten Childhood': American Play and the Progressive Era's Elizabethan Past," *American Quarterly* 32 (1980): 351–68. On the Chicago Play Festival, see Graham R. Taylor in *Charities and The Commons,* 1 Aug. 1908, 539–45; and Ida Tarbell, "An Old World Fete in Industrial America," *Charities and The Commons,* 1 Aug. 1908, 546–48 (also the reports of the following years).

57. Taylor in *Charities and The Commons,* 1 Aug. 1908, 545.

58. Philpott, *The Slum and the Ghetto,* 88; also (if not with reference to Chicago): Roy Rosenzweig, "Middle-Class Parks and Working-Class Play: The Struggle over Recreational Space in Worcester, Massachusetts, 1870–1910," *Radical History Review* 21 (Fall 1979), 31–46.

59. Addams, *The Spirit of Youth,* 98.

60. Thus the management of Riverview Park advertised in the *ChAZ* with an "open reply to Mr. Farwell, the enemy of Riverview," *ChAZ,* 8 Aug. 1908. (Arthur Farwell was the president of the Law and Order League.) The *ChAZ* also argued with irony and anger against the attempt to close down the "five-cent theaters," 6 Nov. 1907.

61. This is the thesis of Kasson as well as May. A contemporary document—from which I have taken the terms "culture of hilarity" and "culture of decorum"—points toward the same direction: Rollin L. Hartt sees in the new amusement parks an instrument of subversion—the destruction of an ideal of bourgeois personality, "The Amusement Park," *Atlantic Monthly* 99 (1907): 667–77.

62. *ChAZ,* 6 May 1912.

63. *ChAZ*, 21 July 1914; Horowitz, *Culture and the City*, 212.

64. Graham R. Taylor, "The Chicago Industrial Exhibit," *Charities and The Commons* 18 (6 April 1907): 39–45.

65. *ChAZ*, 10 March 1910.

Index